THE AMERICAN CHALLENGE READER

VOLUME II

Second Edition

THE AMERICAN CHALLENGE READER

VOLUME II

Second Edition

Keith J. Volanto

Michael Phillips

Design and Production: Abigail Press
Typesetting: Abigail Press
Typeface: AGaramond
Cover Art: Sam Tolia

The American Challenge Reader
Volume II

Second Edition, 2019
Printed in the United States of America
Translation rights reserved by the publisher
ISBN 1-890919-74-8 13-digit 978-1-890919-74-0

Copyright @ by Abigail Press Inc., 2050 Middleton Dr., Wheaton, IL 60189

All rights reserved. No part of the material protected by the copyright notice may be reproduced or utilized in any form or by any means, electronic or mechanical, including photocopy, recording, or any information storage and retrieval system, without permission in writing from the publisher.

Table of Contents

Chapter Seventeen
A Broken Promise of Freedom: Reconstruction, 1863-1877
Documents
Abraham Lincoln, Preliminary Emancipation Proclamation, September 22, 1862	231
General William Tecumseh Sherman, Special Field Order No. 15	234
Blanche K. Bruce, "Speech in the Senate on The Mississippi Elections"	236
Andrew Johnson State of the Union Address, Decembet 3, 1867	238

Vignettes
Lincoln in Richmond	240
A Celebration of Freedom: Juneteenth	241
The Legacy of Newton Knight and "The Free State of Jones"	242
Confederados	245

Chapter Eighteen
Indian Expulsion and White Settlement in the Trans-Missouri West
Documents
The Charlotte Democrat, "Terrible battle with Indians: General Custer, 15 officers, and every man of five companies slain," July 10, 1876	247
Denis Kearney and H.L. Knight, "Appeal from California," February 28, 1878	249
The Dawes Severalty Act (1887)	251
Condition of the Indian Tribes, Report of the Joint Special Committee	253

Vignettes
No Man's Business to Divide the Land: Chief Joseph and Indian Resistance	255
Frederic Remington and the Mythology of the American West	257
Documenting Dishonor: Helen Hunt Jackson	259
Lyda Conley: A Legal Voice for Native Peoples	261

Chapter Nineteen
Wealth, Poverty, and the Gilded Age, 1870-1900
Documents
Edward Bellamy, *Looking Backward, 2000-1887* (1888)	263
Andrew Carnegie, "The Gospel of Wealth" (1889)	266
Eugene V. Debs, "Unity and Victory" (1908)	268
Booker T. Washington, Up from Slavery, 1901	271

Vignettes
The Tyranny of the Clock	273
Lifestyles of the Rich and Famous in the Gilded Age	274
The Open Shop Movement	276
"The United States of Lyncherdom"	277

Chapter Twenty
The Imperial Republic
Documents
Queen Liliuokalani's Official Protest against the Treaty of Hawaiian Annexation	281
The "De Lôme Letter"	284
Platform of the American Anti-Imperialist League	286
The Platt Amendment	288

Vignettes
What Destroyed the *Maine*?	290
The Anti-Imperialist League	291
Man versus Mosquito	293
Theodore Roosevelt and the "Great White Fleet"	295

Chapter Twenty-one
The Progressive Reformation of Industrial America
Documents
The Case for "Municipal Housekeeping"	297
Petition to Congress Opposing a Constitutional Suffrage Amendment	300
Theodore Roosevelt on Conservation	301
The Hetch Hetchy Debate	302

Vignettes
Influences upon Progressivism	306
The Strands of Progressivism	307
The Workers' Compensation Movement	308
Robert La Follette and the "Wisconsin Idea"	309

Chapter Twenty-two
The "Great War": World War I
Documents
President Wilson's Declaration of Neutrality	311
The Zimmermann Telegram	313
Excerpts from Eugene Debs's Canton, Ohio Anti-War Speech	314
Patriotic Housekeeping: Good Housekeeping Recruits Kitchen Soldiers	316

Vignettes
Social Experimentation in the Military	319
The War against the Socialists	320
The Camp Logan Riot	321
The "Spanish Flu" Pandemic	323

Chapter Twenty-three
The Contentious Twenties
Documents
An El Paso Musician Laments the Popularity of Jazz	325
"Mother Not to Blame for Flapper's Flapping"	326
On the "Limits of Commercial Aviation"	329

	The Motion Picture Producers and Distributors of America's List of "Don'ts" and "Be Carefuls"	331

Vignettes

Mass Advertizing and Credit Fuels the 1920s Economic Boom	334
Margaret Sanger and the Birth Control Movement	335
The Misappropriation of Sigmund Freud	336
The Sacco and Vanzetti Case	337

Chapter Twenty-four
The Great Depression and the New Deal

Documents

An Afternoon in a Pushcart Peddlers' Colony	339
Two Displaced Texas Sharecroppers Write to the Secretary of Agriculture	341
"I'd Rather Not Be on Relief"	343
The National Recovery Administration "Blanket Code"	344

Vignettes

FDR's "Splendid Deception"	348
The Real Bonnie and Clyde	350
The Dust Bowl: A Man-Made Disaster	352
Marian Anderson Performs at the Lincoln Memorial	353

Chapter Twenty-five
Democracy, Fascism and Communism at War, 1921-1945

Documents

Albert Einstein Urges FDR to Build the Atomic Bomb	355
FDR's Pearl Harbor Address to Congress	357
Justice Frank Murphy's Dissent in the Korematsu Case	358
A WASP Remembers Her Basic Training at Avenger Field in Sweetwater, Texas	362

Vignettes

The Kellogg-Briand Pact	364
Roosevelt vs. Lindbergh	365
The Push for Civil Rights during World War II	367
The New President	367

Chapter Twenty-six
The Origins of the Cold War

Documents

President Harry Truman Slams Joseph McCarthy	369
President Eisenhower Rejects Clemency for the Rosenbergs	372
President Eisenhower Bids Farewell and Warns of the "Military-Industrial Complex"	374
Ho Chi Minh Declares Vietnamese Independence	377

Vignettes

The Berlin Airlift: A Logistical Marvel	380
Branch Rickey: Man of Baseball, Man of God	382

Nixon's "Checkers Speech"   383
Two Americans Take on Joseph McCarth   385

Chapter Twenty-seven
American Culture From 1945-1960
Documents
Harry Truman, Executive Order 9981, 1948   387
"Employment of Homosexuals and Other Sex Perverts in Government"   389
The United States Supreme Court, *Brown vs. Board of Education of Topeka* (1954)   392
Charles Alexander, Letter About Integration in Little Rock, Arkansas   394
Vignettes
Racial Violence and a President's Conscience   396
Porn in the U.S.A.   398
Out of Bounds: Pro Sports and the Tackling of Jim Crow   400
Up In Smoke: Tobacco and American Culture after World War II   402

Chapter Twenty-eight
Kennedy & Johnson and the Vietnam War
Documents
John F. Kennedy, Inaugural Address, January 20 1961   405
John F. Kennedy, Report to the American People on Civil Rights, June 11, 1963   408
Lyndon Johnson, Special Message to the Congress Proposing a Nationwide War on the Sources of Poverty March 16, 1964   411
Report of the President's Commission on the Assassination of President Kennedy, September 24, 1964   414
Vignettes
The Burning of Norman Morrison   416
Black and White in American Film and Television   418
Celebrities against the Vietnam War   420
Agent Orange   421

Chapter Twenty-nine
The Nightmare Year; 1968
Documents
Excerpt from Report of the National Advisory Commission on Civil Disorders, February 29, 1968   423
President Lyndon Baines Johnson, Address to the Nation, March 31, 1968   426
Robert F. Kennedy Address, Cleveland City Club, April 5, 1968   428
Senator Edward M. Kennedy Tribute to Robert F. Kennedy   431
Vignettes
The Seizure of the *Pueblo*   433
Murder and Uncommon Valor at My Lai   435
The Age of Aquarius   437
American Fighting Men   438

Chapter Thirty
American Frustration and Decline in the 1970s
    Documents

Transcript: Conversation between President Richard Nixon and White House Counsel John Dean, March 21, 1973	441
Gerald R. Ford's Remarks Upon Taking the Oath of Office as President August 9, 1974	444
Jimmy Carter, Address to the Nation on Energy and National Goals, July 15, 1979	446
The United States Supreme Court, *Roe Et Al. v. Wade*	448

    Vignettes

Against Our Will	451
Roots	452
The People's Temple	454
Spiritual Quests and the "New Narcissism"	455

Chapter Thirty-one
A Period of Transition: The Reagan Revolution, End of the Cold War, and the Gulf War 1980-1992
    Documents

A Post-Summit Letter from Ronald Reagan to Mikhail Gorbachev	457
"Senator, You're No Jack Kennedy"	459
Former President Reagan Reveals His Alzheimer's Diagnosis	462
When AIDS Was Funny	463

    Vignettes

The U.S. Aids Muslim Insurgents in Afghanistan	465
The Once Controversial Vietnam Veterans Memorial	466
A Window to the Universe: The Hubble Space Telescope	467
The Impact of the Americans with Disabilities Act	469

Chapter Thirty-two
American Divided and United, 1993-2008
    Documents

Bill Clinton Calls for a "New Covenant"	471
Bill Clinton's 1996 State of the Union Address	474
Excerpts from President George W. Bush's "Mission Accomplished" Speech aboard the *USS Abraham Lincoln*	476
President George W. Bush Discusses the No Child Left Behind Act	479

    Vignettes

Proposition 187 and the End of Republican Control of California	483
The Capture of the Unabomber	484
They Called Him "Dr. Death"	486
Al Gore Becomes an Environmental Rock Star	487

Chapter Thirty-three
Barack Obama and Contemporary America
Documents
President Obama's Bin Laden Death Announcement	489
President Obama's Eulogy for Reverend Clementa Pinckney of the Charleston Nine	492
Excerpts from President Obama's Farewell Address	496
President Trump Discusses His Desire for a Border Wall	500

Vignettes
President Obama's "Beer Summit"	503
The Controversial "Sequel" to Harper Lee's *To Kill a Mockingbird*	504
The Growing Public Awareness of CTE	506
The Deep Water Horizon Explosion and the Gulf Oil Spill	507

Chapter 17

A Broken Promise of Freedom: Reconstruction, 1863-1877

Documents

Abraham Lincoln
Preliminary Emancipation Proclamation, September 22, 1862

An executive order issued as a military measure in the middle of the Civil War, Abraham Lincoln's Emancipation Proclamation stands as one of the most important civil rights measures in American history. On September 22, 1862, Lincoln issued the proclamation, which declared the freedom of all slaves in states or portions of states still in rebellion against the United States government as of January 1, 1863.

Confederate states ignored the deadline. Due to Lincoln's order, and Confederate inaction, the Civil War transformed into a war of liberation. The Emancipation Proclamation also made it politically impossible for England and France, which had depended on slave-grown southern cotton for their textile industries before the war, to politically, economically, and diplomatically support the Confederate States of America. By the 1860s, the British and French public opposed slavery. With the Emancipation Proclamation Lincoln made it clear that slavery would die if the Union won the war. Siding with the Confederacy was allying with forced servitude. The British-French-Confederate axis against the Union never materialized.

The Emancipation Proclamation did not free the slaves owned by those loyal to the Union, and provided for the return of escaped slaves owned by Union loyalists. There were still four slaves states in the Union—Kentucky, Missouri, Delaware, and Maryland—and Lincoln did not want to provoke those states into seceding by being perceived as an outright abolitionist. When the proclamation became public, Lincoln still supported the concept of "colonization" in which freed slaves would be sent to Africa upon emancipation. Lincoln did not yet embrace the concept of racial equality and was not convinced that African Americans could compete successfully with whites as freed people. However, he would evolve toward a position of supporting at least limited African-American citizenship and voting rights by the end of the war, and he would spend his last months backing an amendment to the United States Constitution that forever banned slavery in all American states and territories. As he put it, "If slavery is not wrong, nothing is wrong,"

By the President of the United States of America.
A Proclamation.

I, Abraham Lincoln, President of the United States of America, and Commander-in-Chief of the Army and Navy thereof, do hereby proclaim and declare that hereafter, as heretofore, the war will be prosecuted for the object of practically restoring the constitutional relation between the United States, and each of the States, and the people thereof, in which States that relation is, or may be, suspended or disturbed. That it is my purpose, upon the next meeting of Congress to again recommend the adoption of a practical measure tendering pecuniary aid to the free acceptance or rejection of all slave States, so called, the people whereof may not then be in rebellion against the United States and which States may then have voluntarily adopted, or thereafter may voluntarily adopt, immediate or gradual abolishment of slavery within their respective limits; and that the effort to colonize persons of African descent, with their consent, upon this continent, or elsewhere, with the previously obtained consent of the Governments existing there, will be continued.

That on the first day of January in the year of our Lord, one thousand eight hundred and sixty-three, all persons held as slaves within any State, or designated part of a State, the people whereof shall then be in rebellion against the United States shall be then, thenceforward, and forever free; and the executive government of the United States, including the military and naval authority thereof, will recognize and maintain the freedom of such persons, and will do no act or acts to repress such persons, or any of them, in any efforts they may make for their actual freedom.

That the executive will, on the first day of January aforesaid, by proclamation, designate the States, and part of States, if any, in which the people thereof respectively, shall then be in rebellion against the United States; and the fact that any State, or the people thereof shall, on that day be, in good faith represented in the Congress of the United States, by members chosen thereto, at elections wherein a majority of the qualified voters of such State shall have participated, shall, in the absence of strong countervailing testimony, be deemed conclusive evidence that such State and the people thereof, are not then in rebellion against the United States.

. . . All officers or persons in the military or naval service of the United States are prohibited from employing any of the forces under their respective commands for the purpose of returning fugitives from service or labor, who may have escaped from any persons to whom such service or labor is claimed to be due, and any officer who shall be found guilty by a court martial of violating this article shall be dismissed from the service.

. . . All slaves of persons who shall hereafter be engaged in rebellion against the government of the United States, or who shall in any way give aid or comfort thereto, escaping from such persons and taking refuge within the lines of the army; and all slaves captured from such persons or deserted by them and coming under the control of the government of the United States; and all slaves of such persons found on (or) being within any place occupied by rebel forces and afterwards occupied by the forces of the United States, shall be deemed captives of war, and shall be forever free of their servitude and not again held as slaves.

. . . [N]o slave escaping into any State, Territory, or the District of Columbia, from any other State, shall be delivered up, or in any way impeded or hindered of his liberty, except for crime, or some offence against the laws, unless the person claiming said fugitive shall first make oath that the person to whom the labor or service of such fugitive is alleged to be due is his lawful owner, and has not borne arms against the United States in the present rebellion, nor in any way given aid and comfort thereto . . .

. . . [T]he executive will in due time recommend that all citizens of the United States who shall have remained loyal thereto throughout the rebellion, shall (upon the restoration of the constitutional relation between the United States, and their respective States, and people, if that relation shall have been suspended or disturbed) be compensated for all losses by acts of the United States, including the loss of slaves.

In witness whereof, I have hereunto set my hand, and caused the seal of the United States to be affixed.

Done at the City of Washington this twenty-second day of September, in the year of our Lord, one thousand, eight hundred and sixty-two, and of the Independence of the United States the eighty seventh.

[Signed:] Abraham Lincoln
By the President

[Signed:] William H. Seward
Secretary of State

Source: https://www.archives.gov/exhibits/american_originals_iv/sections/transcript_preliminary_emancipation.html

THOUGHT QUESTIONS:

1. What effects did the Emancipation Proclamation have on the course of the Civil War?

2. President Abraham Lincoln was trying to reach which audiences with his proclamation?

3. How did the Emancipation Proclamation reflect Lincoln's attitudes towards slavery and race relations midway through the Civil War?

General William Tecumseh Sherman, Special Field Order No. 15

One of the chief obstacles freedmen faced after Lincoln issued the Emancipation Proclamation and the states ratified the 13th Amendment abolishing slavery was their utter poverty. Most freedmen had little or no financial resources after a lifetime of work and did not own land. This financial reality meant that although they were no longer human property, the freedmen would for the most part have to depend on their former masters for their livelihoods. This unequal financial relationship gave the white landowners the power to set the terms by which freedmen they employed worked and immense leverage as they tried to control them politically.

With the exception of Union General William Tecumseh Sherman, no major figure in the Reconstruction period—presidents Abraham Lincoln and Andrew Johnson or the United State Congress—made any attempt to deal with the former slaves' lack of financial resources. As the Civil War ground to its conclusion, freedmen faced cold, hunger, and retaliation from bitter whites in the crumbling Confederacy who blamed the former slaves for the South's rapidly approaching defeat. The freedmen followed Union troops, such as those commended by Sherman, seeking protection and food. Still fighting the Confederate Army, Sherman felt overwhelmed by the additional task of protecting and caring for the freedmen.

Sherman led a force of 60,000 troops and conquered Confederate territory from Tennessee to, in September 1864, the city of Atlanta. Sherman had no interest in providing social services to the impoverished freed slaves and wanted to focus on winning the war. He came up with an innovative solution. On January 16, 1865, Sherman announced Special Order No. 15. The Union Army seized land that had been abandoned by owners who had supported the Confederacy in the Georgia Sea Islands, the South Carolina low country, and part of northern Florida's Atlantic Coast. Under Sherman's order, the land was redistributed to freedmen. Freedmen families could apply for use of 40 acres. Upon request, the military also loaned each family a mule

As of June 1865, 40,000 freedmen had started successfully farming on 400,000 acres of what came to be known as "Sherman land." Andrew Johnson, a former slave owner who became president upon Lincoln's assassination, however, saw Sherman's initiative as a dangerous experiment in socialism and as promoting the equality of the races. Johnson reversed Special Order No. 15 and ordered the land returned to the previous white owners. Sherman's directive became yet one more example of freedom promised and the taken away from African Americans in the South during the Reconstruction Era.

The islands from Charleston, south, the abandoned rice fields along the rivers for thirty miles back from the sea, and the country bordering the St. Johns River, Florida, are reserved and set apart for the settlement of the negroes now made free by the acts of war and the proclamation of the President of the United States.

. . . At Beaufort, Hilton Head, Savannah, Fernandina, St. Augustine and Jacksonville, the blacks may remain in their chosen or accustomed vocations—but on the islands, and in the settlements hereafter to be established, no white person whatever, unless military officers and soldiers detailed for duty, will be permitted to reside; and the sole and exclusive management of affairs will be left to the freed people themselves, subject only to the United States military authority and the acts of Congress. By the laws of war, and orders of the President of the United States, the negro is free and must be dealt with as such. He cannot be subjected to conscription or forced military service, save by the written orders of the highest military authority of the Department, under such regulations as the President or Congress may prescribe. Domestic servants, blacksmiths, carpenters and other mechanics, will be free to select their own work and residence, but the young and able-bodied negroes must be encouraged to enlist as soldiers in the service of the United States, to contribute their share towards maintaining their own freedom, and securing their rights as citizens of the United States . . .

Whenever three respectable negroes, heads of families, shall desire to settle on land, and shall have selected for that purpose an island or a locality clearly defined, within the limits above designated, the Inspector of Settlements and Plantations will himself, or by such subordinate officer as he may appoint, give them a license to settle such island or district, and afford them such assistance as he can to enable them to establish a peaceable agricultural settlement. The three parties named will subdivide the land, under the supervision of the Inspector, among themselves and such others as may choose to settle near them, so that each family shall have a plot of not more than (40) forty acres of tillable ground, and when it borders on some water channel, with not more than 800 feet water front, in the possession of which land the military authorities will afford them protection, until such time as they can protect themselves, or until Congress shall regulate their title. The Quartermaster may, on the requisition of the Inspector of Settlements and Plantations, place at the disposal of the Inspector, one or more of the captured steamers, to ply between the settlements and one or more of the commercial points heretofore named in orders, to afford the settlers the opportunity to supply their necessary wants, and to sell the products of their land and labor . . .

BY ORDER OF MAJOR GENERAL W. T. SHERMAN:

Source: Special Field Orders, No. 15, Headquarters Military Division of the Mississippi, 16 Jan. 1865, Orders & Circulars, ser. 44, Adjutant General's Office, Record Group 94, National Archives.

THOUGHT QUESTIONS:

1. In what ways might African-American poverty limit their freedom after they were emancipated as slaves?

2. On what grounds might the army justify seizing land from owners who supported the Confederacy and on what legal basis might this seizure be challenged?

3. What inspired President Andrew Johnson to reverse Sherman's Special Field Order No. 15 and what might that suggest about his attitude towards the freedmen?

Blanche K. Bruce
"Speech in the Senate on The Mississippi Elections"
March 31 1876

After African Americans were granted citizenship by the 14th Amendment, ratified in 1868, and states were banned from denying the right to vote based on race, color and previous servitude under the 15th Amendment, ratified in 1870, Republicans briefly ruled states across the old Confederacy. Beginning in 1871, however, white so-called "Redeemer" Democrats began regaining control of the region. The Redeemers accused Republicans of spending too much money, raising taxes too high, embezzling government funds, and of having handed the region over to corrupt and incompetent "negro rule." As Reconstruction wound to a close between 1875-1877, Redeemer campaigns became more openly racist and violent. In Mississippi, Redeemers launched a campaign of terror against Republicans in 1875. The "Mississippi Plan" utilized armed gangs, strategic murders, threats, and bribes to prevent African Americans from voting. In one black majority county there, not a single African American voted. Democrats raided Republican Party meetings. Some African Americans were forced at gunpoint to vote for Democrats. In other counties, Redeemers altered Republican ballots or ballot boxes were stuffed. In September, thugs attacked a Republican Party-sponsored barbecue in Clinton, sparking an exchange of gunfire. Armed Redeemers combed the area, gunning down African Americans indiscriminately. "They just hunted the whole country clean out, just every [African American] man they could see they were shooting at him just the same as birds," said one witness. Estimates of the number killed in the "Clinton Massacre" range from 30-50 with children numbering among the victims. A massacre of blacks in Vicksburg may have claimed as many as 80 lives. The Democrats won the November statewide elections in a landslide, with the new legislature impeaching the Republican lieutenant governor and forcing Governor Adelbert Ames to resign or face a similar fate the following year. In March of 1876, Senator Blanche K. Bruce, who in 1874 became Mississippi's first (and so far only) African-American Senator, condemned the state's 1875 elections as an undemocratic travesty.

The conduct of the late election in Mississippi affected not merely the fortunes of partisans—as the same were necessarily involved in the defeat or success of the respective parties to the contest—but put in question and jeopardy the sacred rights of the citizen

. . . The evidence in hand and accessible will show beyond peradventure that in many parts of the State corrupt and violent influences were brought to bear upon the registrars of voters, thus materially affecting the character of the voting or poll lists; upon the inspectors of election, prejudicially and unfairly thereby changing the number of votes cast; and, finally, threats and violence were practiced directly upon the masses of voters in such measures and strength as to produce grave apprehensions for their personal safety and as to deter them from the exercise of their political franchises.

It will not accord with the laws of nature or history to brand colored people a race of cowards. On more than one historic field, beginning in 1776 and coming down to this centennial year of the Republic, they have attested in blood their courage as well as a love of liberty—I ask Senators to believe that no consideration of fear or personal danger has kept us quiet and forbearing under the provocations and wrongs that have so sorely tried our souls. But feeling kindly toward our white fellow-citizens, appreciating the good purposes and politics of the better classes, and, above all, abhorring a war of races, we determined to wait until such time as an appeal to the good sense and justice of the American people could be made.

. . . The unanimity with which the colored voters act with a party is not referable to any race prejudice on their part. On the contrary. They invite the political cooperation of their white brethren, and vote as a unit . . . They deprecate the establishment of the color line by the opposition, not only because the act is unwise and wrong in principle, but because it isolates them from the white men of the South, and forces them, in sheer self-protection and against their inclination, to act seemingly upon the basis of a race prejudice that they neither respect nor entertain. As a class they are free from prejudices, and have no uncharitable suspicions against their white fellow-citizens, whether native born or settlers from the Northern States. They not only recognize the equality of citizenship and the right of every man to hold, without proscription any position of honor and trust to which the confidence of the people may elevate him; but owing nothing to race, birth, or surroundings, they, above all other classes in the community, are interested to see prejudices drop out of both politics and the business of the country, and success in life proceed only upon the integrity and merit of the man who seeks it. . . .

I have confidence, not only in this country and her institutions, but in the endurance, capacity, and destiny of my people. We will, as opportunity offers and ability serves, seek our places, sometimes in the field of letters, arts, sciences, and the professions. More frequently mechanical pursuits will attract and elicit our efforts; more still of my people will find employment and livelihood as the cultivators of the soil. The bulk of this people—by surroundings, habits, adaptation, and choice—will continue to find their homes in the South, and constitute the masses of its yeomanry. We will there probably, of our own volition and more abundantly than in the past, produce the great staples that will contribute to the basis of foreign exchange, aid in giving the nation a balance of trade, and minister to the wants and comfort and build up the prosperity of the whole land. Whatever our ultimate position in the composite civilization of the Republic and whatever varying fortunes attend our career, we will not forget our instincts for freedom nor our love of country.

Source: *Congressional Record*, 44th Congress, 1st Session, March 31, 1876.

THOUGHT QUESTIONS:

1. In the 1870s, what accusations did Redeemer Democrats level against Republicans in the South?

2. What methods did Redeemers use to suppress the Republican vote in the South?

3. What explanation did Senator Blanche Bruce give for why African Americans in the former Confederacy almost unanimously supported the Republican Party in the Reconstruction Era?

Andrew Johnson
State of the Union Address
December 3, 1867

The assassination of Abraham Lincoln on April 15, 1865, brought into the presidency a man uniquely ill-suited for the times. Andrew Johnson was a slave owner from Tennessee; his human property had been taken from him by the state because he stayed loyal to the Union. Lincoln tapped the one-time senator as a running mate in 1864 because the president wanted to send a message of regional forgiveness and unity as the Civil War ground to its bloody climax.

The times called not just for regional but racial healing as well. Unfortunately, throughout his political career Johnson vigorously defended slavery, insisting that the U.S. Constitution guaranteed property rights and that this protection extended to slaves. He denied that the federal government or even states had the right to abolish slavery. And he frequently expressed the deep-seated racism that would shape his policies toward freedmen during this presidency. While serving in Congress, Johnson argued that, "the black race of Africa were inferior to the white man in point of intellect – better calculated in physical structure to undergo drudgery and hardship – standing as they do, many degrees lower in the scale of gradation . . . than the white man."

Before becoming vice president, Johnson blamed Southern slave owners for the war and blasted them as a "swaggering aristocracy," but now that he was in the White House he believed that only they could keep the region from falling into economic misery and prevent the anarchy he believed African American freedmen would bring unless they were kept under tight control by their former masters. He adamantly denounced the widespread granting of voting rights to African Americans. Nevertheless, in the Reconstruction Acts passed over his vetoes in 1867, Congress set black suffrage as a condition for Southern states to re-enter the Union. Johnson bitterly denounced this move in his State of the Union address that year.

The subjugation of the States to Negro domination would be worse than the military despotism under which they are now suffering. It was believed beforehand that the people would endure any amount of military oppression for any length of time rather than degrade themselves by subjection to the Negro race. Therefore they have been left without a choice. Negro suffrage was established by act of Congress, and the military officers were commanded to superintend the process of clothing the Negro race with the political privileges torn from white men . . .

The peculiar qualities which should characterize any people who are fit to decide upon the management of public affairs for a great state have seldom been combined. It is the glory of white men to know that they have had these qualities in sufficient measure to build upon this continent a great political fabric and to preserve its stability for more than ninety years, while in every other part of the world all similar experiments have failed. But if anything can be proved by known facts, if all reasoning upon evidence is not abandoned, it must be acknowledged that in the progress of nations Negroes have shown less capacity for government than any other race of people. No independent government of any form has ever been successful in their hands. On the contrary, wherever they have been left to their own devices they have shown a constant tendency to relapse into barbarism. In the Southern States, however, Congress has undertaken to confer upon them the privilege of the ballot.

Just released from slavery, it may be doubted whether as a class they know more than their ancestors how to organize and regulate civil society. Indeed, it is admitted that the blacks of the South are not only regardless of the rights of property, but so utterly ignorant of public affairs that their voting can consist in nothing more than carrying a ballot to the place where they are directed to deposit it. I need not remind you that the exercise of the elective franchise is the highest attribute of an American citizen, and that when guided by virtue, intelligence, patriotism, and a proper appreciation of our free institutions it constitutes the true basis of a democratic form of government, in which the sovereign power is lodged in the body of the people . . . It ought, therefore, to be reposed in none except those who are fitted morally and mentally to administer it well . . .

Yesterday, as it were, 4,000,000 persons were held in a condition of slavery that had existed for generations; to-day they are freemen and are assumed by law to be citizens. It can not be presumed, from their previous condition of servitude, that as a class they are as well informed as to the nature of our Government as the intelligent foreigner who makes our land the home of his choice. . . . The great difference between the two races in physical, mental, and moral characteristics will prevent an amalgamation or fusion of them together in one homogeneous mass. If the inferior obtains the ascendency over the other, it will govern with reference only to its own interests for it will recognize no common interest--and create such a tyranny as this continent has never yet witnessed. Already the Negroes are influenced by promises of confiscation and plunder. They are taught to regard as an enemy every white man who has any respect for the rights of his own race. If this continues it must become worse and worse, until all order will be subverted, all industry cease, and the fertile fields of the South grow up into a wilderness. Of all the dangers which our nation has yet encountered, none are equal to those which must result from the success of the effort now making to Africanize the half of our country.

Source: James Daniel Richardson, ed., *A Compilation of the Messages and Papers of the President, 1789-1897*, Volume 9 (Washington, D.C.: United States Congress Joint Committee on Printing, 1897. https://babel.hathitrust.org/cgi/pt?id=umn.31951002635755v;view=1up;seq=4

THOUGHT QUESTIONS:

1. Under what circumstances did Andrew Johnson end up as vice president and then as president?

2. What role did Johnson see for former slave owners in the post-Civil War South?

3. What did he see as the potential dangers of granting African Americans suffrage?

Vignettes

Lincoln in Richmond

Just before he died, Abraham Lincoln got a glimpse of the new world he had created. The Union Army had captured Richmond, Virginia, the now former capital of the Confederacy, a sure sign that the end finally neared for the Civil War. Welcoming any chance to get out of Washington, D.C., Lincoln on April 4, 1865 travelled to Richmond with his son Tad who celebrated his 12th birthday that same day. Lincoln wanted to inspect this slice of the South he knew he had changed forever.

Guarded by a small number of sailors, Lincoln and his son walked through an urban hellscape, with fires still raging from the recently concluded battle for control of the city. Richmond's African Americans knew about Lincoln's Emancipation Proclamation that had declared an end to slavery in the rebel states, and they also knew that the Confederate surrender in Richmond meant that they had won freedom.

They immediately asserted themselves. When word spread that "the President" was strolling through Richmond's chaotic streets, some freedmen thought it was Jefferson Davis, the dethroned Confederate president. They thought he had been arrested for treason and was being marched to prison. "Hang him! Hang him!" they began chanting. When the former slaves came face-to-face with the presidential visiting party, however, they soon realized they had met not their chief oppressor, but a man they hailed as their liberator.

A Boston reporter covering the president's trip informed a freedwoman about the visitor's identity. "That's President Lincoln?" the woman asked and upon confirming the news, she began leaping in the air and shouting, "Glory!" even as a larger group of African Americans gathered and cheered. The president may not have realized the full personal impact of the Emancipation Proclamation on millions of black lives until that moment, but it must have become clear as he walked through a crowd showering him with praise and greeting him with the words, "God bless you."

An elderly freedman removed his hat and bowed to the president, saying through tears, "May the good Lord bless you." Lincoln shattered centuries-old racial rules that demanded whites always assume a position of superiority. The president removed his famous stovepipe hat and quietly bowed back. Lincoln capped off the day by visiting the executive mansion Davis had used as Confederate president and eased into his counterpoint's easy chair. "I wonder if I could get a drink of water," Lincoln simply asked.

The next week he would publicly embrace limited black suffrage for the first time and soon thereafter faced his fatal rendezvous with a bitter, Confederate-sympathizing actor, John Wilkes Booth, who would murder the president at Ford's Theater the evening of April 14, 1865.

THOUGHT QUESTIONS:

1. What do the freedmen's reactions at the time of Lincoln's visit to Richmond suggest about their feelings about their new status and towards their old masters?

2. Based on his reaction to the freedmen he encountered in Richmond, what might have been Lincoln's attitudes towards African Americans and how did they vary from the norms of the time?

3. What emotions might have inspired Lincoln to want to visit the former capital of the Confederacy as the Union approached victory in the Civil War?

A Celebration of Freedom: Juneteenth

On June 19, 1865, more than two months after Robert E. Lee, commander of the Army of Northern Virginia, surrendered to the Union Army's commanding officer, Ulysses S. Grant, thus effectively ending the Civil War, another northern officer, General Gordon Granger, came ashore in Galveston, Texas. Granger announced to those assembled that the United States Army's General Order No. 3 had taken effect and had the force of law in Texas. The order read in part, "The people of Texas are informed that, in accordance with a proclamation from the Executive of the United States, all slaves are free. This involves an absolute equality of personal rights and rights of property between former masters and slaves, and the connection heretofore existing between them becomes that between employer and hired labor."

News of Abraham Lincoln's Emancipation Proclamation declaring free all slaves in states or parts of states in rebellion as of January 1, 1863, and of the Confederate armed surrender, reached Texas before Granger arrived. The now former slaveowners in Texas, however, kept freedmen toiling as if they remained legal property. The crack of the whip could still be heard in the East Texas cotton fields in the weeks following Lee's encounter with Grant. Granger's arrival not only proclaimed black freedom in the Lone Star State, it also marked the military's enforcement of the emancipation order in Texas.

Approximately 50,000 federal troops would occupy Texas in the months after Granger read his decree. One army report issued in October 1865 noted that in more remote parts of the state whites "still claim and control [slaves] as property, and in two or three instances recently bought and sold them." African Americans who insisted on acting as free people met with violence, with one state government committee claiming that between 1865 and 1868, whites killed approximately 400 African Americans. That number is almost certainly a serious underestimate. Meanwhile, whites punished freedmen who celebrated their new status. Historian Randolph Campbell notes that a slave patrol lashed 100 freedmen in Crockett for publicly expressing joy over emancipation while elsewhere a former master fired pistol shots between a freedman's feet when the just-liberated man jumped in the air at news of Granger's order.

Nevertheless, the state's freedmen embraced June 19th, the date of Granger's proclamation, as a black July 4th, a day to celebrate freedom. The day came to be known as "Juneteenth." It was first marked in1866, and it became a major black holiday following a massive parade held by freedmen in Austin in 1867. African Americans marked Juneteenth with family gatherings, feasts, parades, and spirituals. The tradition spread from its Texas birthplace to the neighboring states of Arkansas and Louisiana. As African Americans migrated from the South across the country, it came to be observed in most states. Juneteenth now inspires barbecues, parties, and other gatherings from San Francisco to Minneapolis to Washington, D.C.

During the 1950s through the 1970s, younger African Americans for a time shunned Juneteenth. Some disdained its association with slavery and saw the celebrations as backwards-looking at a time civil rights activists wanted to focus on the fight for a better tomorrow. Juneteenth enjoyed a rebirth, however, when Houston Democrat Al Edwards successfully steered a bill through the Texas Legislature declaring Juneteenth a state holiday in 1979. Texas held its first official state Juneteenth observance in 1980.

Now, Juneteenth is recognized in the District of Columbia and all but five of the fifty states. Repeated efforts have been made to designate June 19 as a national holiday, including an intense lobbying campaign by 90-year-old Opal Lee of Fort Worth who in 2017 made her case before Congress and tried to get action on the matter from President Barack Obama before he left office. So far these efforts have fallen short. America's other "Independence Day" remains widely celebrated, but is not yet on the federal calendar.

THOUGHT QUESTIONS:

1. How did Texas slaveowners maintain human bondage in the months following the Confederacy's defeat in the Civil War?

2. Why did Juneteenth become controversial in the Civil Rights Era that followed World War II?

3. In spite of its nationwide popularity, why do you think that Juneteenth has not yet become an official national holiday?

The Legacy of Newton Knight and "The Free State of Jones"

Clearly, the United States was a divided nation at the time of the Civil War, enough so that eleven slave states seceded from the Union and fought a bloody war to separate from the Union. The Confederate States of America, however, also badly fractured during its four-year struggle against the Union. Obviously, the four million slaves languishing in the Confederacy did not support the secessionists' cause. In addition, poor whites across the Confederate states increasingly resented having their crops and livestock seized to support the southern war effort and fighting and dying to preserve the enormous wealth of the major slaveowners.

Numerous parts of the Confederate States of America supported the Union during the war. West Virginia broke off from the rest of the Virginia Commonwealth in order to back the federal government. Other anti-CSA strongholds included Eastern Tennessee, parts of Northwestern Alabama, and Northwestern Arkansas. The Hill Country in Central Texas fought against secessionists, as did many in North Central Texas and the "Big Thicket" country in the eastern part of the state. The Confederate Army fiercely battled not only the Union troops, but anti-Confederates from their own region, even as the Confederate ranks dwindled due to an estimated 100,000 or so desertions.

Due to a recent Hollywood movie one of those deserters—Newton Knight—has become famous. Born in 1837 in Jones County, Mississippi, a swampy region thick with trees in which poor farmers struggled to eke out a living, Knight raised livestock and cultivated grain. The extremely wealthy plantation owners who ran Mississippi could not be found here. Knight's father, a Baptist preacher, saw slavery as sinful, and others in the county shared the elder Knight's attitude. In the 1860 election, Jones County voters overwhelmingly supported an anti-secession candidate.

Although he opposed secession, Knight enlisted in the Confederate Army. Scholars disagree why, but some believe that he might have because he probably would have been drafted anyway. Knight and many other soldiers from the "Piney Woods" section of Mississippi, however, grew disgusted by the high cost in human life caused by a war that benefitted only the rich, and their anger deepened as incompetent officers delivered them into unnecessary danger. After months of being poorly fed, Knight and others from the Piney Woods deserted after the Second Battle of Corinth, October 3-4, 1862, a Confederate defeat in which more than 4,000 of the southern forces died, suffered wounds, or were captured.

Returning home to Jones County, Knight saw first-hand the devastating impact of a Confederate tax that allowed the southern military to seize farm animals, crops, or any other supplies it needed from farmers without compensation. Meanwhile, as poor farmers began to suffer hunger, slaveowners with 20 or more slaves had been granted a draft exemption by the Confederate Congress.

The Confederate Army captured Knight in the first months of 1863, but by the end of the year, after another Confederate defeat at Battle of Vicksburg, Jones went absent without leave again. He probably fatally shot a Confederate officer dispatched to round up deserters. In 1864, Jones and more than 120 fellow deserters and escaped slaves formed a militia that battled Confederate troops. Hiding in the swamps, they seceded from Mississippi and declared the territory they controlled "The Free State of Jones."

An enduring myth of Reconstruction is that after the war, when slavery had been abolished and citizenship and voting rights had been granted African Americans, the Union Army imposed "Negro" rule on the South. In fact, although just emancipated African Americans made more than 60 percent percent of the Southern Republican Party, white Southerners who opposed secession during the war, like Knight, made up a significant part of the Republican governing coalition during Reconstruction.

Mississippi remained as divided, along lines of race and class, after the war. Some struggling white farmers made common cause with freedmen during the period. Although he was already married to a white woman, Knight lived with a freedwoman named Rachel. The couple eventually had five children and raised four children who had been fathered by several of Rachel's former masters. At a time when the local Democratic Party used terrorism to suppress black political participation, Knight led a militia that provided physical safety for African-American voters and forced landowners to release African Americans illegally kept in slavery.

When the Democrats regained control of the state through Ku Klux Klan violence, Jones and his interracial family relocated to Jasper County in Southeastern Mississippi, not far from the Alabama border. Knight outlived his many enemies, passing away—perhaps from a heart attack—at the age of 84 in 1922. His headstone bears the inscription, "He Lived for Others."

Knight's family grew into a sizeable tribe in the post-war years. Rachel died in 1889. One year later, the state of Mississippi passed a law banning interracial marriage. (Former Confederate states began passing such "anti-miscegenation" laws during Reconstruction, starting with Tennessee in 1870. Such laws aimed at driving a deeper wedge between blacks and whites in an era of segregation.) Not quite fitting into the black community, and shunned by most whites because of their mixed-race heritage, some of the Knight children began marrying cousins. Light-skinned Knights moved, hid their family past, and married white spouses or married other mixed-race individuals. Authorities arrested Knight's light-skinned descendant, Davis Knight, following his marriage to white woman in 1948 when a resentful relative exposed his mixed-race heritage.

The Mississippi Supreme Court reversed Davis's conviction in 1948, saying that the prosecution had been unable to prove the racial identity of Davis' ancestor Rachel so long after she died. The film *The Free State of Jones*, based on the story of Newton Knight and his descendant Davis and starring Matthew McConaughey in the title role, was released in 2016 to mixed reviews.

THOUGHT QUESTIONS:

1. How did economic inequality possibly contribute to the Confederacy's defeat in the Civil War?

2. What does the Newton Knight story indicate about the makeup of the Reconstruction Era Republican Party in the South?

3. What motives possibly inspired anti-miscegenation laws (statutes banning interracial marriage) beginning during Reconstruction?

Confederados

About 200,000 people in the eleven Confederate states fled their homes as the Union Army advanced during the Civil War. Few refugees travelled farther and had a more unusual fate than the *Confederados*, the white Southerners who abandoned the American South in the Reconstruction years and settled in Brazil, where slavery would not be abolished until 1888.

After the Civil War, many Confederates feared they might face treason trials in the United States. Others were too bitter to remain in their homeland and be reminded daily that they lost the war. Some worried that they could not survive financially if they had to pay their labor force.

A number of defeated Confederates therefore escaped, resettling as far as the South Pacific, where they established a slave trade selling captive Polynesians and Melanesians. Historians estimate that anywhere between 3,000 and 20,000 former slave owners, mostly from South Carolina, Georgia, Alabama, Mississippi, Louisiana, and Texas fled to locations across Latin America, to places like Mexico and Venezuela. Succumbing to the racist ideas of the time, the governments of these Latin American countries saw white settlers as particularly desirable and offered free or nearly free land to Dixie refugees. South American governments believed in white supremacy and thought their economies were being held back by the racial inferiority of their indigenous populations. The Confederate refugees often were well educated and many had also been successful farmers in their homeland.

Brazil was particularly welcoming. Emperor Dom Pedro II had supported the American South during the war and offered land grants between 1865 and 1875 to former Confederates who settled in the state of São Paulo in the southern part of the country. Some white Southerners brought their slaves with them and continued to hold them in bondage.

The more successful *Confederados*, as they came to be called, also bought new slaves in Brazil at much lower prices than had prevailed in the United States before the Civil War. The newcomers introduced modern plows and other advanced equipment, which helped produce impressive yields not just in cotton but also in food crops, sugar cane, and coffee. Such *Confederados* grew fabulously rich. On the other hand, approximately half of the southern refugees found life in Brazil harder than they expected, returning to their home country or dying from tropical illnesses.

The first *Confederado* generation resisted assimilating into the surrounding culture, building homes with wraparound porches in the style of the American South, holding on to English as their language, and dining on buttermilk biscuits and gravy and fried chicken at dinnertime. American immigrants from the South did all they could to stifle the growing abolitionist movement in Brazil as slavery began to crumble in the South American nation. By the 1880s, Brazil and the Spanish colony in Cuba were the last bastions of legal slavery in the Western Hemisphere. About 75 percent of Brazil's African-descended population was free at that point, slaves frequently escaped, and, since the British had successfully suppressed the trans-Atlantic slave trade, pressure increased for exploiting cheap labor from Italy and other poor European countries as a substitute for chattel.

Although abolitionism developed much more slowly in Brazil than in the United States, by the 1880s it had become a potent force. Transplanted Americans provided some of the dwindling resistance to the movement. A *Confederado* mob carried out the assassination of an abolitionist police chief in southern Brazil the same year slavery was finally abolished in that country.

Over the generations, the *Confederado* community blended in with their Brazilian neighbors. The descendants of American slaveowners now speak Portuguese, and many married into Brazilian families. More than half of all Brazilians have at least some known African heritage, and some are now related to the *Confederados* as well. The modern *Confederado* community is multi-racial and speaks Portuguese, but they keep one foot in the Old South. They yearly hold a *Festa Confederada* ("Confederate Party") in which revelers display the Confederate battle flag and listen to bands singing country and western songs in English. It's a blended community their American ancestors could never have imagined.

THOUGHT QUESTION:

1. What worries prompted the exodus of some slaveowners from the United States after the war?

2. Why did Latin American governments desire immigration from the American South after the Civil War?

3. How do you think the *Confederados* imagined the future of their descendants in Brazil and what would surprise them about that community today?

Indian Expulsion and White Settlement in the Trans-Missouri West

Documents

The Charlotte Democrat
"Terrible battle with Indians:
General Custer, 15 officers, and every man of five companies slain"
July 10, 1876

The federal government created the Great Sioux Reservation, located within modern-day South Dakota, under the 1868 Treaty of Fort Laramie, which granted the Sioux the right to hunt and to live in the Black Hills range "as long as the grass shall grow." As had happened so often in the relationship between the United States government and indigenous people, authorities broke their promise once they realized that native peoples possessed something of value, in this case rich gold deposits discovered by white prospectors.

U.S. Army Colonel George Armstrong Custer directed his troops to conduct a surveying mission in 1874 to determine the extent of the gold and other precious metals in the fields. Custer's men confirmed that the Black Hills contained riches. Suspecting that a white invasion loomed, the Oglala Sioux, Cheyenne, and Arapaho formed an alliance and prepared for battle. The Oglala were led by Crazy Horse, a man already renowned for his skills as a military leader due to his triumph over U.S. Army Captain William J. Fetterman and a force of 80 men in a battle that whites called the Fetterman Massacre. Crazy Horse proved uncompromising in his defense of his people's right to their land.

The U.S. War Department ordered the Oglala and other indigenous nations onto reservations. Four columns of American troops arrived, and, in a series of skirmishes, the Army killed numerous Native Americans and destroyed 100 Indian lodges. White scouts located a major Sioux encampment in a valley the Oglala called Greasy Grass. Custer led 225 men into the valley on June 25, 1876, where the soldiers soon found themselves surrounded by between 2,000 and 4,000 Cheyenne and Sioux warriors who killed 268 soldiers, including Custer, and wounded more than 50 in what came to be known as Battle of the Little Bighorn.

Custer's humiliating defeat stirred genocidal anti-Indian feeling across the United States as "Custer's Last Stand" became an iconic symbol of supposed Indian brutality. The Battle of Little Bighorn became the battle most frequently depicted in American paintings, art prints, and newspaper illustrations. The legend of the "massacre" started with the first newspaper accounts of the battle, such as the one below:

The men were without water 36 hours. They determined to reach water at all hazards, and Col. Benton made a sally and routed the main body, guarding the main approach to the water.

The water was gained with one killed and seven wounded. The fighting ceased for the night, during which Maj. Reno proposed to resist further attacks. They had now been 48 hours fighting with no word from Gen. Custer. Twenty-four hours more of suspense and fighting ended, when the Indians abandoned their village in . . . haste . . .

Soon, an officer came rushing into camp, and related that he had found Gen. Custer dead and stripped naked, and near him his two brothers, Col. Tom and Boston Custer, his brother-in-law Col. Calhoun, and his nephew Col. Yates, Col. Keogh, Capt. Smith, Lieut. Crittenden, Lieut. Sturgis, Col. Cooke, Lieut. Porter, Lieut. Harrington, Dr. Lord, Maj. Kellogg, the *N. Y. Tribune* correspondent, and one hundred and ninety men and scouts. Gen. Custer went into battle with Companies C, L, I, F and E, of the 7th cavalry, and the staff and non-commissioned officers of his regiment, and a number of scouts, and only one scout remained to tell the tale all were killed.

Gen. Custer was surrounded on every side by the Indians, and men and horses fell as they fought on the skirmish line or in line of battle.

Custer was among the last who fell, but when his cheering voice was no longer heard, the Indians made easy work of the remainder.

The bodies of all save the newspaper correspondents were stripped and most of them were horribly mutilated. Custer was shot through the body and through the head. The troops cared for the wounded and buried their dead and returned to their camp for supplies and instructions from the General of the army.

Col. Smith arrived at Bismarck last night with 35 of the wounded. The Indians lost heavily in the battle. The Crow scout survived by hiding in a ravine.

He believes the Indians lost more than the whites. The village numbered 1,500 and it is thought there were 4,000 warriors.

Source: *The Charlotte* [North Carolina] *Democrat*, July 10, 1876

THOUGHT QUESTIONS:

1. Why did Native Americans form a military response so quickly when they detected white surveyors in the Black Hills county?

2. Why did the newspaper provide details such as the fact that the bodies of white casualties had been stripped and what was the likely response of readers to these details?

3. Did the newspaper provide no context explaining the battle intentionally and, if so, for what purpose?

Denis Kearney and H.L. Knight, "Appeal from California," February 28, 1878

Perhaps no group of immigrants in the American West inspired greater racist backlash in the late nineteenth century than Chinese immigrants. Between 1850 and 1880, the number of immigrants from China in the United States zoomed from 7,520 to 105,465, with such newcomers comprising almost 9 percent of California's total population and about 25 percent of the state's total workforce. The Chinese worked for low wages in dangerous jobs in railroad construction, including the construction of the Sierra Nevada section of the United States' first transcontinental line, a project that resulted in thousands of deaths. Chinese immigrants toiled as well manufacturing cigars, at textile mills, shoe factories, and as domestic servants. Ninety-five percent of the Chinese immigrants were men.

White workers despised these new arrivals, accusing them of taking jobs away from Americans and lowering wages for all workers. Employers sometimes hired the immigrants as replacement workers when whites went on strike, deepening the resentments. Ugly rumors spread about the Chinese. The press accused them of causing an epidemic of opium addiction, kidnapping white women and forcing them into prostitution, and of routinely overcharging white customers at the laundries and other businesses they owned.

Whites sometimes besieged Chinese communities, such as during a riot in Rock Springs, Wyoming, in which twenty-eight Chinese were killed and fifteen were wounded. An Irish immigrant named Denis Kearney arose as one of the major instigators of anti-Chinese violence. He formed the Workingman's Party of California in 1878 in San Francisco, home to the nation's largest Chinese population, "Treason is better than to labor beside a Chinese slave," the party's platform proclaimed. At other times, Kearney warned that railroad executives would eventually face lynching if they did not fire all their Chinese workers. Kearney's party enjoyed no electoral success, but his movement and others pressured the Congress to pass the Chinese Exclusion Act in 1882. This law blocked further immigration of Chinese laborers into the United States. Here, Kearney makes his most famous anti-Chinese appeal, which ties the importation of Chinese labor to the larger issue of nineteenth-century corporate greed:

Our moneyed men have ruled us for the past thirty years. Under the flag of the slaveholder they hoped to destroy our liberty . . . We have permitted them to become immensely rich against all sound republican policy, and they have turned upon us to sting us to death. They have seized upon the government by bribery and corruption. They have made speculation and public robbery a science . . . They have grasped all to themselves, and by their unprincipled greed brought a crisis of unparalleled distress on forty millions of people . . .

Such misgovernment, such mismanagement, may challenge the whole world for intense stupidity, and would put to shame the darkest tyranny of the barbarous past.

. . . In our golden state all these evils have been intensified. Land monopoly has seized upon all the best soil in this fair land. A few men own from ten thousand to two hundred thousand acres each. The poor Laborer can find no resting place, save on the barren mountain, or in the trackless desert . . . Here, in San Francisco, the palace of the millionaire looms up above the hovel of the starving poor with as wide a contrast as anywhere on earth.

To add to our misery and despair, a bloated aristocracy has sent to China—the greatest and oldest despotism in the world—for a cheap working slave. It rakes the slums of Asia to find the meanest slave on earth—the Chinese coolie—and imports him here to meet the free American in the Labor market, and still further widen the breach between the rich and the poor, still further to degrade white Labor.

These cheap slaves fill every place. Their dress is scant and cheap. Their food is rice from China. They hedge twenty in a room, ten by ten. They are whipped curs, abject in docility, mean, contemptible and obedient in all things. They have no wives, children or dependents.

They are imported by companies, controlled as serfs, worked like slaves, and at last go back to China with all their earnings. They are in every place, they seem to have no sex. Boys work, girls work; it is all alike to them.

The father of a family is met by them at every turn. Would he get work for himself? Ah! A stout Chinaman does it cheaper. Will he get a place for his oldest boy? He can not. His girl? Why, the Chinaman is in her place too! Every door is closed. He can only go to crime or suicide, his wife and daughter to prostitution, and his boys to hoodlumism and the penitentiary.

Do not believe those who call us savages, rioters, incendiaries, and outlaws. We seek our ends calmly, rationally, at the ballot box. So far good order has marked all our proceedings. But, we know how false, how inhuman, our adversaries are. We know that if gold, if fraud, if force can defeat us, they will all be used. And we have resolved that they shall not defeat us. We shall arm. We shall meet fraud and falsehood with defiance, and force with force, if need be.

We are men, and propose to live like men in this free land, without the contamination of slave labor, or die like men, if need be, in asserting the rights of our race, our country, and our families.

California must be all American or all Chinese. We are resolved that it shall be American, and are prepared to make it so.

Source: Denis Kearney, President, and H. L. Knight, Secretary, "Appeal from California. The Chinese Invasion. Workingmen's Address," *Indianapolis Times*, 28 February 1878.

THOUGHT QUESTIONS:

1. What do Denis Kearney and H.L. Knight see as the reasons California employers sought Chinese immigrant workers?

2. What were the harmful effects of Chinese immigration on American workers, according to Kearney and Knight?

3. How have anti-Chinese stereotypes changed and how have they stayed the same since the late nineteenth century?

The Dawes Severalty Act (1887)

The federal government not only seized land from Native Americans but also sought to shatter their cultures, to replace millennia of Indian traditions with white customs. Congress passed the Dawes Severalty Act in 1887. The law enabled the president to distribute land to individual Indians provided they broke all ties to their tribes. Racism in part motivated the law. White authorities assumed that the Indian tradition of holding land in common was "uncivilized" and that advanced peoples embraced private ownership and capitalist competition. The federal government also wanted to break up Indian nations and isolate them family-by-family in order to make Native American military and political resistance more difficult. Greed also played a role.

Aware that Plains Indians had no experience with white currency and the United States legal system, and that the Indians had been left with poorly irrigated land, sponsors of the legislation counted on the Indian small farmers to fail. Indians would then sell to speculators what had once been tribal land. The already small amount of land controlled by Indians shrank even further, declining from 155 million acres in 1881 to 78 million acres two decades later.

An Act to provide for the allotment of lands in severalty to Indians on the various reservations, and to extend the protection of the laws of the United States and the Territories over the Indians, and for other purposes.

Be it enacted by the Senate and House of Representatives of the United States of America in Congress assembled, That in all cases where any tribe or band of Indians has been, or shall hereafter be, located upon any reservation created for their use, either by treaty stipulation or by virtue of an act of Congress or executive order setting apart the same for their use, the President of the United States be, and he hereby is, authorized, whenever in his opinion any reservation or any part thereof of such Indians is advantageous for agricultural and grazing purposes, to cause said reservation, or any part thereof, to be surveyed, or resurveyed if necessary, and to allot the lands in said reservation in severalty to any Indian located thereon in quantities as follows:

To each head of a family, one-quarter of a section;

To each single person over eighteen years of age, one-eighth of a section;

To each orphan child under eighteen years of age, one-eighth of a section; and

To each other single person under eighteen years now living, or who may be born prior to the date of the order of the President directing an allotment of the lands embraced in any reservation, one-sixteenth of a section:

... And if any religious society or other organization is now occupying any of the public lands to which this act is applicable, for religious or educational work among the Indians, the Secretary of the Interior is hereby authorized to confirm such occupation to such society or organization, in quantity not exceeding one hundred and sixty acres in any one tract, so long as the same shall be so occupied, on such terms as he shall deem just; but nothing herein contained shall change or alter any claim of such society for religious or educational purposes heretofore granted by law.

... Every Indian born within the territorial limits of the United States to whom allotments shall have been made under the provisions of this act, or under any law or treaty, and every Indian born within the territorial limits of the United States who has voluntarily taken up, within said limits, his residence separate and apart from any tribe of Indians therein, and has adopted the habits of civilized life, is hereby declared to be a citizen of the United States, and is entitled to all the rights, privileges, and immunities of such citizens, whether said Indian has been or not, by birth or otherwise, a member of any tribe of Indians within the territorial limits of the United States without in any manner affecting the right of any such Indian to tribal or other property.

... That nothing in this act contained shall be so construed to affect the right and power of Congress to grant the right of way through any lands granted to an Indian, or a tribe of Indians, for railroads or other highways, or telegraph lines, for the public use, or condemn such lands to public uses, upon making just compensation.

... That nothing in this act shall be so construed as to prevent the removal of the Southern Ute Indians from their present reservation in Southwestern Colorado to a new reservation by and with consent of a majority of the adult male members of said tribe.

Approved, February, 8, 1887.

Source: https://www.ourdocuments.gov/print_friendly.php?flash=false&page=transcript&doc=50&title=Transcript+of+Dawes+Act+(1887)

THOUGHT QUESTIONS:

1. What were the intentions of the United States government in passing and implementing the Dawes Act?

2. What impact did the law likely have on Native Americans socially and politically?

3. How does the law allow encroachment of whites on Indian land and intervention in their culture?

Condition of the Indian Tribes
Report of the Joint Special Committee
March 26, 1867

As the murder and mayhem of the Civil War ground to a close, the United States government began turning its attention to what was widely called "the Indian Problem." The spread of the railroads and the discovery or rich veins of gold, silver, and other precious metals in the West, along with federal legislation encouraging westward migration, resulted in violent white conquest of lands held by indigenous people. In Colorado, natives forced onto poor land and lacking game like buffalo began raiding trains for food supplies. In retaliation, on November 29, 1864, a militia called the Colorado Volunteers murdered 200 Cheyenne men, women, and children, in some cases scalping the victims, in what came to be known as the Sand Creek Massacre.

Covered heavily by the press, the slaughter and the subsequent mutilation of bodies at the Sand Creek Reserve provoked more outrage in Washington, D.C., than most anti-Indian violence. In 1865, the Congress empaneled a special joint committee chaired by Sen. James R. Doolittle of Wisconsin to study the causes of such incidents, and condition of indigenous nations, and to recommend future policy toward original Americans.

The committee would not complete its more than 500-page report until two years later. It attributed the sharp decline in the Indian population in the West to epidemics and the loss of traditional hunting grounds to whites. Anti-Indian violence, the "Doolittle Report" said, stemmed from weak local governments and the greed and ruthlessness of white settlers. The committee also depicted tragedies such as happened at Sand Creek as the predictable result when a "superior" race encountered a supposedly inferior one.

The committee did not call for protecting Indians or ending white violation of Indian territory. Instead it declared that Indians could no longer continue as nomadic hunters. Native peoples would be expected to accept confinement on reservations, depend on farming (regardless of the poor soil often available), and "walk the white man's road." Acting on the report, the federal government accelerated assignment of Western native nations to ever-shrinking, crowded reservations.

"The Indians everywhere, with the exception of the tribes in the Indian territory are rapidly decreasing in numbers from various causes: By disease; by intemperance; by wars among themselves and with the whites; by the steady and resistless emigration of white men into the territories of the west, which confining the Indians to still narrower limits, destroys that game, which in their normal state, constitutes their principal means of subsistence; and by the irrepressible conflict between a superior and inferior race when brought in the presence of each other . . .

The committee are of the opinion that in a large majority of cases, Indian wars are to be traced to the aggressions of lawless white men, always to be found upon the frontier, or boundary line between savage and civilized life.

... Colonel Kit Carson, who has lived upon the plains and in the mountains since 1826, and has been all that time well acquainted with Indian tribes in peace and in war, confirms this statement. He says, 'as a general thing, the difficulties arise from aggressions on the part of the whites . . . The whites are always cursing the Indians and not willing to do them justice . . .'

From whatever cause wars might be brought on, either between different Indian tribes or between Indians and whites, they are very destructive not only of the lives of the warriors engaged in it, but of the women and children also, often becoming a war of extermination. Such is the rule of savage warfare, and it is difficult, if not impossible, to restrain white men, especially white men upon the frontiers, from adopting the same mode of warfare against the Indians. The indiscriminate slaughter of men, women, and children has frequently occurred in the history of Indian wars . . .

Another potent cause of [Indians'] decay is to be found in their loss of their hunting grounds and in the destruction of that game upon which the Indians subsist. This cause, always powerful, has of late greatly increased. Until the white settlements crossed the Mississippi, the Indians could still find hunting grounds without limit and game, especially the buffalo, in great abundance upon the western plains.

But the discovery of gold and silver in California and in all the mountain territories, poured a flood of hardy and adventurous miners across the plains, and into all the valleys and the gorges of the mountains from the east . . .

Even after territorial governments are established over them in form by Congress, the population is so sparse, and the administration of the civil law so feeble that the people are practically without any law but their own will. In their eager search for gold or fertile tracts of land, the boundaries of the Indian reservations are wholly disregarded; conflicts ensue; exterminating wars follow in which the Indian is, of course, at the last, overwhelmed if not destroyed.

Source: Condition of the Indian Tribes: Report of the Joint Special Committee, Appointed Under Joint Resolution of March 3, 1865 (Washington, D.C.: Government Printing Office, 1867). https://babel.hathitrust.org/cgi/pt?id=hvd.32044051726057;view=1up;seq=9

THOUGHT QUESTIONS:

1. What contributed to the increase of the white population in the West?

2. To what did the Doolittle Report attribute the deteriorating living conditions of native peoples in the West?

3. Was the Doolittle Report intended to help Native Americans in the West or rationalize the seizure of more of their land?

Vignettes

No Man's Business to Divide the Land: Chief Joseph and Indian Resistance

The Nez Percé Indians were a small tribe living peacefully in the beautiful Wallowa Valley of Oregon, a fertile area of mountain forests, meadows, winding rivers, and a pure blue lake. Earlier in their history, when the half-starved and illness-weakened Lewis and Clark expedition entered their territory, Nez Percé had welcomed the whites, supplied them with food, and looked after their horses. In seventy years of contact, they had never killed a white settler.

In the 1850s, the Christian, "progressive" branch of the tribe agreed to turn over large tracts of mineral-rich land to the federal government. They accepted the white man's offer to live on a large reservation set aside for them in Idaho. In 1863, the discovery of gold greatly diminished this reservation. However, a new leader emerged at this time, the dignified and statesman-like Hin-mah-too-yah-lat-kekt, whose name in the Nez Percé language means "Thunder Rolling Down the Mountain." Whites called him 'Chief Joseph."

Joseph refused to sign any treaty giving up more land. Joseph reflected the views of most Native Americans when he declared: "The earth was created by the assistance of the sun, and it should be left as it was. . . . The country was made without lines of demarcation, and it is no man's business to divide it." While most whites saw the land and its resources as there to be exploited, Native Americans believed that people were a part of nature, not its master. Chief Joseph affirmed, "The earth and myself are of one mind. The measure of the land and the measure of our bodies are the same." Like other Indians, he felt that land could be used but could no more be owned than the air all people breathed.

An advocate of peaceful coexistence with whites, Joseph and his tribe were able to survive on their little piece of paradise until the 1870s. White settlers began to covet this prime area. They pressured the government into forcing the rest of the Nez Percé onto the Idaho reservation in 1877. With a heavy heart, Joseph convinced his people that resistance was futile, and they began their long journey from the land they loved to the reservation. On the way, however, some of the younger men in the band, angered by their treatment and fortified by alcohol,, killed four whites they saw as invaders of their land.

Joseph understood that retribution would be swift and terrible. He persuaded his people to flee with him, hoping to gain sanctuary in Canada where many Sioux Indians had received refuge. At the battle of White Bird Canyon, he was able to drive off the pursuing American troops. Then the Nez Percé scattered in many directions. Joseph led the largest group of 200 men and 350 women, children, and old people. A remarkable chase followed through Idaho and Montana. The Nez Percé traveled east through Yellowstone Park where they frightened some of the astonished tourists and almost encountered General Sherman fishing in the area. Then they headed north. The weary band of Indians covered 1,321 miles in 75 days, hunted by some 5,000 embarrassed government troops. Fascinated readers of Eastern newspapers, uniformly sympathetic to the underdog Indians, eagerly followed each day's story. (Native Americans had long since been eliminated there, so Easterners could far more easily feel tolerance toward the Indian.) The embarrassed generals explained their ineptitude by dubbing Joseph, "the red Napoleon."

The army regiments finally caught up with the Nez Percé within sight of the Canadian border. Some bands of resolute warriors were able to slip across the border where Sitting Bull in his Sioux Canadian village welcomed them. But Joseph and most of his tribe surrendered, exhausted, freezing, and broken hearted. Of the four hundred Nez Percé left, only eighty-seven were fighting men. General Nelson Miles, who greatly admired Joseph's efforts for his people, agreed to allow the band to return to the Idaho reservation. After meeting with the general, Joseph declared, "Hear me, my chiefs. I am tired; my heart is sick and sad. From where the sun now stands, I will fight no more forever." Then, the chief swept his blanket across his face as a symbol of mourning and surrendered. It had cost almost $2 million to vanquish Joseph and his followers.

The American government reneged on the promise General Miles had made to the Nez Percé. Rather than sending them to the Idaho reservation, it moved them from one desolate place to another, finally settling them in a flatlands reservation in Oklahoma. Many died from malnutrition and disease, including Joseph's six children. In 1885, the government transferred the survivors to a reservation near Spokane, Washington, where their descendants remain to this day. Chief Joseph puzzled Buffalo Bill Cody when he joined the "Wild West" shows. The chief was willing to repeat his famous speeches, but he always refused to don war paint and re-enact the end of his people's quest. He died in 1904. The Indian agency physician listed the cause of death as "a broken heart."

THOUGHT QUESTIONS:

1. How did the Nez Percé conception of land use differ from that of most white Americans?

2. What were the chief turning points in the relationship between the Nez Percé and the United States government?

3. Why were whites living in the Eastern United States more likely to view Chief Joseph as a hero than whites in the Western U.S.?

Frederic Remington
and the Mythology of the American West

Few individuals had as much impact on how the world remembered—and misremembered—the late nineteenth-century West than the artist and writer Frederic Remington. Remington's paintings and sculptures largely depicted the white conquest of the land west of the Mississippi River in the late nineteenth century. He reveled in scenes of shootouts between cowboys and Indians, scouts exploring bleak desert landscapes, Native American buffalo hunts, and the U.S. Army cavalry charging on Native American warriors, who are sometimes depicting as scalping and committing other atrocities on white settlers.

Remington rarely saw his father, who was an officer in the Union Army, during the first four years of his life. As an only child he was spoiled, and when his father Seth Remington returned from the front, he patiently supported his undisciplined son. Frederic started drawing as a young man and entered Yale University where he studied art, but he was far more interested in sports.

Frederic's college career halted abruptly at the age of 19 when his father died of tuberculosis. After proposing to his girlfriend and being rejected by the woman's father, Remington took his inheritance and headed west on a journey of self-discovery that took him first to Montana in 1881.

He would later claim that while there, a conversation with a freighter—someone who loads and receives items for transportation—provided the theme that would animate Remington's art and writing. Remington said that the old man told him that "there [was] no more West." Remington's art reflected this view. The West, in his mind, had been where an heroic, manly American identity had been forged, the scene where an advanced civilization had triumphed over inferior savages. The frontier, however, had closed. Remington and other white elites mourned the end of that historical chapter and feared that the future promised only drift and decadence.

Women barely existed in Remington's works. Men shaped the world, he thought, and largely through violence. Individuals shaped time, not mass movements. History consisted of a struggle by white men to subdue both harsh nature and savage, "inferior" races. Remington both romanticized Native Americans as a dying breed that lived close to purifying nature and demonized them as bloodthirsty primitives.

In the mid-1880s, he began selling sketches depicting big news events for magazines, such as the U.S. Army's pursuit of Chiricahua Apache leader Geronimo who led a band that escaped the Apache reservation in hopes of finding freedom in Mexico.

Remington became a popular illustrator and painter and prided himself in the accuracy with which he captured horse anatomy and the movement of men and animals in mortal combat. In all, he produced more than 3,000 paintings, sketches, and sculptures, along with a voluminous journalism, a novel and even a Broadway play.

He obsessed over the West because he believed that the rugged terrain and the struggle against indigenous people had shaped white manhood and made the country strong. By the 1890s, however, like famed historian Frederick Jackson Turner, he feared that the

West had been settled and that the country would grow listless and soft once the pioneering instinct had been extinguished.

Rather than conquering, Remington feared whites faced conquest by a vast, inferior herd of immigrants from Asia and from Southern and Eastern Europe. A racist friend wrote Remington a letter that described a future race war that whites might have to fight against the swarming horde of outsiders. The artist seemed to relish this violent fantasy. "I've got some Winchesters [rifles], and when the massacring begins which you speak of, I can get my share of 'em and what's more, I will," he wrote. "Jews—injuns—Chinamen—Italians—Huns [Germans], the rubbish of the earth I hate." Remington saw the new immigrants as corrupt, deceitful, and predatory, while by the 1890s he mourned the defeated Indians as child-like but brave and strong. Remington served as illustrator for an 1894 *Harpers' Magazine* article, "The Russian and His Jew," which argued that Jews were persecuted in the Russian Empire because of their greed and dishonesty.

Remington saw labor unions, filled with the immigrants he despised, as the new savages but who lacked the rough nobility of Native Americans. In his writings about the Pullman Strike, a job walk-off by railroad workers in 1894, Remington said that the strikers might "have to be shot up a little" like the cavalry had earlier shot up Indians.

In 1898, he was hired by newspaper kingpin William Randolph Heart to draw battle scenes in Cuba from the Spanish-American War, but by that point he began to focus more on writing. In poor health, his weight reached nearly 300 pounds, which created complications when he underwent surgery for an emergency appendectomy and died the day after Christmas in 1909. Remington's Western sculptures, paintings and sketches, inspired decades of movies and, beginning in the 1950s, TV shows set in the so-called "Wild West."

THOUGHT QUESTIONS:

1. According to Frederic Remington, what significance did the West hold for American history?

2. How did Frederic Remington view Native Americans?

3. What were Remington's feelings about late nineteenth-century immigrants to the United States?

Documenting Dishonor:
Helen Hunt Jackson

Just as Harriet Beecher Stowe's novel *Uncle Tom's Cabin* mobilized a mass readership against slavery before the Civil War, Helen Hunt Jackson's *A Century of Dishonor*, an 1881 nonfiction work, inspired calls to end the federal government abuse of Native Americans and for implementation of more humane policies towards Indians. The child of a linguistics professor at Amherst College in Massachusetts, Hunt possessed a curious, skeptical mind even as a child. After marrying an army officer who was transferred from station to station, she got to befriend many important literary figures across the country, such as Emily Dickinson. In the 1860s she began a career as a poet, a writer of children's books, and author of short stories in numerous popular journals.

Her writing had always been apolitical, but that changed after her she attended a reception in Boston in 1879 with her husband and encountered emissaries from the Ponca and Omaha nations whose lands were being seized by the United States government in spite of previous treaties. Additionally, the government had slashed promised annuities to the native peoples, who were also denied access to their traditional buffalo hunting grounds. The Poncas and Omahas had been left with poor farming land and faced starvation during that year's harsh winter.

Jackson was horrified by the plight of the Ponca and the Omaha peoples and in 1881 authored *A Century of Dishonor*. The book outlined the tragic history of how the American government systematically violated treaties and robbed resources, including land, from seven different Native American peoples: the Cherokees, Cheyenne, Delaware, Nez Perce, Ponca, Sioux, and Winnebago nations. Ridiculing whites who insisted they were doing the native peoples a favor by forcibly removing them from their historical lands and denying them the ability to support themselves through buffalo hunts, Hunt at one point wrote the following acid observation:

> If it is "an appeal to men's better natures" to remove them by force from a healthful Northern climate, which they love and thrive in, to a malarial Southern one, where they are struck down by chills and fever—refuse them medicine which can combat chills and fever, and finally starve them—there indeed, might be said to have been most forcible appeals made to the "better natures" of these Northern Cheyennes.

Indifferent due to their racism and sexism, many male readers dismissed the volume as impractical female sentimentality for supposed savages. Nevertheless, partly inspired by Jackson, Philadelphia churchwomen established a "Friends of the Indians" group in 1883. The group lobbied for the government to build more Indian schools and to improve the quality of education at those institutions, to provide a 160-acre homestead for each indigenous person, and for the federal government to honor its previous commitments to Native American nations.

Similarly, Jackson called for an abolition of the reservation system and its replacement with individual Indian land ownership. This reform effort had unintended consequences. The passage of the Dawes Severalty Act in 1887 aimed at this goal, but mainly resulted in the breakup of Indian tribes and the further acquisition of Native American territory by unscrupulous land agents.

Jackson continued writing on Native American subjects, co-authoring a government-sponsored work, the 1883 *Report on the Conditions and Needs of the Mission Indians*, and a popular novel, *Ramona*, written between 1883-1884.

The later book told the tale of an orphan born of a white man and a Native American woman. Ramona is raised by a foster mother who keeps the girl's Native American heritage a secret. The foster mother, Señora Gonzago Moreno, is able to accept the girl because of her white father, but she despises Indians and fights to prevent Ramona from marrying a young indigenous man, Alessandro. The couple runs away to Alessandro's people and marries anyway. Hunt depicts the fierce prejudice and hardship Indians face. The couple's child dies due to the family's poverty and lack of medical care. Later in the book, a white man murders Alessandro.

Hunt would again be frustrated by the response of readers, who paid less attention to the tragic lives of the Native American characters and more to what they saw as the exotic and romantic "Spanish American" setting for the story. Jackson thought the novel had failed in its mission. She died of stomach cancer the following year in San Francisco at the age of 54 but she laid a foundation for later revisionist histories of Native American treatment at the hands of the white majority.

THOUGHT QUESTIONS:

1. For what reasons was Helen Hunt Jackson's research on the treatment of Native Americans dismissed by many readers when *A Century of Dishonor* was published in 1881?

2. What were some of the hardships experienced by Native Americans in the nineteenth century exposed by Jackson?

3. Did the specific reforms Jackson called for backfire in any way and how did she influence the attitudes of some whites towards Native Americans?

Lyda Conley: A Legal Voice for Native Peoples

The Wyandot Nation had a long history of producing strong, independent women. Jesuit priests, who worked to Christianize them in the 1600s, gave up trying to adapt them to the European idea of male supremacy. Whites took the Wyandots' matriarchal and matrilineal social structure as signs of Indian barbarism. Wyandot women enjoyed property rights to a far greater degree than contemporary European women, helped choose the leaders of their people, and played a central role in religious ceremonies. It was perhaps not surprising that a Wyandot, Lyda Conley, would become only the third woman, the second female attorney, and the first Native American woman to argue a case before the United States Supreme Court.

The Wyandots originally called the region around modern-day Ontario home, but by the mid-nineteenth century, the group had been pushed out of ancestral lands into Ohio and Kansas. In the mid-1850s, they were offered U.S. citizenship if they met white definitions of civilization, which included individual ownership of land. Other Wyndots resettled on a reservation the U.S. government had established in the Indian Territory in modern-day Oklahoma. The Oklahoma Wyndots retained control of some land in Kansas, including a burial ground that came to be known as the Huron Cemetery.

Lyda was born in Kansas in the late 1860s to an English-descended father and a Wynandot mother. She attended Park College in Missouri before she began teaching at a business school. In 1900, she entered the Kansas City College of Law, one of four women in her class. She graduated in 1902, earning admission to the bar. She did not get a lot of clients and thus had to continue teaching classes at Spaulding Business College. But her education and modest practice left her well prepared for what became the critical legal case of her career.

In 1906, the Wyandot Nation in Oklahoma decided to sell the Huron Cemetery, located in Kansas City, Kansas. The land had become highly valuable. Since sale of Indian land could only occur with authorization of the federal government, the Interior Department created a three-member commission, including two members of the Wyandot Nation, that prepared to take bids on the graveyard. However, various relatives of Lyda Conley were buried there, including her grandmother, mother, and one sister. Conley strongly objected to the sale of what she considered sacred ground, a sale that could possibly result in the disinterment of loved ones and the conversion of the plot into a commercial development.

To halt the proceedings, Conley and her sister posted a sign at the cemetery that summer warning, "Trespassers, Beware." Conley and her sister reportedly guarded the site with rifles to ward off intruders. They even built a hut that one slept in while the other sister served as a lookout. The Conley women's bravery won support from whites, particularly middle-class women in Kansas City, and efforts to sell the property stalled.

Conley argued that burial sites held a particularly important place in Native American culture. "History tells us that a superstitious reverence for and burial of the dead has been found a distinguishing trait of Indian character—to some extent we believe this to be true—as graves of the redmen were their only monuments, so traditions were their only history," she said.

Conley filed a petition in a U.S. District court on June 11, 1907 to halt the sale. She argued that such a transaction violated an 1855 treaty between the Wyandot people and the United States government. She lost, but her appeal went all the way to the United States Supreme Court in December 1909.

She presented her case to the justices, thus making history, arguing that the Wyandot graves deserved no less respect than that "of [President George] Washington at Mount Vernon." Her presentation was moving, but nevertheless three weeks later Justice Oliver Wendell Holmes, writing for the majority, ruled that the planned sale of the graveyard was legal. Only the tribe, he said, and not individual Wyandots had the right to determine the disposition of the property.

Conley was not ready to give up. She and her sister resumed squatting at the cemetery, building a shack and then rebuilding it several times when federal marshals knocked it down. Eventually authorities gave up. By now, the Conleys were national celebrities. Kansas Senator Charles Curtis visited the site and subsequently introduced a bill that would prohibit the cemetery's sale. Congress passed legislation, making the Huron Cemetery a national monument on February 13, 1913.

Lyda Conley died May 28, 1946, and the Wyandot Nation in Oklahoma almost immediately lobbied for a new law that would rescind the gravesite's monument status and allow a sale of the grounds, but such legislation failed to gain enough support to pass. Lena Conley, who had stood guard at the site with her sister, died in 1958, and her gravestone in Kansas City declares, "Cursed be the villain that molests their graves."

The Wyandot Nation finally gave up their efforts to sell the land, and, in 2016, the cemetery was declared a National Historic Landmark. It was more than 70 years after her death, but Lyda Conley finally won a permanent victory, insuring that the graves of the Wyandot dead in Kansas will not be disturbed.

THOUGHT QUESTION:

1. What did Lyda Conley see as the significance of burial sites to Native American culture?

2. What tactics did Conley use to prevent the gravesites' sale?

3. What impact did Conley's efforts to preserve the graves have on white public opinion?

Chapter 19

Wealth, Poverty, and the Gilded Age, 1870-1900

Documents

Edward Bellamy
Looking Backward, 2000-1887
(1888)

Late-nineteenth-century so-called "Robber Barons" (super-rich business tycoons like John D. Rockefeller) presided over business empires and lived like royalty in mansions while the children of the industrial working class sometimes died of preventable diseases in the cellars of squalid tenements in urban slums. The suppression of labor unions led to workplace violence, such as the bombing at Haymarket Square in Chicago. Author Edward Bellamy described a much better world more than 100 years in the future in his best-known novel, **Looking Backward: 2000-1887**.

Published in 1888, the novel imagined a utopian socialist future: In the year 2000, war has been abolished and economic inequality has vanished. The state owns all industry and ensures jobs for all citizens. Their comfort and security ensured, citizens pursue education. Crime has vanished, as have all signs of crass commercialism.

Bellamy's idealistic utopian fantasy became the third-highest-selling novel of the nineteenth century, second only to **Uncle Tom's Cabin** *and* **Ben-Hur: A Tale of the Christ**. *More than 1 million copies sold in spite of the fact that the tale, similar in some ways to Rip Van Winkle, consists of series of conversations between Julian West, a man hypnotized into a deep sleep who awakens 113 years later and Dr. Leete, a man of the future who shows him the marvels of his time. Leete explains how humanity climbed from the squalor and greed of* *the late-nineteenth-century Gilded Age to a time in which every material good is distributed equally.*

Bellamy's novel anticipates such twentieth-century innovations as shopping malls and credit cards and imagines that the citizen of the year 2000 will be able to retire in comfort with a full government pension at age 45. Leete explains to West how the government nationalized all major industries in order to provide abundance for all citizens and fostered a belief in that population that the common good outweighed individual ambition.

After publication of the novel, "Nationalist Clubs" dedicated to the ideas embodied in **Looking Backward** *formed all over the country. Bellamy's followers became involved in Populism, a farmers' movement in the 1880s and 1890s that called for (among other reforms) government ownership of the railroads and telegraph lines. The book also influenced Eugene Debs, a labor leader who became the Socialist candidate for president five times between 1900 and 1920.*

Bellamy concerned himself not just with economic fairness but also women's rights, such as women's suffrage. Bellamy's next books such as the sequel to **Looking Backward***, 1897's* **Equality***, received much less attention. He died of tuberculosis in his home state of Massachusetts in 1898 at the age of 48.*

"You have not yet told me what was the answer to the riddle which you found," I said. "I am impatient to know by what contradiction of natural sequence the peace and prosperity which you now seem to enjoy could have been the outcome of an era like my own."

"Excuse me," replied my host, "but do you smoke?" It was not till our cigars were lighted and drawing well that he resumed. ". . . The Bostonians of your day had the reputation of being great askers of questions, and I am going to show my descent by asking you one to begin with. What should you name as the most prominent feature of the labor troubles of your day?"

"Why, the strikes, of course," I replied.

"Exactly; but what made the strikes so formidable?"

"The great labor organizations."

"And what was the motive of these great organizations?"

"The workmen claimed they had to organize to get their rights from the big corporations," I replied.

"That is just it," said Dr. Leete; "the organization of labor and the strikes were an effect, merely, of the concentration of capital in greater masses than had ever been known before. . . . The individual laborer, who had been relatively important to the small employer, was reduced to insignificance and powerlessness over against the great corporation, while at the same time the way upward to the grade of employer was closed to him. Self-defense drove him to union with his fellows."

"The records of the period show that the outcry against the concentration of capital was furious. Men believed that it threatened society with a form of tyranny more abhorrent than it had ever endured. They believed that the great corporations were preparing for them the yoke of a baser servitude than had ever been imposed on the race, servitude not to men but to soulless machines incapable of any motive but insatiable greed."

"Meanwhile, without being in the smallest degree checked by the clamor against it, the absorption of business by ever larger monopolies continued. In the United States there was not, after the beginning of the last quarter of the century, any opportunity whatever for individual enterprise in any important field of industry, unless backed by a great capital. During the last decade of the century, such small businesses as still remained were fast-failing survivals of a past epoch, or mere parasites on the great corporations, or else existed in fields too small to attract the great capitalists. Small businesses, as far as they still remained, were reduced to the condition of rats and mice, living in holes and corners, and counting on evading notice for the enjoyment of existence."

". . . [A]vast increase had gone chiefly to make the rich richer, increasing the gap between them and the poor; but the fact remained that, as a means merely of producing wealth, capital had been proved efficient in proportion to its consolidation."

". . . Early in the last century the evolution was completed by the final consolidation of the entire capital of the nation. The industry and commerce of the country, ceasing to be conducted by a set of irresponsible corporations and syndicates of private persons at their caprice and for their profit, were intrusted to a single syndicate representing the people, to be conducted in the common interest for the common profit. The nation, that is to say, organized as the one great business corporation in which all other corporations were absorbed; it became the one capitalist in the place of all other capitalists, the sole employer, the final monopoly in which all previous and lesser monopolies were swallowed up, a monopoly in the profits and economies of which all citizens shared. The epoch of trusts had ended in The Great Trust. In a word, the people of the United States concluded to assume the conduct of their own business."

. . . [There] was something which followed as a matter of course as soon as the nation had become the sole capitalist. The people were already accustomed to the idea that the obligation of every citizen, not physically disabled, to contribute his military services to the defense of the nation was equal and absolute. That it was equally the duty of every citizen to contribute his quota of industrial or intellectual services to the maintenance of the nation was equally evident, though it was not until the nation became the employer of labor that citizens were able to render this sort of service with any pretense either of universality or equity."

Source: Edward Bellamy, *Looking Backward, 2000-1887* Boston: Ticknor and Company, 1888).

THOUGHT QUESTIONS:

1. What social conditions of the Gilded Age likely inspired Edward Bellamy's novel *Looking Backward*?

2. How did society in the year 2000 differ from 1887, as depicted in Bellamy's novel?

3. What political impact did Bellamy's writing have in the late nineteenth century?

Andrew Carnegie
"The Gospel of Wealth" (1889)

Two ideas dominated elite thinking during The Gilded Age. One was Social Darwinism. In this worldview, the human society is not much different from nature. Humans, like animals in the wild, compete for food, shelter, and other advantages in an unforgiving world. The "fittest"—the smartest, the bravest, the most innovative, and the most determined—prevail, while the "unfit"—the least intelligent, the laziest, and the fearful—fall to the bottom. Wealthy individuals like Andrew Carnegie, John D. Rockefeller, and Jay Gould were able to build their fortunes, the Social Darwinists argued, because they were the most biologically fit, while the poor were unfit. Social Darwinism reinforced the other major concept shaping the elite conscious in the late nineteenth century, laissez-faire.

Believers in laissez-faire held that the federal and state governments should not interfere in the workings of the economy in terms of regulating wages, working conditions, or prices, or forbidding trusts. To do so would stifle ambition and rob the rewards the wealthy had supposedly earned through their creativity and determination.

Steel magnate Andrew Carnegie offered an alternative to pure laissez-faire and Social Darwinism in an article he authored in June 1889, "Wealth," published in the **North American Review***, an essay that later became known as "The Gospel of Wealth." Carnegie worried that modern means of production created alienation between workers and capitalists and fueled calls for socialism and communism. He chided others of his class for conspicuous consumption, warning that the lavish lifestyles of the superrich yielded resentment and radicalism among the poor.*

He disdained the recipients of inherited wealth and advocated high taxes on inheritances to force heirs to work their way up as he thought he had. He advocated that excess wealth be used to underwrite a trust fund to create opportunities for the less advantaged to climb the economic ladder, but he also rejected traditional forms of charity, such as providing direct financial aid to the poor. Carnegie's admonitions won few converts among other Robber Barons. In any case, his behavior as a business manager did not align with his printed words. Many critics pointed out that the type of philanthropy Carnegie engaged in and advocated in his essay ignored that he had millions to give away because he paid his workers such miserable wages.

We assemble thousands of operatives in the factory, in the mine, and in the counting-house, of whom the employer can know little or nothing, and to whom the employer is little better than a myth. All intercourse between them is at an end. Rigid Castes are formed, and, as usual, mutual ignorance breeds mutual distrust. Each Caste is without sympathy for the other, and ready to credit anything disparaging in regard to it. Under the law of competition, the employer of thousands is forced into the strictest economies, among which the rates paid to labor figure prominently, and often there is friction between the employer and the employed, between capital and labor, between rich and poor. Human society loses homogeneity.

... Objections to the foundations upon which society is based are not in order, because the condition of the race is better with these than it has been with any other that has been tried. Of the effect of any new substitutes proposed we cannot be sure. The Socialist or Anarchist who seeks to overturn present conditions is to be regarded as attacking the foundation upon which civilization itself rests, for civilization took its start from the day that the capable, industrious workman said to his incompetent and lazy fellow, "If thou dost not sow, thou shalt not reap," and thus ended primitive Communism by separating the drones from the bees. One who studies this subject will soon be brought face to face with the conclusion that upon the sacredness of property civilization itself depends—the right of the laborer to his hundred dollars in the savings bank, and equally the legal right of the millionaire to his millions. To those who propose to substitute Communism for this intense Individualism the answer, therefore, is: The race has tried that. All progress from that barbarous day to the present time has resulted from its displacement. Not evil, but good, has come to the race from the accumulation of wealth by those who have the ability and energy that produce it.

... There are but three modes in which surplus wealth can be disposed of. It can be left to the families of the decedents; or it can be bequeathed for public purposes; or, finally, it can be administered during their lives by its possessors ...

There remains, then, only one mode of using great fortunes; but in this we have the true antidote for the temporary unequal distribution of wealth, the reconciliation of the rich and the poor—a reign of harmony—another ideal, differing, indeed, from that of the Communist in requiring only the further evolution of existing conditions, not the total overthrow of our civilization ... Under its sway we shall have an ideal state, in which the surplus wealth of the few will become, in the best sense the property of the many, because administered for the common good, and this wealth, passing through the hands of the few, can be made a much more potent force for the elevation of our race than if it had been distributed in small sums to the people themselves. Even the poorest can be made to see this, and to agree that great sums gathered by some of their fellow-citizens and spent for public purposes, from which the masses reap the principal benefits, are more valuable to them than if scattered among them through the course of many years in trifling amounts.

... This, then, is held to be the duty of the man of Wealth: First, to set an example of modest, unostentatious living, shunning display or extravagance; to provide moderately for the legitimate wants of those dependent upon him; and after doing so to consider all surplus revenues which come to him simply as trust funds, which he is called upon to administer, and strictly bound as a matter of duty to administer in the manner which, in his judgment, is best calculated to produce the most beneficial results for the community—the man of wealth thus becoming the mere agent and trustee for his poorer brethren, bringing to their service his superior wisdom, experience and ability to administer, doing for them better than they would or could do for themselves.

Source: Andrew Carnegie, *The Gospel of Wealth and Other Timely Essays* (New York: The Century Company, 1901).

THOUGHT QUESTIONS:

1. What did Andrew Carnegie think were the three alternatives the wealthy had in distributing their fortunes upon death and which did he think was the wisest?

2. What realities did Carnegie think that socialists and communists ignored in their call for the confiscation of wealth from the upper classes and its redistribution to the poor?

3. What behavior did Carnegie urge the rich to adopt in order to ensure social cohesion and forestall revolution?

Eugene V. Debs
"Unity and Victory" (1908)

Eugene Debs grew up during the 1850s and 1860s in a humble home in Terre Haute, Indiana, one of six children born to Jean Daniel and Marguerite Mari Debs, French immigrants who operated a grocery story in a two-story house. As crowded as the surroundings were, the Debs family shared an intellectual hunger that drove the future five-time Socialist presidential candidate for the rest of his life.

Debs left school when he had only reached the age of 14 to become a paint scraper and car cleaner for the Terra Haute and Indianapolis Railroad until one night he was asked to replace a fireman who hadn't shown up for work. (Firemen tended the fire that generated the power for steam engines.) Debs held that job for three years until he took a position working in a grocery store and attending business school at night. At the age 19, in 1875, he joined a union for the first time, the Brotherhood of Local Firemen. He quickly saw a connection between labor's struggle for fair working conditions and political activism, and he won election as a Democrat to the Indiana House of Representatives in 1884.

Debs served only one term before devoting himself fulltime to union organizing, and he helped build several railway workers' unions, such as the Brotherhood of Railroad Brakemen. By the early 1890s he became increasingly interested in the leftist politics of author Edward Bellamy and particularly in socialism. He played a major role in the 1894 strike against the Pullman Palace Car Company, a manufacturer of railroad sleeping cars that laid off hundreds of workers and slashed wages by about 33 percent one year after the start of a major depression. Debs led the 150,000-member American Railway Union. The ARU staged a strike calling for a rollback in pay cuts and a reduction in rents at company housing. The strike spread nationwide, with railroad workers refusing to handle trains carrying Pullman Cars.

The strike provoked a brutal response from President Grover Cleveland. As a federal court issued an injunction calling on strikers to return to work, Cleveland dispatched 12,000 troops to crush the uprising and reopen rail lines. Federal marshals shot two strikers to death in Kensington, Illinois, not far from Chicago, while authorities arrested Debs and put him in prison for defying the court order by continuing the strike. He stayed in prison for six months, an experience that deepened his commitment to radical politics.

He won the Social Democratic Party's nomination for president in 1900. He would earn the presidential nomination of the Socialist Party of America in 1904, 1908, and 1912. He went from winning 0.6 percent of the popular vote in his first race to almost 6 percent in the 1912 election. He ran for the White House one last time in 1920, this time from prison, after being convicted of sedition for urging workers to resist the military draft during World War I, which he called a capitalist plot to divide workers by nationality and generate profits for the arms industry. He was sentenced to 10 years in prison, but Republican President Warren Harding commuted his sentence. The prison term wrecked his health, and he died of heart failure in 1926 at the age of 70. Below is a speech he made during his 1908 presidential campaign:

Until quite recently the average trade unionist was opposed to having politics even mentioned in the meeting of his union. The reason for this is self-evident. Workingmen have not until now keenly felt the necessity for independent working class action. They have been divided between the two capitalist parties and that very suggestion that the union was to be used in the interest of one or the other was in itself sufficient to sow the seeds of disruption. So it isn't strange that the average trade unionist guarded carefully against the introduction of political questions in the union. But within the past two or three years there have been such changes that workingmen have been compelled to take notice of the fact the labor question is essentially a political question, and that if they would protect themselves against the greed and rapacity of the capitalist class they must develop their political power as well as their economic power, and use both in their own interest.

. . . According to the Declaration of Independence, man has the inalienable right to life. If that be true it follows that he has also the inalienable right to work.

If you have no right to work you have no right to life because you can only live by work. And if you live in a system that deprives you of the right to work, that system denies you the right to live. That is sufficient proof, and if he has the right to life, it follows that he has the right to all the means that sustain life. But how is it in this outgrown capitalist system? A workingman can only find work on condition that he finds somebody who will give him permission to work for just enough of what his labor produces to keep him in working order.

. . . A half a century ago all a man needed was a trade and having this he could supply himself with the simple tools, then used, produce what he needed, and enjoy the fruit of his labor. But this has completely changed. The simple tool has disappeared and the great machine has taken its place. The little shop is gone and the great factory has come in its stead. The worker can no longer work by and for himself. He has been recruited into regiments, battalions, and armies and work has been subdivided and specialized; and now hundreds and thousands and tens of thousands of workingmen work together cooperatively to produce in great abundance, but not for themselves, however, for they no longer own the tools they work with. What they produce belongs to the capitalist class who own the tools with which they work. A man fifty years ago who made a shoe owned it. Today it is possible for that same worker, if still alive, to make a hundred times as many shoes, but he doesn't own them now. He works today with modern machinery which is the property of some capitalist who lives perhaps a thousand miles away and who owns all the products because he owns the machinery.

... The bigger the tool and the more generally it is applied, the more it produces, the sharper competition grows between the workers for the privilege of using it, and the more are thrown out of employment. Every few years, no matter what party is in power, no matter what our domestic policy is, how high the tariff or what the money standard, every few years the cry goes up about "over-production" and the working class is discharged by the thousands and thousands, and are idle . . .

No work, no food, and after a while, no credit, and all this is in the shadow of the abundance these very workers have created.

Don't you agree with me, my brothers, that this condition is an intolerable and indefensible one and that whatever may be said of the past, this system no longer answers the demands of this time? . . .

. . . There is one fact, and a very important one, that I would impress upon you, and that is the necessity for revolutionary working class political action . . .

Let me impress this fact upon your minds: the labor question, which is really the question of all humanity, will never be solved until it is solved by the working class. It will never be solved for you by the capitalist. It will never be solved for you by the politicians. It will remain unsolved until you yourselves solve it. As long as you can stand and are willing to stand these conditions, these conditions will remain: but when you unite all over the land, when you present a solid class-conscious phalanx, economically and politically there is no power on earth that can stand between you and complete emancipation.

As individuals you are helpless but united you represent an irresistible power.

Source: Eugene Debs, "Unity and Victory." Speech Before the State Convention of the American Federation of Labor, Pittsburg, Kansas, August 11, 1908, *Labor and Freedom: The Voice and Pen of Eugene V. Debs*, (St. Louis: Phil Wagner, 1916).

THOUGHT QUESTIONS:

1. Why did Eugene Debs believe that unions tried to stay out of partisan politics in the late nineteenth and early twentieth century?

2. What did Debs see as the connection between the right to live and the right to work?

3. How does Debs' view of American society compare and contrast with those of Edward Bellamy and Andrew Carnegie?

Booker T. Washington
Up from Slavery
1901

In his lifetime, Booker T. Washington became the white man's favorite black man. Born a slave in Virginia in 1856, Washington in many ways had a remarkable life. Always a curious child, he developed a lifelong love affair with learning shortly after the Emancipation Proclamation took effect across Virginia in 1865.

Shortly after freedom, Washington began teaching himself to read and received his first formal education. Working as a coal miner and in other hard, dangerous, low-wage jobs in West Virginia, he set aside enough money to attend the Hampton Institute, a black college in his home state, as well as Wayland Seminary in the nation's capital. In 1881, he earned appointment as the first president of the Tuskegee Normal and Industrial Institute, a black institution of higher learning just established in Alabama. He came to Tuskegee in an era in which white political and cultural leaders like journalist Henry Grady promoted the vision of a "New South" that would no longer be almost exclusively dependent on the production of cotton. Grady hoped to bring industrialization to the South just as Washington hoped to provide a wide range of vocational training to his Tuskegee students.

The 1880s were also a grim time for the state's racial politics, a time when African Americans began to lose political rights gained in Reconstruction, and lynchings became regular public spectacles. In the face of these horrors, Washington urged caution and restraint. He emphasized education and economic progress for blacks and urged African Americans to put aside issues of political and social equality. In an 1895 speech that came to be known as the "Atlanta Compromise," he proposed that "In all things that are purely social we [blacks and whites] can be as separate as the fingers, yet one as the hand in all things essential to mutual progress."

Washington's acceptance of segregation and disenfranchisement appealed to whites North and South, who awarded the so-called "Wizard of Tuskegee" with generous donations. He hoped that his students' successes might increase white acceptance of African Americans, but the "New South" remained a dangerous, frightening place. Even Washington could not escape ominous white resentment of his success. When he was invited to meet for lunch with President Theodore Roosevelt and his wife and daughter, Senator Benjamin Tillman (D) of South Carolina grumbled that "we shall have to kill a thousand niggers to get them back in their places." Washington summarized his cautious political and educational philosophy in his autobiography, **Up from Slavery,** *first published in 1901.*

The years from 1867 to 1879 I think may be called the period of Reconstruction . . . During the whole of the Reconstruction period two ideas were constantly agitating in the minds of the coloured people, or, at least, in the minds of a large part of the race. One of these was the craze for Greek and Latin learning, and the other was a desire to hold office.

It could not have been expected that a people who had spent generations in slavery, and before that generations in the darkest heathenism, could at first form any proper conception of what an education meant. In every part of the South, during the Reconstruction period, schools, both day and night, were filled to overflowing with people of all ages and conditions, some being as far along in age as sixty and seventy years. The ambition to secure an education was more praiseworthy and encouraging. The idea, however, was too prevalent that, as soon as one secured a little education, in some unexplainable way he would be free from most of the hardships of the world and, at any rate, could live without manual labour.

Naturally, most of our people who received some little education became teachers or preachers. While among those two classes there were many capable, earnest, godly men and women, still a large proportion took up teaching or peaching as an easy way to make a living. Many became teachers who could do little more than write their names.

. . . During the whole of the Reconstruction period our people throughout the South looked to the Federal Government for everything, very much as a child looks to its mother. This was not unnatural. The central government gave them freedom, and the white Nation had been enriched for more than two centuries by the labour of the Negro . . . I cannot but help feeling it would have been wiser if some plan could have been put in operation which would have made the possession of a certain amount of education or property, or both, a test for the exercise of the franchise, and a way provided by which this test should be made to apply honestly and squarely to both the white and the black races.

… I felt that the Reconstruction policy, so far as it related to my race, was in large measure on a false foundation, was artificial and forced. In many cases, it seemed to me that the ignorance of my race was being used as a tool with which to help white men into office, and that there was an element in the North which wanted to punish the Southern white men by forcing the Negro into positions over the heads of the Southern whites. I felt that the Negro would be the one to suffer for this in the end. Besides, the general political agitation drew the attention of our people away from the more fundamental matters of perfecting themselves in the industries at their doors and in securing property.

Source: Booker T. Washington, *Up from Slavery* (Garden City, N.Y.: Doubleday & Co., 1901) http://www.gutenberg.org/files/2376/2376-h/2376-h.htm#link2HCH0005

THOUGHT QUESTIONS

1. How does Booker T. Washington portray Reconstruction Era freedmen in Up from Slavery, and is this depiction aimed primarily at a black or white audience?

2. Why does Washington think federal policy toward African Americans during Reconstruction rested on a "false" and "artificial" foundation?

3. What does Washington think should have been the focus of federal policies toward Southern African Americans during Reconstruction, and is it likely that whites and African Americans responded differently to his overall message of self-improvement?

Vignettes

The Tyranny of the Clock

The rise of big business in the late nineteenth century seemed to intrude into every aspect of American life. Before railroads spread across the nation, for instance, standard time did not exist. Few owned mechanical clocks, and in the country's vast farmlands, Americans still mainly kept time by observing the position of the sun in the sky. Those few clocks and watches were calculated on when "high noon" took place. Time could be set differently by 10 minutes or more from town to town.

Such varying estimates of minutes and hours could not persist in the age of railroads. More precise timekeeping was a matter of life and death. Railroad companies had to accurately schedule the comings and goings of trains speeding along thousands of miles of intersecting track to prevent collisions. In any case, the arrival and departure of trains had to be more closely timed so passengers could know when to arrive at a station. The rise of industrialization led to an increased use of mechanical timepieces and the spread of telegraph lines that made synchronization of these devices possible.

Sanford Fleming, a Canadian born in Scotland, first developed the concept of standard time. In the 1870s, he proposed creating a 24-hour clock for the world, based on the time at the British Royal Observatory in Greenwich near the Thames River in England, what he called Greenwich Mean Time. Railroad companies began to lobby state legislatures to adopt standard time: the creation of time zones roughly along lines of longitude that eventually reduced about 300 local time zones to four in the contiguous states and territories. American and Canadian Railroad companies adopted this system on November 18, 1883.

This reform generated intense resistance, particularly from farmers. Some saw standard time as an intrusion upon the domain of God, who alone could control time. Other opponents of standard time, who filed lawsuits to stop it in Nebraska, Kentucky, Minnesota, North Dakota, Utah, New York and California between 1890 and 1917, had a more earthly, pragmatic concern. They saw the government's creation of time zones as evidence of the ever-expanding power of corporate America, particularly railroad companies that repeatedly victimized farmers through excessive freight fees.

Standard time reinforced the tyranny of the clock under which workers labored as the nineteenth century progressed. Mechanical clocks began appearing in American mills in the 1830s, which allowed supervisors to more tightly police the working hours of their employers.

As indoor electricity spread across the United States in the 1880s and 1890s, factories increasingly operated around the clock and supervisors told workers to speed up production or get fired. Some factories hid clocks from workers in order to trick employees to toil past the end of their shift. The presence of clocks increased the consciousness by employers of each passing second and would prompt a cult of "efficiency" in the early twentieth century lead by industrial engineer Frederick Winslow Taylor. Taylor's 1911 book *Principles of Scientific Management* urged supervisors to measure every motion taken by factory workers, in order to streamline every second of the production process, and workers were chided for each wasteful movement.

THOUGHT QUESTIONS:

1. How was time kept before the widespread use of mechanical clocks in the United States?

2. Why were railroad companies in particular interested in creating standard time?

3. Why was there opposition to standard time, and how did mechanical timekeeping change the workplace?

Lifestyles of the Rich and Famous in the Gilded Age

Industrialization created both fabulous riches and devastating poverty, and in big cities both realities sat side-by-side. By the late 1800s, more than 2 million of New York City's working poor crammed into 80,000 foul smelling and poorly ventilated tenement buildings often lacking in basic amenities such as indoor plumbing. Some of the buildings had no fire escapes, and it was not unusual for six to eight people to share a single room just 13 feet across. Tenement buildings, usually about seven stories high, swarmed with rats and provided a rich environment for the spread of infectious diseases.

Side-by-side with such grinding poverty stood opulence. The Robber Barons, as the top business elites were called in the late nineteenth and early twentieth centuries, enjoyed access to riches rarely seen in the United States, and embraced conspicuous consumption, flaunting wealth to enhance one's social standing.

The Gilded Age's super rich lived like royalty in places like San Francisco's "Nob Hill," the name derived from the word "nabob," a term referring to a person of high status. San Francisco residents liked to sneer at the rich neighborhood as "Snob Hill." There, railroad executive Mark Hopkins ordered construction of a 40-room Gothic mansion that took three years to build starting in 1875, cost $1.5 million to construct, and remained unfinished before he died in 1876. The mansion featured medieval-style columns, turrets, and towers that one local writer compared to a garish candy castle on an elaborate cake.

Cornelius Vanderbilt II inherited part of the fortune created by his grandfather, Cornelius "Commodore" Vanderbilt, the founder of the New York Central Railroad. The younger Vanderbilt's mansion, constructed in 1883 and located at 1 West 57th Street, took up an entire block. It still holds the record as the largest-ever private dwelling in New York City. At the time Vanderbilt moved in, eight family members shared 130 rooms lit by gilt chandeliers.

Also in New York City, builders covered the bottom two floors of the Fifth Avenue mansion of one-time Navy officer Edward Berwind, a king of the coal industry, in limestone. The second story included a massive ballroom. The estate featured sculpted cherubs, classic Greek columns, and a reception hall covered with a domed roof on which an artist had painted a starry night.

Charles Schwab, president of U.S. Steel, resided in a 50,000-square-foot, 75-room mansion on Riverside Drive in Manhattan that sported a great view of the Hudson River, a gymnasium, a bowling alley, a pool, and three elevators. Mrs. Stuyvesant Fish spent part of her riches to throw a dinner party for her dog. At a time when the average worker made $500 a year (a little more than $13,000 in today's dollars), Fish bedecked her pet with a $15,000 diamond collar.

Ms. Fish showered her dog in jewels while blocks away her poorer neighbors in Manhattan suffered chronic malnutrition. Social Darwinists, who believed that human society was engaged in a struggle for survival similar to that in nature, justified such luxurious living at a time of great want, arguing that great wealth was the reward the supposedly biologically fit earned by winning their struggle for survival against the unfit poor. Having such a mindset allowed one to indulge such conspicuous consumption free of embarrassment or guilt. Such inequality, however, also inspired the rise of labor unions, social justice crusades, and radical political movements such as socialism, communism, and anarchism.

THOUGHT QUESTIONS:

1. What was conspicuous consumption and how was it reflected in the lifestyles of the wealthiest Americans during the Gilded Age?

2. What living conditions did the poor suffer in urban centers like New York City during the Gilded Age and how did Social Darwinism rationalize the era's income inequality?

3. What might have been the political impact of the vast fortunes accumulated by the Gilded Age's wealthiest families?

The Open Shop Movement

The quickening pace of union activism, and the climbing number of strikes in the late nineteenth and early twentieth century frightened corporate America, which launched an intense propaganda campaign that came to be known as the "Open Shop" movement. Labor activists at the time battled to turn their worksites into "closed shops," places where all the workers were represented by a union that could determine who got hired or fired, promoted or demoted. Closed shops would prevent employers from the unfair advantage of bargaining in bad faith and then hiring strikebreakers when workers walked off the job over low wages or working hours.

Across the nation, corporate leaders and business organizations funded lobbying campaigns to get states to ban the closed shop. By 1901, according to historian Chad Pearson's book *Reform or Repression: Organizing America's Anti-Union Movement*, about 1,600 open-shop organizations had been established to ensure that their businesses became "union-free" environments. The businessmen behind these open-shop organizations presented themselves as advocates of democracy and defenders of workers' rights.

Open shop advocates depicted unions as dictatorial extortionists who wanted to force their peers to fork over union membership dues that labor leaders supposedly spent lavishly for private luxury. Leaders of the campaign, like John Kirby, Jr., of the National Association of Manufacturers, in 1906 claimed that unions did not unite but divided workers among themselves and workers against employers. Kirby said that the open shop movement represented "the strongest defense of all against the tyranny of the labor trust." The National Association of Manufacturers and other corporate-sponsored organizations used sophisticated advertising techniques to persuade the middle class that unions posed a threat to the country's economic and social stability.

Open shop leaders like N.F. Thompson, secretary of the Huntsville, Alabama Chamber of Commerce, described unions as a threat not only to the bottom lines of employers, but the "greatest menace" to the United States government. Thompson, who came from a slave-owning Tennessee family, often waxed nostalgic about what he thought had been the harmonious and productive work environment of his father's antebellum plantation. After the Civil War, Thompson became an early leader of the Reconstruction Era Ku Klux Klan. An intense campaigner for Prohibition, Thompson also plunged into the Open Shop campaign in the South, supporting an "Individual Rights Bill" passed by the Alabama state legislature in 1903. The law punished, through fines and imprisonment, anyone guilty of "boycotting, blacklisting, [or] picketing" businesses or "assaulting" the rights of strikebreakers. He would return to Tennessee in 1905 and edit an anti-union publication, *Tradesmen*, which would tout the South as a superior business environment to the North because of its anti-union political environment. Elsewhere, open-shop advocates used violence to stop unions, employing company-hired goons and police to beat strikers and placed spies in labor groups to tip off employers and the police about impending job walk-offs.

In spite of this violence, the Open Shop Movement won the support not only of the most conservative members of the business community, but also pro-reform and modernization advocates like President Theodore Roosevelt. This corporate-funded movement bore legislative fruit in the mid-twentieth century when so-called "Right to Work" laws banning closed shops passed at the federal, state, and local level.

As of 2016, 26 states had passed "right-to-work" laws. The Taft-Hartley Act enacted by Congress in 1947, meanwhile, outlawed closed shops. The Open Shop campaign was one of many factors leading to a sharp decline in organized labor in the second half of the twentieth century. Union membership peaked in 1954 at about 35 percent of the work force. As of 2017, only about 11 percent of workers belong to organized labor.

THOUGHT QUESTIONS:

1. What motivated business owners to participate in the "Open Shop" movement of the late nineteenth and early twentieth centuries?

2. What tactics did the Open Shop Movement use against labor unions?

3. What legislative success did Open Shop advocates enjoy?

"The United States of Lyncherdom"

On October 26, 1934, a mob as large as 7,000 people spent several hours torturing Claude Neal, a 23-year-old African-American man. They cut off body parts, burned him with hot irons, and hoisted him up by a noose until he started to choke to death and then let him down to prolong his agony. Finally, they killed him.

The lynching had been publicized in advance, in newspapers and on the radio, as people from eleven southern states travelled to Jackson County, Florida, to witness the spectacle. Police had arrested Neal for the murder of 20-year-old Lola Cannady and held him in a cell, but the jailors handed him over to the mob when it arrived. A member of the Florida state legislature was at the scene and made a speech not to encourage the crowd to respect Neal's legal right to a trial, but to joke that everyone should behave themselves as they committed an act of public murder.

Sadly, Claude Neal's ordeal was not unique. According to the National Association for the Advancement of Colored People, between 1882-1968, mobs lynched 4,736 men, women, and even children in the United States. That number is almost certainly a serious underestimate. Among the victims, 3,446, or 72.7 percent, were African Americans. The non-black victims included Chinese and Italian immigrants, Mexicans and Mexican Americans and, in one infamous case, Leo Frank, the Jewish manager of a pencil factory outside of Atlanta accused in 1913 of murdering a 13-year-old girl, Mary Phagan. Most of the non-black lynching victims, therefore, belonged to groups considered non-white in the late nineteenth and early twentieth century.

Lynchings happened in 44 of the 50 states but mostly in the South. About 79 percent of lynchings happened in southern states; and three former Confederate states ranked at the top for numbers of lynching: Mississippi with 581 such incidents, followed by Georgia with 531 and Texas with 493. Some lynchings aren't included in the statistics because mobs killed and buried the victims in a remote location, and the deed failed to attract attention. It is also only recently that historian Benjamin Heber Johnson revealed that as many as 5,000 Mexicans and Mexican Americans were slaughtered by the Texas Rangers law enforcement agency, sheriff departments, and local police as well as private vigilantes in the decade following the 1910 Mexican Revolution.

Perhaps what is most terrifying about lynching was that so many people participated and that in their day-to-day lives most of those involved seemed perfectly normal—farmers, businessmen, teachers, doctors, lawyers, and other "respectable" persons who committed their grisly deeds of torture and then went on with their regular routines, playing with their children, tossing a baseball back and forth, and bringing food over to ill neighbors.

The many defenders of lynching claimed that these killings were spontaneous acts of rage incited by an epidemic of black men raping white women. Rape, however, was only alleged in 19.2 percent of the cases and was highly unlikely in many of the other cases. Rape almost always occurs within racial groups, not between them and, in any case, some of the lynching victims were elderly, disabled, very young, or female, not the typical profile of a rapist.

Lynching became a common phenomenon after African Americans achieved citizenship and voting rights, ran for office, as some began to achieve financial success, and as more demanded fairer treatment from their employers. In the end, lynching was an act of terrorism. African-American men, women, and children were murdered for random reasons, such as speaking to white people before they were spoken to or for not getting out of the way of whites fast enough. The aim was to make the entire African-American community feel vulnerable and powerless. If whites could get away with the public torture and murder of black people for the most trivial of reasons, the message was then that African Americans better not fight for political freedom,

The wealthy and the powerful reacted violently any time African Americans achieved fame or influence, and would call for violence. Thus, when Booker T. Washington was invited to lunch at the White House by Theodore Roosevelt and dined with the president and his wife and daughters, Senator Benjamin Tillman (D) of South Carolina said "we shall have to kill a thousand niggers to get them back in their places."

Lynching was so common an occurrence that Mark Twain in one 1901 essay called this nation the "United States of Lyncherdom." He mocked the hypocrisy of Americans sending Christian missionaries to China while white churches refused to condemn lynching. Rather than converting the Chinese, Twain suggested, whites here should have been sending preachers to the American South to "Christianize the Christians."

A few men and women were brave enough to condemn these public spectacles of murder. None showed more courage than African-American journalist Ida B. Wells, who exposed the evils of lynching, revealing (at great danger to herself), that African Americans were murdered by mobs most often because they were too successful, they were seen as displaying too much pride, for being what was seen as insufficiently deferential to whites, or because whites wanted their property. She discovered that lynchings increased in hard economic times, such as the so-called "Long Depression" from 1873-1896. As the money supply shrank and cotton supplies dropped, destroying the income of white farmers, she reported, violence against African Americans increased.

Jesse Daniel Ames, a white woman who spent much of her life in Texas, in 1930 formed the Association of Southern Women for the Prevention of Lynching. She argued that lynching was inspired by sexism as well as racism. Lynchings skyrocketed as the women's suffrage movement peaked. Lynchers tried to convince women that they were weak and vulnerable to attack by black men. Lynching, and the urban myths about black rapists, fostered in white southern women a dependency on white men that undermined whatever confidence they gained in winning the vote.

Repeatedly, southern senators filibustered proposed federal anti-lynching laws, but the lobbying of Ames and others had an impact. From 1882 to 1901, there were more than 100 lynchings a year in all but one year in that two-decade period. The worst year, 1892, saw 230 mob murders. Lynching declined in the late 1920s, but it almost vanished in the 1930s. For the first time since it started compiling statistics, the NAACP recorded no lynchings in 1953, 1954, and 1955. The rise of defense industries in the South starting during World War II increased pay in the region, relieving the economic anxiety that provoked racial violence, and drew northern immigrants to the region who were less steeped in the South's unfortunate racial traditions. Beginning in 1946, the federal government also began investigating lynchings and actually won criminal convictions against some involved in these crimes. The epidemic receded though racial violence remains a problem in the United States today.

THOUGHT QUESTION:

1. How commonplace was lynching, where did it happen, and who were its primary victims?

2. What social factors contributed to lynchings between 1882 and 1968?

3. What led to the drop in lynchings after World War II?

The Imperial Republic

Documents

Queen Liliuokalani's Official Protest against the Treaty of Hawaiian Annexation

In 1893, under the leadership of Sanford B. Dole and aided by a cadre of U.S. marines based at Pearl Harbor, American sugar planters overthrew Queen Liliuokalani of Hawaii. The planters then asked the U.S. government to formally annex the islands. In the United States, Republican congressional leaders and President Benjamin Harrison both supported annexation, but Harrison had recently been defeated in his reelection bid by Democrat Grover Cleveland, and the Republicans lost control of the Senate and House of Representatives. Before assuming office, President-elect Cleveland successfully convinced Senate Democrats during the lame-duck session to stall on a proposed annexation treaty before they formally took over control of Congress in the next session. The queen then issued a formal protest to the U.S. government, displayed below, demanding the return of her kingdom and her lands. After an investigation revealed the role of U.S. marines in the insurrection and the fact that most native Hawaiians preferred the return of the queen, Cleveland refused to pursue annexation any further, telling the planters to give up control of the islands. The planters refused, instead declaring the independence of the "Republic of Hawaii" under the presidency of Sanford Dole. In 1898, after the conclusion of the Spanish-American War, the U.S. finally annexed Hawaii during Republican William McKinley's presidency by joint resolution of Congress.

June 17, 1897

I, Liliuokalani of Hawaii, by the will of God named heir apparent on the tenth day of April, A.D. 1877, and by the grace of God, Queen of the Hawaiian Islands on the seventeenth day of January, A.D. 1893, do hereby protest against the ratification of a certain treaty, which, so I am informed, has been signed at Washington by Messrs. Hatch, Thurston, and Kinney, purporting to cede those Islands to the territory and dominion of the United States. I declare such a treaty to be an act of wrong toward the native and part-native people of Hawaii, an invasion of the rights of the ruling chiefs, in violation of international rights both toward my people and toward friendly nations with whom they have made treaties, the perpetuation of the fraud whereby the constitutional government was overthrown, and, finally, an act of gross injustice to me.

BECAUSE the official protests made by me on the seventeenth day of January, 1893, to the so-called Provisional Government was signed by me, and received by said government with the assurance that the case was referred to the United States of America for arbitration.

BECAUSE that protest and my communications to the United States Government immediately thereafter expressly declare that I yielded my authority to the forces of the United States in order to avoid bloodshed, and because I recognized the futility of a conflict with so formidable a power.

BECAUSE the President of the United States, the Secretary of State, and an envoy commissioned by them reported in official documents that my government was unlawfully coerced by the forces, diplomatic and naval, of the United States; that I was at the date of their investigations the constitutional ruler of my people.

BECAUSE neither the above-named commission nor the government which sends it has ever received any such authority from the registered voters of Hawaii, but derives its assumed powers from the so-called committee of public safety, organized on or about the seventeenth day of January, 1893, said committee being composed largely of persons claiming American citizenship, and not one single Hawaiian was a member thereof, or in any way participated in the demonstration leading to its existence.

BECAUSE my people, about forty thousand in number, have in no way been consulted by those, three thousand in number, who claim the right to destroy the independence of Hawaii. My people constitute four-fifths of the legally qualified voters of Hawaii, and excluding those imported for the demands of labor, about the same proportion of the inhabitants.

BECAUSE said treaty ignores, not only the civic rights of my people, but, further, the hereditary property of their chiefs. Of the 4,000,000 acres composing the territory said treaty offers to annex, 1,000,000 or 915,000 acres has in no way been heretofore recognized as other than the private property of the constitutional monarch, subject to a control in no way differing from other items of a private estate.

BECAUSE it is proposed by said treaty to confiscate said property, technically called the crown lands, those legally entitled thereto, either now or in succession, receiving no consideration whatever for estates, their title to which has been always undisputed, and which is legitimately in my name at this date.

BECAUSE said treaty ignores, not only all professions of perpetual amity and good faith made by the United States in former treaties with the sovereigns representing the Hawaiian people, but all treaties made by those sovereigns with other and friendly powers, and it is thereby in violation of international law.

BECAUSE, by treating with the parties claiming at this time the right to cede said territory of Hawaii, the Government of the United States receives such territory from the hands of those whom its own magistrates (legally elected by the people of the United States, and in office in 1893) pronounced fraudulently in power and unconstitutionally ruling Hawaii.

Therefore I, Liliuokalani of Hawaii, do hereby call upon the President of that nation, to whom alone I yielded my property and my authority, to withdraw said treaty (ceding said Islands) from further consideration. I ask the honorable Senate of the United States to decline to ratify said treaty, and I implore the people of this great and good nation, from whom my ancestors learned the Christian religion, to sustain their representatives in such acts of justice and equity as may be in accord with the principles of their fathers, and to the Almighty Ruler of the universe, to him who judgeth righteously, I commit my cause.

Done at Washington, District of Columbia, United States of America, this seventeenth day of June, in the year eighteen hundred and ninety-seven.

Liliuokalani

Source: National Archives and Records Administration

THOUGHT QUESTIONS:

1. On what major points does the queen base her protest against the annexation treaty?

2. To what degree was her protest forceful in pushing her claim for reinstatement to the crown and to regain control over her lands?

3. What are your feelings with regard to the benefits to the United States of annexing Hawaii balanced against the manner in which the islands were acquired?

Chapter Twenty

The "De Lôme Letter"

*In the midst of the Cuban rebellion against Spanish rule, riots broke out in Havana led by Spanish troops upset that their commander, Valeriano Weyler, had been recalled by the Spanish government. Responding to the possible threat to American lives and property in the provincial capital, President William McKinley sent the **U.S.S. Maine** to Havana harbor. Enrique Dupuy de Lôme, the Spanish ambassador to the United States then sent a letter to a diplomat in Cuba, José Canalejas, heavily criticizing McKinley. What he did not anticipate was the theft of the letter by friends of the insurgents before it could be delivered, let alone the publication of its contents in a New York newspaper owned by William Randolph Hearst. The resulting furor in the United States, which led to the ambassador's resignation, was just beginning to die down when the **Maine** exploded, leading to the spiraling of events that culminated in the Spanish American War. Below is a translation of the famous "De Lôme Letter" in its entirety:*

His Excellency
Don José Canalejas

My Distinguished and Dear Friend:
You have no reason to ask my excuses for not having written to me, I ought also to have written to you but I have put off doing so because overwhelmed with work and *nous sommes quittes*.

The situation here remains the same. Everything depends on the political and military outcome in Cuba. The prologue of all this, in this second stage [phase] of the war, will end the day when the colonial cabinet shall be appointed and we shall be relieved in the eyes of this country of a part of the responsibility for what is happening in Cuba while the Cubans, whom these people think so immaculate, will have to assume it.

Until then, nothing can be clearly seen, and I regard it as a waste of time and progress, by a wrong road, to be sending emissaries to the rebel camp, or to negotiate with the autonomists who have as yet no legal standing, or to try to ascertain the intentions and plans of this government. The [Cuban] refugees will keep on returning one by one and as they do so will make their way into the sheep-fold, while the leaders in the field will gradually come back. Neither the one nor the other class had the courage to leave in a body and they will not be brave enough to return in a body.

The Message has been a disillusionment to the insurgents who expected something different; but I regard it as bad [for us].

Besides the ingrained and inevitable coarseness with which is repeated all that the press and public opinion in Spain have said about Weyler, it once more shows what McKinley is, weak and a bidder for the admiration of the crowd besides being a would-be politician who tries to leave a door open behind himself while keeping on good terms with the jingoes of his party.

Nevertheless, whether the practical results of it [the message] are to be injurious and adverse depends only upon ourselves.

I am entirely of your opinions; without a military end of the matter nothing will be accomplished in Cuba, and without a military and political settlement there will always be the danger of encouragement being given to the insurgents, by a part of the public opinion if not by the government.

I do not think sufficient attention has been paid to the part England is playing. Nearly all the newspaper rabble that swarms in your hotels are Englishmen, and while writing for the Journal they are also correspondents of the most influential journals and reviews of London. It has been so ever since this thing began.

As I look at it, England's only object is that the Americans should amuse themselves with us and leave her alone, and if there should be a war, that would the better stave off the conflict which she dreads but which will never come about.

It would be very advantageous to take up, even if only for effect, the question of commercial relations and to have a man of some prominence sent hither, in order that I may make use of him here to carry on a propaganda among the senators and others in opposition to the Junta and to try to win over the refugees.

So, Amblard is coming. I think he devotes himself too much to petty politics, and we have got to do something very big or we shall fail.

Adela returns your greeting, and we all trust that next year you may be a messenger of peace and take it as a Christmas gift to poor Spain.

Ever your attached friend and servant,

ENRIQUE DUPUY de LÔME.

Source: *Papers Relating to the Foreign Relations of the United States, 1898.* Washington, D.C., Government Printing Office, 1901. 1007-8.

THOUGHT QUESTIONS:

1. What specific insults toward President McKinley are revealed in this letter?

2. Despite token overtures to the rebel side, under what terms does the ambassador believe, as laid out in the letter, actual peace will depend upon?

3. What parallels and differences can be seen between the theft and publication of the letter with various kinds of government leaks today?

Platform of the American Anti-Imperialist League

The American Anti-Imperialist League was founded in June 1899 after the Spanish-American War in an effort to prevent the annexation of the Philippines. While a majority of Americans supported overseas expansion, many noteworthy citizens in the United States (including individuals from such disparate backgrounds as Andrew Carnegie, Mark Twain, Clarence Darrow, and Samuel Gompers) were greatly troubled by the prospect of American imperialism, citing a wide range of economic, legal, and moral objections. Below is the founding principles of the organization spelled out in their platform:

We hold that the policy known as imperialism is hostile to liberty and tends toward militarism, an evil from which it has been our glory to be free. We regret that it has become necessary in the land of Washington and Lincoln to reaffirm that all men, of whatever race or color, are entitled to life, liberty and the pursuit of happiness. We maintain that governments derive their just powers from the consent of the governed. We insist that the subjugation of any people is "criminal aggression" and open disloyalty to the distinctive principles of our Government.

We earnestly condemn the policy of the present National Administration in the Philippines. It seeks to extinguish the spirit of 1776 in those islands. We deplore the sacrifice of our soldiers and sailors, whose bravery deserves admiration even in an unjust war. We denounce the slaughter of the Filipinos as a needless horror. We protest against the extension of American sovereignty by Spanish methods.

We demand the immediate cessation of the war against liberty, begun by Spain and continued by us. We urge that Congress be promptly convened to announce to the Filipinos our purpose to concede to them the independence for which they have so long fought and which of right is theirs.

The United States have always protested against the doctrine of international law which permits the subjugation of the weak by the strong. A self-governing state cannot accept sovereignty over an unwilling people. The United States cannot act upon the ancient heresy that might makes right.

Imperialists assume that with the destruction of self-government in the Philippines by American hands, all opposition here will cease. This is a grievous error. Much as we abhor the war of "criminal aggression" in the Philippines, greatly as we regret that the blood of the Filipinos is on American hands, we more deeply resent the betrayal of American institutions at home. The real firing line is not in the suburbs of Manila. The foe is of our own household. The attempt of 1861 was to divide the country. That of 1899 is to destroy its fundamental principles and noblest ideals.

Whether the ruthless slaughter of the Filipinos shall end next month or next year is but an incident in a contest that must go on until the Declaration of Independence and the Constitution of the United States are rescued from the hands of their betrayers. Those who dispute about standards of value while the foundation of the Republic is undermined will be listened to as little as those who would wrangle about the small economies of the household while the house is on fire. The training of a great people for a century, the aspiration for liberty of a vast immigration are forces that will hurl aside those who in the delirium of conquest seek to destroy the character of our institutions.

We deny that the obligation of all citizens to support their Government in times of grave National peril applies to the present situation. If an Administration may with impunity ignore the issues upon which it was chosen, deliberately create a condition of war anywhere on the face of the globe, debauch the civil service for spoils to promote the adventure, organize a truth-suppressing censorship and demand of all citizens a suspension of judgment and their unanimous support while it chooses to continue the fighting, representative government itself is imperiled.

We propose to contribute to the defeat of any person or party that stands for the forcible subjugation of any people. We shall oppose for reelection all who in the White House or in Congress betray American liberty in pursuit of un-American ends. We still hope that both of our great political parties will support and defend the Declaration of Independence in the closing campaign of the century.

We hold, with Abraham Lincoln, that "no man is good enough to govern another man without that other's consent. When the white man governs himself, that is self-government, but when he governs himself and also governs another man, that is more than self-government—that is despotism." "Our reliance is in the love of liberty which God has planted in us. Our defense is in the spirit which prizes liberty as the heritage of all men in all lands. Those who deny freedom to others deserve it not for themselves, and under a just God cannot long retain it."

We cordially invite the cooperation of all men and women who remain loyal to the Declaration of Independence and the Constitution of the United States.

Source: *Speeches, Correspondence, and Political Papers of Carl Schurz*, vol. 6, ed. Frederick Bancroft (New York: G.P. Putnam's Sons, 1913), p. 77.

THOUGHT QUESTIONS:

1. What main arguments against imperialism did the League espouse in its platform? What types of counter-arguments would supporters of imperialism use to defend the acquisition of territories such as the Philippines?

2. What threats did League members make against those politicians who pursued a policy of imperialism?

3. How do advocates of various causes today try to mobilize ideas about "traditional American beliefs" to buttress their points of view?

The Platt Amendment

U.S. troops remained in Cuba for several years after the conclusion of the Spanish-American War. Three years after the war's end, Senator Orville Platt of Connecticut attached a rider to the Army Appropriations Bill of 1901 containing a series of guidelines with respect to future U.S.-Cuba relations that came to be known as the Platt Amendment. Cuban delegates to a convention crafting their new national constitution were notified that the U.S. Congress expected the Amendment's provisions to be incorporated into their finished product. The rigid terms stipulating conditions for U.S. intervention in Cuban affairs and barring Cuba from making treaties with other powers ensured that while Cuba would be an independent nation, the island country would exist as a virtual U.S. protectorate.

The Platt Amendment, shown below, became the justification for American military interventions in Cuban affairs on four separate occasions between 1906 and 1920. By 1934, however, rising Cuban nationalism and deep-seated resentment toward the Platt Amendment led its repeal as part of Franklin D. Roosevelt's Good Neighbor policy toward Latin America. The United States, nevertheless, retained its lease on the Guantánamo Bay naval base in eastern Cuba and later supported the regime of Fulgencio Batista until the general was overthrown by rebel forces led by Fidel Castro in 1959.

Whereas the Congress of the United States of America, by an Act approved March 2, 1901, provided as follows:

Provided further, That in fulfillment of the declaration contained in the joint resolution approved April twentieth, eighteen hundred and ninety-eight, entitled "For the recognition of the independence of the people of Cuba, demanding that the Government of Spain relinquish its authority and government in the island of Cuba, and withdraw its land and naval forces from Cuba and Cuban waters, and directing the President of the United States to use the land and naval forces of the United States to carry these resolutions into effect," the President is hereby authorized to "leave the government and control of the island of Cuba to its people" so soon as a government shall have been established in said island under a constitution which, either as a part thereof or in an ordinance appended thereto, shall define the future relations of the United States with Cuba, substantially as follows:

I. That the government of Cuba shall never enter into any treaty or other compact with any foreign power or powers which will impair or tend to impair the independence of Cuba, nor in any manner authorize or permit any foreign power or powers to obtain by colonization or for military or naval purposes or otherwise, lodgment in or control over any portion of said island.

II. That said government shall not assume or contract any public debt, to pay the interest upon which, and to make reasonable sinking fund provision for the ultimate discharge of which, the ordinary revenues of the island, after defraying the current expenses of government shall be inadequate.

III. That the government of Cuba consents that the United States may exercise the right to intervene for the preservation of Cuban independence, the maintenance of a government adequate for the protection of life, property, and individual liberty, and for discharging the obligations with respect to Cuba imposed by the Treaty of Paris on the United States, now to be assumed and undertaken by the government of Cuba.

IV. That all Acts of the United States in Cuba during its military occupancy thereof are ratified and validated, and all lawful rights acquired thereunder shall be maintained and protected.

V. That the government of Cuba will execute, and as far as necessary extend, the plans already devised or other plans to be mutually agreed upon, for the sanitation of the cities of the island, to the end that a recurrence of epidemic and infectious diseases may be prevented, thereby assuring protection to the people and commerce of Cuba, as well as to the commerce of the southern ports of the United States and the people residing therein.

VI. That the Isle of Pines shall be omitted from the proposed constitutional boundaries of Cuba, the title thereto being left to future adjustment by treaty.

VII. That to enable the United States to maintain the independence of Cuba, and to protect the people thereof, as well as for its own defense, the government of Cuba will sell or lease to the United States lands necessary for coaling or naval stations at certain specified points to be agreed upon with the President of the United States.

VIII. That by way of further assurance the government of Cuba will embody the foregoing provisions in a permanent treaty with the United States.

Source: U.S. Statutes at Large, Chapter 803, 31 Stat. 895-98

THOUGHT QUESTIONS:

1. Why might many Cubans be upset with many of the Platt Amendment's provisions? How did the Platt Amendment undermind notions of Cuban independence?

2. By what article(s) in the amendment was the United States allowed to set up naval bases in Cuba such as the Guantanamo Bay facility outpost? By what article(s) were other nations forbidden from doing the same?

3. Under what provisions and what set of circumstances was the United States granted the ability to militarily intervene in Cuban affairs?

Vignettes

What Destroyed the *Maine*?

On the evening of February 15, 1898, the U.S. battleship *Maine*, sitting at anchor in Havana Harbor, suddenly exploded and sank, killing 260 officers and men. In the daylight, only twisted portions of the wreck could be visible above the water. The *Maine* had arrived only three weeks prior in response to riots by Spanish soldiers against Cuban citizens, foreigners, and their property that erupted when the troopers' popular commander was relieved of his duties by Spanish authorities. President William McKinley had ordered the ship to Havana to be prepared to evacuate any Americans needing to leave but also to send a message to Spanish authorities that he was monitoring the situation in Cuba very closely.

Yellow journalists in the United States were quick to place blame for the explosion on the Spanish, who they accused of sabotage either by direct orders or through the actions of renegade troopers. Why the Spanish would attack the *Maine* was not exactly clear, but such an action fit the running narrative that publishers William Randolph Hearst and Joseph Pulitzer, owners of the *New York Journal* and the *New York World*, had been promoting—portraying the Spanish as brutish barbarians quick to use violent atrocities in order to get the upper hand in Cuba over their rebel adversaries—all in an effort to outsell their rival in the sales of their respective newspapers.

Hawkish senators and the Assistant Secretary of the Navy Theodore Roosevelt immediately demanded war, but President McKinley first wanted to see if the Navy could investigate the wreckage and determine a cause. Within a month, a U.S. Naval Inquiry Board, after taking testimony from survivors, witnesses, and divers sent down to investigate the wreckage, concluded that the *Maine* blew up as the result of an "external explosion," probably from a mine that subsequently detonated the ammunition stored in the magazines aboard the ship. The investigators placed much weight on the statements of witnesses who heard two separate explosions, plus a portion of the battleship's keel was found to be bent inwards. This hasty determination prevented any real effort at preventing a war from erupting over the incident. By the end of April, the Spanish-American War was underway.

A dozen years later, the U.S. Navy ordered a second inquiry in response to the Cuban government's desire to remove the wreck from Havana Harbor. While taking care to also remove the remaining corpses of sailors trapped within the vessel, a more thorough investigation could also be undertaken. In late 1910, engineers began work on a cofferdam built around the wreckage site followed by the pumping out of seawater to expose the remnants of the ship. For two weeks, investigators inspected the *Maine* and eventually concluded that an external explosion had triggered the explosion of its magazines.

There matters stood until 1974, when yet another exploration of the *Maine* was undertaken by Hyman Rickover, the esteemed admiral who had earned the nickname "Father of the Nuclear Navy" for directing the conversion of the modern U.S. Navy to nuclear propulsion. The admiral had become interested in the story of the *Maine* disaster and sought a private investigation using updated scientific methods. Using reports examining numerous ships damaged by internal and external explosions to compare with the Navy's two official *Maine* inquiries, as well as data obtained on the design and construction of the battleship and the type of ammunition on board, Rickover determined that the *Maine* was not destroyed by a mine. Instead, he concluded that a spontaneous combustion occurring in the coal bunker situated next to the magazine was the most likely culprit rather than the nefarious work of Spanish intriguers. (The bituminous coal used aboard the ship frequently released gases that could ignite under certain conditions.) The admiral published a book about this investigation, *How the Battleship Maine Was Destroyed*, in 1976. This theory has now been accepted as the consensus explanation for a tragic event that cost many lives and led to a conflict that would cost many more.

THOUGHT QUESTIONS:

1. What did the U.S. Navy investigators conclude in its first two inquiries into the destruction of the *Maine*? What led them to their conclusions?

2. Who reinvestigated the explosion aboard the *Maine* many decades later and what evidence did he employ to come to a totally different conclusion for what probably happened?

3. What other historical subjects are you aware in which investigators have used current technology or new forms of evidence to reexamine previous conclusions drawn by others in the past?

The Anti-Imperialist League

Established in June 1898, the American Anti-Imperialist League organized in an effort to prevent U.S. annexation of the Philippines following the conclusion of the Spanish-American War. Formed in Boston by prominent local leaders who opposed the war, its first president was James Boutwell, a former Republican Massachusetts Governor and Senator who openly broke with President William McKinley over the latter's decision to endorse the annexation of the Philippines. A total of 18 (later increased to 40) prominent civic and government leaders filled the group's ceremonial vice presidential positions, including former U.S. President Grover Cleveland, steel magnate Andrew Carnegie, and American Federation of Labor leader Samuel Gompers.

The League attempted to establish a network of local organizations in an effort to decentralize and expand the group's publicity efforts. By February 1899, the League claimed to have over 25,000 members in over 100 local branches. Well-known members of the League included 1896 presidential candidate William Jennings Bryan, social reformer Jane Addams, and the author Mark Twain.

The production and distribution of leaflets and pamphlets meant to rail against American imperialist activities became one of the primary activities of the League. These publications made extensive use of quotations from various Founding Fathers attempting to demonstrate basic contradictions between the Republic's ideals and designs for colonial expansion advanced by many national political leaders. Because the major cause of the American Revolution had been the perceived mistreatment of the American colonies by an overseas power, for the United States to conquer and rule over non-Americans with limited rights would be hypocritical.

Other, less ideological motives also explain the group's opposition to annexation of the Philippines. Some members were uneasy about the large costs involved in setting up a military and diplomatic establishment in the Philippines. Though capitalists like Carnegie could be found among the more altruistic anti-imperialists, many others joined the cause out of self-interest. U.S. sugar producers, for example, feared competition from Filipino producers. Trade unionists, such as Gompers, worried that cheap Filipino labor would come to the United States and flood the American labor market resulting in reduced wages. Finally, many anti-imperialists were devout Social Darwinists already anxious about the massive influx of southern and eastern Europeans, and these opponents of imperialism feared the effects that a surge of new "inferior" Asian immigrants would have on their country.

Ultimately, an anti-annexation coalition in the Senate failed by one vote to prevent the ratification of the Treaty of Paris in February 1899. The Anti-Imperialist League continued as the nation's moral conscience on expansion-related issues, supporting Bryan's failed 1900 presidential rematch against McKinley before slowly fading away and dissolving in 1921 three years after the end of World War I.

THOUGHT QUESTIONS:

1. What idealistic reasons did the Ant-Imperialist League often promote to explain the group's opposition to the annexation of the Philippines?

2. Which non-idealistic, more pragmatic reasons explains why other members supported the Leagues goals?

3. What forces do you think are at work projecting American power abroad today? Economic? Ideological? National defense? Other concerns? Which of these are the most important and why?

Man versus Mosquito

At the turn of the twentieth century, American engineers made a bold attempt to conquer the jungles of Central America by building a canal across the Isthmus of Panama in order to link the great Atlantic and Pacific Oceans. A previous effort begun by a French company in 1881 had ended in bankruptcy eight years later after more than 20,000 workers lost their lives to the ravages of malaria and yellow fever. While the health risks of working in such a tropical environment were understood, the causes of how malaria and yellow fever spread among humans had yet to be discovered by the medical community.

Malaria is caused by a victim being exposed to a single-celled parasite leading to severe chills, head and body aches, fever, fatigue, and nausea. In its worst manifestation, kidney failure occurs leading to death. Yellow fever, caused by exposure to a particular virus, has a higher death rate and even worse symptoms. While initially experiencing headaches, fever, and muscle pain, the disease can reach an advanced stage characterized by jaundiced skin (hence the term yellow fever) and a dark black vomit caused by internal bleeding followed by kidney failure, delirium, coma, and death. A host of theories were still being floated during the 1800s for the causation of both maladies, especially those of the airborne variety—everything from toxic swamp gas spreading unhealthy air to noxious fumes being emitted from trash and animal waste ("malaria" comes from the Italian mala aria, or "bad air").

By the late 1890s, some physicians began to suspect that both malaria and yellow fever had a connection to mosquitos, though they did not immediately understand exactly how. A British doctor serving in India named Ronald Ross made a major breakthrough after dissecting a specific type of mosquito—Anopheles—that had bitten a malaria patient. He found the malaria-causing parasite growing within the insect's stomach and salivary gland, concluding that malaria was transmitted to other humans only after the female of that type of mosquito (male mosquitos feed off fruit juice and nectar rather than blood) bit someone after previously biting into (and therefore receiving the parasite) from an already-infected human. Soon to win the Nobel Prize for his monumental discovery, Ross suggested that the way to prevent future malaria outbreaks was to exterminate the Anopheles wherever possible.

Several physicians contributed to the discovery of the link between mosquitos and the spread of yellow fever. Pioneering work had been undertaken in Cuba by Carlos Finlay, who isolated a specific mosquito—Stegomyia fasciata (later renamed Aedes aegypti)—as responsible for transmitting the virus, although he had been unable to definitively prove his allegation. The proof would come with the work of the U.S. Army Yellow Fever Commission, sent to Havana, Cuba by the Army Surgeon General to investigate the disease, which had been a debilitator and killer of U.S. troops there ever since the Spanish American War of 1898. Headed by Dr. Walter Reed who was intrigued by Finlay's theories, the Commission's doctors and staff undertook a series of experiments (sometimes on themselves with lethal effects) in order to demonstrate that bad air, dirty conditions, and the clothing of infected patients had no relation to the spread of yellow fever whatsoever. Instead, the virus was only passed among humans by the bite of the Aedes aegypti mosquito after it had previously bitten someone who had recently contracted the virus but not yet displayed any symptoms and after a twelve to twenty-day incubation period within the insect.

A member of the Commission staff, Dr. William Gorgas, remained skeptical of Reed's work despite the growing evidence, but insisted that there was only one way to find out—a massive effort should be organized to eradicate the mosquito from the city. Reed did not think it was possible but allowed Gorgas to try. Begun in February 1901, Gorgas's campaign involved a two-prong attack. First, to interfere with the ability of the mosquitos to breed, standing water was eliminated across the city to prevent the female mosquitos from laying their eggs—puddles were filled up, ponds were drained, bowls and jugs of water in houses were covered, water barrels outdoors had lids placed on them or thin layers of oil were added to the surface to prevent the larvae from receiving air. Second, systematic efforts were undertaken to directly kill as many of the insects as possible through the fumigation of every house and building. The results were astonishing. During the previous year, over 1,400 cases of yellow fever had been reported in Havana. In 1901, there were only 37. The next year, there were none. (Instances of malaria also declined sharply, from 325 deaths to 77.)

Building upon these remarkable developments, confidence was high that methods could be developed to keep yellow fever and malaria in check while constructing the Panama Canal. William Gorgas was named chief sanitation officer for the canal project but immediately ran into difficulties with the architects, project engineers, and Canal Zone governor who arrogantly refused to belief the notion that the jungle's harmful diseases were spread by mosquitoes. However, after a yellow fever outbreak made the Chief Engineer and about a quarter of the workforce flee Panama, Gorgas found the new project leader, John Stevens, to be an important ally. Despite not completely convinced that the project should be slowed down by a seemingly vain attempt to clear the Zone of mosquitos, Stevens shut down most work to allow Gorgas to give his proposed mosquito control program a try. Though certainly a more daunting task than the impressive effort to cleanse Havana (the Canal Zone had one city on each coast with 30 villages and over 50 miles of dense jungle in between), Gorgas believed that a thoroughly organized and executed plan could be successful. In the summer of 1905, more than 4,000 workers began a yearlong effort to prevent the region's mosquitos from depositing their eggs within the Zone. As in Havana, all houses and buildings were fumigated. Standing pools of water were drained. The practice of using domestic water containers was eliminated as the area was provided with running water via underground pipes or concrete ditches free of obstructions so water would always be moving. Once again, the results were amazing: a 90 percent decline in the death rate and hospitalization rate of workers due to yellow fever and malaria. As a result of the work of Gorgas's "mosquito brigades," successful completion of the Panama Canal would be virtually assured.

THOUGHT QUESTIONS:

1. What are the symptoms of malaria and yellow fever? How are these diseases transmitted to humans?

2. How were malaria and yellow fever controlled in Havana and the Canal Zone?

3. What diseases are the main threats to Americans today? What degree of research is currently underway to find cures for them? What efforts are underway to educate the public about them?

Theodore Roosevelt and the "Great White Fleet"

In a bold publicity stunt designed to impress the world's major powers, Theodore Roosevelt near the end of his administration ordered 16 battleships of the United States fleet to embark on a fourteen-month, 45,000-mile world tour with stops at every major port-of-call, including Tokyo Bay. Hoping to project America's military might to the world, especially Japan, the president believed that there would be no better way to accomplish this purpose than for the new, steel-hulled ships to steam around the world and visit their ports.

Officially, Roosevelt stated that the goal of the operation was to help the Navy train its crews in navigation, communication, coal consumption, and fleet maneuvering, though circumnavigating the globe was hardly necessary to achieve these ends. Roosevelt was criticized by many congressmen. Some asserted the tour would be too expensive to undertake. Others argued that the operation would unnecessarily weaken America's coastal defenses. Some even brought up the possibility that the trek might provoke a military response from Japan or some nation. The president ignored his critics, and after congressional funding was secured, the flotilla began to make its preparations.

The squadron embarked from Hampton Roads, Virginia, on December 16, 1907, stopping in Trinidad off the coast of Venezuela before steaming to Rio de Janeiro, Brazil. Because the Panama Canal had not yet been completed, the ships went "around the Horn"—the tip of South America—through the Straits of Magellan to reach the Pacific Ocean. After stopping at Chilean and Peruvian ports, the "Great White Fleet," so nicknamed because the vessels' hulls were painted white as was traditional for the U.S. Navy's ships in peacetime, propelled onward to Baja California. Thus far, the American sailors had experienced no serious difficulties and were enthusiastically received in all foreign ports visited, but they received near-royal treatment when they arrived at the American West Coast ports on their itinerary—San Diego, Los Angeles, Santa Barbara, Monterrey, Santa Cruz, San Francisco, Seattle, and Tacoma. Huge crowds came out to see the battleships, and the crews were regaled with praiseworthy speeches, grand banquets, and elaborate balls.

The accolades continued as the fleet made its way to Hawaii, New Zealand, Australia, Manila Bay, and (after encountering a major typhoon off the coast of Formosa) eventually Yokohama and other ports of call in Japan. After steaming back to Manila, the fleet trekked into the Indian Ocean, stopping in Ceylon (modern Sri Lanka) off the southeastern coast of India before celebrating the Christmas of 1908 in the Indian Ocean while en route to the Arabian Sea.

After traversing the Suez Canal in Egypt, the fleet's commander received word that a severe earthquake had devastated Messina, Sicily and dispatched two of the ships to set a course for Messina at top speed. When they arrived, the sailors provided food and other forms of aid to the residents of the stricken city. The other ships split into several parties after leaving Egypt and visited Algiers, Tripoli, Naples, Marseille, Athens, and Malta before regrouping at Gibraltar on February 6, 1909, before steaming into the Atlantic toward home, arriving at Hampton Roads sixteen days later to a tumultuous crowd led by prideful Theodore Roosevelt who had two weeks remaining in his presidency.

The cruise of the Great White Fleet was an overall success on many fronts for Roosevelt. From an operational standpoint, the cruise was a great success as it became the largest group of vessels to undertake a circumnavigation of the globe. Initially, critics had questioned the ability of the vessels to make such a global transit, but no serious maintenance issues or breakdowns had occurred. Diplomatically, the cruise projected American military strength in grand fashion, showing the world that the United States could bring a major force to bear anywhere in the world if needed. At the same time, the tour was also designed to be a peace mission fostering goodwill between the U.S. and the visited nations. The most improved relations took place with Japan, which had always been the main diplomatic target of the expedition. As Roosevelt hoped, Japanese officials were not provoked by the visit. Indeed, they seemed to have been genuinely impressed by the display of America's naval might and cognizant of its implications for their growing rivalry with the U.S. in the Pacific.

THOUGHT QUESTIONS:

1. What were Theodore Roosevelt's intentions in ordering the Great White Fleet to circumnavigate the globe? What did he hope to gain by this publicity stunt?

2. Was the expedition a success in terms of its goals? Why or why not?

3. In what ways do nations try to "flex their military muscles" in today's age? Is there any way that a country could organize an equivalent of the Great White Fleet today?

Chapter 21

The Progressive Reformation of Industrial America

Documents

The Case for "Municipal Housekeeping"

Much of the conservative opposition to the involvement of women in Progressive Era reforms was often centered on the idea that a woman's "proper place" was in the home rather than in the "dirty world" of male-dominated politics. Given this environment, savvy female Progressives understood that such opposition to their public activism could often be successfully countered by framing their efforts as an extension of their traditional position within the domestic sphere as protector of the home—what they often referred to as "municipal housekeeping."

In a pamphlet written for the National Woman Suffrage Association, excerpts from which appear below, Progressive reform icon Jane Addams justifies granting women the vote as an extension of municipal housekeeping necessitated by the changes created by the rise of the modern industrial metropolis.

We all know that the modern city is a new thing upon the face of the earth, and that everywhere its growth has been phenomenal, whether we look at Moscow, Berlin, Paris, New York or Chicago. With or without the medieval foundation, these cities are merely resultants of the vast crowds of people who have collected at certain points which have become manufacturing and distributing centers.

As the city itself originated for the common protection of the people, and was built about a suitable center of defense which formed a citadel, so we can trace the beginnings of the municipal franchise to the time when the problems of municipal government were still largely those of protecting the city from rebellion from within and from invasion from without. A voice in city government, as it was extended from the nobles who alone bore arms, was naturally given solely to those who were valuable to the military system. There was a certain logic in giving the franchise only to grown men, when the existence and stability of the city depended upon their defense, and when the ultimate value of the elector could be reduced to his ability to perform military duty. It was fair that only those who were liable to a sudden call to arms should be selected to decide as to the relations which the city bore to rival cities, and that the vote for war should be cast by the same men who bore the brunt of battle and the burden of protection. We are told by historians that citizens were first called together, in those assemblages which were the beginning of popular government, only if a war was to be declared or an expedition to be undertaken.

But rival cities, even St. Louis and Chicago, have long since ceased to settle their claims by force of arms, and we shall have to admit, I think, that this early test of the elector is no longer fitted to the modern city.

It has been well said that the modern city is a stronghold of industrialism, quite as the feudal city was a stronghold of militarism; but the modern cities fear no enemies and rivals from without, and their problems of government are solely internal affairs, for the most part, are going badly in these great new centers, in which the quickly-congregated population has not yet learned to arrange its affairs satisfactorily. Unsanitary housing, poisonous sewage, contaminated water, infant mortality, the spread of contagion, adulterated food, impure milk, smoke-laden air, ill-ventilated factories, dangerous occupations, juvenile crime, unwholesome crowding, prostitution and drunkenness, are the enemies which the modern cities must face and overcome, would they survive. Logically, their electorate should be made up of those who can bear a valiant part in this arduous contest, those who in the past have at least attempted to care for children, to clean houses, to prepare foods, to isolate the family from moral dangers; those who have traditionally taken care of that side of life which inevitably becomes the subject of municipal consideration and control as soon as the population is congested. To test the elector's fitness to deal with this situation by his ability to bear arms is absurd. These problems must be solved, if they are solved at all, not from the military point of view, not even from the industrial point of view, but from a third, which is rapidly developing in all the great cities of the world—the human-welfare point of view....

A city is in many respects a great business corporation, but in other respects it is enlarged housekeeping. If American cities have failed in the first, partly because officeholders have carried with them the predatory instinct learned in competitive business, and cannot help "working a good thing" when they have an opportunity, may we not say that city housekeeping has failed partly because women, the traditional housekeepers, have not been consulted as to its multiform activities? The men of the city have been carelessly indifferent to much of its civic housekeeping, as they have always been indifferent to the details of the household. They have totally disregarded a candidate's capacity to keep the streets clean, preferring to consider him in relation to the national tariff or to the necessity for increasing the national navy, in a pure spirit of reversion to the traditional type of government which had to do only with enemies and outsiders.

It is difficult to see what military prowess has to do with the multiform duties which, in a modern city, include the care of parks and libraries, superintendence of markets, sewers and bridges, the inspection of provisions and boilers, and the proper disposal of garbage. It has nothing to do with the building department, which the city maintains that it may see to it that the basements are dry, that the bedrooms are large enough to afford the required cubic feet of air, that the plumbing is sanitary, that the gas pipes do not leak, that the tenement house court is large enough to afford light and ventilation, that the stairways are fireproof. The ability to carry arms has nothing to do with the health department maintained by the city, which provides that children are vaccinated, that contagious diseases are isolated and placarded, that the spread of tuberculosis is curbed, that the water is free from typhoid infection. Certainly the military conception of society is remote from the functions of the school boards, whose concern it is that children are educated, that they are supplied with kindergartens, and are given a decent place in which to play. The very multifariousness and complexity of a city government demand the help of minds accustomed to detail and variety of work, to a sense of obligation for the health and welfare of young children, and to a responsibility for the cleanliness and comfort of other people.

Because all these things have traditionally been in the hands of women, if they take no part in them now they are not only missing the education which the natural participation in civic life would bring to them, but they are losing what they have always had. From the beginning of tribal life, they have been held responsible for the health of the community, a function which is now represented by the health department. From the days of the cave dwellers, so far as the home was clean and wholesome, it was due to their efforts, which are now represented by the Bureau of Tenement House Inspection. From the period of the primitive village, the only public sweeping which was performed was what they undertook in their divers dooryards, that which is now represented by the Bureau of Street Cleaning. Most of the departments in a modern city can be traced to woman's traditional activity; but, in spite of this, so soon as these old affairs were turned over to the care of the city, they slipped from woman's hands, apparently because they then became matters for collective action and implied the use of the franchise. Because the franchise had in the first instance been given to the man who could fight, because in the beginning he alone could vote who could carry a weapon, it was considered an improper thing for a woman to possess it....

Source: Jane Addams, *The Modern City and the Municipal Franchise for Women* (New York: National Woman Suffrage Association, 1900).

THOUGHT QUESTIONS:

1. What types of modern problems does Addams list as existing in modern cities at the turn of the twentieth century? What did she say was the reason why men alone were not capable of solving these problems?

2. What did Addams believe that women could contribute to solving these problems, and why?

3. Are there issues today at the local, state, or national level that you think garner more attention because women are involved in politics, both as voters and officeholders? On a related note, are there any issues that you think would be ignored if not for the involvement of women in politics as voters and officeholders?

Petition to Congress Opposing a Constitutional Suffrage Amendment

Woman suffrage was a heavily divisive issue during the Progressive Era. Female and male supporters vehemently argued that it was a basic human right being denied to over half the country's population, as well as a much-needed reform that would add to the ability of progressives to achieve other vital societal reforms. In southern states, many white suffragists also favored giving women the vote in order to dilute the collective voting strength of African Americans. Meanwhile, many male and female opponents also emerged to delay state and federal suffrage efforts, arguing everything from states' rights to defending the woman's traditional place to be in the home and not "soiling themselves" through involvement in the dirty world of politics. Below is an appeal to Congress by one anti-suffrage group, the New York State Association Opposed to Woman Suffrage, to reject submission to the states for ratification of a federal constitutional amendment granting women the right to vote.

WHEREAS, it is proposed by those advocating suffrage for women to introduce at this session of Congress a bill providing for the amendment to the Federal Constitution, giving women the ballot, and

WHEREAS, it is our best judgment that according to the Constitution and the fundamental principles of our government, it is the sole province of each state to decide this question for itself, and

WHEREAS, in most of the states where this question has been submitted to the people, their verdict has been adverse to granting suffrage to women,

We, the undersigned, believing that the passage of such a bill would be antagonistic to the sovereign rights of the several states, hereby earnestly protest against such action and respectfully petition the members of both Houses of the Congress of the United States to reject any bill which has for its object [the enforcing] of woman suffrage upon unwilling states by means of a federal constitutional amendment.

Source: National Archives

THOUGHT QUESTIONS:

1. On what basis did the group state that it was opposing Congress approving of the proposed constitutional amendment?

2. How might this tactic of opposition be used to effectively delay or defeat its acceptance?

3. Are there issues today in which groups use similar tactics to prevent a national policy from being accepted? Explain.

Theodore Roosevelt on Conservation

In 1908, President Theodore Roosevelt created the National Conservation Commission, chaired by Chief Forester Gifford Pinchot and consisting largely of members of Congress, government bureaucrats, and professors who were charged with studying the nation's water, forest, land, and mineral resources and making recommendations regarding their conservation. The following year, the Commission delivered its report to the president, providing an inventory of the nation's natural resources along with several conservation recommendations. Roosevelt expressed his personal conservation views in a letter that he attached to the report, which he forwarded the report to Congress. Excerpts from that letter are included below.

I transmit herewith a report of the National Conservation Commission, together with the accompanying papers. This report, which is the outgrowth of the conference of governors last May, was unanimously approved by the recent joint conference held in this city between the National Conservation Commission and governors of States, state conservation commissions, and conservation committees of great organizations of citizens. It is therefore in a peculiar sense representative of the whole nation and all its parts. . . .

The great basic facts are already well known. We know that our population is now adding about one-fifth to its numbers in ten years, and that by the middle of the present century perhaps one hundred and fifty million Americans, and by its end very many millions more, must be fed and clothed from the products of our soil. With the steady growth in population and the still more rapid increase in consumption, our people will hereafter make greater and not less demands per capita upon all the natural resources for their livelihood, comfort, and convenience. It is high time to realize that our responsibility to the coming millions is like that of parents to their children, and that in wasting our resources we are wronging our descendants. . . .

I desire to make grateful acknowledgment to the men, both in and out of the government service, who have prepared the first inventory of our natural resources. They have made it possible for this nation to take a great step forward. Their work is helping us to see that the greatest questions before us are not partisan questions, but questions upon which men of all parties and all shades of opinion may be united for the common good. Among such questions, on the material side, the conservation of natural resources stands first. It is the bottom round of the ladder on our upward progress toward a condition in which the nation as a whole, and its citizens as individuals, will set national efficiency and the public welfare before personal profit.

The policy of conservation is perhaps the most typical example of the general policies which this Government has made peculiarly its own during the opening years of the present century. The function of our Government is to insure to all its citizens, now and hereafter, their rights to life, liberty, and the pursuit of happiness. If we of this generation destroy the resources from which our children would otherwise derive their livelihood, we reduce the capacity of our land to support a population, and so either degrade the standard of living or deprive the coming generations of their right to life on this continent. If we allow great industrial organizations to exercise unregulated control of the means of production and the necessaries of life, we deprive the Americans of to-day and of the future of industrial liberty, a right no less precious and vital than political freedom. Industrial liberty was a fruit of political liberty, and in turn has become one of its chief supports, and exactly as we stand for political democracy so we must stand for industrial democracy....

All this is simply good common sense. The underlying principle of conservation has been described as the application of common sense to common problems for the common good. If the description is correct, then conservation is the great fundamental basis for national efficiency. In this stage of the world's history, to be fearless, to be just, and to be efficient are the three great requirements of national life. National efficiency is the result of natural resources well handled, of freedom of opportunity for every man, and of the inherent capacity, trained ability, knowledge, and will, collectively and individually, to use that opportunity.

Source: Library of Congress

THOUGHT QUESTIONS:

1. Why does Roosevelt believe that conservation of natural resources is such an urgent matter?

2. What responsibility does Roosevelt say that Americans have with regard to providing for future generations of Americans?

3. In today's times, what are some of the biggest threats, environmental and otherwise, that we as Americans can work on now to provide for a better tomorrow for future Americans?

The Hetch Hetchy Debate

Between 1908 and 1913, Congress debated whether to preserve a beautiful wilderness area carved by ancient glaciers within Yosemite National Park known as the Hetch Hetchy Valley, or to construct a dam and allow the site to be flooded in order to create a large reservoir to serve as a steady water supply for San Francisco, California. National opinion split between those in favor of providing the city with access to a steady supply of clean drinking water after a devastating 1906 earthquake and those favoring other options in order to preserve the valley from development.

At the heart of the debate was the conflict between conservationists, such as Chief Forester Gifford Pinchot who believed that the nation's resources should definitely be used but used wisely to benefit society, and preservationists such as Sierra Club founder John Muir who believed that nature should be left alone to maintain its beauty and protected from human interference. In this fight, the citizens of San Francisco generally supported the conservationists, arguing that the reservoir was vital to the health and growth of their city. On the other side, preservation-

ists argued that Congress should protect the Hetch Hetchy Valley from destruction, forcing San Francisco to seek other options.

Organizations and private citizens from across the country contacted Congress to voice their opinions on the issue. Ultimately, Congress passed legislation authorizing the creation of the 430-foot high O'Shaughnessy Dam in the Hetch Hetchy Valley, and President Woodrow Wilson signed the bill into law on December 19, 1913. Below are two surviving artifacts of the Hetch Hetchy fight—petitions to Congress sent by supporters and opponents of the dam, each preserved in the National Archives.

Today, the Hetch Hetchy Reservoir still serves as part of San Francisco's water supply, and falling water from O'Shaughnessy Dam continues to provide hydroelectric power for the city. Ironically, while the beauty of the larger Yosemite Valley continues to lure millions to its grandeur every year, threatening to permanently disrupt its ecology, Hetch Hetchy has escaped this annual rush of humanity and, with the exception of its flooded valley floor, has in some ways become the more preserved of the two sites.

Hon. Frank P. Flint San Francisco, February 5, 1910
U.S. Senator

Dear Sir:
The Hypatia Women's Club of San Francisco has voted to request that the permission granted by the Government to San Francisco to take water from Lake Eleanor and the Hetch-Hetchy Valley be not revoked, for the following reasons:

1st. San Francisco has no other available supply of pure water that is sufficient.

2nd. Under the permit Lake Eleanor is to be first developed.

3rd. The Yosemite Park is an immense tract, while the Hetch-Hetchy Valley, where a reservoir is proposed, is a very small space not over a mile wide and not more than three or four miles long and is often flooded for long periods during storms and high water and the making the same as a permanent reservoir rather beautifies than injures this small piece of land.

4th. Yosemite Park of which this valley is so minute a portion, is a vast domain of almost inaccessible mountains, lakes and streams at a very high altitude and largely a region of perpetual snow. It is not, or never will be visited by large numbers of people at any one time.

5th. This vast supply of pure water is running away to the ocean while San Francisco is suffering for a supply of pure water.

6th. The individual who adores every bush or tree that has ever become a familiar object and who would sacrifice the rights and needs of a great city for pure water to a more aesthetic desire to permit the slightest modification of scene, is irrational and unjust.

7th. This matter has been fully discussed in every phase at Washington, D. C., for many years before the permit was granted and Government experts have fully reported to President Roosevelt's Administration favorably.

8th. After complete campaigns in San Francisco, the vote to issue bonds for such a water supply was substantially unanimous.

9th. It is not at all denied that at all times since this permit was first applied for, that its chief and open opponent has been the Spring Valley Water Co., which has a monopoly of the present undesirable and inadequate water supply of San Francisco.

Respectfully submitted by Edith Webster, Secretary Hypatia Women' s Club, San Francisco, California.

San Francisco, June 27, 1913
Hon. George E. Chamberlain,
Senate Chamber, Washington, D.C.

Dear Sir:

The Yosemite National Park is not only the greatest and most wonderful national playground in California, but in many of its features it is without a rival in the whole world. It belongs to the American people and in world wide interest ranks with the Yellowstone and the Grand Canyon of the Colorado. It embraces the head waters of two rivers—the Merced and the Tuolumne. Yosemite Valley is in the Merced basin and the Hetch Hetcby Valley, the Grand Canyon of the Tuolumne, and the Tuolumne Meadows are in the Tuolumne Basin. Excepting only the Yosemite Valley, the Tuolumne basin in its general features is the more wonderful and larger half of the Park.

The Hetch Hetchy Valley is a wonderfully exact counterpart of' the great Yosemite, not only in its cliffs and waterfalls and peaceful river, but in the gardens, groves, meadows and camp grounds of its flowery park-like floor.

At a recent session of Congress a most determined attack was made by the City of San Francisco to get the right to use the Hetch Hetchy Valley as a reservoir site, thus depriving ninety millions of people of one of their most priceless possessions for the sake of saving San Francisco dollars.

As soon as this scheme became manifest, public-spirited citizens all over the country entered their protests, and before the session was over, the Park invaders saw that they were defeated, and permitted the bill to die without bringing it to a vote, so as to be able to try again.

Ever ready to take advantage of every political change, a bill having the same destructive purpose has been re-introduced at this session of Congress and is now pending before the Public Lands Committee, and its supporters are speciously urging that it should be rushed through at this special session as an emergency measure when in reality nothing like an emergency exists.

San Francisco may be in immediate need of an increased supply of water but her own engineers admit that the present supply can be more than doubled by adding to present nearby sources and that is the first and most economic plan of development before the city eventually goes to the Sierra for additional water.

The advisory Board of Army Engineers "is of the opinion that there are several sources of water supply that could be obtained and used by the city of San Francisco and adjacent communities to supplement the nearby supplies as the necessity develops. From any one of these sources the water is sufficient in quantity and is, or can be made, equitable in quality."

We are preparing data based on the reports of the Army Engineers which will demonstrate that San Francisco can obtain abundance of pure water from other sources than the Tuolumne Hetch Hetchy.

So important a bill should not be rushed through Congress without mature consideration and time allowed for its opponents to be heard. Anything less would be unjust to the American people, therefore in behalf of all who appreciate our mountain parks and believe that they should be preserved, we call on you to aid us in postponing consideration of this destructive bill until the regular session of Congress, for we have not even seen a copy of the bill now being considered. Ever since the establishment of the Yosemite National Park by Act of Congress, October 8th, 1890, constant strife has been going on around its boundaries and is likely to go on as part of the universal tattle between good and evil however much its boundaries may be broken or wild beauty destroyed.

When this application was first made over ten years ago the Secretary of the Interior then holding office emphatically denied the right saying in part:

"Presumably the Yosemite National Park was created such by law because of the natural objects, of varying degrees of scenic importance, located within its boundaries, inclusive alike of its beautiful small lakes, like Eleanor, and its majestic wonders, like Hetch Hetchy and Yosemite Valley. It is the aggregation of such natural scenic features that makes the Yosemite Park a wonderland which the Congress of the United States sought by law to preserve for all coming time as nearly as practicable in the condition fashioned by the hand of the Creator -- a worthy object of national pride and a source of healthful pleasure and rest for the thousands of people who may annually sojourn there during the heated months."

In behalf of all of the people of the nation we ask your aid in putting an end to these assaults on our great national parks, and to prevent this measure from being rushed through before it can be brought to the attention of the ninety millions of people who own this park.

Faithfully yours,
John Muir
E.T. Parsons
Wm. F. Bade

Source: National Archives

THOUGHT QUESTIONS:

1. What do you think were the strongest arguments made by the dam's supporters in the first petition? What were the weaker ones?

2. What do you think were the strongest arguments made by Muir and the dam's opponents in the second petition? What were the weaker ones?

3. What criteria would you use when balancing the preservation of the nation's historical sites and places of beauty, the conservation of vital natural resources, and the need to use those resources for national development?

Vignettes

Influences upon Progressivism

Progressive Era reformers responded to numerous influences that guided their thoughts and actions, some having more impact than others. The legacy of late-nineteenth century political reform efforts, for example, continued to stimulate thought and provoke action. Protests against laissez-faire capitalism levied by Socialists provided a vigorous critique of the status quo. Memories of the "Mugwump" political reformers kept alive the ideal of a government run by honest public servants. Populist demands for more active government involvement to solve the nation's economic problems became more accepted dogma.

New stimuli from religious organizations reacting to the pronounced changes brought about by the Industrial Revolution also influenced reformers across the country. Initially arising in evangelical Protestant churches (but eventually seeping into many Catholic churches and Jewish synagogues), a reform spirit soon to be labeled the "Social Gospel" began to take hold as religious leaders such as Walter Rauschenbusch and their followers sought to better the lives of their fellow men on Earth and rid the world of the evils produced by industrialization. Harkening back to the antebellum religious reform tradition that sought, for example, to end alcohol consumption and slavery, evangelical Progressives believed that it was their Christian duty to fight for the downtrodden and to better society through reform.

Historians have also noted the impact of new scientific thought on reformers. By the turn of the century, colleges and universities produced many new professionals who often sought to apply the latest developments in their fields to the problems of society. Whether they were trained in the natural or social sciences, this slew of new educators, economists, sociologists, social workers, medical doctors, city planners, and civil engineers believed that the scientific approach provided the best means to bring order to the nation. Problems needed to be investigated with accurate data obtained, proposals for reform initiated (often through the passage of new laws), and solutions implemented to eradicate the problems.

THOUGHT QUESTIONS:

1. What were the main influences upon Progressive Era reforms coming from the political world, religious thought, and scientific developments?

2. Identify some examples of individuals applying the "Social Gospel" to aspects of life in the United States today.

3. How do individual reformers and reform groups today, as many Progressives did at the turn of the twentieth century, attempt to use scientific data to legitimize their positions? Provide a modern example.

The Strands of Progressivism

As Progressivism became a reality at the local, state, and national levels, the reforms reflected the great variety of the individuals and groups who had supported them. Seemingly contradictory actions by different groups of reformers often occurred. For example, while some social Progressives sought to aid foreign immigrants in American cities, other reformers with an equal claim to the Progressive mantle lobbied to bar immigrants from entering the country altogether. While the variance of progressivism was pronounced, historians often group the types of reforms produced during the Progressive Era into three main categories, or strands, based upon the reformers' varying motivations.

The demand for social justice comprised one major strand of Progressivism. Large numbers of men and women supported a wide range of reforms designed to improve the lives of urban residents and industrial workers. Whether referring to an outraged middle-class parent appalled by the notion of nine-year old children toiling in a factory somewhere, or a sociologist convinced that long working hours by women had a detrimental effect on families, or a social worker endeavoring to provide a decent home life for urban residents, social progressives fought for a wide range of municipal and labor reforms that they hoped would improve the living and working environment of the urban masses.

Equally progressive were the efforts by many reformers to constrain various individuals through numerous social controls. Many advocates believed that ethnic minorities possessed traits needing to be mitigated. Among the most well-known reform efforts coming from the period that bore this strain—prohibition of alcohol, foreign immigration restrictions, and southern laws enforcing segregation and disenfranchisement of African Americans—were efforts to employ social coercion in order to "improve" society. In their endeavors on behalf of these and related causes, reformers also used the classic Progressive formula of investigation, data collection, the use of moralistic rhetoric to persuade others, along with a call for increased government action to alleviate the problems.

One last strand of Progressivism involved the efforts of efficiency experts in numerous fields who sought to apply scientific methods promoted by their profession to solve a host of local, regional, and national problems. City planners seeking a more orderly environment through the application of zoning laws or a more efficient urban layout reflected this strand of reform. Engineers seeking more efficient production methods, doctors resolving to end quackery in their profession, and even trained foresters desiring to limit wanton waste of the nation's timberlands though scientific conservation methods would also fit into this broad category.

THOUGHT QUESTIONS:

1. What were the main strands of reforms during the Progressive Era?

2. Identify an example of a Progressive Era reform from each strand that continues to exist today and another that has since been discarded.

3. In modern times, what examples do you see of reform-minded groups taking very different, if not contradictory, approaches to solving what they see as a problem in society?

The Workers' Compensation Movement

Passage of the nation's first workers' compensation laws by several states marked a significant advance for American laborers during the Progressive Era. By 1900, numerous industrializing countries in Western Europe had already established insurance systems to compensate those injured or killed on the job. However, in the United States, where industrial accidents numbered in the hundreds of thousands per year, the only recourse for workers and their families was to sue in court—an often long, drawn-out, and expensive process (for workers and companies alike) that seldom produced adequate compensation. Using the standard progressive tools of data acquisition and publicity, reformers gathered statistical evidence and published reports showing the toll that industrial accidents took on the nation's workforce as well as business productivity. Crystal Eastman was one such progressive. Published in 1910, her book *Work Accidents and the Law* was based on painstakingly studying over a thousand cases of worker accidents in Pittsburgh, noting the nature of each incident and the economic effects of the resulting injuries and deaths on the workers' families. She found that, contrary to the arguments of employers, worker carelessness caused only a minority of the accidents. Workers and their families also bore the brunt of the economic cost of those mishaps. She calculated that a majority of families who had workers killed on the job received less than $100. Of those injured on the job, most employers paid hospital costs but only a third received any subsequent payment.

Continued agitation by progressive reformers, along with improvements in technology and plant design and a growing realization by companies that reducing accidents made business sense, provided an impetus to greatly improve factory and mine safety. Workers' compensation began to be accepted increasingly not only as a means to aid victims of industrial accidents but also as a strong preventative device. Crystal Eastman had argued in her book that if employers had an economic incentive to reduce hazards in the workplace they would implement such improvements.

The workers' compensation systems passed during the Progressive Era were rather conservative in nature and thus favored by the business community. When accidents occurred, claimants did not go to the employer but, rather, sought compensation from a state pool, funded by businesses or their insurance companies, according to a set pay schedule determined by law and based on the nature of the disability (or death). In this manner, employers found it cheaper and more manageable to operate with predictable costs deposited into the state fund rather than having to deal with the unpredictable nature of variable numbers of accidents and legal costs to cover litigation, not to mention the protection now provided from the occasional large court award from a judge or jury. Reliance on the state fund for compensation also shifted the emphasis of the debate in that the system lent credence to the notion that frequent accidents were a normal part of factory or mine work in the industrial era. Organized labor initially opposed the establishment of such compensation systems but increasingly came to see them as a better means to reduce accidents since the amount of employer payments and their accident insurance premiums were based upon their individual safety ratings. Overall, these first systems produced a slightly better process for laborers to receive something for injuries and deaths. By 1921, 46 states had workers' compensation laws in effect and the entire concept would later be expanded to the national level during the 1930s when the idea was written into the Social Security Act.

THOUGHT QUESTIONS:

1. How did Crystal Eastman employ techniques popular among Progressive Era reformers in her book on worker safety in Pittsburgh?

2. How did the passage of workers' compensation laws during the Progressive Era benefit American laborers when compared to how injury and death claims were typically handled during the early decades of the Industrial Revolution?

3. Why did the business community increasingly accept the workers' compensation systems that were developed in the states during the first couple of decades of the twentieth century?

Robert La Follette and the "Wisconsin Idea"

Under its vibrant governor Robert M. La Follette, Wisconsin proved to be a leader in state-level progressive innovation. A former Republican congressman who broke with his party's establishment because of his belief that they were in the pockets of corporate business interests, La Follette spent much of the 1890s building up a coalition of rank-and-file members in an effort to seize the gubernatorial nomination. He finally succeeded in 1900 and won in the general election.

For the next six years, "Battlin' Bob" worked tirelessly to reform his party and his state. He successfully campaigned for state legislature candidates who supported his call for the direct primary (his main proposal for achieving government accountability and corporate regulation) and other key elements of his reform agenda, including workers' compensation, creation of a state railroad commission, a comprehensive civil service law, and a state income tax on the wealthy, which were eventually adopted.

Before leaving the governorship in 1906 to fill a vacant U.S. Senate seat, La Follette worked closely with faculty members of the University of Wisconsin (his alma mater) to craft legislation geared toward addressing public policy issues. Soon to be known as the "Wisconsin Idea," La Follette relied on these collegiate experts to examine specific problems in society and government, gather evidence, and propose legislative solutions. To aid the state government in this endeavor, the legislature created the Legislative Research Library to provide an agency with state funds to aid in the development of new laws. Often called the "laboratory of democracy," Wisconsin during the Progressive Era produced many pioneering reforms that influenced the way in which states across the country reacted to similar concerns.

THOUGHT QUESTIONS:

1. How did Robert La Follette seek to promote reform in Wisconsin while remaining within the Republican Party?

2. What barriers and what possible benefits might La Follette have expected to encounter if he sought change by creating a third party?

3. How did La Follette employ classic Progressive Era techniques to promote an assortment of reforms in Wisconsin?

Chapter 22

The "Great War": World War I

Documents

President Wilson's Declaration of Neutrality

Upon the outbreak of war in Europe following the assassination of Archduke Franz Ferdinand of Austria and the failure of the continent's leaders to avert the colossal struggle to come, President Woodrow Wilson appeared before Congress on August 19, 1914, to lay out the position of his administration: specifically, that the U.S. government would declare and enforce a strict neutrality. In the course of his remarks, shown below in their entirety, Wilson noted how the war might become an incredibly divisive issue among Americans, but he famously asked his countrymen to be "impartial in thought as well as action." The president was able to maintain American neutrality throughout his first term, but within a few months after his reelection, he would appear before Congress again, this time asking for a declaration of war against Germany.

MY FELLOW COUNTRYMEN: I suppose that every thoughtful man in America has asked himself, during these last troubled weeks, what influence the European war may exert upon the United States, and I take the liberty of addressing a few words to you in order to point out that it is entirely within our own choice what its effects upon us will be and to urge very earnestly upon you the sort of speech and conduct which will best safeguard the Nation against distress and disaster.

The effect of the war upon the United States will depend upon what American citizens say and do. Every man who really loves America will act and speak in the true spirit of neutrality, which is the spirit of impartiality and fairness and friendliness to all concerned. The spirit of the Nation in this critical matter will be determined largely by what individuals and society and those gathered in public meetings do and say, upon what newspapers and magazines contain, upon what ministers utter in their pulpits, and men proclaim as their opinions on the street.

The people of the United States are drawn from many nations, and chiefly from the nations now at war. It is natural and inevitable that there should be the utmost variety of sympathy and desire among them with regard to the issues and circumstances of the conflict. Some will wish one nation, others another, to succeed in the momentous struggle. It will be easy to excite passion and difficult to allay it. Those responsible for exciting it will assume a heavy responsibility, responsibility for no less a thing than that the people of the United States, whose love of their country and whose loyalty to its Government should unite them as Americans all, bound in honor and affection to think first of her and her interests, may be divided in camps of hostile opinion, hot against each other, involved in the war itself in impulse and opinion if not in action.

Such divisions amongst us would be fatal to our peace of mind and might seriously stand in the way of the proper performance of our duty as the one great nation at peace, the one people holding itself ready to play a part of impartial mediation and speak the counsels of peace and accommodation, not as a partisan, but as a friend.

I venture, therefore, my fellow countrymen, to speak a solemn word of warning to you against that deepest, most subtle, most essential breach of neutrality which may spring out of partisanship, out of passionately taking sides. The United States must be neutral in fact as well as in name during these days that are to try men's souls. We must be impartial in thought as well as action, must put a curb upon our sentiments as well as upon every transaction that might be construed as a preference of one party to the struggle before another.

My thought is of America. I am speaking, I feel sure, the earnest wish and purpose of every thoughtful American that this great country of ours, which is, of course, the first in our thoughts and in our hearts, should show herself in this time of peculiar trial a Nation fit beyond others to exhibit the fine poise of undisturbed judgment, the dignity of self-control, the efficiency of dispassionate action; a Nation that neither sits in judgment upon others nor is disturbed in her own counsels and which keeps herself fit and free to do what is honest and disinterested and truly serviceable for the peace of the world.

Shall we not resolve to put upon ourselves the restraints which will bring to our people the happiness and the great and lasting influence for peace we covet for them?

Source: 63rd Cong, 2nd Session, Senate Document No. 566 (Washington, 1914), pp. 3-4.

THOUGHT QUESTIONS:

1. What benefits does Wilson see for the United States, and for the prospects of peace in Europe, if the United States declared and maintained neutrality?

2. Why does Wilson think Americans would be divided on whether to support the Allies or the Central Powers in the "Great War" when it broke out in 1914?

3. In today's times, what factors do you think influence whether the United States will choose to intervene in a foreign conflict?

The Zimmermann Telegram

Reelected president in 1916 with the help of the slogan "He Kept Us out of War," Woodrow Wilson soon found the situation much changed by early 1917. Frustrated with continued American aid to the western Allies that they could not enjoy because of the effectiveness of the British naval blockade, German leaders in February 1917 declared unrestricted submarine warfare in an effort to limit supplies, especially from America, from reaching England and France. In response, Wilson severed diplomatic relations with Germany.

In January 1917, British spies were able to tap into phone lines and intercept a brief telegram sent from German Foreign Minister Arthur Zimmermann to the German ambassador to Mexico. Codebreakers were able to determine the startling contents of the message—that if the U.S. and Germany declared war on each other, Germany wished to entice Mexico to declare war on the United States in an effort to distract America from the war in Europe. After the British delivered the decoded telegram (shown below) to President Wilson in late February, he sat on the information for a week before finally revealing its contents to the American people, helping to inflame public opinion and setting the stage for acceptance of Congress's declaration of war after German U-boats began sinking American merchant ships.

We intend to begin on the first of February unrestricted submarine warfare. We shall endeavor in spite of this to keep the United States of America neutral. In the event of this not succeeding, we make Mexico a proposal or alliance on the following basis: make war together, make peace together, generous financial support and an understanding on our part that Mexico is to reconquer the lost territory in Texas, New Mexico, and Arizona. The settlement in detail is left to you. You will inform the President of the above most secretly as soon as the outbreak of war with the United States of America is certain and add the suggestion that he should, on his own initiative, invite Japan to immediate adherence and at the same time mediate between Japan and ourselves. Please call the President's attention to the fact that the ruthless employment of our submarines now offers the prospect of compelling England in a few months to make peace.

Signed, ZIMMERMANN.

Source: National Archives and Records Administration

THOUGHT QUESTIONS:

1. What specific offer did Germany make to Mexico? Regardless of the plausibility regarding whether the offer would be accepted, how would such a deal potentially benefit Germany?

2. What benefit did England have in providing the contents of the intercepted message to Wilson? What benefit did Wilson see in revealing the telegram to the public?

3. Explain the importance of technological espionage for governments today, i.e., how important is it for countries to be able to acquire information from rivals as well as prevent information from falling into the wrong hands? Discuss with a few modern examples.

Excerpts from Eugene Debs's Canton, Ohio Anti-War Speech

On June 18, 1918, Eugene Debs, the labor leader and recent presidential nominee of the Socialist Party of America, delivered a scathing speech to supporters in Canton, Ohio condemning U.S. participation in the First World War. In response to his address, Debs was arrested, tried, and convicted in federal court for violating the Espionage Act. He was sentenced to ten years in prison. After his conviction was upheld by the Supreme Court, he remained imprisoned until 1921 when he was pardoned by the new president, Warren Harding. Over 50,000 came out to greet Debs upon his return home to Terre Haute, Indiana. Below are portions from the lengthy speech that landed him in trouble with U.S. authorities.

Comrades, friends and fellow-workers, for this very cordial greeting, this very hearty reception, I thank you all with the fullest appreciation of your interest in and your devotion to the cause for which I am to speak to you this afternoon.

To speak for labor; to plead the cause of the men and women and children who toil; to serve the working class, has always been to me a high privilege; a duty of love.

I have just returned from a visit over yonder, where three of our most loyal comrades are paying the penalty for their devotion to the cause of the working class. They have come to realize, as many of us have, that it is extremely dangerous to exercise the constitutional right of free speech in a country fighting to make democracy safe in the world.

I realize that, in speaking to you this afternoon, there are certain limitations placed upon the right of free speech. I must be exceedingly careful, prudent, as to what I say, and even more careful and prudent as to how I say it. I may not be able to say all I think; but I am not going to say anything that I do not think. I would rather a thousand times be a free soul in jail than to be a sycophant and coward in the streets. They may put those boys in jail—and some of the rest of us in jail—but they cannot put the Socialist movement in jail. Those prison bars separate their bodies from ours, but their souls are here this afternoon. They are simply paying the penalty that all men have paid in all the ages of history for standing erect, and for seeking to pave the way to better conditions for mankind.

If it had not been for the men and women who, in the past, have had the moral courage to go to jail, we would still be in the jungles....

Yes, my comrades, my heart is attuned to yours. Aye, all our hearts now throb as one great heart responsive to the battle cry of the social revolution. Here, in this alert and inspiring assemblage our hearts are with the Bolsheviki of Russia. Those heroic men and women, those unconquerable comrades have by their incomparable valor and sacrifice added fresh luster to the fame of the international movement. Those Russian comrades of ours have made greater sacrifices, have suffered more, and have shed more heroic blood than any like number of men and women anywhere on earth; they have laid the foundation of the first real democracy that ever drew the breath of life in this world. And the very first act of the triumphant Russian revolution was to proclaim a state of peace with all mankind, coupled with a fervent moral appeal, not to kings, not to emperors, rulers or diplomats but to the people of all nations. Here we have the very breath of democracy, the quintessence of the dawning freedom. The Russian revolution proclaimed its glorious triumph in its ringing and inspiring appeal to the peoples of all the earth. In a humane and fraternal spirit new Russia, emancipated at last from the curse of the centuries, called upon all nations engaged in the frightful war, the Central Powers as well as the Allies, to send representatives to a conference to lay down terms of peace that should be just and lasting.

Here was the supreme opportunity to strike the blow to make the world safe for democracy. Was there any response to that noble appeal that in some day to come will be written in letters of gold in the history of the world? Was there any response whatever to that appeal for universal peace? No, not the slightest attention was paid to it by the Christian nations engaged in the terrible slaughter.

It has been charged that Lenin and Trotsky and the leaders of the revolution were treacherous, that they made a traitorous peace with Germany. Let us consider that proposition briefly. At the time of the revolution Russia had been three years in the war. Under the Czar she had lost more than four million of her ill-clad, poorly-equipped, half-starved soldiers, slain outright or disabled on the field of battle. She was absolutely bankrupt. Her soldiers were mainly without arms. This was what was bequeathed to the revolution by the Czar and his regime; and for this condition Lenin and Trotsky were not responsible, nor the Bolsheviki. For this appalling state of affairs the Czar and his rotten bureaucracy were solely responsible. When the Bolsheviki came into power and went through the archives they found and exposed the secret treaties—the treaties that were made between the Czar and the French government, the British government and the Italian government, proposing, after the victory was achieved, to dismember the German Empire and destroy the Central Powers. These treaties have never been denied nor repudiated. Very little has been said about them in the American press. I have a copy of these treaties, showing that the purpose of the Allies is exactly the purpose of the Central Powers, and that is the conquest and spoilation of the weaker nations that has always been the purpose of war.

Wars throughout history have been waged for conquest and plunder. In the Middle Ages when the feudal lords who inhabited the castles whose towers may still be seen along the Rhine concluded to enlarge their domains, to increase their power, their prestige and their wealth they declared war upon one another. But they themselves did not go to war any more than the modern feudal lords, the barons of Wall Street go to war. The feudal barons of the Middle Ages, the economic predecessors of the capitalists of our day, declared all wars. And their miserable serfs fought all the battles. The poor, ignorant serfs had been taught to revere their masters; to believe that when their masters declared war upon one another, it was their patriotic duty to fall upon one another and to cut one another's throats for the profit and glory of the lords and barons who held them in contempt. And that is war in a nutshell. The master class has always declared the wars; the subject class has always fought the battles. The master class has had all to gain and nothing to lose, while the subject class has had nothing to gain and all to lose—especially their lives.

They have always taught and trained you to believe it to be your patriotic duty to go to war and to have yourselves slaughtered at their command. But in all the history of the world you, the people, have never had a voice in declaring war, and strange as it certainly appears, no war by any nation in any age has ever been declared by the people.

And here let me emphasize the fact—and it cannot be repeated too often—that the working class who fight all the battles, the working class who make the supreme sacrifices, the working class who freely shed their blood and furnish the corpses, have never yet had a voice in either declaring war or making peace. It is the ruling class that invariably does both. They alone declare war and they alone make peace: "Yours not to reason why; Yours but to do and die."

That is their motto and we object on the part of the awakening workers of this nation. If war is right let it be declared by the people. You who have your lives to lose, you certainly above all others have the right to decide the momentous issue of war or peace....

Source: *The Call*, June 27, 1918

THOUGHT QUESTIONS:

1. How does Debs respond to the understanding that the words he speaks during his speech might land him in jail?

2. Who did Debs blame for the current conflict? Who did he blame for all wars in general? Who did he say ends up bearing the burden for the wars of all nations, hence his opposition to involvement in World War I?

3. What are your feelings with regard to the freedom of speech in times of war or national emergency? Should certain types of speech be curtailed or forbidden? Should other types of public opposition to a war be resisted under any circumstances? Explain.

Patriotic Housekeeping: Good Housekeeping Recruits Kitchen Soldiers

---

Upon U.S. entry into World War I, Herbert Hoover was named the director of the U.S. Food Administration, charged with overseeing efforts to ensure that Americans had enough agricultural goods for both military and civilian needs. Hoover rejected calls for mandatory government food rationing, instead preferring appeals to patriotism and voluntarism to accomplish his agency's goals. Citizens were encouraged to plant home gardens, voluntarily ration food, and avoid wasteful practices. Enlisted for help in this endeavor, **Good Housekeeping** *published a December 1917 editorial, shown below, seeking "recruits for an army of kitchen soldiers," asking the magazine's readers to sign a voluntary pledge to conserve food for the duration of the war.*

Good Housekeeping Institute
Mildred Maddocks, Director
Wanted: Recruits for an Army of Kitchen Soldiers!
If the Allied Peoples and Their Soldiers Are to Have Enough to Eat Next Year, You Must Fight Your Battles in Your Kitchen Now!
Will You Sign this?

I, the member of the household entrusted with the handling of food, do hereby enlist as Kitchen Soldier for Home Service and pledge myself to waste no food and to use wisely all food purchased for this household, knowing that by so doing I can help conserve the foods that must be shipped to our soldiers and our Allies.

Name

Address

Women of America, this is a call to you to enlist in an army of food conservation. It is an opportunity to fight a battle that is being waged as earnestly, as bravely, and as skillfully as any battle overseas. It is a call to put your heart and soul into winning this war—to be a Kitchen Soldier!

From Washington, the Government is working with a giant's strength. But the first official request is for cooperation. The Food Administration can make us think, can lay down great, broad, general plans, can tell us what our country and our Allies need. But then the burden comes to us—to work out for ourselves the details of the ways in which each one can serve best.

And that is where Good Housekeeping knows that it can aid you by acting as a central point of contact, a clearing-house of ways and means, a vast recruiting station for the women of this country in their fight!

The plan we have is simply to intensify the work begun from Washington, to add our power to the force of Mr. Hoover and his able staff, to carry further for our readers the working out of our national home defenses from the inside. So this is our proposal:

If you are willing to play an active, vital part in saving food and making every meal a blow for freedom, send us your name to be enlisted in the Kitchen Soldiers' Army. As a symbol of your devotion to the cause in which the Allied nations are engaged, you will receive from us a richly printed certificate. Hang it upon your kitchen wall—to remind you of your pledge!

This is a movement for the woman who is actually dealing in the food of American homes. We want employers and employees to join our forces. A soldier may be one who fights just with her brain or one who fights by doing with her hands the work of women in this crisis.

She may be one whose ancestors have lived here for generations or she may be one whose parents have seen war's horrors pass their very door abroad, whose brothers bear the arms of England, or France, or Italy, or Russia, or any other Allied country.

Once you have enlisted as a Kitchen Solider, your kitchen is your battle-field. There you must fight your fight. There you must plan and experiment just as we, in the kitchen of the Good Housekeeping Institute, have been planning and experimenting with redoubled efforts since the war began.

When you hit upon a good idea, sit down and write to us. Tell us how you found that you could get along without some food that may mean life and comfort to a soldier in a foreign trench. Tell us new combinations, new substitutes, new short cuts.

We want a flood of letters bearing your discoveries. For years we have invited new ideas in cooking, and thousands of attractive, money-saving recipes have been printed—recipes that represented also daintiness and tastefulness, foods fit for the epicure.

But from our Kitchen Soldiers we want new ways to save food, not merely how to make it attractive. For food must be saved. The women of this country are now in deadly earnest in their fight to save it, and we want ideas to deal out as ammunition in their battle.

Each good idea received will be tried out here in our kitchen. For each one that proves satisfactory we will pay one dollar. It will be printed in the pages set aside for the exclusive use of Kitchen Soldiers.

Those pages in Good Housekeeping will be yours to make as truly useful and valuable as you can make them. When you enlist as a Kitchen Soldier, you contribute, through our pages, to the welfare of the family of every reader of this magazine. From month to month those pages will increase in value; we know that all your brains applied to this great task will greatly multiply the usefulness of the department. Two heads can think of more than one, and once you put your hundreds—yes, your thousands and your tens of thousands of heads at work on Kitchen Soldiery, then we can win this war!

Remember you are fighting not only to save the family gathered round you. You are fighting for the families in every city, village, and town in this broad country. One discovery that you make may send tons of grain or sugar to the nations fighting "over there." So you are fighting, too, for all the women, all the children, all the soldiers of the Allies—for democracy everywhere.

So, now, enlist! Become a Kitchen Soldier. The time has passed to do your bit. It's time to do your best! Enlist!

Source: "Wanted: Recruits for an Army of Kitchen Soldiers!" *Good Housekeeping*, December 1917, p. 71.

THOUGHT QUESTIONS:

1. Identify some of the everyday actions that women were encouraged to do in this article to help the war effort.

2. According to the editors, how would a woman's participation in such acts help the war effort?

3. In today's time of relative peace, what are some examples of how citizens are encouraged to volunteer to help their local communities? How does citizen voluntarism reduce the expenditures and degree of direct involvement by government in tackling local problems?

Vignettes

Social Experimentation in the Military

During World War I, Progressive reformers believed it would be crucial to protect innocent young servicemen from potential vices that they might encounter near training camps, not to mention the "sinful temptations" existing while being stationed in France. Limiting access to alcohol became one of their first goals. Consequently, they succeeded in pressuring Congress to extend an existing ban on the sale of alcohol on military bases by adding a section to the Selective Service Act that prohibited the purchase of intoxicating beverages "in and near military camps," which the War Department soon defined as within a five-mile radius around its outposts. In the same legislation, Congress outlawed the sale of intoxicating beverages to any member of the armed forces while in uniform, though this provision proved nearly impossible to enforce.

The army also launched a massive campaign against sexual vice, giving most of the young men their first exposure to sex education. The military distributed Margaret Sanger's article "What Every Girl Should Know" (twice banned as obscene), which contained the birth control advocate's take on puberty, sexual impulses, and the prevention of venereal diseases. Another distributed pamphlet reassured men that wet dreams were normal, and masturbation would not cause insanity, despite their grandmothers' warnings. The implication was clear—both were preferable to dangerous sexual encounters with unfamiliar women since "a man who is thinking below the belt is not efficient." Camps were plastered with posters declaring, "A German Bullet is Cleaner than a Whore." Another pamphlet asked, "How could you look the flag in the face if you were dirty with gonorrhea?"

This sexual purity campaign was somewhat hampered overseas by what the American commanding general in France, John Pershing, diplomatically described as "the difference between the French attitude and our own." French Premier Georges Clemenceau offered to provide Americans with the same type of licensed, inspected houses of prostitution available to French troops. A horrified Secretary of War Newton D. Baker supposedly responded to the communique by exclaiming: "For God's sake . . . don't show this to the president or he'll stop the war!" The army preferred to punish sternly any soldiers who contracted a venereal disease. Though approximately 15 percent of American servicemen did acquire a form of venereal disease during the war years, the War Department believed its campaign greatly reduced the rate of infection. Certainly the widespread distribution of condoms aided in the post-war birth control campaign, and the frank discussions of sexual matters helped to change American mores after the war.

THOUGHT QUESTIONS:

1. How did the Progressives who supported Prohibition use the war to justify their efforts to reduce the consumption of alcohol in the country? In what ways were they successful?

2. What did General Pershing mean by "the difference between the French attitude and our own" when it came to regulating sexual conduct among the troops?

3. Though Progressive reformers remained active during the war, as evidenced by the efforts of social reformers described above, how did America's preoccupation with the war reinforce the fear among other Progressives that the conflict would detract the movement to achieve other significant social and economic reforms?

The War against the Socialists

Despite President Woodrow Wilson's warning: "Woe be to the man that seeks to stand in our way in this day of high resolution," some courageous dissenters continued to criticize the war despite the potential backlash from the government and the general public. These war opponents not only included avowed pacifists, but also dedicated socialists who viewed the conflict as a conflict between European nations primarily to expand their empires and for the benefit of their capitalists—the bankers who financed the governments and the manufacturers who provided the munitions and other supplies for their militaries.

U.S. government officials, already predisposed to despise the Socialists, used American entry into World War I to crack down on the Socialist Party by suppressing its ability to publish and distribute informational materials and harassing its leaders. Attorney General Thomas Gregory, who actively sought to curb internal dissent against involvement in the war, instructed Postmaster General Albert Burleson to censor and, if necessary, discontinue delivering any letters, magazines, or newspapers deemed to be "anti-American or pro-German." Burleson used this newfound power to effectively suppress Socialist Party periodicals and even moderately leftist journals that expressed any doubts about participation in the war.

Congress, via the Espionage Act (1917) and the Sedition Act (1918), prescribed prison sentences for hindering the draft or making statements containing "disloyal, profane, scurrilous or abusive language" about the government, the flag, or the military. Eugene Debs, the Socialist Party candidate for president in 1912 who received almost one million votes was sentenced to ten years in prison for a speech condemning the military draft. Even after the war had ended, a self-righteous Woodrow Wilson denied him a presidential pardon, declaring: "'While the flower of American youth was pouring out its blood to vindicate the cause of civilization, Debs stood behind the lines sniping, attacking and denouncing them." (Wilson's successor, Warren Harding, finally pardoned Debs in 1921.)

When Wisconsin voters in a U.S. House of Representatives election chose Victor Berger, a Socialist Party founder and organizer who was under federal indictment for violating the Espionage Act by publishing anti-war tracts, the House denied Berger his seat. After his conviction, the voters re-elected him in a special election, but the House refused to seat him for a second time. Berger served two years of a twenty-year prison sentence before he won his case on appeal after the war.

THOUGHT QUESTIONS:

1. What motivations did U.S. government officials have to limit speech and writings during World War I, for the public in general and the Socialists in particular?

2. In what ways did the federal government seek to suppress the Socialist Party and other anti-war opponents?

3. To what extent do you agree (or disagree) with Supreme Court Justice Oliver Wendell Holmes's statement in the *Schenck v. United States* (1919) decision defending the government's ability to tightly regulate speech during wartime if such speech was determined by the government to present a "clear and present danger" to the public or the war effort?

The Camp Logan Riot

During the summer of 1917, in Houston, Texas, sweltering temperatures and lingering resentment against the system of Jim Crow led to the most severe outbreak of racial violence to occur during the Great War. Known as the "Camp Logan Riot," the incident involved African-American troops sent to the Houston area to guard the construction of Camp Logan, a training base established outside the city.

Like their counterparts in other parts of the South when similar circumstances occurred, white Houstonians were worried that the presence of black soldiers wearing the uniform of their county might inspire African Americans within their communities to resist segregation laws and other racist restrictions. Societal norms in Houston with regard to race relations meant strict adherence to segregated public facilities. African Americans could not ride on many trolleys, eat at restaurants with white customers, or congregate in large groups in most public places. From the moment of their arrival, the black soldiers faced repeated episodes of discrimination whenever they went into the city while off duty. Houston's all-white law enforcement establishment proved to be especially rough in their treatment of soldiers within the city limits while on leave. Though most of the soldiers were Southerners and therefore quite familiar with the system of segregation, as servicemen, they did expect better treatment than they received.

Trouble occurred on a hot, sticky August day when a young African-American recruit tried to stop a Houston policeman's beating of a black female in the street of her residential neighborhood. The officer had dragged the woman outside after she protested his entering her home in pursuit of a suspect from a craps game that he and his partner had just broken up. When the soldier intervened, the cop turned his club against him, soon helped out by fellow officers who beat the trooper unconscious and hauled him off to jail. Upon hearing of the soldier's arrest, Corporal Charles Baltimore went to the police station to broker his release. As soon as he arrived, harsh words were exchanged, and officers attacked Baltimore, who fled but was soon captured, beaten, and arrested.

When the news of Baltimore's incarceration reached Camp Logan, the rest of the outfit became enraged, determined to set him free. Though the injured Corporal Baltimore was released later that day, about 150 soldiers gathered their weapons and marched on Houston to attack the police, engaging in firefights with officers and attacking white civilians along the way. In all, 14 whites died, including five policemen, before the men began to lose heart and returned to their base after a group of them accidentally killed a white National Guard officer arriving on the scene from Camp Logan. Three black soldiers died in the melees (later determined in every case to have resulted from fire by fellow soldiers) while one of their leaders, Sergeant Vida Henry, soon killed himself.

After an investigation by United States Army officials, 63 African-American troops were charged with mutiny. (No white citizens or police officers were tried for any role in the events of that day and evening). At the first of several courts-martial—the largest in U.S. military history—13 black soldiers were found guilty and sentenced to death, including Corporal Baltimore. Six more troops were executed after the second trial, and dozens imprisoned with sentences ranging from 24 months to life at the final court martial proceedings.

Army officials used the Camp Logan incident to justify reduced enrollment of black soldiers as soon as the war ended. During the Great Depression, white Texas civic leaders and politicians would frequently bring up the violence that took place in Houston to justify their opposition to the placement of black Civilian Conservation Corps (CCC) camps near white population centers, fearing the outbreak of violence despite the fact that the CCC facilities never housed weapons of any kind.

THOUGHT QUESTIONS:

1. How did the actions of local police before the riot contribute to the violent state of affairs to come?

2. Though most were Southerners, why were many of the soldiers especially enraged at the treatment that they had received in Houston?

3. Without justifying their actions, what ultimately led the soldiers to escalate matters to the point of committing random acts of violence?

The "Spanish Flu" Pandemic

America experienced a tumultuous social and economic transition period following the First World War. Even before the conflict ended, the nation weathered a biological calamity in the form of an influenza pandemic that ultimately killed five times as many Americans as the number of soldiers lost during the Great War. Grossly mislabeled the "Spanish flu" because Spanish King Alfonso XIII became an early celebrity affected by the sickness, the pandemic actually began in the Southern Plains of the United States. In the spring of 1918, the first reported cases of the illness (caused by a virus probably spread from birds to swine and then to humans) were noted at Fort Riley, Kansas. This particular strain of flu virus attacked the body by forcing the immune system to turn against itself, producing pneumonia. This process explains why most victims were otherwise young healthy individuals rather than infants or the elderly, as is often the case with influenza. Close soldiers' quarters led to the spread of the disease among American military personnel and, by the fall of 1918, to the civilian population.

Troop movements spread the flu quickly from Middle America to the Atlantic coast, then to Europe and beyond. Current estimates suggest that the pandemic killed perhaps 50 million people across the globe with few populated areas being spared. Confusion and fear of the unknown reigned across the country as it would again thirty years later when the polio outbreak occurred. Ordinary residents wearing surgical masks became a common sight in towns and cities across the country. Public places such as dance halls, theaters, and even churches closed as citizens and their governments desperately tried to limit the epidemic even though its exact cause was unknown at the time. By the summer of 1920, when the disease ran its course, over 500,000 American citizens had died.

THOUGHT QUESTIONS:

1. What were the origins of the flu pandemic? Why was it mislabeled the "Spanish Flu"?

2. What caused the spread of the flu pandemic? How extensive were the effects of the pandemic geographically?

3. What was the toll of the flu on human lives in the U.S., and how did that number compare to the number of combat deaths during World War I?

Chapter 23

The Contentious Twenties

Documents

An El Paso Musician Laments the Popularity of Jazz

Though existing for many years in African-American communities, jazz music gained mainstream popularity across the country during the 1910s and 1920s when white Americans discovered the art form. Many younger Americans went crazy over the music, attracted to its liveliness, syncopated rhythms, and improvisational nature. Predictably, there was a large backlash against jazz, especially among the older generations, as exhibited in the responses given by a musician when interviewed about the subject by a curious local newspaper reporter in El Paso.

It is sad. Indeed, that the atmosphere of El Paso that once charmed the ears of the tourist with the entrancing strains of the Mexican serenade; whose plazas sent forth the sweet concord of sounds that made it talked of in all corners of the country has at last been polluted with that thunderous jazz racket that echoes from the underworld....

Can anyone doubt the evil effects of a music so coarse and sensual?

Most business musicians, when asked if they like jazz, will answer in the negative, but will say they play it because the public demands it. I do not believe the general public wants it: but only a small percent consisting mostly of the rounders and sports of the town, who have enough money and social influence to force the managers of amusement places to cater to their whims. Consequently, the skilled musician is displaced by the jazz player who is usually a fakir but who fills the bill to the satisfaction of this racket loving element.

I think it time that the musicians and music loving people were organizing a crusade to fight the noise demon and recover the lost art of music.

What is the popular song of today? The lyrics consist of a lot of silly, foolish twaddle that would not be tolerated anywhere but in a song or the insane asylum; or of vulgar suggestions that are only understood in the underworld. Yet the innocent young music student buys it, takes it home and drums at it until she learns this perfectly lovely jazz melody; then she goes to the dance hall and there swings to its degrading rhythm in the arms of some young man who labors under the delusion that Orpheus and Terpsichore have collaborated to give him the latest artistic creation—the classic jazz fox trot.

I am rearing two daughters and, from my own observations as a dance player, they shall never enter the dance hall so long as the present popular jazz style of dancing prevails. I have been a professional violinist for 20 years and many times I have thanked the good Lord that he bestowed a bit of the divine art on me, for both artistic and business reasons, until the recent jazz innovations, and now I feel like smashing my violin to pieces and crying out for the wash board or sewing machine, the hum of which would be a relief to the loathsome jazz racket.

Source: *El Paso Herald*, Jan. 28, 1919

THOUGHT QUESTIONS:

1. What criticisms of jazz music did this musician offer?

2. What were her objections to the lyrics of jazz songs and the accompanying dance moves?

3. What similarities do you see between this woman's criticism of jazz and later generations' criticism of rock and roll, hip-hop, and other forms of music popular among the nation's youth?

"Mother Not to Blame for Flapper's Flapping"

The flapper phenomenon is one of the iconic images of the "Roaring Twenties" aspect of the 1920s. Social commentators and average citizens alike commented frequently in the media about the young women who chose to defy previous conventions by dressing and acting more freely in public than their Victorian Era mothers and grandmothers. In this lively piece appearing in a New York City newspaper, reporter Fay Stevenson has fun relaying the attitudes of a conservative female congresswoman and a conservative education professor as they both try, through the prism of their world view, to determine the degree to which the flapper's mother is responsible for her behavior.

For one brief moment, it seemed as if the flapper solution were settled once and for all—"The flapper flaps because her mother flaps."

No less a person than Representative Alice Robertson of Oklahoma, the only woman in Congress, has just come forth with this statement.

"You can blame the flapper's mother every time," said Miss Robertson. "As the mothers flap, so flap the youngsters. Mother sets the pace and her daughter follows. While mother is flapping around at an afternoon tea or at a reception or bridge game, daughter goes out flapping in an auto. It's only natural. Let the mothers stay at home then they would find that their daughters would come flapping home, flap into an apron, and spend their out-of-school hours in a thoroughly wholesome way. But you can't expect a young girl to stay home and knit when her mother is out playing cards or flapping around."

Let us repeat—for one brief moment, it all seemed clear—perfectly so.

With this idea fixed in our head and our teeth gritted against the flapperish mother who has brought such comment upon her little innocent daughter's head, we trotted up to see Prof. Herman Horne of New York University. Prof. Horne panned the flapper pretty well the other day in an address to graduates of Washington Irving High School. He said:

"A flapper is a person who prefers ignorance to the truth. A flapper has a conscience which does not bother her."

Therefore we thought we would find out how clever Prof. Horne was at panning the flapper-mother. But here is where we met our Waterloo. Here is where Representative Alice Robertson's "flapper-mother" solutions fell through.

"I do not agree with Miss Robertson at all," declared Prof. Horne. "I know too many mothers of flappers.

While flappers flap, mothers mourn.

"But mothers, yes, mothers of fifty and grandmothers of seventy, flap around in low-cut blouses, skirts to their knees, and smoke cigarettes," we persisted, still trying to defend the flapper.

Prof. Horne raised his eyebrows as he said "a few, perhaps, in New York City, but what of the mothers in the suburbs, of the mothers all around us in New Jersey, Brooklyn, Staten Island and on the outskirts of all this city, and in the heart of it, too? No, no, I have met too many mothers of flappers to say that the mother leads in the flapping.

Let me repeat, "While flappers flap, mothers mourn."

"The flapper is a sophisticated youngster who could tell her mother lots of things, but usually doesn't.

"Mothers have changed but little with the changing times; flappers have outchanged the changing times.

"A mother is usually willing to listen; the flapper knows it already.

"Mothers like to help their daughters catch their beaus; the flapper catches hers all by herself.

"Mothers still believe in some form of oversight of adolescent girls, but flappers chaperone themselves.

"The American mother still rejects the intimacies of Lady Nicotine, whom the flapper makes her patron saint.

"Mothers much prefer their daughters should not know some of the seamy side of life, while flappers turn the garment of life inside out."

After this outburst of philosophy we were convinced that the flapper is quite original in her own artistic, flapping way. After all, she is a problem and we must still keep on criticizing her. But she makes delicious copy and splendid models for magazine covers!

"The flapper movement is worldwide," continued Prof. Horne. "In the new Germany it is known as the 'Youth Movement.' All over the world youth has declared war on the old customs and the old schools, but mothers are still conservative."

"Mothers still take slight comfort in the thought when flappers marry and become mothers they will cease to flap. But there is the disquieting thought that to the all-knowing flapper marriage does not mean motherhood."

"You are hitting the flapper pretty hard," we remarked.

"I am defending the flapper's mother," replied Prof. Horne. "You see, I know them both well, the flappers and the mothers. The modern mother is ready to play the game, the game of girlish pranks and catching a husband, but not to the flapping limit."

Source: *The Evening World* (New York)—February 3, 1922

THOUGHT QUESTIONS:

1. Who did congresswoman blame for the flapper's "flapping" behavior? Why did she think that way?

2. What did the professor say was behind the phenomenon? To what extent did he hold the mothers of flappers accountable? What did he say he based his opinion on?

3. What parallels, if any, do you see between the flappers and the youth (male or female) of today with regard to dress and behavior? What parallels or differences do you see between how parents and older people in society then viewed the flappers and the youth of today?

On the "Limits of Commercial Aviation"

Founded in 1885, **The Forum** *was once one of the most respected magazines in the United States, popular for its use of a symposium style in which guest authors debated important social and political issues of the day. In 1928, the journal pondered the commercial possibilities of aircraft, pondering the question: "Has Aviation a Future?" While U.S. Navy aviator and polar explorer Richard Byrd asserted in his piece that airplanes definitely had a commercial future, Alfred Dewar, a pilot serving as the chief of the Historical Section of the British Royal Navy, expressed his belief (excerpts presented below) that airplanes would never provide efficient transport, serving at best as "an auxiliary to sea transport."*

When one speaks of a future for commercial aviation, one means a future not merely of daring enterprise and heavily subsidized routes, but a future in terms of definite commercial success on a large scale. Every new instrument of man's invention attracts around it a ring of ardent enthusiasts who paint its future in roseate hues. But sooner or later they find that it is encompassed about with definite and inevitable limitations, inherent in its own nature, which cannot be overcome. It reaches a certain point of development which it can only surpass at the cost of vastly disproportionate labor and expense.

It has been so with the locomotive and steamship, and it will be so with aircraft. Limitations may be imposed as surely by considerations of economic expediency as by the more rigid restrictions of natural laws. . . . Nowhere do these limitations apply more forcibly than to aircraft. A plane has to contend directly against gravity. Before it can carry anything, it has first to lift itself, and then lift its load. This is a staggering handicap. Approximately four fifths of the horsepower of a big plane is absorbed merely in maintaining the craft and its load in the air. Air transport can never contend seriously with transport by land and water, where the actual weight is carried by the earth and sea and the engine has merely to push or pull its load along. . . .

It comes finally to this, that a passenger plane developing 1,155 horsepower is capable of a comparatively short voyage of say two hundred miles with fourteen passengers and seven hundred pounds of freight, or approximately three pounds of paying load to the horsepower. . . .

In one word, power load is an insuperable bar to air transport on a big scale. Apart from all questions of convenience and comfort—in which land and water transport must always be infinitely superior—no form of transport which is forced to measure its weights in skimpy figures of pounds and fractional ounces can ever be more than an emergency or supplementary means of locomotion. . . .

. . . In the United States two thirds of the cost of the Air Mail Service is met from government funds. The expenditure may be justified in terms of utility, and the advantages of a speedy mail service may be worth the expense involved. But the same argument cannot apply to the ordinary run of traffic, and the fact remains that even in the transport of mails, the air cannot compete economically with the rail or road.

The partisans of aviation reply airily that the plane is only in its infancy. But is it? Every machine must at some time reach its zenith of development. The steam engine took nearly a century to reach maturity. But time runs faster now: ten years of the present century can easily outstrip fifty of the last. Aircraft had seen over twenty years of forced and precocious development, and are probably well within sight of their zenith.

Whatever may be their line of development, the fact remains irrefutable that in any question of transport in bulk, the plane is hopelessly outclassed. The freight of an ordinary train carrying a load of one hundred tons would require at least twenty or thirty large planes, while the dead-weight cargo of a moderate-sized tramp steamer carrying five thousand tons would require hundreds of planes and involve a long series of transshipments.

But in using large planes in large numbers, there are limits of common-sense convenience. The large plane is an intolerably bulky and inconvenient vehicle to load and unload, and considering the small load it can carry, it may safely be said that there would be an actual loss, rather than a saving of time, in the transport of any considerable volume of freight by air.

Again, though speed is the ace of air transport, it is not the ace of trumps. What is required in world transport is regularity. The prime essential of traffic on a large scale is the maintenance of a regular schedule. Speed may be very important on some occasions, but it is not a primary consideration. . . .

It is precisely in this requisite of regularity that aircraft are notoriously deficient. They are slaves of weather and cannot run to a strict schedule on voyages of any length. They are governed by the wind. Here one meets with the dominant consideration governing navigation in the air. Aircraft do not struggle against the wind. The wind is merely a moving current of air and they are carried bodily along in it, just as a ship is carried by the tide. . . .

It is not contended, of course, that there is no place for air transport. There is a place, and, in certain exceptional circumstances, possibly a considerable place—but never a great place. Across stretches of difficult and undeveloped country, where the rail and road do not run, on short routes for carrying goods of little weight and bulk, when speed is of primary importance, when a businessman wants to expedite an important interview, when a film must be rushed to Chicago or New York, then the airplane will be used. But the bulk of traffic will always go by land and sea, because earth and water can sustain great weight and air cannot. . . .

What then is the sum of the whole matter? There is no large and growing future for commercial aviation, because the future will never be much more than the present. There is a place for short range traffic in places to carry mails and those few passengers whom necessity impels to save time at the expense of comfort. But their number is not great. Recent sensational achievements in aviation have blinded its exponents to the inevitable obstacles. The feats of heroism and endurance performed in long oceanic flights are merely a token of the stern limitations which beset them. "Thou hast placed bounds upon them which they shall not pass." [Psalm 104:9]

The devotees of new instruments can never see anything else. The princes of the power of the air wax sarcastic over what they call "the Noah's Ark school" of transport. But the Ark could carry a considerable freight and bore it in safety. Noah used flight merely as an auxiliary to sea transport, and that is all it is good for.

Source: *The Forum*, August 1928

THOUGHT QUESTIONS:

1. What barriers to the widespread use of airplanes for commercial transport did the author cite? Did he address if these limitations would always exist? With the use of hindsight, how might he be proven wrong?

2. What positive tasks, if any, did the author cite regarding the use of aircraft for transport purposes? What small benefits did the author concede that air transport had over its rivals?

3. What modern examples can you think of regarding some product or invention that some people that would never amount to anything but later became an essential part of society?

The Motion Picture Producers and Distributors of America's List of "Don'ts" and "Be Carefuls"

Hollywood motion pictures fell under intense scrutiny in many sections of the country during the 1920s. After a U.S. Supreme Court decision found that free speech guarantees did not apply to film, many states and localities began to institute censorship boards to oversee the content of movies shown in their jurisdictions. The large Hollywood studios also responded to the decision, naming William H. Hays to be the first president of the newly formed Motion Picture Producers and Distributors of America, soon to be known as the Motion Pictures Association of America (MPAA). A former chairman of the Republican National Committee, Hays had served as Warren Harding's campaign manager in the 1920 presidential campaign before becoming Postmaster General in the Harding Administration. Studio executives chose Hays to lead the MPAA because he was an elder in the Presbyterian Church who could help Hollywood clean up its image with the public and avoid federal government regulation.

Hays endeavored to develop a standard voluntary code for filmmaking designed to produce films without objectionable material that would also save the studios money by not having to constantly edit their movies to comply with the desires of the myriad of local censors around the country. Hays began with a list of suggested "Don'ts and Be Carefuls"—a set of general rules based on the most frequent objections of local censorship boards. This list (presented below) became the basis for the future Motion Picture Production Code, often referred to as the "Hays Code," which began to be enforced by the motion picture industry's Production Code Administration (PCA). After 1934, all films had to be approved by the PCA before they could be released to the general public. The Hays Code governed the content of Hollywood films for the next 35 years until replaced by the Movie Ratings System used in modified form today.

Resolved, That those things which are included in the following list shall not appear in pictures produced by the members of this Association, irrespective of the manner in which they are treated:

1. Pointed profanity – by either title or lip – this includes the words "God," "Lord," "Jesus," "Christ" (unless they be used reverently in connection with proper religious ceremonies), "hell," "damn," "Gawd," and every other profane and vulgar expression however it may be spelled;
2. Any licentious or suggestive nudity – in fact or in silhouette; and any lecherous or licentious notice thereof by other characters in the picture;
3. The illegal traffic in drugs;
4. Any inference of sex perversion;
5. White slavery;
6. Miscegenation (sex relationships between the white and black races);
7. Sex hygiene and venereal diseases;
8. Scenes of actual childbirth – in fact or in silhouette;
9. Children's sex organs;
10. Ridicule of the clergy;
11. Willful offense to any nation, race or creed;

And be it further resolved, That special care be exercised in the manner in which the following subjects are treated, to the end that vulgarity and suggestiveness may be eliminated and that good taste may be emphasized:

1. The use of the flag;
2. International relations (avoiding picturizing in an unfavorable light another country's religion, history, institutions, prominent people, and citizenry);
3. Arson;
4. The use of firearms;
5. Theft, robbery, safe-cracking, and dynamiting of trains, mines, buildings, etc. (having in mind the effect which a too-detailed description of these may have upon the moron);
6. Brutality and possible gruesomeness;
7. Technique of committing murder by whatever method;
8. Methods of smuggling;

9. Third-degree methods;
10. Actual hangings or electrocutions as legal punishment for crime;
11. Sympathy for criminals;
12. Attitude toward public characters and institutions;
13. Sedition;
14. Apparent cruelty to children and animals;
15. Branding of people or animals;
16. The sale of women, or of a woman selling her virtue;
17. Rape or attempted rape;
18. First-night scenes;
19. Man and woman in bed together;
20. Deliberate seduction of girls;
21. The institution of marriage;
22. Surgical operations;
23. The use of drugs;
24. Titles or scenes having to do with law enforcement or law-enforcing officers;
25. Excessive or lustful kissing, particularly when one character or the other is a "heavy."

Source: Motion Picture Producers and Distributors of America (October 1927)

THOUGHT QUESTIONS:

1. Are there any "Don'ts" or "Be Carefuls" that you are surprised were placed on either list? Explain.

2. Think of a modern film that you have seen recently. Would there be one or more items from the above lists that would potentially cause the film to be censored and therefore prevented from being released during the 1920s according to these recommendations? If so, give some examples.

3. What are the benefits and negative aspects of the current ratings system for movies today? Should there be a movie ratings system in place today? Should it modified or ended? Explain.

Vignettes

Mass Advertizing and Credit Fuels the 1920s Economic Boom

While the availability of jobs and the increase in average workers' incomes provided the fuel for the economic recovery of the 1920s, extensive advertising efforts by the first generation of modern corporate marketers often determined the direction in which consumer money would flow. During the post-World War I decade, companies paid marketers billions of dollars to lure consumers to their products over the radio, in movie houses, and the traditional print media.

Under the weight of saturation advertising, consumers were bombarded with messages that often conflicted with more traditional values of thrift and savings. Indulgence was celebrated: the Eastman Kodak Company in 1928 began to sell its "Vanity Kodak," a handheld camera directly marketed to women. Not only were the cameras available in five different colors—"Sea Gull" (gray), "Cockatoo" (green), "Redbreast" (red), "Bluebird" (blue), and "Jenny Wren" (brown)—the implication in the company's ad was that women should own all five versions of the camera in order to limit the possibility of the device's color clashing with their wardrobes. Advertisers often emphasized the notion that buyers needed to be current with the latest styles: "Was your present watch in style when Uncle Tom's Cabin came to town?" asked one ad from 1927 for the Elgin Watch Company. Other ads directly played on consumers' insecurities, such as the famous advertisement for Listerine that depicted a sad, lonely woman with the caption: "Often a bridesmaid, but never a bride." Her problem being that she had chronic "halitosis"—a phrase invented by a New York marketing firm to describe bad breath.

In addition to the power of advertising, companies lured new buyers to their products through increased use of installment buying. Though increasing sales by expanding consumer purchasing power, installment buying led many irresponsible consumers to overextend themselves with large amounts of personal debt. A contemporary study made during the mid-1920s found that 25 percent of jewelry, 50 percent of sewing machines, radios, and electric refrigerators, 65 percent of vacuum cleaners, 75 percent of washing machines, 75 percent of automobiles, 80 percent of phonographs, and 90 percent of furniture purchases were made on credit. These numbers portended dire consequences for the economy if consumer spending could not be maintained at levels necessary to sustain prosperity.

THOUGHT QUESTIONS:

1. Can you think of any modern examples of advertising similar to the "Vanity Kodak" campaign of the 1920s? How specifically are they similar?

2. What modern examples of advertisements can you think of that are similar to the famous Listerine ad of the 1920s? How can these types of ads successfully target people from all walks of life?

3. How could large proportion of consumer purchasing on credit potentially lead to disastrous consequences for an economy in the long run?

Margaret Sanger and the Birth Control Movement

In addition to the flamboyant flappers, Margaret Sanger also radically challenged traditional ideas concerning women during the 1920s by launching the modern birth control movement. Even before she began working as a nurse to the poor in the Lower East Side slums of Manhattan, Sanger witnessed firsthand how large families could wear down women. Born the sixth of eleven children to a mother who also had seven miscarriages, Sanger was greatly affected by her mother's early death (at the age of 48) and the struggle to help her parents raise her siblings. After her nursing training, she met and married an architect, gave birth to three children, and started promoting the use of contraceptives among the immigrant poor in violation of state and federal laws. To Sanger, birth control was not only a means to relieve the burdens of unwanted pregnancies and prevent amateur abortions, which could maim or kill poor women, but also a representation of freedom and equal rights. "No woman can call herself free," she wrote, "until she can choose conscientiously whether she will or will not be a mother."

Many religious groups, as well as some immigrant groups, opposed Sanger's activities on moral grounds, believing contraceptives to be against their religious beliefs or simply inviting women to be more promiscuous without ramifications. New York State authorities jailed Sanger in 1916 for operating a birth control clinic in Brooklyn where she distributed information about diaphragms and other contraceptive techniques. Though found guilty and sentenced to a thirty-day sentence, an appeals court later ruled that while Sanger was duly convicted, it would be legal for licensed physicians to prescribe contraceptives as a means to prevent the spread of diseases. As a result, she organized the American Birth Control League in 1921 to educate the public about "the dangers of uncontrolled procreation" and to operate family planning clinics where doctors could give women reliable methods of birth control.

Sanger's support for some aspects of the pseudo-scientific eugenics movement led to dissension with many birth control advocates. Running counter to the viewpoint of a majority of old Progressives who believed that one's environment served as the major factor in determining human behavior, the supporters of eugenics argued that hereditary factors predominated, thus society would benefit from selective breeding. While Sanger never advocated euthanasia of those determined to be "unfit," (often defined as the mentally disabled or repeat criminals), she publicly supported their sterilization as a way to prevent children with the supposedly inherited defective traits from being born. Many states passed legislation authorizing compulsory sterilization of certain classes of criminals and the mentally incompetent—a practice affirmed by a 1927 U.S. Supreme Court decision.

Though she resigned the presidency of the American Birth Control League in 1928 over differences with members due to her support of eugenics and her management style, Sanger continued to advocate for women's fertility rights for the next 40 years and helped to change perceptions about birth control in the nation. The American Birth Control League also continued under new directors. Renamed Planned Parenthood in 1942, the organization continues to dispense family planning information and remains a leader in defending female reproductive rights in the modern era.

THOUGHT QUESTIONS:

1. What in Sanger's background motivated her to campaign for birth control?

2. What forms of resistance did Sanger encounter as she attempted to spread her views?

3. How did Sanger's flirtation with eugenics tarnish her legacy among some who otherwise supported her birth control efforts?

The Misappropriation of Sigmund Freud

The theories of Sigmund Freud, often in perverted form, found a ready audience in the United States during the 1920s. The Austrian founder of psychoanalysis had pioneered the clinical approach of treatment through dialogue with patients. Among his most influential theories was the assertion that a person's sexual drives buried within the subconscious mind, rather than rational thought, environmental factors, or supernatural influences, served as the driving force of human life. Only a small portion of a person's mind, what Freud dubbed the "ego," dealt with consciousness and rationality. A much larger part, which the psychologist labeled the "id," referred to the assortment of irrational passions and inner impulses that bore a strong influence on human behavior. At the core of the id, Freud posited, lay a person's sexual drive, or the "libido." Within every individual, Freud surmised, there is conflict between the ego and the id. Humans try to control the power of the id through reason or by channeling the id to more productive ends. Too much repression of one's subconscious drives, Freud believed, led to many of the anxieties of the modern era. Therefore, the main goal of the psychoanalyst should be helping the patient use their ego to discipline the id while still allowing for meaningful expression of inner desires.

Freud's ideas were spread across the country by educated members of the middle class, but often oversimplified by those looking for an easy justification of their Bohemian lifestyle. Taking the doctor's findings and arguments totally out of context, they justified their challenges to prevailing social conventions on the supposed scientific basis that sexual self-restraint was unnatural and unhealthy. Nevertheless, the popularity of Freud proved to be just a part of the broader postwar development of sexual topics being discussed more openly than in the past.

THOUGHT QUESTIONS:

1. What was Sigmund Freud's contribution to psychology as a field of study?

2. How did some people (who often never deeply read Freud's published works) alter Freud's theories during the 1920s to justify nontraditional lifestyles?

3. Can you think of an example today where some people take a simplified version of someone's more complex work and use it to justify a point of view or action? Explain.

The Sacco and Vanzetti Case

In addition to immigration restriction, nativist prejudice during the 1920s manifested itself in other ways. Many western states prohibited Japanese residents from leasing or owning land. A majority of justices on the U.S. Supreme Court in 1922 ruled that Japanese Issei, or first-generation immigrants, as nonwhites, could never become naturalized citizens. Like other groups, Italian immigrants also suffered sporadic attacks, such as occurred in West Frankfort, Illinois in August 1920 when mobs terrorized Italian miners and their families for three days in an effort to drive them out before state troopers arrived to restore order.

No individual case revealed the deep divisions in society along nativist lines during the decade more than the saga of Italian immigrants Nicola Sacco and Bartolomeo Vanzetti. Arrested for a 1920 robbery of a shoe factory in South Braintree, Massachusetts that involved the murder of the company paymaster and a security guard, Sacco and Vanzetti gained the support of many inside and outside the United States who believed that the pair were being tried merely for being political radicals who followed Luigi Galleani, an Italian anarchist who advocated revolutionary violence against governments around the world.

Historians who have intensely studied every aspect of the case have failed to reach a solid consensus about Sacco and Vanzetti's guilt. Though they had no prior criminal records, the men definitely had an association with Galleani's supporters and may have taken part in the robbery to amass funds for revolutionary activities. Still, plenty of grounds for reasonable doubt existed—the testimony of eyewitnesses proved to be inconclusive and there can be no doubt that the presiding judge, Webster Thayer, exhibited strongly biased behavior against the defense inside and outside of the courtroom.

After a jury found them guilty of first-degree murder, Thayer sentenced Sacco and Vanzetti to death, leading to a highly-publicized six-year effort by radicals, intellectuals, Italian American groups, and other interested citizens to secure a stay of execution. After uncovering new evidence, including a confession for the murders by a convicted killer, the governor of Massachusetts appointed a three-man advisory panel to review the case. The board headed by Harvard University President Abbott Lowell (a member of the Immigration Restriction League), however, determined that the judge and jury had addressed the evidence fairly and saw no reason to overturn the conviction.

The subsequent execution of Sacco and Vanzetti in the electric chair on August 23, 1927, led to a series of random protest bombings around the world by sympathetic anarchists and occasional explosions targeting the trial participants, including an attack on Judge Thayer's home that wounded his wife and demolished their residence.

THOUGHT QUESTIONS:

1. What were some ways in which anti-immigrant prejudice manifest itself during the 1920s?

2. How were Sacco and Vanzetti's political beliefs and ethnicity used against them during their legal proceedings?

3. Identify a case from today like Sacco and Vanzetti's in which groups have rallied to retry an imprisoned person for a crime they may or may not have committed but the groups believed that the accused had not received a fair trial. In what ways is the current case both similar and different from Sacco and Vanzetti's?

Chapter 24

The Great Depression and the New Deal

Documents

An Afternoon in a Pushcart Peddlers' Colony

While three quarters of the workers for the New Deal's Works Progress Administration (WPA) labored on construction projects for the government, the WPA also developed some creative programs to help men and women perform non-construction work. The most well-known of these projects proved to be the programs for unemployed artists, actors, and musicians, but the WPA also created the Federal Writers' Project to support unemployed writers during the Great Depression. The Writers' Project produced an assortment of well-received works, including state travel guides, local histories, slave narratives based on oral interviews with former slaves, and life histories of other Americans. In the following excerpt from one of these life histories, the writer describes a visit to a group of New York City men who survived during the Great Depression by scrounging and peddling junk items out of pushcarts.

It was snowing and, shortly after noontime, the snow changed to sleet and beat a tattoo against the rocks and board shacks that had been carelessly thrown together on the west bank of the Harlem [River]. It was windy too and the cold blasts that came in from the river sent the men shivering for cover behind their shacks where some of them had built huge bonfires to ward off the icy chills that swept down from the hills above.
    Some of them, unable to stand it any longer, went below into the crudely furnished cabins that were located in the holds of some old abandoned barges that lay half in, half out of the water. But the men did not seem to mind. Even the rotting barges afforded

them some kind of shelter. It was certainly better than nothing, not to mention the fact that it was their home; address, the foot of 133rd Street at Park Avenue on the west bank of the Harlem River; depression residence of a little band of part-time pushcart peddlers whose cooperative colony is one of the most unique in the history of New York City.

These men earn their living by cruising the streets long before daylight, collecting old automobile parts, pasteboard, paper, rags, rubber, magazines, brass, iron, steel, old clothes or anything they can find that is saleable as junk. They wheel their little pushcarts around exploring cellars, garbage cans and refuse heaps. When they have a load, they turn their footsteps in the direction of the American Junk Dealers, Inc., whose site of wholesale and retail operations is located directly opposite the pushcart colony at 134th Street and Park Avenue. Of the fifty odd colonists, many are ex-carpenters, painters, brick-masons, auto mechanics, upholsterers, plumbers and even an artist or two.

Most of the things the men collect, they sell, but once in a while they run across something useful to themselves, like auto parts, pieces of wire, or any electrical equipment, especially in view of the fact that there are two or three electrical engineers in the group. . . .

After being introduced to some of the boys, we went down into Oliver's barge. It was shaky, weather-beaten and sprawling, like the other half-dozen that surrounded it. Inside, he had set up an old iron range and attached a pipe to it that carried the smoke out and above the upper deck. On top of the iron grating that had been laid across the open hole on the back of the stove were some spare ribs that had been generously seasoned with salt, pepper, sage and hot sauce. Later I discovered a faint flavor of mace in them. The small and pungency of spices filled the low-ceilinged room with an appetizing aroma. The faces of the men were alight and hopeful with anticipation.

There was no real cause for worry, however, since Oliver had more than enough for everybody. Soon he began passing out tin plates for everyone. It makes my mouth water just to think of it. When we had gobbled up everything in sight, all of us sat back in restful contemplation puffing on our freshly-lighted cigarettes. Afterwards there was conversation, things the men elected to talk about of their own accord. . . .

The conversation drifted along until I was finally able to ease in a query or two. "Boys," I ventured, "how is it that none of you ever got on Home Relief? You can get a little grub out of it, at least, and that would take a little of the load off you, wouldn't it?" At this they all rose up in unanimous protest.

"Lis'en," one of them said, "befo' I'd take Home Relief I'd go out in duh street an' hit some bastard oveh de haid an' take myse'f some'n'. I know one uv duh boys who tried to git it an' one of dem uppity little college boys ovah dere talked tuh him lak he was some damn jailbird or some'n'. If it had been me, I'd a bust hell outn' him an' walked outa duh place. What duh hell do we wants wid relief anyhow? We is all able-bodied mens an' can take it. We can make our own livin's."

This, apparently, was the attitude of every man there. They seemed to take fierce pride in the fact that every member of Joe Elder's National Negro Civil Association (it used to be called the National Negro Boat Terminal) was entirely self-supporting. They even had their own unemployment insurance fund that provided an income for any member of the group who was ill and unable to work. Each week the men give a small part of their earnings toward this common fund and automatically agree to allow a certain amount to any temporarily incapacitated member. In addition to that, they divide among themselves their ill brother's work and provide a day and night attendant near his shack if his illness is at all serious. After chatting awhile longer with them, I finally decided to leave. "Well boys," I said, getting up, "I guess I'll have to be shoving off. Thanks, a lot, for the ribs. See you again sometime." . . .

Outside the snow and sleet had turned to rain and the snow that had been feathery and white was running down the river bank in brown rivulets of slush and mud. It was a little warmer but the damp air still had a penetrating sharpness to it. I shuddered, wrapped my muffler a little tighter and turned my coat collar up about my ears.

There was wind in the rain, and behind me lay the jagged outline of the ramshackle dwellings. I hated to think of what it would be like, living in them when there was a scarcity of wood or when the fires went out.

Source: Library of Congress

THOUGHT QUESTIONS:

1. What type of work did these peddlers do before the Great Depression arrived?

2. How did these men come together communally to provide for each other if any of the members got sick and could not care for themselves?

3. What was the common attitude among the peddlers to the idea of going on government relief? How did they explain their position?

Two Displaced Texas Sharecroppers Write to the Secretary of Agriculture

In response to the collapse in farm prices caused by the combination of chronic overproduction and the great drop in consumer demand due to the Great Depression, Congress passed the Agricultural Adjustment Act in 1933 creating a new agency—the Agricultural Adjustment Administration (AAA)—to oversee the government's plans to adjust the supply of seven major farm commodities to existing demand. By encouraging farmers to produce less through the inducement of subsidies (payments), the AAA hoped to infuse farmers with cash while taking surpluses out of the market in an effort to raise the prices of the crops that they did raise and sell in the marketplace. Though the program proved to be a lifesaver for farm owners everywhere, the reduction of land for production purposes hurt southern sharecroppers particularly hard because of the reduced need for farm labor. Though the AAA cotton contract stipulated that landowners were expected to reduce production without upsetting the number of workers on their land "as much as possible," in practice, hundreds of thousands of sharecroppers, mostly involved in cotton production, were simply thrown out of work across the South. In Texas alone, the number of cropper families was reduced from 105,122 in 1930 to 39,821 by 1940, a reduction of 62 percent over the entire decade.

Though their lives were often characterized by immense poverty, living off the land by raising a cotton crop was the only lifestyle large numbers of sharecroppers ever knew. Some were able to find work on another farm, but large numbers were simply set adrift, unable to find steady work, forcing many of them into small towns and cities to seek employment or relief on the government dole. Thousands of southern sharecroppers wrote government officials to explain their situation. The anxiety felt by these people is clearly revealed in these two sample letters written by desperate Texas croppers to the Secretary of Agriculture Henry A. Wallace. G.H. Summers to Secretary of Agriculture Henry Wallace, Hale Center, TX

"in reguard to the triple A Plan I cant say I am against it. But Will Say this. It has Put more Families on the relief than any one thing Because the man that has got the land wont let a man have any of it Because he wants all of those checks that he gets from the goverment to run his Big Auto. Then in the fall he gets a Big Bunch of Mexicans to gather the cotton and wont hardly hire a white Family. It wood Bea all right if a man could get some land to work. I am with my wife and three groan girls and cant get no land to work. Some men work in 2 or 3 Sections and wont let a man have any of it on the account of them checks he gets from the Goverment. So you See that puts lots of Families on the releaf. I have farmed all my life But cant get any land now. But I aint the only one. There are thousands in the same Fix I am in now. Mr Wallace you study this over and see what you think about it."

W.A. Harrick (Floyd County sharecropper) to Secretary of Agriculture Henry Wallace, January 10, 1935

"I am writing you a few lines in regards to the farm that I am renting. I work the place last year on the halves. The landlord never said any thing about me not staying here this year until yesterday the 9th. That he wanted the place to handle him self. That he was going to have it work different this year. They would not let me sind up for eny of the cotton reduction. . .

So I am forced to move to a town and get on the relief, something I have never in all my life had to do, unless the goverment help a little farmer. I have a wife and six children age 18 to 2 years old. We want to stay on the land but how can we, with such landlords?"

Source: National Archives and Records Administration

THOUGHT QUESTIONS:

1. Who did the sharecroppers most blame for their predicament? Why?

2. Leaving aside spelling and grammar issues, how well did the croppers articulate their plight?

3. Describe the croppers' feelings toward government relief. Did they refuse to accept it? Did they accept it grudgingly? Ultimately, what did these two sharecroppers desire most?

"I'd Rather Not Be on Relief"

The Dust Bowl was an ecological disaster caused by the combination of harsh weather conditions and harmful farming practices undertaken for many years in the environmentally sensitive region. By the end of the 1930s, over half the population of western Oklahoma, western Kansas, northwestern Texas, and eastern Colorado left the area to seek a new life elsewhere, with many of them heading west. Written by Lester Hunter in 1938, this poem was turned into a song by migrants at a Farm Security Administration camp in California. The words reflect various aspects of Dust Bowl life and the feelings held by many of the people forced to leave the region.

We go around all dressed in rags
While the rest of the world goes neat,
And we have to be satisfied
With half enough to eat.
We have to live in lean-tos,
Or else we live in a tent,
For when we buy our bread and beans
There's nothing left for rent.

CHORUS:
I'd rather not be on the rolls of relief,
Or work on the W.P.A.
We'd rather work for the farmer
If the farmer could raise the pay;
Then the farmer could plant more cotton
And he'd get more money for spuds,
Instead of wearing patches,
We'd dress up in new duds.

From the east and west and north and south
Like a swarm of bees we come;
The migratory workers
Are worse off than a bum.
We go to Mr. Farmer
And ask him what he'll pay;
He says, "You gypsy workers
Can live on a buck a day."

(CHORUS)

We don't ask for luxuries
Or even a feather bed.
But we're bound to raise the dickens
While our families are underfed.
Now the winter is on us
And the cotton picking is done,
What are we going to live on
While we're waiting for spuds to come?

(CHORUS)

Now if you will excuse me
I'll bring my song to an end.
I've got to go and chuck a crack
Where the howling wind comes in.
The times are going to get better
And I guess you'd like to know
I'll tell you all about it,
I've joined the C.I.O.

Source: Charles L. Todd and Robert Sonkin migrant workers collection (AFC 1985/001), American Folklife Center, Library of Congress

THOUGHT QUESTIONS:

1. What are some of examples of the general negative aspects of life during the Great Depression laid out in this poem/song?

2. What attitudes about being on government relief are expressed?

3. Describe ways in which historians and non-historians alike can glean aspects of life during a time period by studying various types of art, such as music, produced during those years.

The National Recovery Administration "Blanket Code"

In a desperate effort to maintain industrial employment while boosting profits for businesses in the midst of the Great Depression, Congress in June 1933 passed the National Industrial Recovery Act creating the National Recovery Administration (NRA)—one of the boldest experiments of the entire New Deal. The new agency supervised the drafting and enforcement of "codes of fair competition" in every commercial and industrial sector in order to maintain profitable prices (by eliminating price cutting and overproduction) while establishing basic labor standards for all businesses to follow within their sector.

To direct the NRA, President Franklin Roosevelt appointed Hugh Johnson, a brash army general with experience in public relations who previously served on the War Industries Board during World War I. Johnson immediately launched a campaign with much fanfare to rally all Americans behind the program. Through parades, public rallies with patriotic speeches, and other assorted hoopla, the general generated massive publicity to convince businessmen and consumers to join the crusade. Johnson made the NRA's logo which he designed, a Native American Thunderbird-like image named "The Blue Eagle," synonymous with cooperation in the collective national endeavor to restore economic prosperity. Only business owners who voluntarily complied with the code for their particular sector could legally display the symbol in their stores, on their products, or in their advertisements. Meanwhile, the government openly encouraged consumers only to purchase goods and services from establishments displaying the Blue Eagle. The NRA's symbol soon sprouted everywhere—on placards in storefront windows, at factory entrances, on company stationery, and newspaper ads, usually accompanied by the slogan "We Do Our Part."

Johnson brought together the largest producers in every business sector and in the NRA's first four months, over seven hundred codes of fair competition were written to govern their affairs. Where one or more large firms dominated an industry, the agency relied on them to prepare the regulations; where no company controlled an industry, the NRA turned to a trade association. When some code-making efforts stalled, Johnson asked business leaders in an industry to accept a standard "blanket code" (shown below) that would guarantee a minimum wage for workers, limit workers' hours, and abolish the use of child labor.

Although the blanket code helped to speed up sign-ups, the NRA ultimately failed to generate full economic recovery and the agency received increasing criticism from a variety of sources. Many industrialists blamed the NRA's labor provisions and complained about the high level of paperwork and general interference with their business practices. Small business owners railed against the big businesses who dominated the code making and code enforcement authorities, believing that wage and price provisions were written for the benefit of the corporate entities at their expense. Workers charged the NRA with failing to accept their unions of choice. Consumers complained that the rise in prices was not offset by a corresponding increase in wages and job opportunities. All began to believe that the oversight committees set up to enforce the codes were powerless to punish violators. By early 1935, it was clear that the NRA had failed. When the Supreme Court declared that the agency's codes were unconstitutional in May 1935, even President Roosevelt was relieved that the NRA experiment was over.

During the period of the president's emergency re-employment drive, that is to say, from August 1 to December 31, 1933, or to any earlier date of approval of a code of fair competition to which he is subject, the undersigned hereby agrees with the president as follows:

1. After August 31, 1933, not to employ any person under 16 years of age, except that persons between 14 and 15 may be employed (but not in manufacturing or mechanical industries) for not to exceed three hours per day and those hours between 7 a m. and 7 p.m., in such work as will not interfere with hours of day school.

2. Not to work any accounting, clerical, banking, office, service or sales employees (excepting outside salesmen -- in any store, office. department, establishment or public utility, or on any automotive or horse-drawn passenger, express, delivery, or freight service, or in any other place or manner, for more than 40 hours in any one week and not

to reduce the hours of any store service operation below 52 hours in any one week, unless such hours were less than 52 hours per week before July 1, 1933, and in the latter case not to reduce such hours at all.

3. Not to employ any factory or mechanical worker or artisan more than a maximum week of 35 hours until December 31, 1933, but with the right to work a maximum week of 40 hours for any six weeks within this period; and not to employ any worker more than eight hours in any one day.

4. The maximum hours fixed in the foregoing paragraphs (2) and (3) shall not apply to employees in establishments employing not more than two persons in towns of less than 2500 population, which towns are not part of a larger trade area; nor to registered pharmacists or other professional persons employed in their profession; nor to employees on emergency maintenance work; nor to employees in a managerial or executive capacity who now receive more than $35 per week; nor to very special cases where restrictions of hours of highly skilled workers on continuous processes would unavoidably reduce production, but in any such special ease, at least time and one third shall be paid for hours worked in excess of the maximum. Population for the purposes of this agreement shall be determined by reference to the 1930 federal census.

5. Not to pay any of the classes of employees mentioned in paragraph (2- less than $15 per week in any city over 500,000 population, or in the immediate trade area of such city; nor less than $14.50 per week in any city of between 250,000 and 500,000 population, or in the immediate trade area of such city; nor less than $14 per week in any city of between 2500 and 250,000 population, or in the immediate trade area of such city; and in towns of less than 2500 population to increase all wages by not less than 20 per cent, provided that this shall not require wages in excess of $12 per week.

6. Not to pay any employee of the classes mentioned in paragraph (3) less than 40 cents per hour unless the hourly rate for the same class of work on July 15, 1929, was less than 40 cents per hour, in which latter cases not to pay less than the hourly rate on July 15, 1929, and in no event less than 30 cents per hour. It is agreed that this paragraph establishes a guaranteed minimum rate of pay regardless of whether the employee is compensated on the basis of a time rate or on a piece work performance.

7. Not to reduce the compensation for employment now in excess of the minimum wages hereby agreed to (notwithstanding that the hours worked in such employment may be hereby reduced) and to increase the pay for such employment by an equitable readjustment of all pay schedules.

8. Not to use any subterfuge to frustrate the spirit and intent of this agreement which is, among other things, to increase employment by a universal covenant, to remove obstructions to commerce, and to shorten hours and to raise wages for the shorter week to a living basis.

9. Not to increase the price of any merchandise sold after the date hereof over the price of July 1, 1933, by more than is necessary by actual increases in production, replacement, or invoice costs of merchandise since July 1, 1933, or by taxes or other costs resulting from action pursuant to the agricultural adjustment act, and in setting such price increases, to give full weight to probable increases in sales volume and to refrain from taking profiteering advantage of the consuming public.

10. To support and patronize establishments which also have signed this agreement and are listed as members of N. R. A. (National Recovery Administration).

11. To cooperate to the fullest extent in having a code of fair competition submitted by his industry at the earliest possible date an in any event before September 1, 1933.

12. Where, before June 16, 1933, the undersigned had contracted to purchase goods at a fixed price for delivery during the period of this agreement, the undersigned will make an appropriate adjustment of said fixed price to meet any increase in cost caused by the seller having signed this president's re-employment agreement or having become bound by any code of fair competition approved by the president.

13. This agreement shall cease upon approval by the president of a code to which the undersigned is subject; or, if the N. R. A. so elects, upon submission of a code to which the undersigned is subject and substitution of any of its provisions for any of the terms of this agreement.

14. It is agreed that any person who wishes to do his part in the president's re-employment drive by signing this agreement, but who assorts that some particular provision hereof, because of peculiar circumstances, will create great and unavoidable hardship, may obtain the benefits hereof by signing this agreement and putting it into effect and then, in a petition approved by a representative trade association of his industry, or other representative organization designed by N. R. A., may apply for a stay of such provision pending a summary investigation by N. R. A., if he agrees in such application to abide by the decision of such investigation.

This agreement is entered into pursuant to section 4 (A) of the National Industrial Recovery Act and subject to all the terms and conditions required by sections 7 (A) and 10 (B) of that act.

Source: National Archives

THOUGHT QUESTIONS:

1. What provisions of the NRA blanket code had the potential to benefit workers? Identify any potential limitations for laborers by its provisions.

2. What provisions of the blanket code sought to benefit businesses suffering from falling prices and ruinous competition in the midst of the Depression?

3. In what ways do you think the very complexity of the NRA model worked to undermine its effectiveness?

Vignettes

FDR's "Splendid Deception"

On August 10, 1921, Franklin Roosevelt fell ill during a family vacation on Campobello Island in New Brunswick, Canada. He soon experienced high fevers, excessive pain, and, eventually, paralysis. Within two weeks Roosevelt was diagnosed as suffering from the effects of poliomyelitis—a viral disease that destroyed cells in his spinal cord and almost killed him. Through his courage, perseverance, and grueling physical therapy sessions over several years, FDR was able to regain some strength in his upper body muscles, but his life would be changed forever as he would never walk without assistance again.

Refusing to adhere to his mother's desire for him to retire to the family estate along the Hudson River, Roosevelt planned to continue his political career but knew that the public's view of his infirmity would greatly impact his chances to return successfully. During the early twentieth century, people with disabilities rarely worked, let alone served in the highest levels of government, as most Americans believed that they would be better off living an inactive life at home or an institution. Roosevelt responded to the challenge by developing an intricate illusion for the public that he was largely unaffected by the illness. With his lower body painfully locked in heavy steel braces, he trained his remaining abdominal and hip muscles to swing his hips while using a cane and leaning on the arm of a family member or aide to propel himself forward as naturally as possible to give the impression that he could actually walk, albeit for short distances. Through his mastery of this maneuver, Roosevelt was able to convince people who did not know him well that he was fine despite their knowledge of his bout with polio. Helping him in the intricate theatrical production that biographer Hugh Gallagher (himself a polio survivor) labeled Roosevelt's "splendid deception" were members of the mainstream press corps who never printed the fact that FDR was unable to walk unassisted and avoided taking pictures of him in his wheelchair. As a result, the American people never understood the toll that polio had actually taken on Roosevelt's body.

In 1928, FDR resumed his political career, winning election as governor of New York. Four years later, he continued to hide the extent of his disability while running for president, with reporters and photographers downplaying his illness. Though acknowledging his experience with polio, the media often described Roosevelt as someone who courageously overcame the disease and only suffered a slight limp while walking. Political cartoons often depicted him leaping or running, projecting an image of strength and vitality.

Throughout his presidency, Roosevelt's staff with the help of the press endeavored to maintain a strict silence with regard to Roosevelt's health. Presidential appearances were carefully staged events. In a time when few buildings were accessible to disabled Americans in wheelchairs, workers constructed temporary ramps hidden from public view by sight-blocking fences that connected the street to building entrances allowing the president to have the private mobility he desired. Roosevelt often delivered public addresses from the back of trains or automobiles. When that was not possible, arrangements were made so that he could perform his awkward gait of simulated walking while holding onto an aide's arm to reach the podium.

There were a few instances when FDR fully recognized the extent of his disability in public, usually during visits to wounded soldiers at military hospitals during World War II. The most noteworthy occasion occurred when Roosevelt appeared seated before Congress to report on the Yalta Conference a few months before his death and began his remarks by saying: "I hope that you will pardon me for this unusual posture of sitting down during the presentation of what I want to say, but I know that you will realize that it makes it a lot easier for me not to have to carry about ten pounds of steel around on the bottom of my legs; and also because of the fact that I have just completed a fourteen-thousand-mile trip."

Fifty years later, attitudes had changed in America. The nation dedicated the FDR Memorial in Washington, D.C. on May 2, 1997, and critics soon pointed out that nowhere on the sprawling grounds of the monument was a depiction of the president's physical impairment. Roosevelt's disability, once again, seemed to be hidden from the public view. Responding to the brewing controversy, Congress soon passed an act calling for a representation of the president that acknowledged his disability, resulting in money being raised for a new sculpture of FDR sitting prominently in a wheelchair.

THOUGHT QUESTIONS:

1. How did FDR learn to disguise his inability to walk unaided from the public? Who helped him in this endeavor?

2. Why did FDR undertake his "splendid deception"? Would a politician in similar circumstances have to do the same today? What if he or she had a disability or infirmity other than paralysis?

3. Do you think it was important to add a depiction of Roosevelt in a wheelchair at the FDR Memorial in Washington, D.C.? If so, to what extent? If not, why not?

The Real Bonnie and Clyde

Even before they died in a hail of bullets at the hands of a Texas Ranger and his posse along a country road in northwest Louisiana, the image of Depression Era-outlaws Bonnie Parker and Clyde Barrow as renegade nonconformists thumbing their noses at authority by robbing banks and outwitting hapless law enforcement officials began to take hold in much of the country's mainstream media. In reality, both were bored criminals who only cared about excitement, were frequently careless and inept, and often lacked mercy as they murdered anyone who got in their way. This depiction was certainly not unique. At a time when public opinion for bankers was at an all-time low due to the role of financial institutions in bringing on the Great Depression, many crooks who robbed banks like John Dillinger, Pretty Boy Floyd, and Baby Face Nelson not only gained notoriety but even some fans who read with interest about their exploits in the newspapers or heard about their acts from movie theater newsreels. Soon, Bonnie and Clyde would join this notorious but legendary pantheon.

Bonnie Parker was born in Rowena, Texas in 1910. After her father, a bricklayer, died when she was four years old, her mother moved the family to West Dallas, an industrial section of the growing city where she found work as a seamstress. Though not yet 16, Parker married Roy Thornton who she knew from their high school. Thornton was frequently absent from their home, often womanizing or committing petty crimes, and she never saw him again after 1929. She moved back in with her mother and began waiting tables at a café when she met Clyde Barrow, a recent migrant to West Dallas from a poor Ellis County sharecropping family. Twenty-one years old in early 1930, Barrow was already involved in various criminal activities, mostly robbing stores and stealing cars, when he was arrested and sent to an East Texas prison farm where he endured grueling work assignments and eventually killed his first person—a fellow inmate who had repeatedly sexually assaulted him. Paroled in 1932, Barrow emerged from prison a bitter young man, hardly rehabilitated, with an abiding hatred for law enforcement officials. He soon assembled a gang, which soon began their famous two-year crime spree ranging from Texas to as far north as Minnesota and Indiana. The group included Bonnie Parker—the bored waitress smitten with the troubled bad boy—Clyde's older brother Buck, and Buck's wife Blanche.

Before their increasingly violent string of bank robberies, gas station holdups, carjackings ended, they had killed at least thirteen people, most of them law enforcement officers, but also some ordinary citizens who somehow interfered with their actions. In their attempt to escape justice, the gang hid out for a time at a garage apartment in Joplin, Missouri, but their raucous, alcohol-fueled card games soon drew suspicion in the quiet residential neighborhood. When local police arrived on April 13, 1933, expecting to arrest bootleggers, the Barrow gang shot their way out, killing two officers in the process. As a result of their hasty escape, the criminals left behind a trove of weapons and ammunition along with a camera. The film in the camera revealed images of gang members hamming it up, most famously of Bonnie cockily leaning against a car packing a pistol at her side while clenching a cigar between her teeth. The publication of the photos greatly elevated their story into an over-glamorized drama making national headlines.

Over the next three months, their crime spree continued across the Plains states, but as the death toll rose, public opinion began to turn strongly against them. Their growing fame began to hinder their operations, and they could no longer risk eating at restaurants or a stay at motels without garnering unwanted attention. Nevertheless, they were forced to check into a motor court to tend to injuries that Bonnie received after Clyde accidentally drove their automobile into a ditch resulting in acid from the car's battery badly burning her right leg. When authorities were alerted, the gang once again had to shoot their way out, but this time Buck Barrow was killed and a seriously wounded Blanche was captured.

The end finally came to Bonnie and Clyde when retired Texas Ranger Frank Hamer was recruited to assemble a posse and track them down. Hamer's big break occurred after Barrow helped a gang member escape from the same prison farm where he formerly did time. Other convicts also escaped and befriended the Barrow gang, leading the father of one of them to arrange a deal that would commute his son's sentence in exchange for revealing the couple's whereabouts. Waiting in ambush along State Highway 154 near Gibsland, Louisiana, Hamer and his cohorts emptied 130 rounds fired from their automatic machine guns into Bonnie and Clyde's car, killing them quickly. After their bullet-ridden bodies and vehicle were displayed to the media, Bonnie and Clyde were largely forgotten for the next 35 years until Hollywood revived their legend with a film version of their lives that did exceptionally well at the box office and won two Academy Awards. Starring Warren Beatty and Faye Dunaway, *Bonnie and Clyde* romanticized the couple as good-looking, impeccably-dressed counterculture figures seeking action as a means of escaping a conformist lifestyle. The movie took great leaps with the truth, not only with its depiction of real-life events, but especially in its portrayal of the two outlaws who, in real life, seem to have had few redeeming qualities. While one should always be leery of seeking role models among habitual lawbreakers, they should be even more reluctant about getting their historical information from Hollywood.

THOUGHT QUESTIONS:

1. What explained the attraction of some individuals to the exploits of Bonnie and Clyde (and other colorful criminals) during the Great Depression?

2. How was the story of Bonnie and Clyde rediscovered and retold during the 1960s? Was it an accurate depiction of the gangsters' story? Why or why not?

3. Do you see any parallels in the way that Bonnie and Clyde have been depicted in the media and some criminal cases today? Explain with examples.

The Dust Bowl: A Man-Made Disaster

Though brought on by the extreme drought that hit the Southern Great Plains during the 1930s, the ecological devastation of the "Dust Bowl" was actually a man-made disaster that was years in the making. While the high heat and lack of rainfall were prime elements necessary to create the mammoth dust storms that wreaked havoc on the region and surrounding areas during the Great Depression years, they do not explain why the unprecedented environmental catastrophe occurred. Other areas of the country, and indeed the world, endure high heat and a dearth of rain without producing immense dust storms registering hundreds of feet high and blowing for hundreds of miles. Indeed, the confluence of multiple factors ultimately produced the Dust Bowl.

The Southern Great Plains is a location noted for frequent high winds over a relatively flat terrain. As historian James Malin documented during the 1940s and 1950s in an unconvincing effort to explain away the dust storms of the 1930s as simply the latest manifestation of a naturally-occurring phenomenon, a large number of newspaper and other accounts from the mid-to-late 1800s abound testifying to the high winds and frequent bouts of Plains residents with dust as a result, especially during periods of low rainfall.

Another contributing factor was the fertile but "flocculant" soil types of the Southern Plains. When the rainfall is sufficient, the soil produces fabulous yields for farmers of wheat and other crops in part because the dirt holds together well when moist. When high heat and extended drought occur, however, the earth simply fails to adhere and blows away easily when the inevitable high winds occur.

Despite all of these natural factors at play, the Dust Bowl disaster could not have taken place had it not been for the increasing number of profit-seeking growers coming onto the Plains during the high-price years of World War I, tearing up the native grasses that held the soil on the landscape, and cultivating large expanses of land without the use of sound soil conservation techniques. The high rainfall of the war years allowed for bumper crops and record profits for the farmers, many of whom weren't even full-time agriculturalists. These itinerant "suitcase farmers" were often townspeople such as realtors, teachers, and other professionals looking to make some extra money on the side to supplement their incomes by planting wheat and leaving the fields to themselves with the hope that the crops would grow enough to produce a bountiful and profitable harvest. If the crops failed and the soil blew away because of bad growing conditions, they often viewed the result as simply a bad investment and hoped to do better the next year. Consecutive years of extreme heat, high winds, little rain, and the growers' replacement of cover grasses with withered crops unable to hold the powdery soil in place made the Southern Plains in the 1930s resemble the Sahara Desert and leading to half its residents to flee the area.

Ultimately, the rain and agricultural prosperity returned during the 1940s, but only after those who remained began to employ contour plowing, land terracing, irrigated farming, and other necessary soil conservation techniques. The federal government contributed by purchasing and removing submarginal farming land from cultivation, reverting over one million worn-out acres into wildlife refuges and national grasslands. As a result of these changes, when a period of extended drought returned to the Southern Plains during the 1950s, the dust blew again (in some instances created massive storms reminiscent of the 1930s Dust Bowl), but the frequency and severity of these storms were notably less than the "black blizzards" of twenty years earlier.

THOUGHT QUESTIONS:

1. What natural factors contributed to the creation of the Dust Bowl of the Southern Plains?

2. In what significant ways was the Dust Bowl a man-made creation?

3. How did the employment of soil conservation techniques reduce the frequency and severity of dust storms on the Southern Plains in subsequent years?

Marian Anderson Performs at the Lincoln Memorial

Marian Anderson had gone far in her career as a world-renowned singer before she became the centerpiece of a highly publicized controversy in 1939 when the Daughters of the American Revolution (DAR) refused to allow the African-American vocalist the honor of performing at Constitution Hall in Washington, D.C. because of her race. The daughter of a schoolteacher and a delivery man in South Philadelphia in 1897, Anderson first caught the attention of her Baptist Church choirmaster who was moved by the beauty, strength, and tremendous range of her voice (she could sing soprano, alto, tenor, or bass). The congregation helped fund her formal lessons, and though she was not accepted into prestigious music academies because she was black, Anderson inevitably caught the attention of important suitors in the music world. In 1925, she entered and won a contest to make a solo appearance with the New York Philharmonic Symphony Orchestra. Three years later, she sang for the first time at Carnegie Hall in New York City. Feeling that she was being held back from success in America because of her race, she traveled to Europe and became a smash hit performing at London's Wigmore Hall, the Paris Opera House, and other venues including multiple command performances before royalty.

Anderson returned to the United States in 1935 and the following year became the first African American to be invited to perform at the White House. Despite finally becoming a huge concert draw in her home country, she was still subject to the racial bias of her day. While on tour, she was restricted like other blacks to staying at "colored" waiting rooms and hotels, but often preferred to spend the night at the homes of local black leaders in a town or city in which she was giving a performance. This treatment, reflecting the pervasive racism of the time, set the stage for the controversy to come.

In 1939, Howard University in Washington, D.C. invited Anderson to sing as part of its concert series. Because of Anderson's growing reputation, the university sought a venue large enough to accommodate the anticipated large crowd. Constitution Hall, with a seating capacity of 4,000, was thought to fit the bill, but the DAR, which owned the Hall, declined. The rebuff became a news story when Eleanor Roosevelt, a supporter of African-American rights and herself a member of the DAR, heard about the organization's decision and promptly resigned from the group in protest, writing a public letter stating "I am in complete disagreement with the attitude taken in refusing Constitution Hall to a great artist . . . You had an opportunity to lead in an enlightened way and it seems to me that your organization has failed."

The First Lady was not done with the matter. When Walter White, the executive secretary of the National Association for the Advancement of Colored People (NAACP), suggested an outdoor concert somewhere in the city, she used her pull within her husband's administration to arrange a performance at the Lincoln Memorial with Secretary of the Interior Harold Ickes. The Secretary led Anderson onto the stage set up on the steps of the memorial on Easter Sunday, April 9, 1939, in front of an integrated audience of 75,000 people, by far the largest crowd before which she would ever perform. Though initially terrified at the immensity of the audience, she was determined to turn in the performance of her life. As she later wrote: "I could not run away from this situation. If I had anything to offer, I would have to do so now." Never a civil rights activist, Anderson agreed to participate in the hope that she could contribute to the end of prejudice through her music if she performed and behaved with dignity.

Accompanied only by a pianist, Anderson began with a solid rendition of the patriotic song "My Country, 'Tis of Thee." She followed with "Nobody Knows the Trouble I've Seen," delivered with tears in her eyes. After "America," she sang an aria from *La Favorite* by Gaetano Donizetti, then Franz Schubert's "Ave Maria." She ended the 30-minute performance with three spirituals, "Gospel Train," "Trampin'" and "My Soul is Anchored in the Lord." The concert received maximum publicity at the time and became a landmark event in American civil rights history.

Four years later, in the midst of World War II, the DAR finally invited Anderson to perform at Constitution Hall in front of an integrated audience at a benefit for the Red Cross. She continued her illustrious career at home and abroad for two more decades. In 1955, Anderson became the first African American to perform at the Metropolitan Opera in New York City. In 1961, she sang the National Anthem at John F. Kennedy's inauguration and two years later returned to the steps of the Lincoln Memorial where she sang at the conclusion of the Martin Luther King-led March on Washington. Living long enough to see great changes take place in her country, she died in 1993 at the age of 96.

THOUGHT QUESTIONS:

1. Why did Howard University desire Anderson to sing at Constitution Hall? What was the response by the Daughters of the American Revolution?

2. How did Eleanor Roosevelt respond to the DAR with respect to her membership and with regard to Anderson performing somewhere else in Washington?

3. What do you believe is the proper role of the First Lady with respect to potentially controversial topics? Should they avoid them at all costs or sometimes engage the public by using their position to generate publicity for a cause that they believe in?

Chapter 25

Democracy, Fascism and Communism at War, 1921-1945

Documents

Albert Einstein Urges FDR to Build the Atomic Bomb

The discovery of uranium fission by German scientists in late 1938 captured the attention of physicists around the world. Physicist Leo Szilard realized that the fission of atoms could be used to create a nuclear chain reaction capable of yielding a vast amount of energy for both electric power and atomic bombs. Working with Enrico Fermi, the two scientists built a nuclear reactor using uranium at Columbia University, conducted a series of important experiments, and concluded that a chain reaction using uranium was possible.

In order to push for government support of further uranium research, they decided to write a letter to President Franklin Roosevelt (shown below) and have someone more prestigious put their name on it—Albert Einstein. Roosevelt decided that the letter had merit and required action, authorizing the creation of the Advisory Committee on Uranium, marking the start of the government's effort to develop an atomic bomb. Other government committees took over the issue of atomic bomb development, but the full-scale effort with the British that would become the Manhattan Project did not commence until 1942.

Sir:
Some recent work by E. Fermi and L. Szilard, which has been communicated to me in manuscript, leads me to expect that the element uranium may be turned into a new and important source of energy in the immediate future. Certain aspects of the situation

which has arisen seem to call for watchfulness and, if necessary, quick action on the part of the Administration. I believe therefore that it is my duty to bring to your attention the following facts and recommendations:

In the course of the last four months it has been made probable—through the work of Joliot in France as well as Fermi and Szilard in America—that it may become possible to set up a nuclear chain reaction in a large mass of uranium by which vast amounts of power and large quantities of new radium-like elements would be generated. Now it appears almost certain that this could be achieved in the immediate future.

This new phenomenon would also lead to the construction of bombs, and it is conceivable—though much less certain—that extremely powerful bombs of a new type may thus be constructed. A single bomb of this type, carried by boat and exploded in a port, might very well destroy the whole port together with some of the surrounding territory. However, such bombs might very well prove to be too heavy for transportation by air.

The United States has only very poor ores of uranium in moderate quantities. There is some good ore in Canada and the former Czechoslovakia, while the most important source of uranium is Belgian Congo.

In view of the situation you may think it desirable to have more permanent contact maintained between the Administration and the group of physicists working on chain reactions in America. One possible way of achieving this might be for you to entrust with this task a person who has your confidence and who could perhaps serve in an inofficial [sic.] capacity. His task might comprise the following:

a) to approach Government Departments, keep them informed of the further development, and put forward recommendations for Government action, giving particular attention to the problem of securing a supply of uranium ore for the United States;

b) to speed up the experimental work, which is at present being carried on within the limits of the budgets of University laboratories, by providing funds, if such funds be required, through his contacts with private persons who are willing to make contributions for this cause, and perhaps also by obtaining the co-operation of industrial laboratories which have the necessary equipment.

I understand that Germany has actually stopped the sale of uranium from the Czechoslovakian mines, which she has taken over. That she should have taken such early action might perhaps be understood on the ground that the son of the German Under-Secretary of State, von Weizsäcker, is attached to the Kaiser-Wilhelm-Institut in Berlin where some of the American work on uranium is now being repeated.

Yours very truly,
A. Einstein

Source: FDR Presidential Library

THOUGHT QUESTIONS:

1. How well did the Einstein letter convey the importance of nuclear fission in the development of atomic weaponry? How technically detailed was its contents?

2. At that early stage in atomic development, what did Einstein write was the most probable way of delivering an atomic bomb?

3. How did the letter explain that the Germans might soon seek to get their hands on uranium for the purposes of developing an atomic bomb?

FDR's Pearl Harbor Address to Congress

Upon hearing of the Japanese attack on Pearl Harbor, Franklin Roosevelt personally began to write and edit the address to Congress asking for a declaration of war that he planned to deliver the following day. Knowing that he already had the votes for war, he focused his words instead on the American public that he knew would be glued to their radios as he gave his speech, seeking to rally their spirits and prepare them for the conflict ahead.

Yesterday, Dec. 7, 1941—a date which will live in infamy—the United States of America was suddenly and deliberately attacked by naval and air forces of the Empire of Japan.

The United States was at peace with that nation and, at the solicitation of Japan, was still in conversation with the government and its emperor looking toward the maintenance of peace in the Pacific.

Indeed, one hour after Japanese air squadrons had commenced bombing in Oahu, the Japanese ambassador to the United States and his colleagues delivered to the Secretary of State a formal reply to a recent American message. While this reply stated that it seemed useless to continue the existing diplomatic negotiations, it contained no threat or hint of war or armed attack.

It will be recorded that the distance of Hawaii from Japan makes it obvious that the attack was deliberately planned many days or even weeks ago. During the intervening time, the Japanese government has deliberately sought to deceive the United States by false statements and expressions of hope for continued peace.

The attack yesterday on the Hawaiian Islands has caused severe damage to American naval and military forces. Very many American lives have been lost. In addition, American ships have been reported torpedoed on the high seas between San Francisco and Honolulu.

Yesterday, the Japanese government also launched an attack against Malaya.
Last night, Japanese forces attacked Hong Kong.
Last night, Japanese forces attacked Guam.
Last night, Japanese forces attacked the Philippine Islands.
Last night, the Japanese attacked Wake Island.

This morning, the Japanese attacked Midway Island.

Japan has, therefore, undertaken a surprise offensive extending throughout the Pacific area. The facts of yesterday speak for themselves. The people of the United States have already formed their opinions and well understand the implications to the very life and safety of our nation.

As commander in chief of the Army and Navy, I have directed that all measures be taken for our defense.

Always will we remember the character of the onslaught against us.

No matter how long it may take us to overcome this premeditated invasion, the American people in their righteous might will win through to absolute victory.

I believe I interpret the will of the Congress and of the people when I assert that we will not only defend ourselves to the uttermost, but will make very certain that this form of treachery shall never endanger us again.

Hostilities exist. There is no blinking at the fact that our people, our territory and our interests are in grave danger.

With confidence in our armed forces—with the unbounding determination of our people—we will gain the inevitable triumph—so help us God.

I ask that the Congress declare that since the unprovoked and dastardly attack by Japan on Sunday, Dec. 7, a state of war has existed between the United States and the Japanese empire.

Source: FDR Presidential Library

THOUGHT QUESTIONS:

1. Describe the tone and basic progression of the speech—was it an address characterized by constant anger from the beginning? Did it start out slow and gradually build up to a feeling of indignation?

2. How well you think FDR rallied Americans for war after the Pearl Harbor attack?

3. How important do you think a president's words are to convince the nation to take a certain course of action? When are they most effective? When are they least effective?

Justice Frank Murphy's Dissent in the Korematsu Case

The internment of Japanese Americans during World War II was a moral and legal travesty, but at the time many Americans did not think so, including government officials. Nevertheless, some internees challenged their imprisonment in federal court, including California native Fred Korematsu, who police arrested for refusing to report to his designated assembly center. In 1944, a majority of Supreme Court justices ruled in the **Korematsu v. United States** *case that the government's internment policy was constitutional, thus continuing the tradition of allowing the executive and congressional branches of the government much leeway in defining "military necessity" in times of war. Not all of the Supreme Court justices agreed with the* *majority in the* **Korematsu** *decision. Three justices wrote dissenting opinions, none stronger than Frank Murphy's displayed below, wherein the justice proclaimed that racism was a prime element in the government's move. His use of the term "racism" marked one of the first times the word was ever used in a Supreme Court opinion.*

This exclusion of "all persons of Japanese ancestry, both alien and non-alien," from the Pacific Coast area on a plea of military necessity in the absence of martial law ought not to be approved. Such exclusion goes over "the very brink of constitutional power," and falls into the ugly abyss of racism.

In dealing with matters relating to the prosecution and progress of a war, we must accord great respect and consideration to the judgments of the military authorities who are on the scene and who have full knowledge of the military facts. The scope of their discretion must, as a matter of necessity and common sense, be wide. And their judgments ought not to be overruled lightly by those whose training and duties ill-equip them to deal intelligently with matters so vital to the physical security of the nation.

At the same time, however, it is essential that there be definite limits to military discretion, especially where martial law has not been declared. Individuals must not be left impoverished of their constitutional rights on a plea of military necessity that has neither substance nor support. Thus, like other claims conflicting with the asserted constitutional rights of the individual, the military claim must subject itself to the judicial process of having its reasonableness determined and its conflicts with other interests reconciled.

What are the allowable limits of military discretion, and whether or not they have been overstepped in a particular case, are judicial questions. The judicial test of whether the Government, on a plea of military necessity, can validly deprive an individual of any of his constitutional rights is whether the deprivation is reasonably related to a public danger that is so "immediate, imminent, and impending" as not to admit of delay and not to permit the intervention of ordinary constitutional processes to alleviate the danger. Civilian Exclusion Order No. 34, banishing from a prescribed area of the Pacific Coast "all persons of Japanese ancestry, both alien and non-alien," clearly does not meet that test. Being an obvious racial discrimination, the order deprives all those within its scope of the equal protection of the laws as guaranteed by the Fifth Amendment. It further deprives these individuals of their constitutional rights to live and work where they will, to establish a home where they choose and to move about freely. In excommunicating them without benefit of hearings, this order also deprives them of all their constitutional rights to procedural due process. Yet no reasonable relation to an "immediate, imminent, and impending" public danger is evident to support this racial restriction, which is one of the most sweeping and complete deprivations of constitutional rights in the history of this nation in the absence of martial law.

It must be conceded that the military and naval situation in the spring of 1942 was such as to generate a very real fear of invasion of the Pacific Coast, accompanied by fears of sabotage and espionage in that area. The military command was therefore justified in adopting all reasonable means necessary to combat these dangers. In adjudging the military action taken in light of the then apparent dangers, we must not erect too high or too meticulous standards; it is necessary only that the action have some reasonable relation to the removal of the dangers of invasion, sabotage and espionage. But the exclusion, either temporarily or permanently, of all persons with Japanese blood in their veins has no such reasonable relation. And that relation is lacking because the exclusion order necessarily must rely for its reasonableness upon the assumption that all persons of Japanese ancestry may have a dangerous tendency to commit sabotage and espionage and to aid our Japanese enemy in other ways. It is difficult to believe that reason, logic, or experience could be marshalled in support of such an assumption.

That this forced exclusion was the result in good measure of this erroneous assumption of racial guilt, rather than bona fide military necessity is evidenced by the Commanding General's Final Report on the evacuation from the Pacific Coast area. In it, he refers to all individuals of Japanese descent as "subversive," as belonging to "an enemy race" whose "racial strains are undiluted," and as constituting "over 112,000 potential enemies . . . at large today" along the Pacific Coast. In support of this blanket condemnation of all persons of Japanese descent, however, no reliable evidence is cited to show that such individuals were generally disloyal, or had generally so conducted themselves in this area as to constitute a special menace to defense installations or war industries, or had otherwise, by their behavior, furnished reasonable ground for their exclusion as a group.

Justification for the exclusion is sought, instead, mainly upon questionable racial and sociological grounds not ordinarily within the realm of expert military judgment, supplemented by certain semi-military conclusions drawn from an unwarranted use of circumstantial evidence. Individuals of Japanese ancestry are condemned because they are said to be "a large, unassimilated, tightly knit racial group, bound to an enemy nation by strong ties of race, culture, custom and religion." They are claimed to be given to "emperor worshipping ceremonies," and to "dual citizenship." Japanese language schools and allegedly pro-Japanese organizations are cited as evidence of possible group disloyalty, together with facts as to certain persons being educated and residing at length in Japan. It is intimated that many of these individuals deliberately resided "adjacent to strategic points," thus enabling them to carry into execution a tremendous program of sabotage on a mass scale should any considerable number of them have been inclined to do so.

The need for protective custody is also asserted. The report refers, without identity, to "numerous incidents of violence," as well as to other admittedly unverified or cumulative incidents. From this, plus certain other events not shown to have been connected with the Japanese Americans, it is concluded that the "situation was fraught with danger to the Japanese population itself," and that the general public "was ready to take matters into its own hands." Finally, it is intimated, though not directly charged or proved, that persons of Japanese ancestry were responsible for three minor isolated shellings and bombings of the Pacific Coast area, as well as for unidentified radio transmissions and night signaling.

The main reasons relied upon by those responsible for the forced evacuation, therefore, do not prove a reasonable relation between the group characteristics of Japanese Americans and the dangers of invasion, sabotage and espionage. The reasons appear, instead, to be largely an accumulation of much of the misinformation, half-truths and insinuations that for years have been directed against Japanese Americans by people with racial and economic prejudices—the same people who have been among the foremost advocates of the evacuation. A military judgment based upon such racial and sociological considerations is not entitled to the great weight ordinarily given the judgments based upon strictly military considerations. Especially is this so when every charge relative to race, religion, culture, geographical location, and legal and economic status has been substantially discredited by independent studies made by experts in these matters.

The military necessity which is essential to the validity of the evacuation order thus resolves itself into a few intimations that certain individuals actively aided the enemy, from which it is inferred that the entire group of Japanese Americans could not be trusted to be or remain loyal to the United States. No one denies, of course, that there were some disloyal persons of Japanese descent on the Pacific Coast who did all in their power to aid their ancestral land. Similar disloyal activities have been engaged in by many persons of German, Italian and even more pioneer stock in our country. But to infer that examples of individual disloyalty prove group disloyalty and justify discriminatory action against the entire group is to deny that, under our system of law, individual guilt is the sole basis for deprivation of rights. Moreover, this inference, which is at the very heart of the evacuation orders, has been used in support of the abhorrent and despicable treatment of minority groups by the dictatorial tyrannies which this nation is now pledged to destroy. To give constitutional sanction to that inference in this case, however well-intentioned may have been the military command on the Pacific Coast, is to adopt one of the cruelest of the rationales used by our enemies to destroy the dignity of the individual and to encourage and open the door to discriminatory actions against other minority groups in the passions of tomorrow.

No adequate reason is given for the failure to treat these Japanese Americans on an individual basis by holding investigations and hearings to separate the loyal from the disloyal, as was done in the case of persons of German and Italian ancestry. It is asserted merely that the loyalties of this group "were unknown and time was of the essence." Yet nearly four months elapsed after Pearl Harbor before the first exclusion order was issued; nearly eight months went by until the last order was issued, and the last of these "subversive" persons was not actually removed until almost eleven months had elapsed. Leisure and deliberation seem to have been more of the essence than speed. And the fact that conditions were not such as to warrant a declaration of martial law adds strength to the belief that the factors of time and military necessity were not as urgent as they have been represented to be.

Moreover, there was no adequate proof that the Federal Bureau of Investigation and the military and naval intelligence services did not have the espionage and sabotage situation well in hand during this long period. Nor is there any denial of the fact that not one person of Japanese ancestry was accused or convicted of espionage or sabotage after Pearl Harbor while they were still free, a fact which is some evidence of the loyalty of the vast majority of these individuals and of the effectiveness of the established methods of combatting these evils. It seems incredible that, under these circumstances, it would have been impossible to hold loyalty hearings for the mere 112,000 persons involved—or at least for the 70,000 American citizens—especially when a large part of this number represented children and elderly men and women. Any inconvenience that may have accompanied an attempt to conform to procedural due process cannot be said to justify violations of constitutional rights of individuals.

I dissent, therefore, from this legalization of racism. Racial discrimination in any form and in any degree has no justifiable part whatever in our democratic way of life. It is unattractive in any setting, but it is utterly revolting among a free people who have embraced the principles set forth in the Constitution of the United States. All residents of this nation are kin in some way by blood or culture to a foreign land. Yet they are primarily and necessarily a part of the new and distinct civilization of the United States. They must, accordingly, be treated at all times as the heirs of the American experiment, and as entitled to all the rights and freedoms guaranteed by the Constitution.

Source: Supreme Court of the United States

THOUGHT QUESTIONS:

1. What does Justice Murphy say with regard to the importance of giving the military a large amount of discretion with respect to military-related decisions in wartime?

2. What are some of the examples that Justice Murphy cites in reaching his conclusion that racism, rather than military necessity, drove the decision to relocate Japanese Americans from the West Coast?

3. What parallels and differences do you see between the internment of the Japanese during World War II and talk among some to track, limit entry, and/or exclude Muslims and Muslim Americans during current times?

A WASP Remembers Her Basic Training at Avenger Field in Sweetwater, Texas

---

In recent years, a renewed interest in the WASPs had led many scholars to track down as many surviving female pilots as possible to collect their thoughts and memories about their wartime experiences. Most of the women fondly remember their time as a WASP. In the following oral history excerpt from the large collection of interviews housed at Texas Women's University, Jean Cole describes her entry in to the WASP program and some memorable aspects of her basic training:

... I heard about the WASPs. I joined, and I went over to Dayton, I think it was, Ohio, to take my physical, and Marge Gilbert also lived in Richmond, Indiana, and we both joined the WASPs together. We went down together, as I remember, on the train, and I can remember the train had open windows, and I'd never seen desert country before.

I was just amazed at Texas, going through Texas. We got to Sweetwater, and I don't quite remember how we got [to Avenger Field], it seems to me we got picked up in the cattle car right at the railroad station, but that could be wrong. I remember the first night I was out there, I could hear these airplanes flying. Oh, it seems though they were flying all night. They would fly right over our barracks and everything just shook, it was the most exciting thing I can imagine. Every night, in fact, from then on, early in the game, at least, I can remember those airplanes flying over the barracks shaking everything.

We had to wear zoot suits, I remember those, and sometimes, first we wore hairnets, they couldn't quite figure out what to do with our hair. Then the hairnets, they didn't like that, so then they decided that we would wear turbans, and we really looked ridiculous, we all had white turbans, and we wore them for a long time. On Saturdays we always had an inspection, and three or four people would come, some from the Army, and we were always trying to hide our booze. And they would find it. We tried all sorts of places, but they would always find it, and take it away from us. Finally we all settled on burying it outside between the barracks so, I think somebody else has already told this story, but we all had a little stick sticking up to mark the place where we had our bottles buried. . . .

What we liked best was the AT-6. I don't know anybody who didn't like the AT-6. It was just a fun airplane . . . One experience I had in the AT-6 was, I think it was sort of a short night crosscountry, or we were somehow, I had to go away from the area, at night, in the AT-6. When I came back, you always had to fly, there were people flying in quadrants over the airport, and they would be flying at different elevations so that they wouldn't run into each other, and all the cross-country people had to come in under them, at 3,000 feet.

So, I can remember, when I got away, I could not get my radio to work, and the only thing I could hear on that radio was Mexican music. So I came in on my Mexican music and came underneath, and I said, three cheers, here's a chance to buzz the tower, because I don't have any radio, so how am I going to get a light to land? It was very windy that night, and I came in and buzzed the tower. That was a lot of fun, and then I went up, circled around, and headed in to land, so they would know that I was the one who buzzed and I wanted to come in. Well, I got a red light, flash, red light, flash, so I went around again. I couldn't see anything wrong, I couldn't see any reason why they were giving me a red light, everything looked fine on the ground, but I came around again and they gave me another red light. I couldn't figure it out, I said maybe they don't know who I am, and I buzzed them again. Then I went around for the third time, and I'm coming in just right, and I got another red light. I said this is nonsense, I've gotta come in, I can't stay up here all night, and I can't talk to them.

So I came heading on in, and landing, and as I got near the ground I sort of noticed that I was going real fast. I put on more flaps, and more flaps, and the more flaps I put on, the faster I went. Well, I was bound I was going to land that airplane anyway, so on about the last third of the runway, which is a no-no, I got the wheels down, but it was still going like a son-of-a-gun. I went right up to the lights at the end of the runway, and had to swing left real fast and almost ground looped to get that thing stopped. The minute I hit the ground, the radio came back on again, and I heard them saying, make your approach to land 180 degrees due south, and I had just landed zero degrees to the north, which is the way I took off. It never occurred to me that the wind would switch 180 degrees in that short time! But then I quick looked over and I saw the tee, there was a lighted tee, so that if you can't hear any radio, you can look at the tee to see which way to land. Which I hadn't even thought of doing. But they didn't know that, and the tee was still pointing north. So they must have just changed it not but a very short time ago, because they hadn't gotten around to switching the tee.

Of course there was an ambulance rushing along as I came in, and there was a fire engine rushing along when I came in, and the guy who was head of the post was there. I got out of the airplane because they were all gathered around, and he said, you know, you just landed downwind. I said, I didn't have any radio, and the tee is pointing north, what was I supposed to do? He said you kept getting red lights, you got three red lights and you came in and landed anyway. I said, I was tired, and I wanted to go to bed. This was about three o'clock in the morning. I looked at him, and he looked at me, and he laughed. I sort of knew I was in, at that point, and he knew that they had made a mistake by having the tee not turned around, so I never got in any trouble for that. I have a feeling that they always liked the girls to be unafraid, they wanted you to be gung-ho and ready to do anything, sort of, so they knew you wouldn't get scared and chicken out on anything. I had always said that one of my little goals, was to land that darned AT-6 downwind. Apparently that had got around, and so he thought I had done that on purpose, and he thought that was sort of neat. Well, I hadn't done it on purpose, and I was scared to death, but since he didn't know that everything went okay. And I didn't have any problems with that. . . .

Source: Women Airforce Service Pilots Oral History Project, The Woman's Collection, Texas Woman's University

THOUGHT QUESTIONS:

1. What did Cole remember about her arrival in Texas and her initial experiences at Avenger Field?

2. What were Cole and the other WASPs trying to hide from Army inspectors? How did they finally succeed in keeping them hidden?

3. Regarding the AT-6 incident mentioned, why did Cole "buzz the tower"? How did the head of the post react when Cole told him why she did it? In Cole's opinion, why did he react that way?

Vignettes

The Kellogg-Briand Pact

During the late 1920s, the United States became a signatory of the Kellogg-Briand Pact, a diplomatic agreement seeking to outlaw war as an instrument of foreign policy. Salmon Levinson, a wealthy Chicago attorney with pacifist beliefs, first floated the notion of making the illegality of war a cornerstone of international law. Though the U.S. did not join the League of Nations, Levinson hoped that American involvement in a treaty with other countries pledging to resolve all differences through negotiations or arbitration might serve the same purpose.

Levinson's efforts were largely ignored by most who were not involved in the peace movement, but French foreign minister Aristide Briand eventually seized upon the American lawyer's idea as a means to draw the United States within his country's security system. Extremely fearful of another conflict with Germany, Briand thought that if he could sign a bilateral treaty with the United States renouncing war, the U.S. would be compelled to aid France if attacked by Germany in the future. In 1927, Briand announced his plans in a speech directed to the American public followed by a formal invitation to Calvin Coolidge's Secretary of State Frank Kellogg.

Neither the president nor Kellogg was amused by Briand's tactics, which included coordinated help in generating publicity for the overture by scores of organizations associated with the peace movement. In the end, Briand's move backfired when Kellogg outmaneuvered him by calling on all nations of the world to sign a multilateral treaty renouncing war. Briand had no recourse but to accept the offer since the proposal was immensely popular with the peace groups.

In August 1928, the United States, France, Great Britain, Japan, Italy, Belgium, Poland, and Czechoslovakia became the first nations to sign the pact outlawing war (with conditions allowing for self-defense), eventually followed by 54 other countries. Like the Washington Naval Conference agreements, the Kellogg-Briand Pact lacked any enforcement provisions beyond the word of the signers and would eventually be ignored. Nevertheless, while providing a later moral and legal basis for resisting aggression in subsequent decades, the efforts on behalf of the Kellogg-Briand Pact demonstrate another example that the United States did not recede into isolationism during the 1920s.

THOUGHT QUESTIONS:

1. Who originally sought to outlaw war as an instrument of a nation's foreign policy and why?

2. How did foreign minister Briand attempt to coopt the effort to outlaw war and how did his effort fall short?

3. Why do you think the Kellogg-Briand Pact ultimately failed?

Roosevelt vs. Lindbergh

President Franklin Roosevelt's actions favoring England and France in response to the outbreak of World War II in Europe, especially the transfer of 50 U.S. Navy destroyers to the British in exchange for the use of British bases in the Western Hemisphere, led the nation's isolationists to launch a desperate counterattack. Through the America First Committee, anti-interventionists condemned Roosevelt and his supporters for policies they believed would needlessly draw the country into another European bloodbath. If the United States focused inwardly on national defense to create a "Fortress America" instead, committeemen argued, the U.S. would have nothing to fear from events occurring in Europe.

Prominent internationalist opponents of the isolationists' position formed the Committee to Defend America by Aiding the Allies under Kansas newspaperman William Allen White in order to influence public opinion toward all-out aid to England short of military intervention, believing such a policy would provide the best means to protect the United States from potential German aggression. By supplying the British with war materiel and other forms of vital aid, White's organization argued, the United States could contribute to Hitler's defeat without sending American soldiers to fight.

The famed aviator Charles Lindbergh emerged as America First's leading spokesman. Sharing the isolationist sentiments of his father (a Minnesota congressman who voted against U.S. entry into World War I), Lindbergh also feared that war would open the door for communist expansion in Europe. Unlike most isolationists, however, the celebrity pilot publicly admired the Nazis for their technical prowess (especially with airplanes) and held blatantly anti-Semitic views. After Lindbergh began to make a series of highly publicized speeches promoting appeasement and openly criticizing Roosevelt, the administration hit back. The president accused Lindbergh of being no different than Clement Vallandigham, a northern Democratic "Copperhead" congressman who sympathized with the Confederacy during the Civil War. Secretary of the Interior Harold Ickes openly mocked Lindbergh as a "Knight of the German Eagle" because the pilot had once accepted a Nazi decoration during a 1938 visit to Germany.

Angrily resigning his commission in the Army Air Corps in protest, Lindbergh continued to speak his mind. Refusing the requests of other isolationists to mix in condemnations of fascism and to express sympathy for Great Britain in his speeches, Lindbergh's criticism of his opponents' viewpoints only became more intense, culminating in a controversial speech at a September 11, 1941 America First rally held in Des Moines, Iowa. Titled "Who Are the War Agitators?" the pilot's address laid the blame for America inching toward war with Germany and Italy squarely at the foot of a conspiracy concocted by the British, the Roosevelt Administration, and Jewish interest groups. Widespread criticism followed, with some sharp venom coming from isolationist and anti-Roosevelt circles who believed the aviator had gone too far. Norman Thomas soon quit the organization, which became increasingly discredited in the public eye. After the bombing of Pearl Harbor, Lindbergh publicly supported the war effort and took part in 50 combat missions against the Japanese in the South Pacific, officially as a civilian consultant because Roosevelt refused to reinstate his Army Air Corps colonel's commission.

THOUGHT QUESTIONS:

1. What were the objections brought up by Lindbergh and others in the America First movement?

2. How did President Roosevelt and others respond to Lindbergh's protests? Were they justified? Why or why not?

3. Are there examples today one can point to where a celebrity is involved in a particular issue, especially one involving foreign affairs, where the celebrity has a large number of followers despite their lack of expertise?

The Push for Civil Rights during World War II

Active participation in the war effort led to increased pride and assertiveness by many African Americans for social change at home even before the war ended. While extolling black citizens to show loyalty to their country by supporting the fight against the nation's enemies, the African-American press continued to stress that the benefits of equal rights should come as a result. The influential Pittsburgh *Courier* led a "Double V" campaign, calling for the defeat of the Axis abroad while continuing to advocate for the end to Jim Crow at home.

In 1942, the Congress of Racial Equality (CORE) organized in Chicago to push for an end to segregation through nonviolent direct action. The successful use of sit-ins by the group's black and white members, two decades before their popularity by antiwar activists and civil rights protesters during the 1960s, led to the desegregation of public facilities in Chicago, Denver, Detroit, and many other cities outside the South. Meanwhile, the legal division of the National Association for the Advancement of Colored People (NAACP) achieved a significant victory when the Supreme Court overturned the Texas white primary law in its 1944 *Smith v. Allwright* decision.

Blacks outside of the South also began to assert themselves politically during the war. With nearly 90 percent of southern black migrants eventually settling in the seven states with the largest electoral vote counts, African American political power rose as these states were very closely balanced between the Democrats and Republicans. As a result, northern politicians from both major parties began to woo black voters who often held the balance of power in close elections—a political development brought about by the war that would serve African Americans well in the postwar years.

THOUGHT QUESTIONS:

1. What position did the advocates of the "Double V" campaign take regarding the war effort?

2. What advances on the civil rights front took place during the war?

3. How did the movement of black migrants out of the South before and during the war add to increased African-American political clout after the war?

The New President

Born in the small town of Lamar, Missouri, in 1884, Harry S Truman in many ways embodied Middle America during the first half of the twentieth century. Hard-working and determined, casually racist, and well-read but lacking a college education, the future president possessed "the manner of a country boy who had made good but never forgot his origins," according to historian David Kennedy. "He was as straightforward as a sentence without commas."

Truman experienced many personal highs and lows before his perseverance began to produce dividends. After high school, he undertook a series of odd jobs and enlisted in the Missouri National Guard. During World War I, Truman served as an artillery captain in France. The war impacted Truman on many levels as he observed the devastation of war firsthand, lived for the first time in a foreign land, and established personal contacts that would make possible his future political career. Upon returning home he briefly entered a business school and took night classes to seek a law degree but quit before finishing either pursuit. He opened a haberdashery in Kansas City with a wartime buddy, but the business closed after a few years.

Truman's fortunes turned when he entered Missouri politics. In 1922, he received support from the Democratic Party political machine in Kansas City run by Thomas Pendergast (the uncle of another wartime comrade) to win election as a county judge. An administrative post rather than a judicial position, Truman served as a loyal member of the political establishment throughout the 1920s. In 1934, Pendergast promoted Truman's candidacy for a U.S. Senate seat, which he won in the Democratic landslide of that year, quickly elevating the inexperienced local politician to the national stage.

While earning a reputation in Washington as a solid New Dealer, Truman largely operated out of public view before Franklin Roosevelt chose him as a political compromise to be his running mate in the 1944 election. Before FDR's decision, Truman had only emerged into the national spotlight on two occasions: his dogged investigation of questionable wartime government contracts that brought the senator his largest degree of positive publicity; and, when he responded to a reporter's query about his views on the German invasion of Russia, by stating bluntly: "If we see that Germany is winning we ought to help Russia, and if Russia is winning we ought to help Germany, and that way let them kill as many as possible." While not received well by the suspicious Joseph Stalin, Truman's sentiments were commonly held by many in the United States and Great Britain. Truman's elevation to the presidency meant that an individual with many positive attributes but also some glaring personal limitations would be directing America's participation in the closing months of World War II, including the use of the atomic bomb.

THOUGHT QUESTIONS:

1. In what ways was Truman's background not likely to portend a rise to the presidency?

2. What accounted for Truman's rise to political prominence and, eventually, the presidency?

3. What type of experience and character should a president possess in the modern era? Which of these attributes, experience or character, is more important and why?

Chapter 26

The Origins of the Cold War

Documents

President Harry Truman Slams Joseph McCarthy

In February 1950, Republican Senator Joseph McCarthy of Wisconsin began his campaign of fear and paranoia over possible communist infiltration of the American government by alleging in a speech in Wheeling, West Virginia that over 200 State Department staff members were members of the Communist Party. During a press conference in March while on vacation in Key West, Florida, President Harry Truman used part of his time to respond boldly to the senator's address, portraying McCarthy as a rank opportunist. That portion of Truman's remarks is presented here:

REPORTER: Do you think that Senator McCarthy can show [if] any disloyalty exists in the State Department?

TRUMAN: I think the greatest asset that the Kremlin has is Senator McCarthy.

REPORTER: Would you care to elaborate on that?

TRUMAN: I don't think it needs any elaboration—I don't think it needs any elaboration.

REPORTER: Brother, will that hit page one tomorrow!

REPORTER: If you think we are going to bust down the fence on what you have got later, that's a pretty good starter. [Laughter]

REPORTER: Mr. President, could we quote that one phrase, "I think the greatest asset the Kremlin has is Senator McCarthy"?

TRUMAN: Now let me give you a little preliminary, and then I will tell you what I think you ought to do. Let me tell you what the situation is. We started out in 1945, when I became President, and the two wars were still going on, and the Russians were our allies, just the same as the British and the French and Brazil and the South American countries. And we won the war together. We organized the United Nations in April 1945, and one of the first questions that was asked me, after I was sworn in at 7:09 o'clock on the 12th of April, was whether or not the San Francisco conference on the United Nations should go ahead. And I said it certainly will. It went ahead and we finally succeeded in getting a charter and getting it agreed to by I think 51 nations, if I remember correctly.

Then our objective was to—as quickly as possible—get peace in the world. We made certain agreements with the Russians and the British and the French and the Chinese. We kept those agreements to the letter. They have nearly all been—those agreements where the Russians were involved—been broken by the Russians. And it became perfectly evident that they had no intention of carrying out the fundamental principles of the United Nations Charter and the agreements which had been made at Teheran, Yalta, and Potsdam. And it became evident that there was an endeavor on the part of the Kremlin to control the world.

A procedure was instituted which came to be known as the Cold War. The airlift to Berlin was only one phase of it. People became alarmed here in the United States then, that there might be people whose sympathies were with the Communist ideal of government—which is not communism under any circumstances, it is totalitarianism of the worst brand. There isn't any difference between the totalitarian Russian Government and the Hitler government and the Franco government in Spain. They are all alike. They are police state governments.

In 1947 I instituted a loyalty program for Government employees, and that loyalty procedure program was set up in such a way that the rights of individuals were respected.

In a survey of the 2,200,000 employees at that time, I think there were some 205-something like that—who left the service. I don't know—a great many of them left of their own accord.

REPORTER: How many, Mr. President?

TRUMAN: Somewhere in the neighborhood of 205. Does anybody remember those figures exactly? It's a very small figure.

REPORTER: Very small.

TRUMAN: An infinitesimal part of 1 percent. We will get the figures for you. And then, for political background, the Republicans have been trying vainly to find an issue on which to make a bid for the control of the Congress for next year. They tried "statism." They tried "welfare state." They tried "socialism." And there are a certain number of members of the Republican Party who are trying to dig up that old malodorous dead horse called "isolationism." And in order to do that, they are perfectly willing to sabotage the bipartisan foreign policy of the United States. And this fiasco which has been going on in the Senate is the very best asset that the Kremlin could have in the operation of the Cold War. And that is what I mean when I say that McCarthy's antics are the best asset that the Kremlin can have.

Now, if anybody really felt that there were disloyal people in the employ of the Government, the proper and the honorable way to handle the situation would be to come to the President of the United States and say, "This man is a disloyal person. He is in such and such a department." We will investigate him immediately, and if he were a disloyal person he would be immediately fired. That is not what they want. They are trying to create an issue, and it is going to be just as big a fiasco as the campaign in New York and other places on these other false and fatuous issues. With a little bit of intelligence they could find an issue at home without a bit of trouble!

REPORTER: What would it be, Mr. President?

TRUMAN: Anything in the domestic line. I will meet them on any subject they want, but to try to sabotage the foreign policy of the United States, in the face of the situation with which we are faced, is just as bad as trying to cut the Army in time of war.

REPORTER: On that question we were just kidding.

TRUMAN: And that gave me a chance to give you an answer. To try to sabotage the foreign policy of the United States is just as bad in this Cold War as it would be to shoot our soldiers in the back in a hot war. I am fed up with what is going on, and I am giving you the facts as I see them.

REPORTER: Mr. President, do you consider the Republican Party as a party [to McCarthy's tactics]?

TRUMAN: The policy of the Republican Party has endorsed the antics of Mr. McCarthy.

REPORTER: That affects the bipartisan—

TRUMAN: That's what it is for—that's what it is for. They are anxious for the return of isolationism.

REPORTER: Do you think that this has torpedoed, then, the bipartisan—

TRUMAN: It is an endeavor to torpedo the bipartisan foreign policy. They are not going to succeed, because the level-headed Republicans do not believe that at all, as note Mr. Stimson, Senator Vandenberg, Senator Saltonstall, and a dozen others I could name, who know exactly what is going on and are trying their best to cooperate. And I am going to try to help them prevent it going under.

REPORTER: Well, Mr. President, to carry that out to its logical conclusion, when these people come up for reelection, with the grace of God and so on, there is nothing that the Democratic Party can do except simply to sit on the sidelines and say, "Well?"

TRUMAN: Well, it's too bad. It's a dangerous situation, and it has got to be stopped. And every citizen in the United States is going to find out just exactly what the facts are when I get through with this thing.

REPORTER: You will stand up on one side, and they will stand up on the other?

TRUMAN: There's only one side that the people will stay on, and that is the side that will lead to peace. That is all we are after. This is just another fiasco to find an issue. This is not it.

REPORTER: Mr. President, would you like to name any others besides Senator McCarthy who have participated in this attempt to sabotage our foreign policy?

TRUMAN: Senator Wherry.

REPORTER: Yes, sir?

TRUMAN: Senator Bridges.

REPORTER: Yes, sir?

TRUMAN: That's about as far as I care to go....

Source: Harry S. Truman Presidential Library

THOUGHT QUESTIONS:

1. In what ways did President Truman try to explain what he meant when he stated his belief that Senator McCarthy was the "best asset" that the Russians had?

2. In Truman's opinion, what was McCarthy's ultimate goal? What did Republicans have to gain for going along with McCarthy?

3. How important do you feel it is for the United States to conduct, as Truman put it, a "bipartisan foreign policy"? What are the political challenges to maintaining such an arrangement? What are some ways in which it can be undermined?

President Eisenhower Rejects Clemency for the Rosenbergs

On June 8, 1953, Clyde Miller, an education professor at Columbia University where Dwight Eisenhower had served as president before being elected President of the United States, wrote Eisenhower requesting that he commute the death sentence issued to Julius and Ethel Rosenberg who had recently been convicted of espionage for the Soviet Union. (Current historical scholarship accepts that while Julius knowingly passed atomic bomb secrets to Soviet agents, Ethel was probably not guilty.) Miller told his friend and former boss that instead of being associated with justice and mercy, the U.S. would "stand for just the opposite among tens of millions the world over." Two days later, the new president penned this response to explain why he would not intervene:

Personal and Confidential

Dear Clyde:

Thank you very much for your thoughts on the Rosenberg conviction. It is extremely difficult to reach a sound decision in such instances. Not all the arguments are on either side.

I started studying the record of the case immediately after Inauguration, and have had innumerable conferences on it with my associates.

Several of the obvious facts which must not be forgotten are these. The record has been reviewed and re-reviewed by every appropriate court in the land, extending over a period of more than two years. In no single instance has there been any suggestion that it was improperly tried, that the rights of the accused have been violated, that the evidence was insufficient, or that there was any factor in the case which justified intervention on the part of the Executive with the function of juridical agencies.

As to any intervention based on consideration of America's reputation or standing in the world, you have given the case for one side. What you did not suggest was the need for considering this kind of argument over and against the known convictions of Communist leaders that free governments—and especially the American government—are notoriously weak and fearful and that consequently subversive and other kind of activity can be conducted against them with no real fear of dire punishment on the part of the perpetrator. It is, of course, important to the Communists to have this contention sustained and justified. In the present case they have even stooped to dragging in young and innocent children in order to serve their own purpose.

The action of these people has exposed to greater danger of death literally millions of our citizens. The very real question becomes how far can this be permitted by a government that, regardless of every consideration of mercy and compassion, is also required to be a just government in serving the interests of all its citizens. That their crime is a very real one and that its potential results are as definite as I have just stated, are facts that seem to me to be above contention.

Another factor that appeals, quite naturally, to Americans is that one of these criminals—indeed the more strong-minded and the apparent leader of the two—is a woman. But the question presents itself—if the Executive should interfere because of this fact, would we be justified in encouraging the Communists to use only women in their spying process?

I assure you that I appreciate receiving your thoughts on the matter. You not only have the right of any citizen to submit your suggestion, bit, of course, our old friendship at Columbia assures that I would give special attention to your convictions. But when it comes to the decision to commute such as sentence—which would mean that these arch criminals would be subject to parole at the end of fifteen years—I must say I have not yet been able to justify such an action.

I have answered your letter at some length. Because I know that you wrote it out of a deep sense of duty and friendship. I realize that your desire to protect America is as great as mine, but I doubt that you have had to consider some of the results that could spring from the action you recommend.

We shall, of course, have another clemency petition presented this week, from which we will see whether there are additional considerations to take into account.

Source: Dwight D. Eisenhower Presidential Library

THOUGHT QUESTIONS:

1. What did Eisenhower say were the main reasons keeping him from sparing the Rosenbergs?

2. What did Eisenhower say with regard to sparing Ethel Rosenberg because she was a woman? What comment did he make in passing about the Rosenbergs being parents of young children?

3. Recognizing that that United States also spies on nations that are friends and foes alike, what factors do you think should be considered when determining the punishment of someone convicted of espionage in this country?

President Eisenhower Bids Farewell and Warns of the "Military-Industrial Complex"

On January 17, 1961, outgoing President Dwight D. Eisenhower delivered his farewell address to the American people broadcast over the nation's television networks live from the Oval Office of the White House. He surprised many people when, during the course of his remarks, he warned Americans about the possible dangers posed by the rise of unwarranted power from the nation's defense industry, which he famously referred to as the "military-industrial complex." Despite his belief in the necessity of having a strong military, the former general was also a fiscal conservative who was concerned about the growing cost and size of the defense establishment, so he worked hard during his presidency to slow the influence of defense industry lobbyists, though not always successfully.

My fellow Americans:

Three days from now, after half a century in the service of our country, I shall lay down the responsibilities of office as, in traditional and solemn ceremony, the authority of the Presidency is vested in my successor.

This evening I come to you with a message of leave-taking and farewell, and to share a few final thoughts with you, my countrymen.

Like every other citizen, I wish the new President, and all who will labor with him, Godspeed. I pray that the coming years will be blessed with peace and prosperity for all....

We now stand ten years past the midpoint of a century that has witnessed four major wars among great nations. Three of these involved our own country. Despite these holocausts, America is today the strongest, the most influential and most productive nation in the world. Understandably proud of this preeminence, we yet realize that America's leadership and prestige depend, not merely upon our unmatched material progress, riches and military strength, but on how we use our power in the interests of world peace and human betterment.

Throughout America's adventure in free government, our basic purposes have been to keep the peace; to foster progress in human achievement, and to enhance liberty, dignity and integrity among people and among nations. To strive for less would be unworthy of a free and religious people. Any failure traceable to arrogance, or our lack of comprehension or readiness to sacrifice would inflict upon us grievous hurt both at home and abroad.

Progress toward these noble goals is persistently threatened by the conflict now engulfing the world [the Cold War]. It commands our whole attention, absorbs our very beings. We face a hostile ideology—global in scope, atheistic in character, ruthless in purpose, and insidious in method. Unhappily, the danger it poses promises to be of indefinite duration. To meet it successfully, there is called for, not so much the emotional and transitory sacrifices of crisis, but rather those which enable us to carry forward steadily, surely, and without complaint the burdens of a prolonged and complex struggle—with liberty the stake. Only thus shall we remain, despite every provocation, on our charted course toward permanent peace and human betterment....

A vital element in keeping the peace is our military establishment. Our arms must be mighty, ready for instant action, so that no potential aggressor may be tempted to risk his own destruction.

Our military organization today bears little relation to that known by any of my predecessors in peacetime, or indeed by the fighting men of World War II or Korea.

Until the latest of our world conflicts, the United States had no armaments industry. American makers of plowshares could, with time and as required, make swords as well. But now we can no longer risk emergency improvisation of national defense; we have been compelled to create a permanent armaments industry of vast proportions. Added to this, three and a half million men and women are directly engaged in the defense establishment. We annually spend on military security more than the net income of all United States corporations.

This conjunction of an immense military establishment and a large arms industry is new in the American experience. The total influence—economic, political, even spiritual—is felt in every city, every state house, every office of the federal government. We recognize the imperative need for this development. Yet we must not fail to comprehend its grave implications. Our toil, resources and livelihood are all involved; so is the very structure of our society.

In the councils of government, we must guard against the acquisition of unwarranted influence, whether sought or unsought, by the military-industrial complex. The potential for the disastrous rise of misplaced power exists and will persist.

We must never let the weight of this combination endanger our liberties or democratic processes. We should take nothing for granted. Only an alert and knowledgeable citizenry can compel the proper meshing of the huge industrial and military machinery of defense with our peaceful methods and goals, so that security and liberty may prosper together.

Akin to, and largely responsible for the sweeping changes in our industrial-military posture, has been the technological revolution during recent decades.

In this revolution, research has become central; it also becomes more formalized, complex, and costly. A steadily increasing share is conducted for, by, or at the direction of, the federal government.

Today, the solitary inventor, tinkering in his shop, has been overshadowed by task forces of scientists in laboratories and testing fields. In the same fashion, the free university, historically the fountainhead of free ideas and scientific discovery, has experienced a revolution in the conduct of research. Partly because of the huge costs involved, a government contract becomes virtually a substitute for intellectual curiosity. For every old blackboard, there are now hundreds of new electronic computers.

The prospect of domination of the nation's scholars by federal employment, project allocations, and the power of money is ever present—and is gravely to be regarded.

Yet, in holding scientific research and discovery in respect, as we should, we must also be alert to the equal and opposite danger that public policy could itself become the captive of a scientific technological elite.

It is the task of statesmanship to mold, to balance, and to integrate these and other forces, new and old, within the principles of our democratic system—ever aiming toward the supreme goals of our free society....

In this, my last good night to you as your President—I thank you for the many opportunities you have given me for public service in war and peace. I trust that in that service you find some things worthy; as for the rest of it, I know you will find ways to improve performance in the future.

You and I—my fellow citizens—need to be strong in our faith that all nations, under God, will reach the goal of peace with justice. May we be ever unswerving in devotion to principle, confident but humble with power, diligent in pursuit of the nation's great goals.

To all the peoples of the world, I once more give expression to America's prayerful and continuing aspiration:

We pray that peoples of all faiths, all races, all nations, may have their great human needs satisfied; that those now denied opportunity shall come to enjoy it to the full; that all who yearn for freedom may experience its spiritual blessings; that those who have freedom will understand, also, its heavy responsibilities; that all who are insensitive to the needs of others will learn charity; that the scourges of poverty, disease and ignorance will be made to disappear from the earth, and that, in the goodness of time, all peoples will come to live together in a peace guaranteed by the binding force of mutual respect and love.

Source: Dwight D. Eisenhower Presidential Library

THOUGHT QUESTIONS:

1. How did Eisenhower describe how American military preparation had necessarily changed since the end of World War II? How did he describe the changing nature of the American defense establishment since that war concluded?

2. What types of specific concerns did Eisenhower have about the rising importance and influence of the "military-industrial complex" on governmental decision-making?

3. What do you think of the state of the relationship between the federal government and the defense industry today? Do you believe that the government spends too much on defense in order to satisfy defense contractors, reward political donors, keep the economy going, etc., or is the amount and type of spending adequate (or not enough) for the country's current needs? Explain.

Ho Chi Minh Declares Vietnamese Independence

On September 2, 1945, Ho Chi Minh read the following proclamation declaring the independence of Vietnam from French colonial rule before a large crowd of supporters packed into Ba Dinh Square, a plaza recently renamed for an earlier unsuccessful anti-French rebellion begun in 1886. He asserted that because of their fight against Japanese occupation during World War II, coupled with the many ways that he listed in which the prewar rule of the French had kept the Vietnamese people in a constant state of subjugation, the Vietnamese people were entitled to self-rule. The proclamation went largely unheeded outside of Vietnam, however, as the French soon moved to restore control over Indochina with the help of the United States whose leaders disregarded Ho's help in fighting against the Japanese because of his sympathy with communist ideology. Vietnam would soon be embroiled in a 30-year conflict, initially between Ho's forces and French troops, before evolving into a more lengthy fight between the Viet Cong resistance and the U.S.-supported non-communist government of South Vietnam.

"All men are created equal. They are endowed by their Creator with certain inalienable rights, among them are Life, Liberty, and the pursuit of Happiness."

This immortal statement was made in the Declaration of Independence of the United States of America in 1776. In a broader sense, this means: All the peoples on the earth are equal from birth, all the peoples have a right to live, to be happy and free.

The Declaration of the French Revolution made in 1791 on the Rights of Man and the Citizen also states: "All men are born free and with equal rights, and must always remain free and have equal rights." Those are undeniable truths.

Nevertheless, for more than eighty years, the French imperialists, abusing the standard of Liberty, Equality, and Fraternity, have violated our Fatherland and oppressed our fellow-citizens. They have acted contrary to the ideals of humanity and justice. In the field of politics, they have deprived our people of every democratic liberty.

They have enforced inhuman laws; they have set up three distinct political regimes in the North, the Center and the South of Vietnam in order to wreck our national unity and prevent our people from being united. They have built more prisons than schools. They have mercilessly slain our patriots; they have drowned our uprisings in rivers of blood.

They have fettered public opinion; they have practiced obscurantism against our people. To weaken our race they have forced us to use opium and alcohol.

In the field of economics, they have fleeced us to the backbone, impoverished our people, and devastated our land. They have robbed us of our rice fields, our mines, our forests, and our raw materials. They have monopolized the issuing of bank-notes and the export trade.

They have invented numerous unjustifiable taxes and reduced our people, especially our peasantry, to a state of extreme poverty. They have hampered the prospering of our national bourgeoisie; they have mercilessly exploited our workers.

In the autumn of 1940, when the Japanese Fascists violated Indochina's territory to establish new bases in their fight against the Allies, the French imperialists went down on their bended knees and handed over our country to them.

Thus, from that date, our people were subjected to the double yoke of the French and the Japanese. Their sufferings and miseries increased. The result was that from the end of last year to the beginning of this year, from Quang Tri province to the North of Vietnam, more than two million of our fellow citizens died from starvation. On March 9, the French troops were disarmed by the Japanese. The French colonialists either fled or surrendered showing that not only were they incapable of "protecting" us, but that, in the span of five years, they had twice sold our country to the Japanese.

On several occasions before March 9, the Vietminh League urged the French to ally themselves with it against the Japanese. Instead of agreeing to this proposal, the French colonialists so intensified their terrorist activities against the Vietminh members that before fleeing they massacred a great number of our political prisoners detained at Yen Bay and Caobang.

Notwithstanding all this, our fellow citizens have always manifested toward the French a tolerant and humane attitude. Even after the Japanese putsch of March 1945, the Vietminh League helped many Frenchmen to cross the frontier, rescued some of them from Japanese jails, and protected French lives and property.

From the autumn of 1940, our country had in fact ceased to be a French colony and had become a Japanese possession.

After the Japanese had surrendered to the Allies, our whole people rose to regain our national sovereignty and to found the Democratic Republic of Vietnam.

The truth is that we have wrested our independence from the Japanese and not from the French.

The French have fled, the Japanese have capitulated, Emperor Bao Dai has abdicated. Our people have broken the chains which for nearly a century have fettered them and have won independence for the Fatherland. Our people at the same time have overthrown the monarchic regime that has reigned supreme for dozens of centuries. In its place has been established the present Democratic Republic.

For these reasons, we, members of the Provisional Government, representing the whole Vietnamese people, declare that from now on we break off all relations of a colonial character with France; we repeal all the international obligation that France has so far subscribed to on behalf of Vietnam and we abolish all the special rights the French have unlawfully acquired in our Fatherland.

The whole Vietnamese people, animated by a common purpose, are determined to fight to the bitter end against any attempt by the French colonialists to reconquer their country.

We are convinced that the Allied nations which at Tehran and San Francisco have acknowledged the principles of self-determination and equality of nations, will not refuse to acknowledge the independence of Vietnam.

A people who have courageously opposed French domination for more than eight years, a people who have fought side by side with the Allies against the Fascists during these last years, such a people must be free and independent.

For these reasons, we, members of the Provisional Government of the Democratic Republic of Vietnam, solemnly declare to the world that Vietnam has the right to be a free and independent country—and in fact is so already. The entire Vietnamese people are determined to mobilize all their physical and mental strength, to sacrifice their lives and property in order to safeguard their independence and liberty.

Source: Ho Chi Minh, *Selected Works* Vol. 3, (Hanoi: Foreign Languages Publishing House, 1960–62), 17–21.

THOUGHT QUESTIONS:

1. What elements of the proclamation, especially at the beginning and near the end of the speech, seem designed to appeal to individuals and leaders of countries outside of Vietnam, specifically the United States?

2. Though opinion was divided among the Vietnamese people with respect to what form of government and economy would best replace French colonial rule, how does Ho Chi Minh try to create the impression that all Vietnamese were united in their beliefs going forward?

3. While we know how events played out after the Truman administration committed to aiding the French attempt to reestablishing their empire in Indochina, what other options were available for the U.S. government going forward in Vietnam at the end of the Second World War? What results, positive and negative to U.S. interests, could have occurred in pursuing each option?

Vignettes

The Berlin Airlift: A Logistical Marvel

Lying deep within the Soviet occupation zone in eastern Germany, West Berlin after World War II resembled a democratic capitalist island in the middle of a communist sea. As per the Yalta agreement with the Soviet government, the western Allied powers of Great Britain, France, and the United States controlled the western portion of the former Nazi capital. Highways and railroads connected the city with the western Allied occupation zones, as well as 20-mile-wide air corridors for transport and cargo planes. The announcement of an independent West German currency in June 1948 (as a first step toward the uniting of the western occupation zones into a new noncommunist country), however, provoked an angry response from Soviet dictator Josef Stalin, who began the "Berlin Blockade" on June 24 by cutting ground access to West Berlin in an effort to starve and freeze out the residents and force the unification of the city under his control.

President Harry Truman had three major options to counter the Russian moves. The most extreme possibilities were unacceptable to him as an initial option—either backing down and allowing the communists to take over West Berlin or commencing major hostilities by having the Allied militaries fight their way to Berlin in order to break the blockade by force. Instead, Truman looked for a middle approach that would show resolve but not in a way that could be perceived as overly belligerent. That modest response proved to be organizing joint operations with the British to supply West Berlin through the air.

The decision immediately created one of greatest peacetime logistical operations in world history. Commanders in Europe were charged with determining all the required elements to perform the task: the amount of supplies needed by the West Berliners; the number of cargo planes, air crews, and ground personnel required; development of flight schedules to maximize efficiency. Logistical experts estimated that the 2 million residents of West Berlin would require a minimum of 2,000 tons of coal and 1,500 tons of food per day to meet basic needs, not to mention other less essential items still deemed important. C-47 aircraft capable of carrying 3 tons of supplies each were ordered to West Germany from scattered bases around Europe while large numbers of larger C-54 transports capable of carrying 10 tons each were ordered in from Alaska, Hawaii, Panama, Japan, and the United States.

Beginning on June 26, the first flights from air bases in West Germany began arriving at air fields in the American and British sectors. Within four days, cargo planes were arriving every eight minutes around the clock, depositing 150 planeloads of supplies daily to be distributed throughout the city or stored in warehouses. Not knowing how long the airlift would be taking place, orders went out to start building two more airfields, which were completed and fully operational within 5 months. Without experience or set protocol for such an operation, the learning curve was steep at the beginning. Crews did not prioritize cargos by importance, and the loading and unloading operations were not well organized. The undermanned air crews flew eight hour shifts, then performed eight hours of ground duty before catching a few hours of sleep. Nevertheless, within the first 10 days, more than 1,000 tons of supplies had arrived daily into the besieged city. By the middle of July, 2,000 tons per day were getting through. As the C-54s began arriving, the daily delivery figures by the end of September rose to an average of 5,000 tons of coal, food, medicine, and gasoline, as well as donated non-essential items to boost civilian morale, such as toys, clothes, and candy.

The arrival of winter caused numerous problems for the pilots, air crews, and maintenance personnel. Planes had to be de-iced regularly and, despite the snow, sleet, and fog, were sent off if there was any chance of getting through with the vital goods. Crashes with loss of life occasionally occurred. On one day in November, only one place arrived in Berlin. Coal reserves for the entire city dwindled to only a week's supply. Not helping matters, the Soviets continued to disrupt operations by aiming glaring searchlights into the cockpits of the cargo planes, interfering with their radio communications, and even occasionally sending fighter planes to fly through their flight paths. In one case, a pilot flew too close and clipped a British passenger plane, leading both planes to crash and the loss of 35 lives. (A total of 75 British and American air crew members would lose their lives by the end of the operation.)

Despite these troubles, the campaign only got more efficient as time went on and the weather improved. By April 1949, deliveries reached almost 8,000 tons daily, and included a record day when 1,400 flights deposited over 13,000 tons of coal without any trouble. Stalin finally realized that the airlift was succeeding, not only logistically, but also from a public relations standpoint as the Americans and their allies were able to frame a narrative in their favor perfectly—that this endeavor was a humanitarian mission delivering much-needed supplies to determined, freedom-loving people. On May 12, 1949, the blockade was lifted, and ground transportation flowed once again to West Berlin. The airlift continued, however, until West Germany was formally declared a nation (the Federal Republic of Germany) in September 1949 to stockpile additional supplies in case Stalin reinstituted the blockade. By the end of the operation, 278,228 flights had delivered 2.3 million tons of supplies to the people in West Berlin, which remained out of communist control for the remainder of the Cold War.

THOUGHT QUESTIONS:

1. What options did President Truman have when Stalin initiated the Berlin Blockade? What benefits from a strategic standpoint did an airlift provide that other options did not?

2. What were the major logistical problems that had to be overcome in order to undertake an operation of this magnitude?

3. What did Stalin hope to gain by instituting the Berlin Blockade, and why did he finally end it after almost an entire year?

Branch Rickey: Man of Baseball, Man of God

Wesley Branch Rickey was a well-established executive long known in the baseball world for his innovations to the sport before he became nationally famous by signing Jackie Robinson and promoting the superstar athlete to the Brooklyn Dodgers roster. For those who knew him well, the move was consistent with his main motivations in life—doing the Lord's work and excelling at producing a quality baseball franchise.

Born on December 20, 1881, into a pious Methodist farming family in south-central Ohio (he was named after John Wesley, the founder of Methodism), Rickey attended local schools before attending Ohio Wesleyan University (a Methodist institution) where he played baseball and football. After playing minor league and semi-pro ball during the summers to help pay for his studies, he was declared ineligible to continue playing and instead became the team's head coach. Rickey personally recruited a talented three-sport black athlete, Charles Thomas, to take his place as the team's catcher. So began a series of dramas: opposing teams hurling racial slurs at Thomas; some colleges forfeiting the scheduled game rather than play against Ohio Wesleyan because of the presence of an African American on their squad; and multiple personal humiliations for Thomas off the field, the most remembered occasion by Rickey being when the team arrived at a hotel in South Bend, Indiana after playing Notre Dame and being told that all the players could check into their rooms except for Thomas because the hotel's personal policy was that the establishment was for whites only. After much persistence, Rickey arranged for Thomas to share a room with him if the player slept on a cot. When Rickey arrived at their room after talking with the other players, he found Thomas quietly weeping and tugging at the skin on his hands, exclaiming "It's my skin. If I could just tear it off, I'd be like everybody else!" Though Thomas persevered (he eventually graduated, became a successful dentist in New Mexico, and maintained a lifelong friendship with Rickey), the memory of the man's disgraceful treatment stuck deep within Rickey for the rest of his life.

Upon graduation, Rickey signed a contract with the Cincinnati Reds to play major league baseball. He eventually played three lackluster seasons for the St. Louis Browns and New York Highlanders (now Yankees), earning a reputation as an average defensive catcher (one team stole 13 bases against him in a game, still the major league record) and a fairly weak hitter. He also upset coaches for his refusal to play games on Sundays on religious grounds.

After his playing days ended, he eventually began a successful career in baseball management, first in a two-year stint as manager of the St. Louis Browns from 1913-15 then (after serving as an officer in World War I), a six-year tenure as manager of the St. Louis Cardinals from 1919 to 1925 before serving as the team's general manager until 1942. During his tenure running the Cardinals, Rickey's use of scouts and minor league teams to develop the talent for his major league rosters marked the birth of the modern baseball "farm system." Rickey moved on to become the new general manager of the Brooklyn Dodgers and continued experimenting with player development techniques such as the first full-time spring training facility in Vero Beach, Florida, as well as new training tools such as batting tees, batting cages, batting helmets, and pitching machines that have become standard equipment in the game today.

Rickey's decision to racially integrate the Dodgers became his greatest "innovation" and resulted from his religious faith, his belief that African-American ballplayers would improve his team, and his ability to view sport within the greater context of American society. For his inaugural player, Rickey understood that success would not be achieved by seeking the best black ballplayer. Rather, he needed to find an athlete with the right combination of talent, intelligence, composure, and good character. After meeting Jackie Robinson, Rickey knew he found the right man for the job. Robinson was a mature 27 years of age at the time of his signing, with a long-time sweetheart that he soon married, he had a college education (from UCLA), and, like himself, was a devout Methodist.

THOUGHT QUESTIONS:

1. Describe Branch Rickey's background and how it influenced his decision to start integrating major league baseball. What event from his college days was seared into Rickey's consciousness?

2. What changes did Rickey bring to major league baseball that contributed to his reputation as an innovator before racial integration of the sport?

3. What traits did Rickey look for when deciding who would be the first black ballplayer to play for the Dodgers?

Nixon's "Checkers Speech"

After securing the Republican Party nomination for president in 1952, Dwight Eisenhower selected Richard Nixon, a 38-year-old senator from California to be his running mate. Though Eisenhower never warmed up to Nixon personally, the senator was popular within the party, represented a state in the quickly growing western region of the country, and provided a youthful balance to the 62-year-old former World War II general. Nixon had endeared himself to the rabid anti-communists within the party for his dogged pursuit of Alger Hiss while a member of House Un-American Activities Committee and for his strong support of Joseph McCarthy after joining the Senate.

No sooner did Nixon become the party's vice-presidential nominee than the press began to report that some wealthy Californians had been contributing to a private fund arranged by his campaign manager to financially assist the senator's ongoing efforts to maintain a high public profile. Nixon issued a statement explaining that the fund was not created to enrich himself and was only being used to defray politically related expenses, but the chairman of the Democratic National Committee nevertheless demanded that Nixon be dropped by the Republicans, saying that both he and Eisenhower knew that the existence of the fund was "morally wrong." Though the amount was modest (about

$16,000), and not illegal as long as the money was not used for the senator's personal benefit, the appearance of impropriety made Eisenhower increasingly apprehensive about keeping Nixon on the ticket.

Though most of Eisenhower's aides wanted the senator to quit, Nixon refused without a fight, choosing to defend himself by addressing the growing scandal in an unprecedented nationally televised broadcast. The Republican National Committee quickly raised the $75,000 needed to buy the air time. On September 23, talking for roughly thirty minutes, Nixon began by describing his modest Quaker upbringing, war service, and close-knit family before attempting to defuse the general impression held by many people that he was using his political fund to enrich himself while granting favors to rich donors. The senator denied that contributors received any special services. His wife Pat, the candidate further explained, did not suddenly possess a mink coat, as some reported, but "she does have a perfectly respectable Republican cloth coat." Nixon then admitted that an admirer from Texas had sent the Nixons a black-and-white-spotted cocker spaniel at the start of the campaign: "Our little girl—Tricia, the six-year-old—named it Checkers. And you know the kids love that dog and I just want to say right now, that regardless of what they say about it, we're going to keep it." (When preparing his remarks, Nixon had recalled Franklin Roosevelt's famous political speech when the president had sarcastically responded to Republican claims that he had sent a U.S. Navy destroyer all the way to Alaska to fetch his dog, Fala. Remembering that his children had recently received the cocker spaniel, wisely thought it would be a good hook to use.)

To the surprise of many, popular reaction to what would become known as the "Checkers Speech" was quite favorable. Relieved by the positive response, Eisenhower decided that Nixon's performance had saved himself with his performance and the California senator was kept on the Republican ticket. Perhaps most important, Nixon illustrated the power of television to influence politics by allowing candidates (as corporate marketers were already doing for their products) to deliver a positive image and carefully crafted message directly into Americans' living rooms. In fact, the 1952 campaign would become the first to make extensive use of television ads. The Republicans alone invested an estimated $1.5 million in television ads to promote Eisenhower's candidacy. Political parties, one observer noted, were "selling the President like toothpaste." Despite the criticism, the use of television coverage had become an indispensable tool in American politics.

THOUGHT QUESTIONS:

1. What were the circumstances that compelled Nixon to deliver the "Checkers Speech"?

2. How did Nixon attempt to humanize his situation as he defused the rumors of malfeasance?

3. Describe the current state of the power of television to influence political opinions as in the past. Is anything new circumventing the previous reliance of political parties on television (especially ads)? Explain.

Two Americans Take on Joseph McCarthy

Joseph McCarthy had reached his zenith by the early 1950s. Through his Permanent Subcommittee on Investigations, the bombastic senator had held numerous public hearings, called hundreds of citizens before his tribunal, and leveled countless charges against those that he believed held communist sympathies. McCarthy's attacks went beyond accusations against individuals. He also targeted government agencies (such as the Defense Department, the Voice of America, and the CIA), colleges, and even churches that he believed were promoting the overthrow of the U.S. government. Although many Republicans initially supported his ramblings because of his usefulness in disparaging the Truman administration, McCarthy increasingly became an embarrassment after Eisenhower's election in 1952. Still, the senator remained popular with many Americans.

McCarthy's downfall began in early 1954, when Edward R. Murrow, one of the nation's most respected radio and television commentators, decided to directly address McCarthy's demagoguery and expose him for the first time on television during a broadcast of his weekly CBS program "See It Now." Murrow largely let McCarthy's bullying words and actions speak for themselves, reserving the end of his program to comment on the senator in rather scathing terms. When McCarthy agreed to appear on the next airing of Murrow's show, he tore into the reporter, calling him "the leader and the cleverest of the jackal pack which is always found at the throat of anyone who dares expose individual communists and traitors." Scholars have debated the impact of Murrow's broadcasts on American viewers, with some asserting that their effect on McCarth's image was negligible, but the episodes definitely got public attention. Soon after Murrow's first broadcast, sponsors began pulling their advertising, demanding that CBS remove Murrow from the air. CBS president Fred Friendly, however, defended Murrow and refused to fire him. "See It Now" not only attracted much controversy, it also inspired others to stand up and publicly criticize the Wisconsin senator.

McCarthy's misplaced attempt to investigate subversive activities in the United States Army effectively ended his public career. The senator's effort was the brainchild of his chief counsel, Roy Cohn, a New York lawyer who at the time was upset that his lover, David Schine, had been recently drafted into the Army. After failing to get Schine released from his two-year commitment, Cohn then tried using influence to get the draftee as many special privileges as possible. When the Army refused to cooperate, Cohn had his boss, McCarthy, unwisely charge that the Army was harboring communists. The resulting furor led to a Senate investigation to hear the charges and countercharges, undertaken by McCarthy's subcommittee but headed by South Dakota Republican Karl Mundt. The nationally televised "Army-McCarthy" hearings began on April 22, 1954 and lasted 36 days. The Army charged that Cohn and McCarthy had employed inappropriate pressure, while the senator and his aide countercharged that the Army deliberately mistreated Schine in an attempt to squelch McCarthy's investigations looking into possible communist infiltration in the U.S. Army. Unlike "See It Now," which was a prime-time evening show, the hearings were televised during the daytime, with an estimated 20 million Americans watching at least part of the inquiry.

For many Americans, the hearings were the first time that they had personally seen McCarthy's antics, and they were appalled by his abusive bullying of witnesses and his sweeping accusations. The most memorable moment of the entire series of hearings occurred on their 30th day during an exchange between Senator McCarthy and Joseph Welch, a well regarded Boston-based lawyer who had been appointed as the Army's special counsel for the proceedings. When Welch asked Cohn to produce Senator McCarthy's supposed list of 130 subversives working in defense plants, McCarthy interjected by suggesting that Welch should check on Fred Fisher, a lawyer in Welch's law firm who the special counsel had planned to have on his hearings staff but dismissed when it became known that he was a member of the National Lawyers' Guild, a liberal lawyer group that had split from the overtly conservative American Bar Association. Welch soon reprimanded McCarthy for his attack on Fisher, saying that "Until this moment, Senator, I think I never really gauged your cruelty or your recklessness." McCarthy dismissed Welch's words and continued his attack on Fisher, at which point Welch angrily cut him short, declaring: "Senator, may we not drop this? We know he belonged to the Lawyer's Guild . . . Let us not assassinate this lad further, Senator; you've done enough. Have you no sense of decency, sir? At long last, have you left no sense of decency?" After Welch ended his remarks, the gallery burst into cheers.

After the hearings ended, the Senate formally censured McCarthy for his behavior. Though he continued to serve for another two and a half years, he quickly became a pariah in Washington, D.C. and the country at large. His colleagues in the Senate largely avoided him, and his speeches on the Senate floor were frequently delivered to near empty chambers. Most important of all, the national press, which had once recorded his every public move, now ignored him. He died in 1957 at the age of 48 from an enflamed liver brought on by his chronic alcoholism. The term "McCarthyism," however, would live on as a euphemism for rampant paranoia, character assassination, guilt by association, and general accusations against groups or individuals without corroborating evidence, often for the purposes of silencing dissent.

THOUGHT QUESTIONS:

1. Describe Edward R. Murrow's efforts to expose Senator McCarthy's antics to a wider television audience.

2. Describe how Joseph Welch's spirited defense of Fred Fisher added to McCarthy's downfall.

3. Can you identify some modern examples of individuals exhibiting McCarthy-like behavior for their cause? With whom do you think such tactics are most effective?

American Culture From 1945-1960

Documents

Harry Truman, Executive Order 9981
1948

Since the 1896 **Plessy vs. Ferguson** *decision in which the United States Supreme Court ruled that segregation was constitutional as long as the accommodations provided African Americans were equal to those open to whites, the federal government looked the other way as blacks in the South were routinely denied, through Jim Crow legislation, the "equal protection of the law" guaranteed by the U.S. Constitution's 14th Amendment. The Cold War between the United States and the Soviet Union that followed World War II, however, changed that equation in American racial politics.*

The Washington political establishment feared that the Soviets sought world domination. As European colonial empires crumbled after 1945, the American government wanted to prevent the Soviets from establishing alliances with newly independent nations in Africa and Asia.

Cases of racial discrimination received wide attention not only in the Soviet press, but also in newspapers and radio broadcasts in just-established nations like India and Ceylon, and in sub-Saharan Africa. The Truman and Eisenhower administrations fretted over losing a global public relations war. In one incident, Alabama police arrested U.S. Senator Glen Taylor, running in 1948 for vice president on the Progressive Party ticket headed by Henry Wallace, when he entered the "colored entrance" to a Birmingham church to make a speech. The Shanghai, China newspaper **Ta Kung Pao** *sharply criticized American hypocrisy.*

"If the United States merely wants to 'dominate' the world, the atomic bomb and the U.S. dollar will be sufficient to achieve this purpose," an editorial said. "However, the world cannot be 'dominated' for a long period of time. If the United States wants to 'lead' the world, it must have a kind of moral superiority in addition to military superiority." The fact that this criticism of American race relations appeared in a newspaper in China, a country engaged in a civil war between a conservative dictatorial regime friendly to the United States and communists, particularly alarmed the American State Department.

Geopolitical concerns shaped President Harry Truman's thoughts about segregation, as explained elsewhere, but post-World War II incidents of racial violence also shocked him. In 1947, he appointed the President's Commission on Civil Rights to explore issues associated with job discrimination, voting rights, and segregation. He then won a bruising battle to get the Democratic National Convention to include a civil rights plank in its national platform: a move that resulted in the walkout of segregationist southern delegates. Truman decided to move ahead on a plan to desegregate the military. On July 26, 1948, Truman issued Executive Order No. 9981, which began the slow process of integrating the service, an effort not completed until the Korean War.

Establishing the President's Committee on Equality of Treatment and Opportunity In the Armed Forces.

WHEREAS it is essential that there be maintained in the armed services of the United States the highest standards of democracy, with equality of treatment and opportunity for all those who serve in our country's defense:

NOW THEREFORE, by virtue of the authority vested in me as President of the United States, by the Constitution and the statutes of the United States, and as Commander in Chief of the armed services, it is hereby ordered as follows:

1. It is hereby declared to be the policy of the President that there shall be equality of treatment and opportunity for all persons in the armed services without regard to race, color, religion or national origin. This policy shall be put into effect as rapidly as possible, having due regard to the time required to effectuate any necessary changes without impairing efficiency or morale.

2. There shall be created in the National Military Establishment an advisory committee to be known as the President's Committee on Equality of Treatment and Opportunity in the Armed Services, which shall be composed of seven members to be designated by the President.

3. The Committee is authorized on behalf of the President to examine into the rules, procedures and practices of the Armed Services in order to determine in what respect such rules, procedures and practices may be altered or improved with a view to carrying out the policy of this order. The Committee shall confer and advise the Secretary of Defense, the Secretary of the Army, the Secretary of the Navy, and the Secretary of the Air Force, and shall make such recommendations to the President and to said Secretaries as in the judgment of the Committee will effectuate the policy hereof.

4. All executive departments and agencies of the Federal Government are authorized and directed to cooperate with the Committee in its work, and to furnish the Committee such information or the services of such persons as the Committee may require in the performance of its duties.

5. When requested by the Committee to do so, persons in the armed services or in any of the executive departments and agencies of the Federal Government shall testify before the Committee and shall make available for use of the Committee such documents and other information as the Committee may require.

6. The Committee shall continue to exist until such time as the President shall terminate its existence by Executive order.

Harry Truman
The White House, July 26, 1948

Source: https://www.trumanlibrary.org/9981a.htm

THOUGHT QUESTIONS:

1. How did American racism complicate the foreign diplomacy of the United States after World War II?

2. What steps did Harry Truman take regarding racial discrimination to improve the American image in the world?

3. What reasons might account for the military taking so long to integrate after Truman's Executive Order No. 9981?

"Employment of Homosexuals and Other Sex Perverts in Government" (1950)

There are no precise numbers, but scholars estimate that approximately one million gay and bisexual men and women served in the military in World War II. However, because members of the gay and bisexual community faced harsh retaliation—including dishonorable discharge from the service, subsequent hardship in finding work, and social condemnation when they returned home—their contribution to the war effort was invisible to the general public.

During the Cold War, in which the Soviet Union and the United States competed for the pre-eminent position in the world, the entire LGBT community suffered an enormous backlash. As the Soviets successfully detonated first an atomic bomb and then a hydrogen weapon, panic spread across the country in the late 1940s and early 1950s about communist spies and saboteurs within the American government and the military. Some charged that homosexuality represented part of a communist conspiracy to undermine American masculinity, the family, and the country's military resolve.

Government officials, including FBI Director J. Edgar Hoover (who many scholars believe was a closeted gay man himself) claimed that gay government workers posed a security risk because they were weak and vulnerable to blackmail by Soviet agents. In 1950, a State Department official revealed that his office had fired dozens of employees for suspected homosexuality. Republican members of Congress charged that gays had infiltrated President Truman's administration. In June 1950, the Senate authorized an investigation into the supposed gay menace lurking in the nation's capital and the armed services.

In December, the government issued a report, "Employment of Homosexuals and Other Sex Perverts in Government." As a result of the report, investigators warned suspected gays in government service, including the military, that their lifestyles would be publicly revealed and they could face criminal prosecution if they did not provide the names of other homosexuals working in federal agencies or serving in the Armed Forces.

The number of government employees dismissed during the "Lavender Scare" increased by twelve times in the period between 1950 and 1953. Shortly after being sworn in as president in January 1953, Dwight Eisenhower issued an executive order prohibiting any gay man or woman from federal employment. The military also launched a gay purge. Annual discharges doubled through the 1950s.

Suspected gay men and lesbians endured constant harassment from superior officers and investigators. Soldiers accused of homosexuality sometimes found themselves confined in "queer stockades" until they received "Undesirable Discharges." When these men and women returned to civilian life, potential employers knew this discharge meant that they had been removed from the ranks because of homosexuality. Such discharges haunted gay Americans, making it much more difficult to find work. Other military careers ended more tragically.

One lesbian soldier, Pat Bond, recalled what happened at her base in Tokyo as 500 were discharged. "They called up one of our kids—Helen," Bond said. "They got her up on the stand and told her that if she didn't give names of her friends they would tell her parents she was gay. She went up to her room on the sixth floor and jumped out and killed herself. She was twenty." The document that launched this anti-gay government purge follows:

Psychiatric physicians generally agree that indulgence in sexually perverted practices indicates a personality which has failed to reach sexual maturity. The authorities agree that most sex deviates respond to psychiatric treatment and can be cured if they have a genuine desire to be cured. However, many overt homosexuals have no real desire to abandon their way of life and in such cases cures are difficult, if not impossible. The subcommittee sincerely believes that persons affiliated with sexual desires which result in their engaging in overt acts of perversion should be considered as proper cases for medical and psychiatric treatment.

. . . In the opinion of this subcommittee homosexuals and other sex perverts are not fit persons to be employed in Government for two reasons; first they are generally unsuitable, and second, they constitute security risks.

. . . Overt acts of sex perversion, including acts of homosexuality, constitute a crime under our Federal, State and municipal statutes and persons who commit such acts are law violators. Aside from the criminality and immorality involved in sex perversion such behavior is so contrary to the normal accepted standards of social behavior that persons who engage in such activity are looked upon as outcast by society generally. The social stigma attached to sex perversion is so great that many perverts go to great lengths to conceal their perverted tendencies . . . This situation is evidenced by the fact that perverts are frequently victimized by blackmailers who threaten to expose their sexual deviations.

In further considering the suitability of perverts as Government employees, it is generally believed that those who engage in overt acts of perversion lack the emotional stability of normal persons. In addition, there is an abundance of evidence to sustain the conclusion that indulgence of acts of sexual perversion weakens the moral fiber of an individual to a degree that he is not suitable for a position of responsibility.

. . . The lack of emotional stability which is found in more sex perverts, and the weakness of their moral fiber, makes them susceptible to the blandishments of the foreign espionage agent. It is the experience of intelligence experts that perverts are vulnerable to interrogation by a skilled questioner and that they seldom refuse to talk about themselves. Furthermore, most perverts tend to congregate at the same restaurants, night clubs, and bars which places can be identified with comparative ease in any community, making it possible for a recruiting agent to develop clandestine relationships which can be used for espionage purposes.

. . . It follows that if blackmailers can extort money from a homosexual under the threat of disclosure, espionage agents can use the same type of pressure to extort confidential information or other material they might be seeking.

. . . It is an accepted fact among intelligence agencies that espionage organizations the world over consider sex perverts who are in possession of or who have access to confidential materials to be prime targets where pressure can be exerted.

. . . It is not possible to determine accurately the number of homosexuals and other sex perverts in government service . . . An individual check of the Federal agencies revealed that since January 1, 1947, the armed services and civilian agencies of Government have handled 4,954 cases involving charges of homosexuality or other types of sex perversion.

The subcommittee also found that the existing criminal laws in the District of Columbia with regards to acts of sex perversion are inadequate . . . It was also discovered that most of the homosexuals apprehended by the police in the District of Columbia were booked on charges of disorderly conduct. In most cases they were never brought to trial but were allowed to make forfeitures of small cash collateral at police stations.

Since the initiation of this investigation considerable progress has been made in removing homosexuals and similar undesirable employees from positions in the Government. However, it should be borne in mind that the public interest cannot be adequately protected unless responsible officials adopt and maintain a realistic and vigilant attitude towards the problem of sex perverts in the government. To pussyfoot, or to take half measures will allow some known perverts to remain in Government and can result in the dismissal of innocent persons.

Source: Senate, 81st Congress, 2d Session, Document 241, Washington, D.C.: United States Government Printing Office, 1950

THOUGHT QUESTIONS:

1. What excuses did the government use to justify the elimination of gay and bi-sexual men and women from federal agencies and the military after World War II?

2. The authors of "Employment of Homosexuals and Other Sex Perverts in Government" employed what stereotypes of the LGBT community?

3. What impact did the "gay purge" have on the LGBT community?

The United States Supreme Court
Brown vs. Board of Education of Topeka (1954)

Since the 1930s, the National Association for the Advancement of Colored People, the leading African American civil rights organization in the United States, had zeroed in on the language of the United States Supreme Court's 1896 **Plessy vs. Ferguson** *decision that maintained that segregation was constitutional as long as the accommodations provided for African Americans—in schools, seating in public transportation, etc.—equaled what was provided white Americans. In this way, they had won cases that opened white law schools to African Americans in cases like* **Murray v. Maryland** *(1936) and* **Sweatt v. Painter** *and* **McLaurin v. Oklahoma**, *both decided in 1950.*

In such cases, NAACP lawyers argued that while blacks and whites were required to attend separate schools, objectively the schools differed widely in terms of funding and quality. The NAACP lawyers did not directly challenge **Plessy** *itself but argued that southern states had failed to live up to the* **Plessy** *"separate but equal" formula.*

Thurgood Marshall, an African-American native of Baltimore who graduated first in his class from Harvard University in 1933, won numerous such "equalization" cases for the NAACP beginning in the 1930s, and he became the executive director of its Legal Defense and Education Fund in 1940. In 1950, Marshall and his legal team launched an all-out assault on segregated schools and represented African-American parents filing lawsuits against "Jim Crow" education in Delaware, Kansas, Louisiana, South Carolina, Virginia, and Washington, D.C.

These suits reached the United States Supreme Court in 1952, the Court consolidating all the cases under the title **Brown et al v. Board of Education of Topeka, et. al.** *The Court announced its decision that exceeded the NAACP's wildest dream on May 17, 1954. In overturning the 1896* **Plessy v. Ferguson** *decision, Chief Justice Earl Warren spoke for a unanimous court in declaring, "In the field of public education, the doctrine of separate but equal has no place. Separate educational facilities are inherently unequal."*

The Supreme Court put off implementation of **Brown** *for a year. The implementation order, issued on May 31, 1955, came to be known as* **Brown II**. *The order set no firm deadline for school districts to achieve integration, only urging local authorities to proceed with "all deliberate speed." Southern states would interpret "deliberate" to mean as slow as possible. The Court failed to define the threshold at which a school district achieved desegregation, leaving that matter to the federal district courts. Finally, the Court provided a list of reasons school districts could use to excuse delayed implementation, such as administrative difficulties.*

The Court unintentionally provided opponents of integration a chance to organize what came to be known as "massive resistance" to the **Brown** *decision. Southern legislatures tried various tricks to avoid complying with the intent of* **Brown** *with school officials in Little Rock, Arkansas, and Norfolk, Virginia, completely shutting down their public schools. Prince Edward County, Virginia, closed its public schools for eight years to avoid admitting African-American students. Some southern states provided white parents vouchers to pay for tuition at private all-white schools. Nevertheless, the* **Brown** *decision began the slow process of ending legal segregation in American public education, even if so-called "white flight," in which white* *parents fled cities with large black and brown populations to suburbs with few people of color, would create a new kind of separate and unequal beginning in the 1960s.*

MR. CHIEF JUSTICE WARREN delivered the opinion of the Court.

These cases come to us from the States of Kansas, South Carolina, Virginia, and Delaware. They are premised on different facts and different local conditions, but a common legal question justifies their consideration together in this consolidated opinion. In each of the cases, minors of the Negro race, through their legal representatives, seek the aid of the courts in obtaining admission to the public schools of their community on a nonsegregated basis. In each instance, they had been denied admission to schools attended by white children under laws requiring or permitting segregation according to race. This segregation was alleged to deprive the plaintiffs of the equal protection of the laws under the Fourteenth Amendment.

... The plaintiffs contend that segregated public schools are not "equal" and cannot be made "equal," and that hence they are deprived of the equal protection of the laws.

... We must consider public education in the light of its full development and its present place in American life throughout the Nation. Only in this way can it be determined if segregation in public schools deprives these plaintiffs of the equal protection of the laws.

Today, education is perhaps the most important function of state and local governments. Compulsory school attendance laws and the great expenditures for education both demonstrate our recognition of the importance of education to our democratic society. It is required in the performance of our most basic public responsibilities, even service in the armed forces. It is the very foundation of good citizenship. Today it is a principal instrument in awakening the child to cultural values, in preparing him for later professional training, and in helping him to adjust normally to his environment. In these days, it is doubtful that any child may reasonably be expected to succeed in life if he is denied the opportunity of an education. Such an opportunity, where the state has undertaken to provide it, is a right which must be made available to all on equal terms.

We come then to the question presented: Does segregation of children in public schools solely on the basis of race, even though the physical facilities and other "tangible" factors may be equal, deprive the children of the minority group of equal educational opportunities? We believe that it does.

In *Sweatt v. Painter* ... in finding that a segregated law school for Negroes could not provide them equal educational opportunities, this Court relied in large part on "those qualities which are incapable of objective measurement but which make for greatness in a law school." In *McLaurin v. Oklahoma State Regents* ... the Court, in requiring that a Negro admitted to a white graduate school be treated like all other students, again resorted to intangible considerations: "... his ability to study, to engage in discussions and exchange views with other students, and, in general, to learn his profession." Such considerations apply with added force to children in grade and high schools. To separate them from others of similar age and qualifications solely because of their race generates a feeling of inferiority as to their status in the community that may affect their hearts and minds in a way unlikely ever to be undone ...

Segregation of white and colored children in public schools has a detrimental effect upon the colored children. The impact is greater when it has the sanction of the law, for the policy of separating the races is usually interpreted as denoting the inferiority of the negro group. A sense of inferiority affects the motivation of a child to learn. Segregation with the sanction of law, therefore, has a tendency to [impede] the educational and mental development of negro children and to deprive them of some of the benefits they would receive in a racial[ly] integrated school system.

... We conclude that, in the field of public education, the doctrine of "separate but equal" has no place. Separate educational facilities are inherently unequal. Therefore, we hold that the plaintiffs and others similarly situated for whom the actions have been brought are, by reason of the segregation complained of, deprived of the equal protection of the laws guaranteed by the Fourteenth Amendment.

Source: https://www.ourdocuments.gov/doc.php?flash=false&doc=87&page=transcript

THOUGHT QUESTIONS:

1. What was the legal strategy the NAACP took in dismantling segregation from the 1930s on?

2. On what basis did the United States Supreme Court in the *Brown* case determine that "Separate educational facilities are inherently unequal?"

3. How did southern states evade complying with the intent of the *Brown* decision?

Charles Alexander
Letter About Integration in Little Rock, Arkansas, 1956

*The 1954 United States Supreme Court decision **Brown v. Board of Education** that ruled school segregation unconstitutional made President Dwight Eisenhower unhappy. He believed that the white South was not ready for school integration and that the attempt to impose it would aggravate racial tensions. "I am convinced that the Supreme Court decision set back progress in the South at least fifteen years," Eisenhower said to an associate, though he generally avoided public comment on **Brown**. Saying he sympathized with white parents who did not want their daughters sitting next to black boys in classrooms, Eisenhower seemed oblivious to the terrible state of black education in the South, and the oppressive lives lived by African Americans there.*

He was also afraid of losing the support of white voters in the four southern states he carried when he won the presidency in 1952: Texas, Tennessee, Florida, and Virginia. Thus, he looked the other way in 1956 when Texas Gov. Alan Shivers ignored a federal court order to integrate Mansfield High School, located in a small community between Dallas and Fort Worth, and sent Texas Rangers to prevent three African Americans from registering. School officials allowed a black effigy to hang near the entrance of the campus, and Mansfield High did not integrate until 1965.

International politics forced Eisenhower to respond differently the next year in Little Rock,

Arkansas. Ordered by a federal court a second time on September 20, 1957, to desegregate Central High School, Gov. Orval Faubus withdrew National Guard troops meant to preserve law and order at the campus as nine African-American teenagers tried to enroll. Faubus promptly left the state as chaos loomed. The story made international headlines, and Eisenhower became deeply worried about the damage the controversy caused to the image of the United States while it competed with the Soviet Union for the support for newly independent nations in Africa and Asia.

Eisenhower federalized the Arkansas National Guard and dispatched a thousand troops of the 101st Airborne Division to Central High to escort the Little Rock Nine safely to the campus. Armed soldiers would accompany the African-American students for several weeks. Before the president made this decision, African Americans across the country, including a sailor named Charles Alexander, wrote pleas to the president to do the right thing.

Mr. President,

My name is Charles Alexander. I am a member of the United States Armed Forces. My race is Negro, and I am eighteen years of age.

The purpose of the letter is to find out, first hand, what is being done about the situation now at hand, in the south concerning the integration problem . . . I am but eighteen years of age, and yet I am willing to lay down my life in defense of a country where my people are not even wanted; I feel very self-conscious about this.

Here in the navy, where both white and others are living together, the problem is still the same, with insults coming from right and left . . .

When two people of different races can't live together something has to be done or disaster follows; and I feel that it is reaching the disaster point now.

The Declaration of Independence states that every man has rights, it doesn't include that his skin must be white to receive them . . .

People being abused because of the color of their skin is not only unconstitutional and indecent, but it is a threat to all humanity, and an open invitation for communists and fascists to move in. If a group of people can't find protection and leadership in their own government they look elsewhere for it.

Something like this could very easily lead to another civil war, with the people of the United States fighting among themselves; other countries would lose confidence in the leadership of this country and things could very easily end up in chaos . . .

Sincerely,
Charles Alexander

Source: *https://www.eisenhower.archives.gov/research/online_documents/civil_rights_citizens_letters/no_date_alexander.pdf*

THOUGHT QUESTIONS:

1. What was Dwight Eisenhower's attitude toward court-mandated school integration and how did that shape his response to events in Mansfield, Texas, in 1956?

2. How did the international political climate change Eisenhower's approach to school integration in Little Rock, Arkansas in 1957?

3. What did Charles Alexander warn could be the consequences for the United States if African Americans were not provided an equal opportunity for a quality education?

Vignettes

Racial Violence and a President's Conscience

President Harry S Truman came from a regional border state (Missouri) and occasionally used anti-black slurs in private conversation. Writing to his daughter Margaret Truman when he was a senator from Missouri, the future president once complained about black waiters at a Washington, D.C. restaurant whom he described as "an army of coons" who thought they were "evidently the top of the black social set in Washington." Once in a 1939 letter to his wife Bess, Truman derided an African American social occasion as "nigger picnic day."

As president, however, Truman worried about the impact of racial injustice in the United States on the Cold War. Pragmatic electoral concerns also shaped his newly found interest in civil rights. From the 1920s through World War II, millions of African Americans had moved north of the Mason-Dixon line and into the West to escape the harassment of southern whites and to find better-paying jobs. Since Roosevelt's second term, African-American voters in the North and West largely supported Democrats, and in states like California and Michigan the black electorate could swing close elections. Black resentment over the influence of southern white segregationists on the Democratic Party, however, caused a drop-off in black support for the Democrats in the 1946 congressional races. Truman wanted to win these voters back.

Post-war racial violence, however, also moved the president. Black activists told Truman of an incident in Monroe, Georgia, in which whites fatally shot two African-American men. The wife of one of the victims recognized one of the white shooters, so the killers assassinated both of the men's spouses, as well. Violence against African-American servicemen in particular shocked the president.

Several grisly attacks on black veterans made headlines across the nation just after World War II. In one incident, the police chief in Aiken, S.C., severely beat Sgt. Isaac Woodard, an African American, with a nightstick and gouged an eye out. Woodard had received his separation papers from the United States Army a mere three hours earlier. Hearing of this attack, Truman reportedly said, "My God. I had no idea it was as terrible as that. We've got to do something!" Truman later said incidents such as the assault on Sgt. Woodard moved him to push for civil rights. Pressed by southern members of Congress to abandon this stand, Truman said, "My forebears were Confederates ... But my very stomach turned over when I learned that Negro soldiers, just back from overseas, were being dumped out of Army trucks in Mississippi and beaten."

On December 5, 1946, Truman established the President's Committee on Civil Rights, to which he predominantly appointed racial liberals. The committee issued its report, "To Secure These Rights," the following October. According to the report, the contrast between the nation's stated ideas of human equality and the widespread practice of racial discrimination served as "a kind of moral dry rot which eats away at the emotional and rational bases of democratic beliefs." With its eyes on America's global competition with the Soviet Union, the report warned that "we cannot ignore what the world thinks of us or our record."

The committee recommended a broad range of reforms including enacting a federal anti-lynching statute (designed to get around southern courts that refused to prosecute violent crimes committed by whites against blacks), a ban on the poll tax (which reduced black voting), prohibiting by federal statute discrimination in private employment, establishing a permanent Commission on Civil Rights, increasing the size of the Justice Department's civil rights division, and strictly enforcing voting rights laws. The Commission also called for federal money to be denied to any public or private agency that practiced segregation and called for the Congress to integrate all facilities in Washington, D.C., including the public school system. President Truman embraced most of these recommendations in a civil rights message to Congress on February 2, 1948.

At the Democratic National Convention that summer, southern delegates walked out when a far-reaching pro-Civil Rights plank was for the first time added to the Democratic Party platform. Led by South Carolina Governor Strom Thurmond, Democrats from the former Confederacy formed the "State's Rights Democratic Party," more commonly called the "Dixiecrats."

In spite of this intense opposition, Truman issued two executive orders on July 26, 1948: one that would eventually desegregate the armed forces and another that prohibited discrimination in the federal civil service. Meanwhile, the Dixiecrats nominated Strom Thurmond for President. Thurmond carried the states of Louisiana, Mississippi, Alabama, and South Carolina, winning almost 1.2 million popular votes and 39 votes in the Electoral College. He almost cost Truman the election, though the Missouri incumbent narrowly prevailed.

Truman first signed Executive Order 9981, ordering the desegregation of the Armed Forces on July 26, 1948, but by January 13, 1949, only one of the Marine Corps' 8,200 officers was African American. Only five of the Navy's 45,000 officers were black. The Army, meanwhile, maintained a 10 percent recruiting quota for African Americans until the Korean War began in 1950. High casualties among white units in the war hastened the integration of black army troops. Not until 1953 could the Army announce that 95 percent of African-American troops served in integrated units.

During the late 1940s, Truman also used his executive powers to empanel a Commission on Higher Education that recommended an end to religious and racial quotas used at universities to limit admission of Jews and blacks. After his presidency, Truman continued to use words like "nigger" in private conversation, dismissed Martin Luther King, Jr., as a "troublemaker," and considered the civil rights movement at least partly inspired by communism, but his presidency nevertheless committed the national Democratic Party to greater support for black voting rights and opposition to segregation.

THOUGHT QUESTIONS:

1. What about President Harry Truman's personal background made him an unlikely supporter of African American civil rights?

2. What issues prompted Truman's shift on racial issues beginning in the late 1940s?

3. What was the reaction of much of the white southern political leadership to Truman's civil rights initiatives?

Porn in the U.S.A.

Perhaps because scientific research conducted by biologist Alfred Kinsey, who revealed that many Americans did not conform to the supposed middle class norms of heterosexuality, waiting for sex until marriage, and observing strict fidelity, or maybe because men and women in the service experienced first-hand the more erotically open European culture during World War II, sexual frankness increased in American popular culture following that war.

"Soldiers who had graced their barracks and even their planes with photos and drawings of 'pinup' girls returned from Europe and Asia laden with pornography obtained abroad," according to John D'Emilio and Estelle B. Freedman in their book *Intimate Matters: A History of Sexuality in the United States*. "They soon found a new genre of magazines available to fill their acquired tastes."

In 1953, Hugh Hefner began publication of *Playboy*, a men's magazine that featured photos of nude women and frank descriptions of sex. Hefner, who earned a psychology degree at the University of Urbana-Champaign, worked as a copy editor at *Esquire Magazine* before he took out a mortgage on his home and raised money from more than 40 investors, including $1,000 from his mother to print *Playboy's* first issue. All 72,000 copies of the first issue, which included a nude calendar photo of the then-unknown aspiring actress Marilyn Monroe, sold. By 1960, readership hit 1 million, and peaked at 7 million in 1972.

As the readership grew and became more prosperous, the magazine eventually also included celebrity interviews, music and movie reviews, and commentary on politics. *Playboy* published stories by some of the best American authors of the mid-twentieth century, such as novelist and essayist James Baldwin, Roald Dahl (who penned *Charlie and the Chocolate Factory*), master of science fiction Ray Bradbury, Ian Fleming (the creator of James Bond), and Gabriel García Márquez (the writer of *One Hundred Years of Solitude*).

Hefner described his attitude toward sex as the "*Playboy* philosophy," and he encouraged his male readership, which reached one million by the end of the 1950s, to "enjoy the pleasures that the female has to offer without becoming emotionally involved." Oblivious or unwilling to acknowledge the toxic harm created by sexism, job and wage discrimination, and the horrors of sexual assault, the publisher presented an upside-down image of American gender politics.

Hefner expressed sympathy with his socially climbing male readership, 25 percent of whom were college-aged, whom he depicted as put upon by money-grabbing women. Hefner characterized marriage as a financial trap, urging men not to become one of the "sorry, regimented husbands trudging down every woman-dominated street in this woman-dominated land."

In the 1960s, *Playboy* Enterprises operated casinos and Playboy Clubs, which served food and drinks served by cocktail waitresses in revealing "Bunny" costumes. Hefner would also host two TV shows between the late 1950s and early 1970s, *Playboy's Penthouse* from 1959-1960 and *Playboy After Dark,* 1969-1970.

Playboy reduced women to the objects of sexual fantasies even as the second great wave of feminism swept the nation and women increasingly sought equal pay for equal work, increased job opportunities, including in supposedly "male" professions, and a bigger voice in politics. So-called men's magazines like *Playboy* and later rivals like *Penthouse* represented an anti-feminist backlash, a way to put women back in their supposed places even as publishers like Hefner presented their products as part of a "sexual revolution." Sexual exploitation was masked as another freedom struggle like the civil rights movement.

Meanwhile, sex scandal-driven periodicals like *Confidential* became the forerunners of today's supermarket tabloids. Magazines posing as male fitness periodicals and featuring muscle-bound male models in swimsuits served as softcore pornography for gay audiences. These publications joined *Playboy* in the escalating eroticization of American culture.

Perhaps sensing the shift in public attitudes toward sex, the United States Supreme Court in the 1950s began to take a more liberal stand on pornography cases brought by prosecutors against writers, photographers, publishers, booksellers and performers of adult material, setting an ever-higher bar for what could be considered "obscene." In the 1957 *Butler v. Michigan* decision, the Court overturned the obscenity conviction of Alfred Butler, a sales manager of Pocket Books in Detroit, whom an undercover police officer arrested for selling a copy of the John H. Griffin novel *The Devil Rides Outside*. A Michigan judge ruled that the book included pornographic language, which could lead to the corruption of minors and thus violated state law. The Supreme Court overturned the Michigan obscenity statute, ruling that the law in question would "reduce the adult population of Michigan to reading only what is fit for a child."

THOUGHT QUESTIONS:

1. Why did sexuality increasingly pervade American culture in the post-World War II era?

2. How did Hugh Hefner's description of gender politics contrast with the experience of women in the mid- and late-twentieth century?

3. What did publications like *Playboy* suggest about the social status of women in the 1950s and 1960s?

Out of Bounds:
Pro Sports and the Tackling of Jim Crow

From the 1940s until the 1960s, Jim Crow began to crumble not only at bus stops and lunch counters, but in professional sports. As television became a presence in most American homes, African-American athletes first became stars in baseball, basketball, and football. Drafted by the National Basketball Association's Boston Celtics in 1956, Bill Russell became the first African-American athlete to completely dominate what had previously been an all-white professional sports league. Russell would guide the team to nine NBA championships in 10 years, his speedy, agile play often inspired by the anger he felt at the racism he encountered across the country.

It was in professional football that integration met some of its fiercest opposition. Pro football had featured African-American stars in the 1920s such as head coach and running back Fritz Pollard of the Akron Pros. The racial politics of the game changed by the early 1930s and African Americans vanished from NFL rosters.

George Preston Marshall became one of the stalwart defenders of Jim Crow in the NFL. Marshall and the other owners convinced themselves that white fans would not support a league that included African-American standouts. In 1932, Marshall bought the financially failing Boston Braves, and moved the squad to Washington, D.C., renaming the franchise the Redskins. He was an innovator who brought to the game a marching band and a team song, "Hail to the Redskins."

The nation's capital was segregated and still culturally a southern city. At the time, it represented the NFL's southern-most franchise. Marshall hoped the entire former Confederacy would embrace the Redskins. To make the Washington franchise Dixie's team, he created a network of sixty radio stations and, by the 1950s, 29 television stations in the South that broadcast the team's games. Marshall cultivated a white southern following, and he was determined to keep the fans' loyalty in part by keeping his team entirely white season after season.

The Los Angeles Rams broke the NFL color barrier in 1946 when they signed two African-American players, Woody Strode and Kenny Washington. Meanwhile a rival to the National Football League, the All-American Football Conference formed and one of its franchises, the Cleveland Browns, would suit up African-American stars such as future Hall of Famer Marion Motley.

Nevertheless, racism poisoned the NFL's first foray into the South itself. The league awarded the failed New York Yanks franchise to Dallas in 1952. Called the Texans, the team roster included two black players, George Taliaferro and Buddy Young. The Texans were an awful team, which contributed to poor attendance during home games at their stadium, the Cotton Bowl. Many observers also believed that white Dallas fans rejected the Texans because fans were not ready to cheer for black athletes. Black fans were forced to sit in a segregated section in the Cotton Bowl end zone, where they squinted directly into the sun. After a few sparsely attended home games, the NFL took over the team and rescheduled the rest of its season on the road. The Dallas Texans died an undignified death, with a record of 1-11 in their only season.

By the 1960s, the NFL faced intense rivalry from an upstart, the American Football League, which proved much more willing to give black players a chance. A new, integrated Dallas Texans team debuted in AFL's first season in 1960 and the appearance of that franchise led the NFL to establish the Dallas Cowboys, that same year. The Cowboys also began play with African American team members.

African-American players increasingly achieved fame and won acceptance, at least on the playing field, but in Washington, Marshall refused to budge. Even as his team sank into yearly, predicable mediocrity, Marshall declined to sign some of the greatest players of the age, like running back Jim Brown, because of their skin color. That became a harder position to sustain as the civil rights struggle filled nightly news broadcasts and Washington, D.C. itself became a blacker city.

Marshall surrendered in 1961 when he sought construction of a new stadium on federal land. John Kennedy's Interior Secretary, Stewart Udall, told Marshall that the team would not be able to use the new playing field in 1962 unless they signed an African-American player. One Sunday afternoon, on September 30, 1962, Bobby Mitchell, Washington's new wide receiver, shredded the secondary of the St. Louis Cardinals, catching seven passes for 147 yards and two touchdowns. Washington thus became the last NFL team to integrate.

Marshall died in 1969. Meanwhile, in recent years the name of the Washington team has become a controversy itself, with many characterizing the term "Redskin" as a racist slur. The Washington Postnewspaper refuses to use the team name in its sports coverage.

THOUGHT QUESTIONS:

1. Why did NFL team owners decide to eliminate African American players from their rosters by the 1930s?

2. What were George Preston Marshall's motives for keeping his team segregated from 1932 until 1962?

3. What impact do you think that successful African American professional athletes might have had on Southern racial politics beginning in the 1960s?

Up In Smoke:
Tobacco and American Culture after World War II

Long before scientific evidence conclusively demonstrated that smoking caused lung cancer and other serious illnesses, the public knew that cigarettes posed a risk to health. As early as the 1890s, the public began referring to cigarettes as "coffin nails." Nevertheless, cigarette use climbed over the next half century.

By the 1800s, Americans found a lot of ways to consume tobacco. They smoked pipes and cigars and chewed tobacco, but these methods of delivering highly addictive nicotine to the body became less popular with increased urbanization. As Richard Kluger, author of *Ashes to Ashes: America's Hundred-Year Cigarette War, the Public Health, and the Unabashed Triumph of Philip Morris* noted, the public increasingly disdained those who chewed tobacco and spat it out because of the fear that spittle could spread tuberculosis. Cigars came to be seen by many as too smelly for crowded urban spaces, and pipes, which required loading and cleaning, seemed too time-consuming as the pace of life quickened in the industrial age.

Pre-rolled and attractively packaged cigarettes, however, were conveniently small, easy to carry, and provided a quick and satisfying way to achieve a nicotine rush even as technological advancements allowed the inexpensive mass production of the product. Cigarettes became the most popular way to consume tobacco in the early twentieth century.

The advertising industry played a major role in convincing the public that smoking was suave and sophisticated. Advertisers were critical in convincing customers to buy a specific type of cigarette since there really wasn't any difference in the brands. R.J. Reynolds Tobacco created perhaps the most recognizable cigarette logo when they launched Camel Cigarettes, which were promoted in the World War I era with the use of "Old Joe," a circus camel that was led through towns and cities as employees distributed free samples. Advertisements featured the slogan "I'd walk a mile for a Camel." R.J. Reynolds soon was spending $10 million a year to promote Camels and other cigarette brands.

In the 1920s, celebrities like singer Al Jolson, the star of 1927's *The Jazz Singer*, started appearing in cigarette promotions. The trend of using celebrity endorsements would continue through the 1960s. Humphrey Bogart, star of the 1942 classic *Casablanca*, smoked continually throughout the film. Cigarette companies became the exclusive sponsors of popular radio shows in the 1930s and 1940s, like those hosted by comedian Jack Benny and the music program "Your Hit Parade."

Tobacco companies provided soldiers free cigarettes during World War II, creating a new generation of tobacco junkies. Consumers of any age were targeted by the cigarette industry. Candy cigarettes in boxes that featured the names of real brands were marketed to children. Two animated characters, Fred Flintstone and Barney Rubble, appeared in an ad for Winston's cigarettes that ran during the popular primetime TV cartoon series *The Flintstones* in the early 1960s. A 1951 Pall Mall ad starred Santa puffing away.

Smokers knew from experience that cigarettes irritated the throat, so in the 1940s, advertisements for Camels emphasized that that brand was "So mild... you can SMOKE ALL YOU WANT." The brand Kool was named in order to distract users from the harshness of cigarette smoke. "GIVE YOUR THROAT A KOOL VACATION," one ad urged consumers. Although they frequently got in trouble with the Federal Trade Commission for such practices, tobacco companies made absurd, untrue claims that cigarettes provided health benefits, such as aiding weight loss and reducing insomnia. One print ad claimed that, "More doctors smoke Camels than any other cigarette."

Cigarette ads filled hours of airtime in the 1950s and 1960s. In ads hyping Philip Morris cigarettes starring Lucille Ball and Desi Arnaz, stars of the most popular situation comedy of the 1950s, *I Love Lucy*, the two praised the brand because it was a "scientific fact" that Philip Morris is the "only brand proved definitely more mild, definitely less irritating, than any other leading brand." Lucy and Desi also promised that, with Philip Morris cigarettes, you could "smoke with pleasure today" and suffer "no cigarette hangover tomorrow."

In 1954, another cigarette company debuted the "Marlboro Man," a cowboy who roped cattle horseback and enjoyed a drag by an outdoor campfire. The ads promoted the idea that smoking was part of rugged individualism and masculinity. At least four of the actors who played the Marlboro Man in print and TV ads over the next seven decades would die of cancer, as would Desi Arnaz.

As public worries over the health problems caused by smoking increased, one of the less successful brands, Lorillard, pioneered the "filtered" cigarette that would supposedly shield the user from the harmful effects of smoking. Some studies later suggested that the filtered cigarettes actually caused smokers to inhale more deeply and to smoke more cigarettes in order to get the same amount of nicotine. In any case, the cigarette filters in the 1950s and 1960s contained asbestos, a cancer-causing flame retardant.

Tobacco companies continued this propaganda campaign even as the evidence mounted that their product was deadly. In a 1954 study by the American Cancer Society published in the *Journal of the American Medical Association*, researchers concluded "that men with a history of regular cigarette smoking have a considerably higher death rate than men who have never smoked or men who have smoked only cigars or pipes." Nevertheless, American per capita cigarette consumption remained high, reaching 11.5 cigarettes in 1960. This journal article inspired a more intense anti-smoking campaign in the medical profession.

A turning point came when the United States Surgeon General in 1964 issued a report that concluded that cigarettes were not only a cause of lung cancer in both men and women but also of chronic bronchitis. As a result of the study, Congress passed the Federal Cigarette Labeling and Advertising Act of 1965, as well as the Public Health Cigarette Smoking Act of 1969. The laws mandated health warnings on cigarette packages and, as of 1970, banned cigarette commercials on television and radio. In 1988, cigarettes were banned on airline flights lasting two hours or less and were prohibited outright on flights in 1998. Increasingly, cigarettes are banned in public spaces. Nevertheless, about 15 percent of all Americans age 18 or older smoke today.

THOUGHT QUESTION:

1. Why did cigarettes become a more popular way to consume tobacco than pipes, cigars, and chewing tobacco in the United States?

2. What role did the advertising industry play in promoting tobacco abuse?

3. How did the advertising industry try to conceal the dangers of tobacco?

Chapter 28

Kennedy & Johnson and the Vietnam War

Documents

John F. Kennedy Inaugural Address, January 20, 1961

The temperature dropped to 22 degrees and eight inches of snow blanketed Washington, D.C. on January 20, 1961, the first of John F. Kennedy's 1,037 days as president. That morning, the 43-year-old Kennedy would become the second-youngest president in American history (Theodore Roosevelt was the youngest at 42), and the first-ever Catholic chief executive. During the 1960 campaign, opponents attacked his age and his religion, not realizing that these qualities were exactly what attracted young voters like Gonzalo Barrientos, who was a University of Texas freshman the day Kennedy took the oath of office.

From a poor rural background, Barrientos dreamed of a financially comfortable life, but Kennedy's inaugural address changed all that. Barrientos would instead pursue a life dedicated to public service, and, in 1974, he won election as one of the first Latino members of the Texas State Legislature. Even though he struggled with anti-Latino racism growing up, Barrientos said that the new president's words made him feel idealistic and hopeful for a more just future. Kennedy, he said, spoke "for all of us . . . whether you were poor, rich, whatever color, whatever background as an American."

It was not just Barrientos who felt this way. Kennedy wordsmith Theodore Sorensen largely penned the speech, the fourth-shortest inaugural address in U.S. history, although Kennedy penned some of the most memorable passages, including "[A]sk not what your country can do for you but what you can do for your country." It struck those attending in Washington, and the larger television audience estimated at 60 million around the world, as an eloquent promise of American resolve to make the world a better place. The president stirred many with this bold notice: "[W]e shall pay any price, bear any burden, meet any hardship, support any friend, oppose any foe, in order to assure the survival and the success of liberty."

Kennedy aimed his comments not just at Americans but to the leadership of the Soviet Union, which he believed was bent on world domination. More than a call to public service, the speech was a declaration of the new administration's determination to stop the spread of communism, a commitment that in the coming years would claim the lives of more than 58,000 American soldiers and $800 billion in modern dollars. That one snowy day, however, the address seemed to herald a new, idealistic age.

We observe today not a victory of party but a celebration of freedom—symbolizing an end as well as a beginning—signifying renewal as well as change. For I have sworn before you and Almighty God the same solemn oath our forbears prescribed nearly a century and three-quarters ago.

The world is very different now. For man holds in his mortal hands the power to abolish all forms of human poverty and all forms of human life. And yet the same revolutionary beliefs for which our forebears fought are still at issue around the globe—the belief that the rights of man come not from the generosity of the state but from the hand of God.

We dare not forget today that we are the heirs of that first revolution. Let the word go forth from this time and place, to friend and foe alike, that the torch has been passed to a new generation of Americans—born in this century, tempered by war, disciplined by a hard and bitter peace, proud of our ancient heritage—and unwilling to witness or permit the slow undoing of those human rights to which this nation has always been committed, and to which we are committed today at home and around the world.

Let every nation know, whether it wishes us well or ill, that we shall pay any price, bear any burden, meet any hardship, support any friend, oppose any foe to assure the survival and the success of liberty.

This much we pledge—and more.

To those old allies whose cultural and spiritual origins we share, we pledge the loyalty of faithful friends.

. . . To those new states whom we welcome to the ranks of the free, we pledge our word that one form of colonial control shall not have passed away merely to be replaced by a far more iron tyranny. We shall not always expect to find them supporting our view. But we shall always hope to find them strongly supporting their own freedom—and to remember that, in the past, those who foolishly sought power by riding the back of the tiger ended up inside.

. . . Finally, to those nations who would make themselves our adversary, we offer not a pledge but a request: that both sides begin anew the quest for peace, before the dark powers of destruction unleashed by science engulf all humanity in planned or accidental self-destruction.

. . . Let us never negotiate out of fear. But let us never fear to negotiate.

. . . Let both sides seek to invoke the wonders of science instead of its terrors. Together let us explore the stars, conquer the deserts, eradicate disease, tap the ocean depths and encourage the arts and commerce.

. . . All this will not be finished in the first one hundred days. Nor will it be finished in the first one thousand days, nor in the life of this Administration, nor even perhaps in our lifetime on this planet. But let us begin.

. . . In the long history of the world, only a few generations have been granted the role of defending freedom in its hour of maximum danger. I do not shrink from this responsibility—I welcome it. I do not believe that any of us would exchange places with any other people or any other generation. The energy, the faith, the devotion which we bring to this endeavor will light our country and all who serve it—and the glow from that fire can truly light the world.

And so, my fellow Americans: ask not what your country can do for you—ask what you can do for your country.

. . . With a good conscience our only sure reward, with history the final judge of our deeds, let us go forth to lead the land we love, asking His blessing and His help, but knowing that here on earth God's work must truly be our own.

Source: https://www.jfklibrary.org/Asset-Viewer/BqXIEM9F4024ntFl7SVAjA.aspx

THOUGHT QUESTIONS:

1. Why did many who listened to John F. Kennedy's inaugural address interpret it as a call to public service?

2. What was the main focus of Kennedy's speech?

3. What message did Kennedy hope to send to the Soviet Union and its allies around the world in this address?

John F. Kennedy, Report to the American People on Civil Rights, June 11, 1963

Nine years after the United States Supreme Court ruled that segregation in public education was inherently unconstitutional, in the 1954 **Brown v. Board of Education** *decision, the state of Alabama had not complied. The University of Alabama in Tuscaloosa did not have a single African American among the more than 8,000 enrolled at the institution. Alabama Governor George Wallace won the office the previous year promising to resist integration. During his inaugural speech on January 14, 1963, he declared, "Segregation now! Segregation tomorrow! Segregation forever!"*

That same year, however, three African Americans—James Hood, Vivian Malone, and Dave McGlathery—applied to the university, and a federal judge ordered their admission. Wallace had pledged to block the students' entrance. Behind the scenes the governor negotiated with President John Kennedy and his brother, Attorney General Robert Kennedy, to arrange a moment of political theater played out in front of TV cameras that would allow Wallace to appear like he was fulfilling his campaign promises while the court order was carried out.

Hood and Malone pre-registered at a Birmingham courthouse. Wallace stood in front of Foster Auditorium, where new students were required to get their class schedules approved and pay tuition, and physically blocked Hood. The Kennedys agreed to allow Wallace to deliver a symbolic speech. "I stand here today," Wallace said, "as governor of this sovereign state and refuse to willingly submit to illegal usurpation of power by the central government." Armed with a court order, Deputy Assistant Attorney General Nicholas Katzenbach had accompanied the two students, and he asked Gov. Wallace to let Hood and Malone enter the doorway. Wallace said no. In Washington, President Kennedy was informed of this and signed an order federalizing the National Guard. A National Guard commander then asked Wallace to step aside, and he complied.

That night in a national broadcast, the president made his strongest statement ever in support of civil rights in a nationally televised address. Kennedy's speechwriter, Ted Sorensen, did not finish his work until minutes before airtime. The same evening Kennedy spoke, the field secretary of the Mississippi NAACP, Medgar Evers, was assassinated in the driveway of his Jackson, Mississippi home. On June 19, 1963, the president submitted to Congress a sweeping civil rights bill that strengthened voting rights laws and empowered the attorney general to file school desegregation lawsuits, among other reforms.

Good evening my fellow citizens:

This afternoon, following a series of threats and defiant statements, the presence of Alabama National Guardsmen was required on the University of Alabama to carry out the final and unequivocal order of the United States District Court of the Northern District of Alabama. That order called for the admission of two clearly qualified young Alabama residents who happened to have been born Negro.

. . . I hope that every American, regardless of where he lives, will stop and examine his conscience about this and other related incidents. This Nation was founded by men of many nations and backgrounds. It was founded on the principle that all men are created equal, and that the rights of every man are diminished when the rights of one man are threatened.

. . . It ought to be possible for American consumers of any color to receive equal service in places of public accommodation, such as hotels and restaurants and theaters and retail stores, without being forced to resort to demonstrations in the street, and it ought to be possible for American citizens of any color to register to vote in a free election without interference or fear of reprisal.

It ought to be possible, in short, for every American to enjoy the privileges of being American without regard to his race or his color. In short, every American ought to have the right to be treated as he would wish to be treated, as one would wish his children to be treated. But this is not the case.

The Negro baby born in America today, regardless of the section of the Nation in which he is born, has about one-half as much chance of completing high school as a white baby born in the same place on the same day, one-third as much chance of completing college, one-third as much chance of becoming a professional man, twice as much chance of becoming unemployed, about one-seventh as much chance of earning $10,000 a year, a life expectancy which is 7 years shorter, and the prospects of earning only half as much.

This is not a sectional issue. Difficulties over segregation and discrimination exist in every city, in every State of the Union, producing in many cities a rising tide of discontent that threatens the public safety.

. . . We are confronted primarily with a moral issue. It is as old as the scriptures and is as clear as the American Constitution.

The heart of the question is whether all Americans are to be afforded equal rights and equal opportunities, whether we are going to treat our fellow Americans as we want to be treated. If an American, because his skin is dark, cannot eat lunch in a restaurant open to the public, if he cannot send his children to the best public school available, if he cannot vote for the public officials who will represent him, if, in short, he cannot enjoy the full and free life which all of us want, then who among us would be content to have the color of his skin changed and stand in his place? Who among us would then be content with the counsels of patience and delay?

. . . We preach freedom around the world, and we mean it, and we cherish our freedom here at home, but are we to say to the world, and, much more importantly, to each other that this is the land of the free except for the Negroes; that we have no second-class citizens except Negroes; that we have no class or caste system, no ghettoes, no master race except with respect to Negroes?

... The fires of frustration and discord are burning in every city, North and South, where legal remedies are not at hand. Redress is sought in the streets, in demonstrations, parades, and protests which create tensions and threaten violence and threaten lives.

We face, therefore, a moral crisis as a country and as a people. It cannot be met by repressive police action. It cannot be left to increased demonstrations in the streets. It cannot be quieted by token moves or talk. It is time to act in the Congress, in your State and local legislative body and, above all, in all of our daily lives.

... Next week I shall ask the Congress of the United States to act, to make a commitment it has not fully made in this century to the proposition that race has no place in American life or law.

... I am, therefore, asking the Congress to enact legislation giving all Americans the right to be served in facilities which are open to the public—hotels, restaurants, theaters, retail stores, and similar establishments.

... I am also asking the Congress to authorize the Federal Government to participate more fully in lawsuits designed to end segregation in public education.

This is one country. It has become one country because all of us and all the people who came here had an equal chance to develop their talents.

... As I have said before, not every child has an equal talent or an equal ability or an equal motivation, but they should have an equal right to develop their talent and their ability and their motivation, to make something of themselves.

We have a right to expect that the Negro community will be responsible, will uphold the law, but they have a right to expect that the law will be fair, that the Constitution will be color blind ...

Source: https://www.jfklibrary.org/Asset-Viewer/LH8F_0Mzv0e6Ro1yEm74Ng.aspx

THOUGHT QUESTIONS:

1. What are the moral arguments President Kennedy made in favor of integration in his June 11, 1963 speech on civil rights?

2. Why did the president, the attorney general, and Alabama Gov. George Wallace choreograph in advance the drama that took place at the entrance of Foster Auditorium when African-American students attempted to pay their tuition at the University of Alabama in 1963?

3. What does President Kennedy suggest might be the effect of continued segregation on the image of the United States in the world?

Lyndon Johnson
Special Message to the Congress Proposing a Nationwide War on the Sources of Poverty, March 16, 1964

Because of his origins in the highly conservative and segregationist state of Texas, liberals worried about Lyndon Johnson's political intentions when John Kennedy's assassination on November 22, 1963 thrust him into the presidency. Johnson, however, skillfully used the memory of the widely mourned Kennedy to win support for anti-poverty legislation, a program he dubbed "The Great Society."

Some called Johnson the "Texas Tornado" during his White House years. Johnson saw the "Great Society" as his destiny. Although it was vague in its original conception, the president wanted the Great Society to complete his hero FDR's mission. In Johnson's mind, in a country as wealthy as the United States, no one should go hungry, no child should be denied a first-class education, and retirement should not be a time of fear and privation.

In the 1964 elections, the Democrats had won 2 additional Senate seats and 37 more seats in the House of Representatives. The Democrats for the first time could pass legislation without watering down proposals in order to win the support of obstructionist conservative southern Democrats. In the first half of 1965 alone, the administration submitted 87 bills to Congress, and by the time Congress recessed in October, 84 laws had passed.

Aimed at the 20 percent of the American population living below the poverty line, Johnson fought what he called the "war on poverty" through programs like the Job Corps designed to provide training to historically underemployed populations. Administered through the Office of Economic Opportunity, under the Job Corps, about 25,000 welfare families received job training, 35,000 college students were placed in work/study programs, and another 35,000 adults were taught how to read and write.

Among other anti-poverty programs, the Johnson administration boosted Social Security payments to senior citizens and created the Neighborhood Youth Corps in 49 cities and 11 rural communities. The NYC provided jobs for young people between ages 16 and 21 to prevent them from dropping out of school because of financial need. Under Volunteers in Service to America or VISTA, 8,000 Americans worked in a domestic version of the Peace Corps in which young Americans offered their services to the poor as teachers, day care workers, job skills counselors, and nutritionists. The availability of financial aid and food stamps for the poor also greatly increased under the more generously funded Aid to Families with Dependent Children (AFDC) program. Johnson made his plea for these programs in the following address:

To the Congress of the United States:

We are citizens of the richest and most fortunate nation in the history of the world. One hundred and eighty years ago we were a small country struggling for survival on the margin of a hostile land.

Today we have established a civilization of free men which spans an entire continent.

With the growth of our country has come opportunity for our people—opportunity to educate our children, to use our energies in productive work, to increase our leisure—opportunity for almost every American to hope that through work and talent he could create a better life for himself and his family.

The path forward has not been an easy one.

But we have never lost sight of our goal: an America in which every citizen shares all the opportunities of his society, in which every man has a chance to advance his welfare to the limit of his capacities.

We have come a long way toward this goal.

We still have a long way to go.

The distance which remains is the measure of the great unfinished work of our society.

To finish that work I have called for a national war on poverty. Our objective: total victory.

There are millions of Americans—one fifth of our people—who have not shared in the abundance which has been granted to most of us, and on whom the gates of opportunity have been closed.

What does this poverty mean to those who endure it?

It means a daily struggle to secure the necessities for even a meager existence. It means that the abundance, the comforts, the opportunities they see all around them are beyond their grasp.

Worst of all, it means hopelessness for the young.

The young man or woman who grows up without a decent education, in a broken home, in a hostile and squalid environment, in ill health or in the face of racial injustice—that young man or woman is often trapped in a life of poverty.

He does not have the skills demanded by a complex society. He does not know how to acquire those skills. He faces a mounting sense of despair which drains initiative and ambition and energy.

... [W]e must ... strike down all the barriers which keep many from using those exits.

... Our fight against poverty will be an investment in the most valuable of our resources—the skills and strength of our people.

And in the future, as in the past, this investment will return its cost many fold to our entire economy.

If we can raise the annual earnings of 10 million among the poor by only $1,000 we will have added 14 billion dollars a year to our national output. In addition we can make important reductions in public assistance payments which now cost us 4 billion dollars a year, and in the large costs of fighting crime and delinquency, disease and hunger.

... Poverty is not a simple or an easy enemy.

It cannot be driven from the land by a single attack on a single front. Were this so we would have conquered poverty long ago.

Today, for the first time in our history, we have the power to strike away the barriers ... to full participation in our society. Having the power, we have the duty.

The Congress is charged by the Constitution to "provide ... for the general welfare of the United States." Our present abundance is a measure of its success in fulfilling that duty. Now Congress is being asked to extend that welfare to all our people.

... We are fully aware that this program will not eliminate all the poverty in America in a few months or a few years. Poverty is deeply rooted and its causes are many.

But this program will show the way to new opportunities for millions of our fellow citizens.

... On similar occasions in the past we have often been called upon to wage war against foreign enemies which threatened our freedom. Today we are asked to declare war on a domestic enemy which threatens the strength of our nation and the welfare of our people.

If we now move forward against this enemy—if we can bring to the challenges of peace the same determination and strength which has brought us victory in war—then this day and this Congress will have won a secure and honorable place in the history of the nation, and the enduring gratitude of generations of Americans yet to come.

Source: *Public Papers of the President of the United States: Lyndon B. Johnson, 1963-1964* (1965)

THOUGHT QUESTIONS:

1. Why were some liberals skeptical of Lyndon Johnson's political priorities when he became president after John Kennedy's assassination?

2. How did the struggles of the poor negatively affect American society as a whole, according to President Lyndon Johnson in his speech announcing a "war on poverty"?

3. In what way does Johnson suggest that tackling poverty is a Constitutional duty of Congress?

Report of the President's Commission on the Assassination of President Kennedy
September 24, 1964

From the moment that Lee Harvey Oswald fired three shots from the Texas School Book Depository in Dallas, Texas, murdering President John F. Kennedy on November 22, 1963, Americans have disbelieved that official account of the assassination: that Oswald, an alienated loner and former Marine sharpshooter who had at one point defected to the Soviet Union, acted alone.

After shooting Kennedy, Oswald left his workplace at the depository in downtown Dallas. Along the way, he fatally shot Dallas police officer J.D. Tippit before hiding in the Texas Theatre, in the Oak Cliff neighborhood, where Dallas police arrested him. Two days later, as Oswald was being transferred to a new cell, a Dallas nightclub owner, Jack Ruby, shot Oswald to death.

The president's murder, and the rapid killing of his suspected assassin, spawned a host of conspiracy theories that blamed the Russians (locked in a Cold War struggle for global domination with the United States), the Cubans (because the Kennedy administration tried to overthrow the communist government of Fidel Castro and tried to kill Castro himself), the Mafia (angered by the work of JFK's brother, Robert Kennedy, as a lawyer for a Senate committee investigating organized crime in the 1950s), Teamsters Union boss Jimmy Hoffa (jailed for corruption after prosecution by the Kennedy administration), and even Vice President Johnson (motivated supposedly by a lust for presidential power). Many African Americans believed that Kennedy had been martyred by white racists because of his support (however tepid) for civil rights.

According to a 2017 poll commissioned by the FiveThirtyEight.com website, only a third of Americans now believe that Oswald was the lone assassin. Sixty-one percent believe that a conspiracy was behind the president's death, that number including a majority in almost every demographic category.

Lyndon Johnson himself had concerns about the possible involvement of Russians and others, and knew that his predecessor's death could dangerously escalate Cold War tensions. Seeking to quell suspicions, he appointed a blue-ribbon panel chaired by Supreme Court Chief Justice Earl Warren and including future President Gerald Ford, then a congressman from Michigan, to investigate the assassination. The Warren Commission, which released its report September 24, 1964, concluded that Oswald acted alone, but doubts persisted. Psychologically, Americans were not willing to accept that a marginal man like Oswald could bring down the most powerful person on Earth and alter the course of American, and even world, history. In the decade that followed Kennedy's death, a period that would see government lies about the Vietnam War exposed and the revelations about the Watergate scandal during the Nixon administration, the assassination in Dallas ushered in an era of cynicism.

These conclusions represent the reasoned judgment of all members of the Commission . . .

The shots which killed President Kennedy and wounded Governor Connally were fired from the sixth floor window at the southeast corner of the Texas School Book Depository . . .

The shots which killed President Kennedy and wounded Governor Connally were fired by Lee Harvey Oswald . . .

Oswald killed Dallas Police Patrolman J. D. Tippitt approximately 45 minutes after the assassination . . .

Within 80 minutes of the assassination and 35 minutes of the Tippitt killing Oswald resisted arrest at the theatre by attempting to shoot another Dallas police officer . . .

The Commission has reached the following conclusions concerning the killing of Oswald by Jack Ruby on November 24, 1963 . . .

There is no evidence to support the rumor that Ruby may have been assisted by any members of the Dallas Police Department in the killing of Oswald . . .

The Commission has found no evidence that either Lee Harvey Oswald or Jack Ruby was part of any conspiracy, domestic or foreign, to assassinate President Kennedy . . .

The Commission could not make any definitive determination of Oswald's motives. It has endeavored to isolate factors which contributed . . .

a) His deep-rooted resentment of all authority which was expressed in a hostility toward every society in which he lived;

(b) His inability to enter into meaningful relationships with people, and a continuous pattern of rejecting his environment in favor of new surroundings;

(c) His urge to try to find a place in history and despair at times over failures in his various undertakings;

(d) His capacity for violence as evidenced by his attempt to kill General Walker;

(e) His avowed commitment to Marxism and communism, as he understood the terms and developed his own interpretation of them; this was expressed by his antagonism toward the United States, by his defection to the Soviet Union, by his failure to be reconciled with life in the United States even after his disenchantment with the Soviet Union, and by his efforts, though frustrated, to go to Cuba . . .

On the basis of these findings the Commission has concluded that Lee Harvey Oswald was the assassin of President Kennedy.

Source: *Report of the President's Commission on the Assassination of President Kennedy* (Washington, D.C.: United States Government Printing Office, 1964), https://www.archives.gov/research/jfk/warren-commission-report/letter.html

THOUGHT QUESTIONS:

1. Why did the public not believe that Lee Harvey Oswald was the sole assassin of John F. Kennedy?

2. Whom did the public blame for President Kennedy's murder?

3. What has been the impact of the Kennedy assassination on the public's trust in the government?

Vignettes

The Burning of Norman Morrison

Norman Morrison committed the most riveting and shocking act in the history of the young anti-Vietnam War movement on November 2, 1965, when the 31-year-old Quaker, inspired by the protest of Buddhist monks in South Vietnam two years earlier, doused himself with gasoline, struck a match, and burned himself to death in front of the Pentagon.

Morrison earlier that day left the family's Baltimore home with their one-year-old daughter, Emily, and drove to the Pentagon complex in northern Virginia, the headquarters of the most powerful military in the world. Accounts vary, but many witnesses said Morrison, a pacifist, handed Emily to someone just before setting himself ablaze at 5:20 in the evening, just under the window of Defense Secretary Robert McNamara's office. Morrison would be one of eight Americans who burned themselves to death in protest of the Vietnam War.

Morrison had been moved by an account about the napalm attack by American forces on the South Vietnamese village of Duc Tho published the previous day in the leftist newspaper *I.F. Stone's Weekly*. The paper quoted a French priest crying, "I have seen my faithful burned up in napalm. I have seen the bodies of women and children blown to bits."

Norman's wife Anne admitted later that her memories of that traumatic day are cloudy, but she believes she discussed the article with her husband just before lunch. After she left, Norman Morrison cut the article out, and before his suicide he stopped by a U.S. Post Office and mailed a letter telling his young wife, "Know that I love thee, but I must act for the children of the priest's village." Ann received the letter after his death became international news.

Secretary of Defense Robert McNamara, who served under presidents John Kennedy and Lyndon Johnson, did not witness Norman Morrison's fiery suicide, but said the event haunted him. In the early 1960s, McNamara pushed for an increased American troop presence in Vietnam, but by the time he resigned as Defense Secretary February 29, 1968, he realized that the war a blunder. Anne Morrison Welsh said it touched her when McNamara admitted his mistakes publicly (though he put ultimate responsibility on President Johnson and not himself).

"In 1995 I read Robert McNamara's *In Retrospect* and felt moved to express my appreciation to him for his acknowledgment that the war was a mistake," she said. "I just felt it was unusual for a public official to admit error, even decades later in hindsight. So I wrote him a letter. It obviously moved him, perhaps in part because most of the reactions to his book were negative, even venomous."

Welsh said McNamara phoned her in response. "We had an amazingly relaxed conversation, almost as if we knew each other. He talked about how he hadn't been able to talk to his family about Norman's death even though they were all deeply affected by it and wanted to talk. I said that I hadn't talked enough about it with my children either in those years."

The reconciliation between McNamara and Anne Morrison Welsh would not be the norm in post-Vietnam America. In the years that followed the Kennedy-Johnson debacle in Vietnam, the war more often divided than united public opinion. Just as the shadow of the Civil War shaped American politics for a half-century after the last shot was fired, political debates since the 1960s have largely centered on the meaning of the war and its ultimately unsuccessful conclusion.

The Vietnam War has been an issue in almost every presidential election in the ensuing four decades. Dissatisfaction with Johnson's war helped Richard Nixon win the presidency in 1968, and Nixon would cruise to reelection in 1972 partly by accusing Democratic nominee George McGovern of being soft on the North Vietnamese and partly by announcing a peace agreement with the communists just before Election Day. Democrat Jimmy Carter promoted his presidential bid by emphasizing his honesty to a public well aware of the dishonesty of Johnson and Nixon on the Vietnam issue.

Republican presidents Ronald Reagan and George H.W. Bush won the White House vowing to restore American military might supposedly lost in the wake of the Vietnam fiasco. After directing a brief and successful war in response to the invasion of Kuwait by Iraqi dictator Saddam Hussein, in 1991, Bush spoke of the U.S. overcoming a "Vietnam Syndrome" of defeatism. Controversies erupted over prominent politicians' use of college deferments or National Guard service to avoid Vietnam combat: Bush's vice president, Dan Quayle; Democratic President Bill Clinton; and Republican President George W. Bush, to name a few.

America was involved in two wars in 2004, in Afghanistan and Iraq, but much of the presidential campaign centered on George Bush's National Guard service and on Republican efforts to discredit the two Purple Hearts earned during the Vietnam War by Democratic nominee John Kerry. What had been the longest war in American history when U.S. involvement ended in 1973 remained a political emotional landmine decades later.

THOUGHT QUESTIONS:

1. What moved Norman Morrison to set himself on fire on November 2, 1965?

2. What do the events that led to the friendship of Anne Morrison Welsh and Robert McNamara suggest about the emotional impact of the Vietnam War on Americans after the conflict's conclusion?

3. How did the Vietnam War shadow American politics in the four decades after the United States withdrew from Southeast Asia in 1973?

Black and White in American Film and Television

In the mainstream media, African Americans had been mostly invisible until the post-World War II era. In the movies, in the 1950s and 1960s, African-American actor Sidney Poitier became the first black movie superstar, but his career revealed the limits of what whites would accept from black performers. The handsome, deep-voiced, Bahamian-born actor worked a series of low-paying jobs and slept in the restroom of a bus terminal when he moved to New York as a teenager. A stage actor, his first big movie break came in the 1950 film *No Way Out* in which he portrayed a doctor with a white racist as a patient.

Even as the civil rights era heated up, Poitier played a series of characters who were imminently reasonable and idealistic and often middle class. By the end of 1950s, he played the leading man in civil rights-friendly films like *The Defiant Ones* (1958) in which he portrayed a convict chained to a white prisoner (Tony Curtis). The two escape, become unchained, and at one point Poitier rescues Curtis, which results in Poitier's recapture. This movie became one of Poitier's biggest hits and earned him his first Oscar nomination for best actor, but white and black audiences perceived the message differently.

Older African Americans took pride in the prominent roles of Poitier and his dignified, intelligent demeanor. They saw the actor as groundbreaking. To many younger African Americans, it seemed that Poitier's characters sacrificed themselves in the interest of white characters. Their hopes, fears and aspirations were surrendered in service to the usual white hero. Poitier's characters struck some younger viewers as "Uncle Toms," black people who deliberately subordinate themselves to whites. Poitier finally won a Best Actor Academy Award for his role in the 1963 film *Lilies of the Field*. Poitier played a likable former soldier traveling across the Arizona desert who discovers a group of white nuns hoping to build a chapel.

In *Guess Who's Coming to Dinner* (1967) he depicted a prosperous, well-respected doctor nominated for the Nobel Prize who travels to the suburbs to meet his white fiancée's parents, played by Katharine Hepburn and Spencer Tracy. Poitier does not wear the African-inspired dashikis popular among many young Black Nationalists of the time, but instead is dressed in a perfect bourgeois suit and tie. Poitier's character does not shout "Black Power!" His future in-laws express the mild discomfort with their daughter's romantic choice necessary for melodrama, but they mouth no ugly racism and everyone is at peace in the end. The film was so tame it did not inspire much controversy, even in the South.

On television, the treatment of African Americans was often similarly condescending. A rare exception challenging such limits placed on black performers was the science fiction series *Star Trek*, cancelled by NBC after just three seasons in 1969. Although its depiction of women was sexist, *Star Trek* highlighted a rare multi-racial, multi-ethnic cast. The Starship *Enterprise* featured an East Asian officer, Mr. Sulu, a nationalistic Russian, Mr. Chekov, and a proudly Scottish engineer stereotypically named "Scotty." The two lead actors, William Shatner and Leonard Nimoy (playing Captain James Kirk and Mr. Spock), both had Jewish ancestry, a rarity in American television at the time. The Mr. Spock character, born of a human mother and a father from the planet "Vulcan," could be seen as a metaphor for the increasingly diverse, hybrid nature of American culture in 1960s.

Meanwhile, the ship's communications officer, Lieutenant Uhura, played by African-American actress Nichelle Nichols, proudly bore an African name. Comedian and actress Whoopi Goldberg later recalled what a powerful impact seeing a beautiful black actress not playing a cleaning lady had on her as a child.

"Well, when I was nine years old *Star Trek* came on. I looked at it and I went screaming through the house, 'Come here, mum, everybody, come quick, come quick, there's a black lady on television and she ain't no maid!' I knew right then and there I could be anything I wanted to be . . ."

Black actors on *Star Trek* often broke out of the subservient roles typical in movies of the era, portraying doctors and other professionals. In one episode, Shakespearean actor William Marshall (who would play an African vampire called "Blacula" in a 1970s film) portrayed a character hailed as the galaxy's greatest computer genius.

In a 1969 episode, "Plato's Stepchildren," Kirk and Uhura engaged in the first interracial kiss on an American dramatic series (the African-American entertainer Sammy Davis, Jr., briefly kissed singer Nancy Sinatra on a variety program two years earlier). Gene Roddenberry, the series producer, struggled with NBC censors who were afraid of negative reaction from TV stations in the South. Even though the amorous Kirk was portrayed in the series as relentlessly pursuing women across the galaxy, even aliens, he and Uhura are depicted as being forced into their kiss by cruel extraterrestrials with telekinetic powers. Nichols later noted, "We received one of the largest batches of fan mail ever, all of it very positive . . . almost no one found the kiss offensive." The audience, even in the South, was apparently ahead of the Hollywood television studio, Desilu, which produced the show.

Though it drew small audiences while broadcast by NBC, *Star Trek* became vastly more popular as reruns in syndication, sparking a revived interest in science fiction and creating an audience for the enormously successful *Star Wars* series of movies, which began in 1977, and several space-themed films by director Steven Spielberg, including *Close Encounters of the Third Kind*.

THOUGHT QUESTIONS:

1. What different reactions did white and black audiences have to Sidney Poitier's film performances in the 1950s and 1960s?

2. In what ways did the *Star Trek* television series revolutionize the depiction of race in the American media?

3. What was the long-term social impact of *Star Trek*?

Celebrities against the Vietnam War

The Vietnam War divided American entertainers, writers, and other celebrities as much as it did the rest of the country. Conservative older Hollywood stars like John Wayne, the star of numerous Westerns and war films, strongly backed the war as did comedian Bob Hope who frequently travelled to Vietnam to entertain the troops in live performances broadcast as television specials.

Other celebrities and artists opposed the war such as the openly gay Beat poet Allen Ginsberg, a longtime leftist. Ginsberg participated in the mass protest at the Army Terminal in Oakland, California, October 15, 1965, in which members of the Hell's Angels motorcycle gang tore down signs and beat protestors they called "communists." Ginsberg, Ken Kesey (the author of the novel *One Flew Over the Cuckoo's Nest*), and others pleaded with Angels' leader Sonny Barger not to disrupt the next day's protests, and they spent the night taking LSD. There was no trouble with the Angels at the next day's protest.

The public reacted with greater surprise when Dr. Benjamin Spock, the author of the 1946 bestseller *Baby and Child Care*, became a peace activist in the early 1960s, joining the Committee for a Sane Nuclear Policy, which opposed the use and spread of nuclear weapons. In 1967 he signed "A Call to Resist Illegitimate Authority," a document that argued "the war is unconstitutional and illegal. Congress has not declared a war as required by the Constitution." Spock and other signatories such as the Reverend William Sloane Coffin encouraged young men not to cooperate with military conscription by refusing to turn in their draft registration cards, to claim conscientious objector status in order to avoid combat duty, and urged soldiers in Vietnam to refuse to follow "illegal and immoral orders."

Jane Fonda, the daughter of film star Henry Fonda who was much beloved by the establishment, became a highly visible anti-war activist in the 1970s and sparked a ferocious backlash when she visited Hanoi, the North Vietnamese capital, in 1972. She accused the American military of intentionally bombing dikes along the Red River in an attempt to cause mass flooding, and disruptions in North Vietnamese farming. She was photographed sitting behind a North Vietnamese anti-aircraft gun as she smiled and laughed. The communist military used such weapons to defend against American air attacks at the time, shooting down American planes. When she returned home, American supporters of the war dubbed her "Hanoi Jane" and called her a traitor.

John Lennon, a singer and guitarist for the British band the Beatles, the most popular rock group in the world, plunged into anti-war activism even before he and his wife, Japanese-born performance artist Yoko Ono, moved to New York City in 1971. He recorded the popular protest anthem "Give Peace a Chance" in 1969 and had one of the biggest hits of his solo career, the pacifist-themed "Imagine," in 1971. His outspokenness against the Vietnam War drew the hostile attention of President Richard Nixon's administration, which would try to deport him from 1972 to 1974.

The boxer Muhammad Ali became the most famous war dissenter not just in the United States but the world. Ali had first gained fame as Cassius Clay, the brash young boxer who claimed a gold medal at the Summer Olympics in Rome in 1960. In a culture that expected deference even from African-American celebrities, Clay taunted his future opponents, proclaiming, "I am the greatest!" and changing his name upon his conversion to Islam by the radical black minister Malcolm X.

In 1967, he refused induction after being drafted, declaring, "I ain't got no quarrel with the Viet Cong. No Viet Cong ever called me Nigger." Ali went further, questioning the justice of the war. "Why should they ask me to put on a uniform and go ten thousand miles from home and drop bombs and bullets on brown people in Vietnam while so-called Negro people in Louisville are treated like dogs and denied simple human rights?" The federal government prosecuted him for draft dodging, and a jury convicted him. He stayed out of prison while lawyers appealed, but boxing authorities stripped him of his heavyweight title and banned him from fighting. He was not allowed to travel, and, instead, he earned a living from speaking fees. Ali lectured at Harvard and other universities where anti-war sentiment grew the strongest. The U.S. Supreme Court overturned his conviction on June 28, 1971. In the 1970s, Ali earned earned back his heavyweight crown in the ring.

THOUGHT QUESTIONS:

1. What kind of influence do celebrities have over American politics?

2. Why did Jane Fonda's visit to North Vietnam in 1972 become so controversial?

3. What likely motivated the federal government's persistent efforts to deport musician John Lennon and to imprison boxer Muhammad Ali?

Agent Orange

For some American soldiers serving in Vietnam, technology made killing an abstract, distant experience. This, in turn, encouraged an indifference to Vietnamese lives. More than 58,000 Americans died in the war, and 300,000 suffered injuries, making it the fourth costliest in American history and creating psychological scars still shaping American politics six decades later. These numbers, however, pale alongside Vietnamese casualties. The South Vietnamese military suffered 224,000 deaths and 1 million injured. The government of Vietnam announced in 1995 that 1.1 million communist troops, including the North Vietnamese Army and the Viet Cong, died; and 600,000 were wounded during the American war from 1964 to 1973. The number of civilian casualties, North and South, remains controversial, but most estimates place the number between 1 and 2 million.

The American air war played a prominent role in Vietnamese military and civilian deaths. In 1961 and 1962, the U.S. military began experimentation with a variety of counter-insurgency tactics aimed at crippling the Viet Cong guerillas. Military scientists developed defoliants aimed at poisoning food supplies for the communist forces and stripping bare the trees in forests and jungles where the VC camped and launched surprise attacks. The plan was to deny the VC food and places to hide. In the six years between 1962 and 1968, the United States military sprayed almost 700,000 acres of farmland with

"Agent Blue," a chemical compound damaging rice crops, which caused hunger among peasants in the Vietnamese countryside.

Pilots participating in Operation Ranch Hand dropped highly carcinogenic chemical compounds like Agent Orange beginning in January 1962, with 100 million pounds dumped over four million acres in South Vietnam over the next eight years. The bombings and the defoliants destroyed about half of the country's timberlands.

Decades after this campaign, Vietnamese, as well as American veterans of the Vietnam War, suffered from side effects of Agent Orange and other defoliants, including chronic lymphocytic leukemia, Hodgkin's disease, lung cancer, non-Hodgkin lymphoma, multiple myeloma, and prostate cancer. After the war, American veterans reported abnormally high rates of children born with spina bifida, or lacking arms and/or legs, or with Down Syndrome. Agencies like the Red Cross estimate that by 2003, a half-million Vietnamese had died from health complications caused by Agent Orange and other chemicals used during the war and that 650,000 still suffered health problems.

Americans also dropped 400,000 tons of bombs containing a petroleum-based jelly made of polystyrene, gasoline and benzene known as Napalm-B. This fire-starting agent burns at 1,000 degrees Fahrenheit, and the military used it to destroy villages suspected of being enemy bases, to clear areas with heavy foliage to allow airborne surveillance, and to terrify the Viet Cong and their supporters. Victims of napalm suffered as the chemical created a burning sensation and ate away skin to the muscle layer.

One American soldier later recalled witnessing an accidental napalm attack against a friendly village to the United States. He watched as another soldier "hurdled the concertina wire [surrounding the village] . . . and pulled [victims] screaming out of the fire, but there was no way to put out napalm; it was made to cling to human flesh and keep eating inward until it burned itself out."

One nurse spent part of her tour of duty working in the "Vietnamese ward" at a hospital in Chu Lai. She frequently dealt with the casualties of America's chemical warfare. "Mostly we had women and children and elderly men," she said. The napalm, she recalled, "had a really pungent odor of burned flesh and chemicals. [The Vietnamese had a] beautiful country and their homes and family were torn apart and yet they managed to survive. They took care of one another and would absorb people from other families who weren't even blood relatives."

THOUGHT QUESTION:

1. Did military technology affect the relationship between American soldiers and Marines and the local population during the Vietnam War?

2. How did America's use of chemical weapons impact the Vietnamese environment?

3. What were the health effects of chemical weapons the United States used during the Vietnamese War like Agent Orange, Agent Blue, and napalm on the health of the Vietnamese population, and that of American soldiers?

Chapter 29

The Nightmare Year, 1968

Documents

Excerpt from Report of the National Advisory Commission on
Civil Disorders, February 29, 1968

President Lyndon Johnson hoped that the blizzard of reform legislation passed early in his presidency, such as the establishment of Medicare and Medicaid, the 1964 Civil Rights Act and the 1965 Voting Rights Act, had laid a solid foundation for what he called "The Great Society." Soon, he hoped, poverty would recede and many racial barriers would be lifted. Though he was not naïve, he must have been surprised by the deep rage at centuries of economic exploitation, police brutality, job discrimination and poverty that erupted in black and brown neighborhoods across the United States in spite of the passage of these measures.

On August 11, 1965, five days after Johnson signed the Voting Rights Act, a riot exploded in the mostly African American Watts neighborhood of Los Angeles. The riot began when a white police officer arrested an African American. Rumors spread rapidly through the crowd that police had beaten the arrested man's mother and pregnant girlfriend. About 5,000 Watts residents, having long suffered racial profiling and rough treatment at the hands of the Los Angeles police, set buildings ablaze, looted stores, and fired handguns. The Watts Riot lasted for six days and took the lives of 34 people (32 of them black), injuring another 900, leaving hundreds homeless, and destroying neighborhood businesses.

Between April and December of 1967, 159 race riots raged across the United States, beginning in Cleveland. Most of these uprisings occurred between June and August, a time that became known as the "long, hot summer." These uprisings cost at least 77 lives and a total of a half-billion dollars in property damage in that three-month period.

Anger over high unemployment, low-quality schools, and police harassment, beatings and arbitrary arrests of young African men ignited rioting between July 12 and 17 of that year in Newark, New Jersey. The worst urban upheaval exploded in Detroit on July 23 after police conducted a series of raids on buildings where after-hours drinking and illegal gambling regularly took place. Police conducted mass arrests, hauling 82 to jail. By 5 A.M., someone had thrown a bottle at a police car window, even as someone else threw a garbage can through a store window.

As a Molotov cocktail set one building on fire, twenty-five mph winds spread the flames across the city. Fire consumed a 100-block area, while violence killed 33 African Americans and 10 whites. This revolt caused $250 million in damages to homes and businesses. Michigan Governor George Romney described Detroit as looking like it "had been bombed on the west side." President Lyndon Johnson impaneled an 11-member commission chaired by Illinois Gov. Otto Kerner, Jr. to examine the causes of the 1967 urban riots and to recommend solutions. What became known as the "Kerner Commission" issued its report early in 1968, a year marked by riots in the wake of Martin Luther King, Jr.'s assassination on April 4. Riots eruped in New York, Washington, D.C., Pittsburgh, Baltimore, Kansas City, Detroit, and in numerous other cities as well as in Chicago during the Democratic National Convention on August 26-29.

The summer of 1967 again brought racial disorders to American cities, and with them shock, fear and bewilderment to the nation.

The worst came during a two-week period in July, first in Newark and then in Detroit. Each set off a chain reaction in neighboring communities.

On July 28, 1967, the President of the United States established this Commission and directed us to answer three basic questions:

What happened?

Why did it happen?

What can be done to prevent it from happening again?

To respond to these questions, we have undertaken a broad range of studies and investigations. We have visited the riot cities; we have heard many witnesses; we have sought the counsel of experts across the country. . .

This is our basic conclusion: Our nation is moving toward two societies, one black, one white—separate and unequal.

. . . This deepening racial division is not inevitable. The movement apart can be reversed. Choice is still possible. Our principal task is to define that choice and to press for a national resolution.

... What white Americans have never fully understood but what the Negro can never forget—is that white society is deeply implicated in the ghetto. White institutions created it, white institutions maintain it, and white society condones it.

... Our recommendations embrace three basic principles:

- To mount programs on a scale equal to the dimension of the problems;

- To aim these programs for high impact in the immediate future in order to close the gap between promise and performance;

- To undertake new initiatives and experiments that can change the system of failure and frustration that now dominates the ghetto and weakens our society.

These programs will require unprecedented levels of funding and performance, but they neither probe deeper nor demand more than the problems which called them forth. There can be no higher priority for national action and no higher claim on the nation's conscience.

Unless there are sharp changes in the factors influencing Negro settlement patterns within metropolitan areas, there is little doubt that the trend toward Negro majorities will continue.

Providing employment for the swelling Negro ghetto population will require ... opening suburban residential areas to Negroes and encouraging them to move closer to industrial centers.

... Cities will have Negro majorities by 1985 and the suburbs ringing them will remain largely all white unless there are major changes in Negro fertility rates, in migration settlement patterns or public policy.

... It is now time to end the destruction and the violence, not only in the streets of the ghetto, but in the lives of people.

Source: Report of the National Advisory Commission on Civil Disorders (Washington, D.C.: U.S. Government Printing Office, 1968).

THOUGHT QUESTIONS:

1. What were the causes of the urban uprisings that happened between 1965 and 1967?

2. What was the nature of American society by 1967 according to the Kerner Commission?

3. What were some solutions offered by the Kerner Commission to the problem of urban unrest?

President Lyndon Baines Johnson
Address to the Nation
March 31, 1968

Inflation, urban riots, and the white backlash against civil rights legislation cast a giant shadow on President Lyndon Johnson's chances for re-election in 1968. The Tet Offensive launched by the communist North Vietnamese government and its allies in the South on January 30, while ultimately stopped by American armed forces, caught Johnson and the U.S. military brass by surprise and destroyed the credibility of the Johnson administration's claims that victory in Southeast Asia was around the corner. The Tet Offensive led to the strong showing of anti-Vietnam War presidential candidate Eugene McCarthy against Johnson in the 1968 Democratic primary in New Hampshire. Newly installed Defense Secretary Clark Clifford and others in the Johnson administration now believed the Vietnam War could not be won.

At a March 25 White House meeting on the war, Johnson's confidant McGeorge Bundy, a former national security advisor, told the president, "We must begin steps to disengage." The president realized that if he no longer had the confidence of his own inner circle, he could not hold the confidence of the American people. Negative feedback inside the White House, and McCarthy's performance in New Hampshire moved the president toward making a decision he had contemplated at least since the fall of 1967.

Johnson was already scheduled to deliver a prime time television speech updating the public on the Vietnam War on March 31. The speech would call for the halt of American bombing in North Vietnam as a gesture aimed at restarting truce talks. Clifford got the president to change the first line of his speech from "I want to talk to you about the War in Vietnam" to "I want to talk to you about peace in Vietnam." Johnson told his speech writers that he would provide the concluding remarks himself.

At the end of his address, Johnson caught his friends, advisors, even his family, and most of all the nation by surprise when he looked up from the paper copy of his speech and said directly into the camera that would not seek another four years as president. The chance for victory in Vietnam and the future he hoped to build, which he called "the Great Society," lay in tatters.

Tonight I want to speak to you of peace in Vietnam and Southeast Asia.

No other question so preoccupies our people. No other dream so absorbs the 250 million human beings who live in that part of the world. No other goal motivates American policy in Southeast Asia.

For years, representatives of our Government and others have traveled the world—seeking to find a basis for peace talks.

. . . Hanoi denounced this offer, both privately and publicly. Even while the search for peace was going on, North Vietnam rushed their preparations for a savage assault on the people, the government, and the allies of South Vietnam.

Their attack—during the Tet holidays—failed to achieve its principal objectives.

. . . They are, it appears, trying to make 1968 the year of decision in South Vietnam—the year that brings, if not final victory or defeat, at least a turning point in the struggle.

This much is clear: If they do mount another round of heavy attacks, they will not succeed in destroying the fighting power of South Vietnam and its allies.

But tragically, this is also clear: Many men—on both sides of the struggle—will be lost. A nation that has already suffered 20 years of warfare will suffer once again. Armies on both sides will take new casualties. And the war will go on. There is no need for this to be so.

There is no need to delay the talks that could bring an end to this long and this bloody war.

. . . So, tonight, in the hope that this action will lead to early talks, I am taking the first step to deescalate the conflict. We are reducing—substantially reducing—the present level of hostilities.

And we are doing so unilaterally, and at once.

Tonight, I have ordered our aircraft and our naval vessels to make no attacks on North Vietnam, except in the area north of the demilitarized zone where the continuing enemy buildup directly threatens allied forward positions and where the movements of their troops and supplies are clearly related to that threat.

. . . Our purpose in this action is to bring about a reduction in the level of violence that now exists.

. . . I call upon [North Vietnamese] President Ho Chi Minh to respond positively, and favorably, to this new step toward peace.

. . . Finally, my fellow Americans, let me say this:

. . . For 37 years in the service of our Nation, first as a Congressman, as a Senator, and as Vice President, and now as your President, I have put the unity of the people first. I have put it ahead of any divisive partisanship.

And in these times as in times before, it is true that a house divided against itself by the spirit of faction, of party, of region, of religion, of race, is a house that cannot stand.

There is division in the American house now. There is divisiveness among us all tonight. And holding the trust that is mine, as President of all the people, I cannot disregard the peril to the progress of the American people and the hope and the prospect of peace for all peoples.

. . . Believing this as I do, I have concluded that I should not permit the Presidency to become involved in the partisan divisions that are developing in this political year.

With America's sons in the fields far away, with America's future under challenge right here at home, with our hopes and the world's hopes for peace in the balance every day, I do not believe that I should devote an hour or a day of my time to any personal partisan causes or to any duties other than the awesome duties of this office—the Presidency of your country.

Accordingly, I shall not seek, and I will not accept, the nomination of my party for another term as your President.

But let men everywhere know, however, that a strong, a confident, and a vigilant America stands ready tonight to seek an honorable peace—and stands ready tonight to defend an honored cause—whatever the price, whatever the burden, whatever the sacrifice that duty may require.

Thank you for listening.

Source: http://www.lbjlibrary.net/collections/selected-speeches/1968-january-1969/03-31-1968.html

THOUGHT QUESTIONS:

1. How did the Vietnam War influence American politics in 1968?

2. Besides Vietnam, what other political difficulties did Lyndon Johnson confront in 1968?

3. Why did Johnson say he was dropping out of the presidential race in his March 31, 1968 speech to the nation?

Robert F. Kennedy Address
Cleveland City Club
April 5, 1968

Senator Robert Kennedy of New York and civil rights leader Martin Luther King, Jr., always shared a fraught relationship. The former attorney general and his late brother, President John Kennedy, frustrated King with their frequent compromises and half-measures on black voting rights and desegregation.

On the other hand, Robert Kennedy resented King because he believed the minister's marches, boycotts, and sit-ins had put his older brother in a bad negotiating position with southern segregationist Democrats in the Congress whose support was needed for key parts of the White House legislative agenda. Robert Kennedy also thought that civil rights demonstrations made the administration look bad on the world stage and harmed the government's international propaganda campaign that sought to convince newly independent nations in Africa and Asia that the United States represented freedom and opportunity while the Soviet enemy stood for tyranny.

In spite of this gulf, Kennedy and King's fates converged in the spring and summer of 1968. After Lyndon Johnson announced that he was not seeking another term as president, Robert Kennedy entered the Democratic primaries. He made poverty in America a primary focus of his campaign. King, meanwhile, after successfully pushing the White House and Congress to pass landmark civil rights and voting rights laws in 1964 and 1965, shifted his attention to economic injustice.

King spent the early months of 1968 planning a Poor People's March, based on his triumphant 1963 March on Washington. King hoped that by focusing on poverty he would be attacking an issue that transcended race. About 13 percent of all Americans lived in poverty in 1968, including 3.6 million whites, with poor whites heavily concentrated in deep southern states like Mississippi and the hills of Kentucky and Tennessee. King gave his support to a strike held by impoverished and overworked sanitation workers in Memphis, Tennessee and was there on the night of April 4, standing on a balcony at the Lorraine Motel, when an escaped convict, James Earl Ray, gunned him down.

That night, Kennedy made a moving speech at Indianapolis in which he paid tribute to King's work and urged his mostly black audience to not surrender to anger or hate because of the murder but to fight for unity and peace. African American leaders asked Kennedy to make similar speeches and for a time, he suspended his campaign. During one speech, in Cleveland, he focused on the prevalence of violence in American society.

This is a time of shame and sorrow. It is not a day for politics. I have saved this one opportunity to speak briefly to you about this mindless menace of violence in America which again stains our land and every one of our lives.

It is not the concern of any one race. The victims of the violence are black and white, rich and poor, young and old, famous and unknown. They are, most important of all, human beings whom other human beings loved and needed. No one—no matter where he lives or what he does—can be certain who will suffer from some senseless act of bloodshed. And yet it goes on and on.

Why? What has violence ever accomplished? What has it ever created? No martyr's cause has ever been stilled by his assassin's bullet.

No wrongs have ever been righted by riots and civil disorders. A sniper is only a coward, not a hero; and an uncontrolled, uncontrollable mob is only the voice of madness, not the voice of the people.

. . . We seemingly tolerate a rising level of violence that ignores our common humanity and our claims to civilization alike. We calmly accept newspaper reports of civilian slaughter in far off lands. We glorify killing on movie and television screens and call it entertainment. We make it easy for men of all shades of sanity to acquire weapons and ammunition they desire.

Too often we honor swagger and bluster and the wielders of force; too often we excuse those who are willing to build their own lives on the shattered dreams of others. Some Americans who preach nonviolence abroad fail to practice it here at home. Some who accuse others of inciting riots have by their own conduct invited them.

. . . [T]here is another kind of violence, slower but just as deadly, destructive as the shot or the bomb in the night. This is the violence of institutions; indifference and inaction and slow decay. This is the violence that afflicts the poor, that poisons relations between men because their skin has different colors. This is a slow destruction of a child by hunger, and schools without books and homes without heat in the winter.

This is the breaking of a man's spirit by denying him the chance to stand as a father and as a man among other men. And this too afflicts us all. . . . When you teach a man to hate and fear his brother, when you teach that he is a lesser man because of his color or his beliefs or the policies he pursues, when you teach that those who differ from you threaten your freedom or your job or your family, then you also learn to confront others not as fellow citizens but as enemies—to be met not with cooperation but with conquest, to be subjugated and mastered.

. . . Our lives on this planet are too short and the work to be done too great to let this spirit flourish any longer in our land.

. . . [P]erhaps remember—even if only for a time—that those who live with us are our brothers, that they share with us the same short movement of life, that they seek—as we do—nothing but the chance to live out their lives in purpose and happiness, winning what satisfaction and fulfillment they can.

Surely this bond of common faith, this bond of common goal, can begin to teach us something. Surely we can learn, at least, to look at those around us as fellow men and surely we can begin to work a little harder to bind up the wounds among us and to become in our hearts brothers and countrymen once again.

Source:https://www.jfklibrary.org/Research/Research-Aids/Ready-Reference/RFK-Speeches/Remarks-of-Senator-Robert-F-Kennedy-to-the-Cleveland-City-Club-Cleveland-Ohio-April-5-1968.aspx

THOUGHT QUESTIONS:

1. What issues often put Robert Kennedy and Martin Luther King, Jr. at odds?

2. What focus did Kennedy and King share in 1968?

3. What kinds of violence did Kennedy address in his speech to the Cleveland Club on April 5, 1968 and how did he claim American culture encouraged violence?

Senator Edward M. Kennedy Tribute to Robert F. Kennedy
St. Patrick's Cathedral, New York City
June 8, 1968

The murder of Martin Luther King, Jr. had taken place only two months and one day earlier, and the civil rights leader's assassin was still on the loose. On June 5, 1968, New York Senator Robert Kennedy had just won the important Democratic presidential primary in California and looked like a strong bet to follow in his late brother's footsteps as not just the party's nominee but possibly the next president of the United States. Shortly after midnight, Sirhan Sirhan, a Jordanian angered at presidential candidate Kennedy's continued support for the state of Israel in the aftermath of the 1967 Six Day War, fired three rounds into the candidate's body.

He died in the middle of the night on June 6. Americans reacted with shock to the news that a second major political assassination had taken place in so short a time and that a bullet had claimed the life of another Kennedy.

Civil Rights crusader John Lewis, a close ally of King who would later represent Georgia in the U.S. House, later remembered his disbelief when he heard that the younger Kennedy brother had been gunned down. "I think I cried all the way from L.A. to Atlanta," he said. "I kept saying to myself, 'What is happening in America?' To lose Martin Luther King Jr. and two months later Bobby." Then, breaking down in tears, he added, "It was too much."

At the funeral, the last surviving Kennedy brother, Sen. Edward Kennedy of Massachusetts, delivered the eulogy. As with services for Abraham Lincoln 103 years earlier, a train bore Robert's body from New York to the nation's capital and eventually to Arlington National Cemetery in Virginia where he would be buried next to President Kennedy. The tombstone for the latest victim of 1960s gun culture bore a simple inscription: "Robert Francis Kennedy, 1925-1968."

On behalf of Mrs. Robert Kennedy, her children and the parents and sisters of Robert Kennedy, I want to express what we feel to those who mourn with us today in this Cathedral and around the world. We loved him as a brother and father and son . . . He gave us strength in time of trouble, wisdom in time of uncertainty, and sharing in time of happiness. He was always by our side.

Love is not an easy feeling to put into words. Nor is loyalty, or trust or joy. But he was all of these. He loved life completely and lived it intensely.

. . . What he leaves us is what he said, what he did and what he stood for. A speech he made to the young people of South Africa on their Day of Affirmation in 1966 sums it up the best, and I would read it now:

" . . . Some believe there is nothing one man or one woman can do against the enormous array of the world's ills. Yet many of the world's great movements, of thought and action, have flowed from the work of a single man. A young monk began the Protestant reformation, a young general extended an empire from Macedonia to the borders of the earth, and a young woman reclaimed the territory of France. It was a young Italian explorer who discovered the New World, and the thirty-two-year-old Thomas Jefferson who proclaimed that all men are created equal.

"These men moved the world, and so can we all . . . . The future does not belong to those who are content with today, apathetic toward common problems and their fellow man alike, timid and fearful in the face of new ideas and bold projects. Rather it will belong to those who can blend vision, reason and courage in a personal commitment to the ideals and great enterprises of American Society."

This is the way he lived. My brother need not be idealized, or enlarged in death beyond what he was in life, to be remembered simply as a good and decent man, who saw wrong and tried to right it, saw suffering and tried to heal it, saw war and tried to stop it.

Those of us who loved him and who take him to his rest today, pray that what he was to us and what he wished for others will some day come to pass for all the world. As he said many times, in many parts of this nation, to those he touched and who sought to touch him:

> "Some men see things as they are and say why.
> I dream things that never were and say why not."

Source: https://www.jfklibrary.org/learn/about-jfk/the-kennedy-family/edward-m-kennedy/edward-m-kennedy-speeches/tribute-to-robert-f-kennedy-st-patricks-cathedral-new-york-city-june-8-1968

THOUGHT QUESTIONS:

1. What appears to have been the motive of Robert Kennedy's assassin, Sirhan Sirhan?

2. What was the reaction to Robert Kennedy's murder and what accounts for the reaction?

3. What did Edward Kennedy want his brother, Robert, remembered for?

Vignettes

The Seizure of the *Pueblo*

As campus demonstrations against the Vietnam War rocked the country in 1968, the United States suffered serious setbacks in foreign policy that seemed to threaten its position in the world. Entering what would be the most difficult year yet for the Vietnam War, the United States almost stumbled into a second war against North Korea.

On January 11, 1968, the *USS Pueblo* departed from a Japanese port on an espionage mission off the North Korean coast. The North Koreans captured the ship and held the crew prisoner for almost a year while the Pyongyang regime presented evidence that the *Pueblo* had entered the communist nation's territorial waters. Conservatives in Congress called for a military strike against North Korea, and President Johnson received angry letters complaining about his perceived failure to respond strongly.

The American command should have seen this incident developing. The Navy had previously come close to mothballing the *Pueblo*, which had a history of problems with navigation, and speed, and with its communication equipment. Yet the Navy sent this vessel to monitor Soviet and North Korean sonar, radar and radio transmissions and to observe the movement of Soviet and North Korean vessels. The *Pueblo*, slow and hard to maneuver, also suffered from inadequate defenses, including guns that overheated and were accurate only from a short range. The ship's translators, Robert Hammond and Robert Chicca, were not up to the jobs assigned them.

"In fact, Hammond's fluency was so poor that while in captivity the North Koreans beat him repeatedly because his personnel file stated that he could speak Korean, but he was so inept at it that they believed he was trying to conceal this ability," wrote historian Mitchell B. Lerner. In spite of all of these problems, the Navy sent the ship near the coast of an enemy with no clear set of commands for the crew on what to do if they were detected and stopped by North Korean ships.

The *Pueblo's* mission took place amid signs that the North Korean government had embarked on a more aggressive course towards the United States and its South Korean ally. The North Korean navy had seized twenty South Korean vessels in the last three months of 1967. On January 17, thirty-one North Korean Army officers had crossed the South Korea border as part of a plot to assassinate President Park Chung Hee. The hit squad reached the South Korean presidential palace on January 22 when stopped by a South Korean policeman. In the ensuing gun battle, eight South Koreans and five members of the assassination squad died. North Korean dictator Kim Il-sung had domestic political reasons for his more aggressive stance towards South Korea and his belligerent approach to the *Pueblo* crisis. The North Korean economy slowed significantly in the 1960s. As industrial and agricultural production fell, the low wages paid North Koreans led most families to suffer as prices rose.

Kim also faced serious challenges within the North Korean communist leadership from moderates who wanted a less provocative foreign policy towards South Korea. Acting aggressively towards a United States vessel, therefore, served Kim's domestic political needs by creating a crisis in which opposition to the dictator would seem like treason. If the United States had viewed North Korea as an independent state rather than as a pawn of the Soviet Union and the People's Republic of China, the military establishment might have been more cautious in how it deployed spy ships near the North Korean coast.

The North Koreans seized the *Pueblo* on January 23, 1968. One crewman died during a faceoff with the North Korean Navy, and the other 82 were taken prisoner. The North Koreans claimed their territorial waters extended 12 miles from their shore and that the *Pueblo* had crossed this line. The seizure of the *Pueblo* proved devastating to American security. The capture of communications equipment and classified documents, combined with information provided by a Soviet-paid spy operating in the United States, Navy Officer John Walker, Jr., allowed the Soviets to decode approximately 1 million American messages. The Soviets were able to tip off the North Vietnamese about American bombing raids in advance, allowing the Hanoi military to prepare defenses, which resulted in downed American bomber planes.

Under torture, the *Pueblo* crew signed several statements indicating they had committed crimes against the North Korean people. To win the release of the prisoners, an American negotiator on December 23 signed a statement written by the North Koreans in which the American government apologized for the incident. The North Koreans released the 82 surviving crew members. The United States, however, was able to avoid armed conflict, a rare foreign policy triumph that year.

THOUGHT QUESTIONS:

1. What role did the American government play in provoking the *Pueblo* incident?

2. What domestic political reasons did North Korean dictator Kim Il-sung have for exploiting the capture of the *USS Pueblo*?

3. What consequences did the incident have on the American war effort in Vietnam?

Murder and Uncommon Valor at My Lai

For four hours on March 16, 1968, American soldiers attacked and massacred civilians in the South Vietnamese village the U.S. military dubbed My Lai 4. The American fighting men attached to "Charlie Company" believed that the villagers were hiding communist guerillas, dubbed the "Viet Cong," who were responsible for lethal attacks on their comrades for several weeks. On March 15, they received orders to clear out local villages of suspected Viet Cong fighters

Many commanding officers in the area, including Captain Ernest Medina, told their men that anyone they found in the village the morning of the operation was probably a Viet Cong fighter. "He [Medina] stated that My Lai . . . was a suspected VC stronghold and that he had orders to kill everybody that was in the village," Max D. Hudson, a weapons squad leader, told the Army Criminal Investigation Unit later.

Fearful and distrusting of the local population, the Americans went on a rampage the next day, raping women at gunpoint and killing everyone they saw—including infants, unarmed men and women, and the elderly. More than 500 civilians in My Lai and the nearby village of My Khe were probably killed that day. Lt. William Calley led soldiers as they mowed down one group of 60 villagers. The lieutenant later stood near a ditch filled with children. A two-year-old climbed away from his mother and got to the top of the ditch. Calley spotted the toddler, yanked up the child, flung him back into the ditch and shot him.

Not all soldiers participated in the slaughter. Individual soldiers tried to save villagers by getting them to hide in their huts, but such men sadly formed a minority at My Lai. Heroism proved to be in short supply, but helicopter pilot Hugh Thompson of Georgia, attached to the 123rd Aviation Battalion, emerged as one of the few brave men in a scene of mass murder.

"Thompson was a character," Michael Bilton and Kevin Sim, historians of the *My Lai Massacre*, later wrote. . . . "Ruthless in winking out the VC, Thompson was also a very moral man. He was absolutely strict about opening fire only on clearly defined targets . . . He wanted to kill them cleanly and made it absolutely clear to his gunners that he wanted to see a weapon first before they opened fire."

Thompson and his crew flew near My Lai 4 to provide assistance if the infantry came under attack, and would also drop smoke sticks marking where he had spotted wounded soldiers and civilians. Thompson dropped a stick near a wounded Vietnamese civilian woman lying in a rice paddy. Thompson watched as a group of soldiers approached the woman. He lowered the chopper near the wounded woman and announced her presence to the soldiers. A man wearing captain's bars approached the unarmed woman, prodded her with his foot and then shot her.

Aware that he was witnessing a war crime, Thompson ordered his men to take off and he spotted a group of 10 civilians, including children, fleeing towards a crudely made bomb shelter. Soldiers from the 2nd Platoon chased them. Thompson ordered his men to land the helicopter between the civilians and the chasing soldiers and told his gunner, Larry Colburn, to shoot the American soldiers if they began to fire upon the villagers. "Open up on 'em—blow 'em away," he screamed to Colburn.

Thompson screamed over the radio to gunship commanders about the unfolding massacre as his men continued to look for survivors. They spotted a ditch that contained at least 100 victims. Thompson could see something moving. As the helicopter crews trained their machine guns on the soldiers of Task Force Barker, Colburn spotted "[a] child, about age 3, covered in blood and slime, but not seriously injured." A soldier handed the child, "limp and . . . like a rag doll" to Colburn. "Thompson, who had a son about the same age, was crestfallen and decided to fly immediately to the ARVN hospital in Quang Ngai. The child, in a clear state of shock, lay across [another soldier's] . . . lap. Colburn noticed the blank look on its face and saw, too, for the second time that day, that tears were streaming down Thompson's cheeks," wrote Bilton and Sim.

When Thompson got the helicopter back to base, he emerged from the craft, throwing his helmet on the ground. He informed his section leader about the massacre, and the information crawled its way up the serpentine military command structure. By this time, Task Force Barker was ordered to cease fire.

In 1970-1971, the military charged 14 officers involved in the My Lai Massacre with suppressing information related to the incident and only one, Colonel Oran K. Henderson, was placed on trial, and he was acquitted. Capt. Medina was also placed on trial and found not guilty of ordering the massacre. On March 29, 1971, a court martial convicted the man most witnesses identified at the chief instigator of violence in My Lai, Lt. William Calley, of 22 murders.

Calley defended himself by saying he was only following orders, but a jury of six officers in Fort Benning, Georgia, rejected the claim and sentenced him to life imprisonment. He was sent to serve his sentence at Fort Leavenworth in Kansas. The American Legion post in Columbus, Georgia, promised to raise $100,000 for Calley's appeal. "What do they give soldiers bullets for—to put in their pockets?" one elevator operator in Boston said. "It sounds terrible to say we ought to kill kids, but many of our boys being killed over there are just kids, too." Others insisted that the story was fake, the result of a liberal conspiracy. "The story was planted by Viet Cong sympathizers and people inside the country who are trying to get us out of Vietnam sooner," one newspaper reader insisted.

Across the country cars sported bumper stickers that demanded "Free Calley" while a Nashville radio station released a record with a reading done in William Calley's voice as "The Battle Hymn of the Republic" played in the background. The record sold 200,000 copies, and some radio stations played the disc around the clock, breaking in only to ask for donations to Calley's defense fund. The White House conducted a poll and found that 78 percent of the American public disagreed with the Calley verdict while about 51 percent wanted him completely exonerated. President Richard Nixon saw an opportunity to ride a growing backlash against anti-war protestors, and he ordered the lieutenant released from the stockade until his appeal was decided.

While he was under house arrest, Calley received 2,000 fan letters a day. His sentence was repeatedly reduced by Nixon and then commuted to time served. He was released in November 1974. Calley resumed a quiet life after his brief reign as an American anti-hero.

THOUGHT QUESTIONS:

1. What circumstances might have contributed to the My Lai Massacre?

2. What role did helicopter pilot High Thompson play in rescuing Vietnamese villagers during the My Lai Massacre?

3. Why did so many Americans embrace Lt. William Calley as a hero after the slaughter in My Lai?

The Age of Aquarius

A musical celebrating hippies, drugs, the anti-war movement, and free love, *Hair: The American Tribal Love-Rock Musical* became one of the surprise Broadway hits in the late 1960s. Opening at the Biltmore Theater in April 1968, the play shocked audiences with its occasional nudity, frequent profanity, embrace of interracial sex, and tolerance of homosexuality. The production mixed an almost naïve hope for peace and love with acidly cynical putdowns of establishment political figures such as Lyndon Johnson and Richard Nixon.

Hair opened with "The Age of Aquarius," a song destined to become a Top 40 hit. The song brimmed with optimism. The lyrics proclaimed the dawn of a new era of human consciousness when peace would prevail and "love will steer the stars."

Featuring music by Galt MacDermot and lyrics by James Rado and Gerome Ragni, the show broke numerous Broadway taboos. Producers worried that the onstage nudity might lead police to shut down the production. They found a New York City ordinance that allowed actors to be undressed as long as they did not move. The creators of the show gave actors the option whether or not to disrobe and one cast member, Diane Keaton (who later won an Oscar for best actress in the Woody Allen comedy *Annie Hall*), chose to remain clothed. Most, however, stood completely uncovered. *Hair* featured a comic, but still likeable, gay character who revels in his crush for Mick Jagger, the singer and songwriter for the popular rock 'n' roll band the Rolling Stones, and one-third of the original cast was African American.

Previous Broadway plays had depicted drug use, but only as a path to ruin and misery. *Hair* celebrated marijuana and the psychedelic drugs as a path to joy and enlightenment. Two songs—"Black Boys" and "White Boys"—hailed the joys of interracial sex while another song, "Colored Spade" ridiculed racism with a recitation of absurd anti-black slurs. Before the environment had become a major focus of the counterculture, the song "Air" whimsically condemned air pollution.

No icon—including Abraham Lincoln and the American flag—was deemed too sacred to lampoon. At a time when most Americans still supported the Vietnam War, *Hair* depicted the war as a demented slaughterhouse and presented draft dodgers as heroes. The writers also directly ridiculed President Lyndon Johnson in the original production, and then Richard Nixon with the change of administrations.

The frequent use of four-letter words, the controversial themes, and the nudity and depictions of sexuality, drew protests from the show's Broadway debut on. Opposition increased as the Broadway cast went on tour and as other cities put on their own productions. Protestors often condemned the show as anti-patriotic and marched in front of theaters where the show was performed. Cities like Boston and Chattanooga sought to stop performances, prompting lawsuits that reached the Supreme Court and in which the producers prevailed. Someone threw a bomb at a Cleveland, Ohio theater in 1971, but the show went on. In spite of such intense opposition, the show was nominated for two Tonys (for best musical and best direction) and a Grammy (for best score from an original cast show album).

Like so much of the 1960s and 1970s, paradox almost overwhelmed *Hair*. In spite of the sunny mood of the opening number, by the climax one of the major characters has decided to not dodge the draft, reports for duty, is sent to Vietnam and, by the closing number, lies dead on the stage as the rest of the cast sings with sadness, "Let the Sunshine In." The emotional kaleidoscope of the 1960s always mixed hues of activism and alienation, new frontiers and apocalyptic doom.

THOUGHT QUESTIONS:

1. What taboos did the Broadway production of *Hair* shatter?

2. What was the likely political agenda of *Hair's* creators?

3. What aspects of the musical likely provoked protests?

American Fighting Men

The Vietnam War brought out the best and the worst in American fighting men. Sandra Collingwood, a community development worker in Vietnam during the war, recalled seeing soldiers sharing food rations with Vietnamese villagers. Journalist Anne Allen remembered meeting a six-year-old Vietnamese boy in Saigon who had been informally adopted by American GIs, who gave him child-sized fatigues that he always wore, and taught him English, including the four-letter words that peppered the troops' daily speech.

The boy, called Dewey, served as a translator for the soldiers and was brought along when the Americans negotiated with prostitutes. Once he finished negotiating terms, the soldiers rewarded Dewey with a soft drink for his translation work, and the boy was sent on his way. Allen reported that Dewey loved "his" GIs.

The Vietnam War included scenes of deep compassion and horrifying cruelty. Doctors serving in Vietnam persuaded friends in the United States to send griseofulvin, a treatment for the terrible cases of ringworm. One doctor, Lawrence H. Climo, described GIs making poverty wages offering to pay for medical care for the daughter of a Montagnard tribesman who had been released from a local charity ward. As the girl's condition worsened from lack of food and water, local soldiers pooled resources to save her life. With money collected from servicemen, Climo was able to place the girl in a "pay" ward at the hospital, where she recovered.

"I save food from the officers' mess (hot dogs, vegetables, etc.) and bring it to a hospitalized Montagnard with nutritional deficiencies and to a young girl low on . . . red blood cells," Climo later recalled. "The hungry family, visitors and other patients gather about me." Meanwhile, the United States Agency for International Development made available powdered milk, protein supplements and wheat for the underfed patients recovering in the Montagnard charity hospital.

Military medical crews provided the first effective care for many Vietnamese suffering from treatable diseases, like tuberculosis and leprosy, that in some cases had almost disappeared in the West. Many of his patients suffered from parasites like pinworm and hookworm. Typhoid fever, malaria, and anemia claimed many Montagnard victims. About 50 percent of the children born near Climo's station died before they reached age five. Many diseases stemmed from haphazard or nonexistent sanitation.

"There were no latrines for the families living with the patients," Climo remembered. "They defecated outside the windows. Behind the surgery ward was a black, foul-smelling, fly-infested streamlet with pooled feces, urine and infected waste." Climo, and the rest of his Army 33rd Advisory Team, spent their time outside of the hospital wards constructing shelters for families, sanitary facilities and hospital furniture.

"I never saw so many guys cry as I did while I was in Vietnam," one nurse said after she returned from the war. "I went over to Vietnam thinking that Army doctors were hard asses. It's just not so," she said. One night a 21-year-old Vietnamese girl cleaned the floors of the medical barracks. A flammable liquid had been used to remove wax, but a soldier struck a match on the floor while the woman was scrubbing the surface, and she burst into flames.

A surgeon named Paul treated her. "When he got to her, she was 100 percent second- and third-degree burns," the nurse said. "Plus, she had inhaled a lot of smoke. Usually these people are going to die, so you let them. The thing was, she was still conscious and talking, and her kidneys were still working. So he had to try and save her . . . Burn victims shed the inside of their lungs. It's like getting sunburned on the inside and peeling. She would cough up her lungs and she'd be bleeding and slowly choking to death. She could speak English. She would hold on to Paul and beg him to not let her die."

The doctor disappeared for an hour, saying he had to think about what treatment he should try next. The nurse found him in a room the size of a closet. "He was in there crying his eyes out," she said. 'What am I going to do? I never should have started that IV on her. I never should have put that catheter in her. But she was alive when she came in and I had to do something. I can't trach her. She'll live six weeks and then she'll die horribly. What am I going to do with her?'" The doctor and the nurse did the only thing they could—as the woman slowly died they changed her dressings and tried to reassure her that they wouldn't let her die, even as they decided to discontinue heroic measures.

THOUGHT QUESTION:

1. What contradictory effects did American technology and medicine have on the Vietnamese people during the war years?

2. Did the different experiences of military medical personnel and members of the infantry lead to conflicting American views of the Vietnamese people?

3. What medical conditions did American military personnel have to deal with when treating Vietnamese, and what were their causes?

Chapter 30

American Frustration and Decline in the 1970s

Documents

**Transcript:
Conversation between President Richard Nixon and
White House Counsel John Dean,
March 21, 1973**

The Watergate scandal began well before the morning of June 17, 1972, when Washington, D.C., police arrested five men employed by Nixon's Committee for the Re-Election of the President (CREEP) after they broke into the Democratic National Committee headquarters located in the Watergate Hotel (just one mile from the White House). Outraged by leaks to the press of Defense Department documents on previously secret American bombings in Cambodia and Laos—what were called the "Pentagon Papers"—President Richard Nixon authorized illegal wiretaps of people the administration suspected of passing classified information to journalists.

Nixon's team also created the so-called "Plumbers Unit," to plug such internal leaks. Nixon's re-election team furthermore wanted the Plumbers to uncover what he thought was a criminal relationship between Democratic National Chair Lawrence O'Brien and the reclusive billionaire Howard Hughes, who also had contributed money to Nixon. The Plumbers planted wiretapping equipment in the DNC offices, but the equipment failed. They broke in a second time on June 17 in order to repair the devices but were caught.

Nixon and his aides quickly became alarmed that the burglars, facing felony charges, might offer to implicate the White House in return for lenient punishments. The scandal was largely ignored for a time, but it grabbed the public's attention in January 1973 when a Washington jury convicted the Watergate burglars, Howard Hunt and G. Gordon Liddy, of conspiracy and burglary charges. One of the burglars, James W. McCord (a security coordinator for the Republican National Committee and the president's reelection committee) began to provide to the court details about the Plumbers and other illegal White House operations.

On March 21, 1973, White House Counsel John Dean discussed the origins of the Watergate break-in with Nixon and the possibility of bribing McCord and others in return for their silence. Unknown to Dean, Nixon had long tape-recorded conversations in the White House in order to preserve the record of what he hoped would be a history-making administration. Unfortunately for him, these secret tapes later provided evidence of White House criminal conspiracies. When courts ordered the release of several hours of White House tapes, Nixon would be forced to resign, which he did on August 9, 1974.

DEAN: I think, I think that, ah, there's no doubt about the seriousness of the problem we're, we've got. We have a cancer—within—close to the Presidency, that's growing. It's growing daily. It's compounding, it grows geometrically now, because it compounds itself. Ah, that'll be clear as I explain, you know, some of the details, ah, of why it is, and basically it's because (1) we're being blackmailed; (2) ah, people are going to start perjuring themself very quickly that have not had to perjure themselves to protect other people and the like.

. . . So, let me give you the sort of basic . . . First of all, on, on the Watergate: How did it all start, where did it start? It started with an instruction to me from [White House Chief of Staff] Bob Haldeman to see if we couldn't set up a perfectly legitimate campaign intelligence operation over at the Re-election Committee . . . [T]hat's when I came up with Gordon Liddy, who. . . had an intelligence background from his FBI service. I was aware of the fact that he had done some extremely sensitive things for the White House while he'd been at the [CREEP] and he had apparently done them well. Uh, going out into [defense analyst] Daniel Ellsberg's [psychiatrist's] . . . office... [to get evidence that Ellsberg leaked the Pentagon Papers] . . . So we talked to Liddy. Liddy was interested in doing it. Took, uh, Liddy over to meet [former U.S. Attorney General and CREEP Director John] Mitchell. Mitchell thought highly of him . . . apparently, . . . Then Liddy was told to put together his plan, you know, how he would run an intelligence operation.

. . . Liddy laid out a million dollar plan that was the most incredible thing I have ever laid my eyes on. All in codes, and involved black bag operations, kidnapping, providing prostitutes, uh, to weaken the opposition, bugging, uh, mugging teams. It was just an incredible thing. (Clears throat) . . . Mitchell just virtually sat there puffing and laughing . . .

I said, "That's the most incredible thing I've ever seen." He said, "I agree." And so then he was told to go back to the drawing boards and come up with something realistic. . . . Uh, at this point, they were discussing again bugging, kidnapping and the like. And at this point I said, right in front of everybody, very clearly, I said, "These are not the sort of things that are ever to be discussed in the office of the Attorney General of the United States"—where he still was—"and I am personally incensed."... And, I thought, at that point the thing was turned off. That's the last I heard of it, when I thought it was turned off, because it was an absurd proposal.

... Mitchell probably puffed on his pipe and said, "Go ahead." And never really reflected on what it was all about. So, they had some plan that obviously had, I gather, different targets they were going to go after. They were going to infiltrate, and bug, and do all this sort of thing to a lot of these targets. This is knowledge I have after the fact.

... Now, where, where are the soft spots on this? Well, first of all, there's the, there's the problem of the continued blackmail ...

President: Right.

Dean: ... which will not only go on now, it'll go on when these people are in prison, and it will compound the obstruction of justice situation. It'll cost money. It's dangerous. Nobody, nothing—people around here are not pros at this sort of thing. This is the sort of thing Mafia people can do: washing money, getting clean money, and things like that. .. we are not criminals and not used to dealing in that business.

President: How much money do you need?

Dean: I would say these people are going to cost, uh, a million dollars over the next, uh,—two years. (Pause)

President: We could get that.

Dean: Uh, huh . . .

President: What I mean is, you could, you could

Source: https://www.nixonlibrary.gov/forresearchers/find/tapes/watergate/trial/exhibit_12.pdf

THOUGHT QUESTIONS:

1. What event inspired the Nixon White House to begin conducting illegal wiretaps?

2. What acts did the Nixon White House hope to uncover by breaking into the headquarters of the Democratic National Committee?

3. What illegal acts were discussed by President Richard Nixon and White House Counsel John Dean during their March 31, 1973 White House conversation and what were the ramifications when this discussion became public?

Gerald R. Ford's Remarks
Upon Taking the Oath of Office as President
August 9, 1974

Throughout his long congressional career, Gerald Ford never pictured himself as president. Ford was entirely a creature of the United States House of Representatives, where he served for almost 25 years. Only a year after being elected to the House representing Grand Rapids, Michigan, he won a spot on the powerful House Appropriations Committee. Ford stood as a strong fiscal conservative, opposing Lyndon Johnson's liberal Great Society programs.

His colleagues respected Ford's integrity, and his genial personality made him popular, but he acquired a reputation, deserved or not, as being out of touch with the struggles of the poor and as being second-rate intellectually. Ford first gained high visibility as a member of the Warren Commission that investigated President John F. Kennedy's assassination, and he became one of the staunchest defenders of its controversial conclusions that Lee Harvey Oswald had acted alone in the president's murder.

In 1965, Ford rose to the position of House Minority leader, and from that point on his ambition was to become House Speaker, which he described as the "greatest job in the world." By 1973, he gave up hope that Republicans would ever gain a majority in the House and decided that he would run for only one more term and return to Michigan. Then, Nixon selected Ford to be vice president to replace Spiro Agnew, who had been forced to resign as part of a bargain that allowed Agnew to avoid prison by pleading "no contest" to bribery charges stemming from when he was Maryland governor.

Ford won easy confirmation as vice president from Congress in December 1973. When Nixon resigned and Ford was sworn in as president, he jokingly contrasted himself with a luxury car, saying he was "a Ford, not a Lincoln." Ford became the first man to become chief executive even though he had never been elected president or vice president. Nevertheless, exhausted by Vietnam and Watergate and the lies that surrounded both issues, Americans responded with relief when Nixon stepped down and Ford assumed the presidency. On the morning Ford assumed the office, the press extensively wrote about how the new president toasted his own English muffins. He asked the Marine Corps Band not to play "Hail to the Chief" at his swearing-in, saying that he would prefer the University of Michigan fight song.

Mr. Chief Justice, my dear friends, my fellow Americans:

The oath that I have taken is the same oath that was taken by George Washington and by every President under the Constitution. But I assume the Presidency under extraordinary circumstances never before experienced by Americans. This is an hour of history that troubles our minds and hurts our hearts.

. . . I am acutely aware that you have not elected me as your President by your ballots, and so I ask you to confirm me as your President with your prayers. And I hope that such prayers will also be the first of many.

If you have not chosen me by secret ballot, neither have I gained office by any secret promises. I have not campaigned either for the Presidency or the Vice Presidency. I have not subscribed to any partisan platform. I am indebted to no man, and only to one woman—my dear wife—as I begin this very difficult job.

I have not sought this enormous responsibility, but I will not shirk it. Those who nominated and confirmed me as Vice President were my friends and are my friends. They were of both parties, elected by all the people and acting under the Constitution in their name. It is only fitting then that I should pledge to them and to you that I will be the President of all the people.

. . . Even though this is late in an election year, there is no way we can go forward except together and no way anybody can win except by serving the people's urgent needs. We cannot stand still or slip backwards. We must go forward now together.

. . . I believe that truth is the glue that holds government together, not only our Government but civilization itself. That bond, though strained, is unbroken at home and abroad.

In all my public and private acts as your President, I expect to follow my instincts of openness and candor with full confidence that honesty is always the best policy in the end.

My fellow Americans, our long national nightmare is over.

Our Constitution works; our great Republic is a government of laws and not of men. Here the people rule. But there is a higher Power, by whatever name we honor Him, who ordains not only righteousness but love, not only justice but mercy.

As we bind up the internal wounds of Watergate, more painful and more poisonous than those of foreign wars, let us restore the golden rule to our political process, and let brotherly love purge our hearts of suspicion and of hate.

In the beginning, I asked you to pray for me. Before closing, I ask again your prayers, for Richard Nixon and for his family. May our former President, who brought peace to millions, find it for himself. May God bless and comfort his wonderful wife and daughters, whose love and loyalty will forever be a shining legacy to all who bear the lonely burdens of the White House.

I can only guess at those burdens, although I have witnessed at close hand the tragedies that befell three Presidents and the lesser trials of others.

With all the strength and all the good sense I have gained from life . . . I now solemnly reaffirm my promise I made to you last December 6: to uphold the Constitution, to do what is right as God gives me to see the right, and to do the very best I can for America.

God helping me, I will not let you down.

Thank you.

Source: https://www.fordlibrarymuseum.gov/library/speeches/740001.asp

THOUGHT QUESTIONS:

1. What reputation had Gerald Ford gained during his long career in the United States House?

2. How did the Watergate scandal shape the tone of Gerald Ford's first speech as president?

3. What were the unusual circumstances by which Ford came to the White House?

Jimmy Carter
Address to the Nation on Energy and National Goals
July 15, 1979

In 1978, the United States began paying a steep price for decades of meddling in Iranian politics. In 1953, the Central Intelligence Agency overthrew the democratically elected government of Prime Minister Mohammad Mossadegh who had seized control of the Anglo-Iranian Oil Company. Mossadegh wanted Iranians to profit from their own oil and for the money to be invested in Iranian schools, colleges, agricultural projects and hospitals. After the coup, absolute power fell to Iran's emperor—called the Shah—Mohammed Reza Pahlavi.

The Shah supported American foreign policy aims by, for instance, establishing friendly relations with the state of Israel. He crushed dissent and spent huge amounts of money on weaponry—$10 billion in the United States alone—between 1972 and 1976. His secret police force, SAVAK, tortured and killed dissidents or had them deported. The Shah seemed oblivious to the suffering of his people, living in vast luxury while many families worried whether they would have enough to eat. In 1971, the Shah threw a massively expensive celebration of the 2,500th anniversary of the establishment of the Persian Empire that cost up to $300 million ($1.5 billion today). This lavish soiree unfolded in a country where the average person earned only $500 a year (about $3,000 today).

In spite of American support, the Shah's regime began to unravel in the late 1970s when an economic slowdown produced rising unemployment and inflation, which reached a catastrophic 50 percent. Riots broke out, starting in January 1978, with protestors in the large cities like the capital, Tehran, numbering in the millions. Strikes by oil workers brought the Iranian economy to a standstill. When soldiers refused to follow orders to shoot at protestors, the Shah realized his life and his family's lives were in danger, and he fled into exile. A new theocracy headed by the Ayatollah Ruhollah Khomeini seized power.

The chaos surrounding the Iranian Revolution caused a drop in the world's supply of oil by 2 million to 2.5 million barrels of oil a day between November 1978 and June 1979, causing crude prices to more than double from $14 to $35 a barrel. Gasoline prices at the pump climbed to an unprecedented 90 cents a gallon (about $3.14 today), and drivers sometimes spent hours in line at the gas stations during the Energy Crisis of 1979. Violence broke out. In Los Angeles, one person attacked a pregnant woman accused of cutting in line. Some carried guns when they went to fill up. Cases of gas poisoning increased as some tried to steal gasoline from their neighbors' cars by sucking on hoses. Angry drivers sported bumper stickers saying "[President] Carter—kiss my gas."

Religious in his orientation, President Jimmy Carter tried to address what he saw as a spiritual crisis besetting the country as a result of Vietnam, Watergate, assassinations, and periodic bouts of inflation and high unemployment. Initial reaction to a July 15, 1979 speech, which came to be known as the "Malaise Speech" even though the president never specifically used that word in his remarks, was strongly positive. Unfortunately, Carter quickly squandered what he gained from the speech, and impulsively asked for resignations of five cabinet officers shortly after the address.

This is a special night for me. Exactly 3 years ago, on July 15, 1976, I accepted the nomination of my party to run for President of the United States. I promised you a President who is not isolated from the people, who feels your pain, and who shares your dreams and who draws his strength and his wisdom from you.

. . . . Ten days ago I had planned to speak to you again about a very important subject—energy. For the fifth time I would have described the urgency of the problem and laid out a series of legislative recommendations to the Congress. But as I was preparing to speak, I began to ask myself the same question that I now know has been troubling many of you. Why have we not been able to get together as a nation to resolve our serious energy problem?

It's clear that the true problems of our Nation are much deeper—deeper than gasoline lines or energy shortages, deeper even than inflation or recession.

. . . So, I want to speak to you first tonight about a subject even more serious than energy or inflation. I want to talk to you right now about a fundamental threat to American democracy.

I do not mean our political and civil liberties. They will endure. And I do not refer to the outward strength of America, a nation that is at peace tonight everywhere in the world, with unmatched economic power and military might.

The threat is nearly invisible in ordinary ways. It is a crisis of confidence. It is a crisis that strikes at the very heart and soul and spirit of our national will. We can see this crisis in the growing doubt about the meaning of our own lives and in the loss of a unity of purpose for our Nation.

The erosion of our confidence in the future is threatening to destroy the social and the political fabric of America.

. . . In a nation that was proud of hard work, strong families, close-knit communities, and our faith in God, too many of us now tend to worship self-indulgence and consumption. Human identity is no longer defined by what one does, but by what one owns. But we've discovered that owning things and consuming things does not satisfy our longing for meaning. We've learned that piling up material goods cannot fill the emptiness of lives which have no confidence or purpose.

The symptoms of this crisis of the American spirit are all around us. For the first time in the history of our country a majority of our people believe that the next 5 years will be worse than the past 5 years. Two-thirds of our people do not even vote. The productivity of American workers is actually dropping, and the willingness of Americans to save for the future has fallen below that of all other people in the Western world.

. . .These changes did not happen overnight. They've come upon us gradually over the last generation, years that were filled with shocks and tragedy.

We were sure that ours was a nation of the ballot, not the bullet, until the murders of John Kennedy and Robert Kennedy and Martin Luther King, Jr. We were taught that our armies were always invincible and our causes were always just, only to suffer the agony of Vietnam. We respected the Presidency as a place of honor until the shock of Watergate.

. . . We know the strength of America. We are strong. We can regain our unity. We can regain our confidence. We are the heirs of generations who survived threats much more powerful and awesome than those that challenge us now. Our fathers and mothers were strong men and women who shaped a new society during the Great Depression, who fought world wars, and who carved out a new charter of peace for the world.

We ourselves are the same Americans who just 10 years ago put a man on the Moon. We are the generation that dedicated our society to the pursuit of human rights and equality. And we are the generation that will win the war on the energy problem and in that process rebuild the unity and confidence of America.

. . . I have seen the strength of America in the inexhaustible resources of our people. In the days to come, let us renew that strength in the struggle for an energy secure nation. In closing, let me say this: I will do my best, but I will not do it alone. Let your voice be heard. Whenever you have a chance, say something good about our country. With God's help and for the sake of our Nation, it is time for us to join hands in America. Let us commit ourselves together to a rebirth of the American spirit. Working together with our common faith we cannot fail.

Source: https://www.jimmycarterlibrary.govJimmy CarterEnergy and National Goals: Address to the NationJuly 15, 1979/documents/speeches/energy-crisis.phtml

THOUGHT QUESTIONS:

1. What was the relationship between the Iranian Revolution and the political crises that President Jimmy Carter faced?

2. What did President Carter diagnose as the ultimate cause of American political and economic woes in the 1970s?

3. What examples from American history did Carter use in an attempt to rally the public to solve the problems the country faced during his administration?

The United States Supreme Court
ROE ET AL. v. WADE,
DISTRICT ATTORNEY OF DALLAS COUNTY
Decided January 22, 1973

Abortion became illegal across the United States in the second third of the 19th century. Early on, abortion laws did not focus on the morality of the issue but instead were aimed at outlawing specific abortion methods said to threaten a mother's health.

The American Medical Association (AMA), which had an all-male membership when it was founded in 1847, campaigned to eliminate competition from female midwives who provided most health care to women. Before the mid-1800s, most women consulted midwives for help in childbirth, natural methods of birth control, abortion, and women's health and nutrition. The AMA used the deaths of women undergoing abortions at the hands of midwives as an excuse to drive midwives out of business. By 1900, the AMA had successfully lobbied states across the Union to ban abortions and at the same time require medical licenses for practitioners, legislation that almost completely eliminated women as health-care providers. Racism also played a role in the anti-abortion campaign, with men like Theodore Roosevelt alarmed that declining birth rates among white women relative to that of immigrants and women of color would result in "race suicide" for the United States

In the 20th century, in Texas and other states where abortion was illegal, women suffered poverty as a result of unwanted pregnancies, died from complications, or during self-induced abortions. In late 1969 two Texas lawyers, Sarah Weddington and Linda Coffee, sought a test case to challenge Texas' abortion law, which criminalized the procedure except if the woman's life was in danger. They found a client in Norma McCorvey, a high school dropout in her early twenties repeatedly brutalized by men who, after losing custody of two children, was pregnant a third time.

McCorvey went to one doctor in her hometown of Dallas and requested help ending the pregnancy. Her doctors told her that abortion was illegal and gave her the name of an attorney, Henry McCluskey, who handled adoptions. McCorvey first went to an illegal abortion clinic. "Nobody was there," she later told authors James Risen and Judy L. Thomas. ". . . I saw dried blood everywhere, and smelled this awful smell." The clinic had been raided and shut down by the Dallas police just before her arrival. McCorvey then consulted Weddington and Coffee, who filed a case in the federal courts arguing that Texas' anti-abortion law violated the 14th Amendment due process clause, privacy rights, and other constitutional liberties. To protect her privacy, McCorvey was identified as "Jane Roe." In its Roe v. Wade decision, handed down on January 22, 1973, the United States Supreme Court ruled by a 7-2 vote that women have a constitutional right to an abortion in the first trimester of pregnancy, that states can impose restrictions in the second trimester, and that states can ban abortion in the third trimester.

The Texas statutes under attack here are typical of those that have been in effect in many States for approximately a century. The Georgia statutes, in contrast, have a modern cast and are a legislative product that, to an extent at least, obviously reflects the influences of recent attitudinal change, of advancing medical knowledge and techniques, and of new thinking about an old issue.

We forthwith acknowledge our awareness of the sensitive and emotional nature of the abortion controversy, of the vigorous opposing views, even among physicians, and of the deep and seemingly absolute convictions that the subject inspires. One's philosophy, one's experiences, one's exposure to the raw edges of human existence, one's religious training, one's attitudes toward life and family and their values, and the moral standards one establishes and seeks to observe, are all likely to influence and to color one's thinking and conclusions about abortion . . .

Jane Roe, a single woman who was residing in Dallas County, Texas instituted this federal action in March 1970 against the District Attorney of that county . . . Rose alleged that she was unmarried and pregnant; that she wished to terminate her pregnancy by an abortion "performed by a competent, licensed physician, under safe clinical conditions"; that she was unable to get a "legal" abortion in Texas because her life did not appear to be threatened by the continuation of her pregnancy; and that she could not afford to travel to another jurisdiction in order to secure a legal abortion under safe conditions. She claimed that the Texas statures were unconstitutionally vague and that they abridged her right of personal privacy protected by the First, Fourth, Ninth, and Fourteenth amendments . . .

In areas other than abortion, the law has been reluctant to endorse any theory that life, as we recognize it, begins before live birth or to accord legal rights to the unborn except in narrowly defined situations and except where the rights are contingent upon live birth . . . In view of all this, we do not agree that by adopting one theory of life, Texas may override the rights of the pregnant woman that are at stake . . .

A state criminal abortion statute of the current Texas type, that exempts from criminality only a lifesaving procedure on behalf of the mother, without regard to pregnancy stage and without recognition of the interests involved is violative of the Due Process Clause of the Fourteenth Amendment . . . For the stage prior to approximately the end of the first trimester, the abortion decision and its effectuation must be left to the medical judgment of the pregnant woman's attending physician . . . For the stage subsequent to approximately the end of the first trimester, the State, in its interest in promoting the health of the mother, may, if it chooses, regulate the abortion procedure in ways that are reasonably related to maternal health . . .For the stage subsequent to viability, the State in promoting its interest in the potentiality of human life may, if it chooses, to regulate, and even proscribe, abortion, except where it is necessary, in appropriate medical judgment, for the preservation of the life or health, of the mother.

Source: https://cdn.loc.gov/service/ll/usrep/usrep410/usrep410113/usrep410113.pdf

THOUGHT QUESTIONS:

1. What motivated laws against abortion in the second half of the 1800s?

2. What arguments did Sarah Weddington and Linda Coffee, attorneys for Norma McCorvey ("Jane Roe") make against the Texas law criminalizing abortion?

3. What interests did the Supreme Court try to balance in its Roe v. Wade decision?

Vignettes

Against Our Will

In the early twentieth century, many Marxists had encouraged workers to reject basing their identity on race, regional identity, or nationality and instead to think of themselves as part of a working class that crossed boundaries of color, culture and language. They encouraged workers to reject what they saw as "false consciousness," identifying with the rich ruling class because of fantasies of economic advancement.

Similarly, feminists in the 1970s challenged women to consider the ways in which they collaborated with sexism: by starving themselves to meet unrealistic societal expectations of thinness; by exposing themselves to poisonous hair dye and makeup to meet unrealistic standards of beauty; by giving up on careers to raise children; and by deferring to domineering fathers, husbands and boyfriends in order to not seem aggressive and "unfeminine." Such women encouraged such personal awareness of sexism and its harmful effects by promoting what they called "consciousness-raising."

A group called the New York Feminist Women pioneered this technique. The group would ask women to gather and speak about topics like rape, unwanted pregnancy, abortion, spousal abuse, economic dependence on men, employment discrimination and so on. Everyone was allowed to speak and to share their experiences. Such talks allowed women to not feel isolated and to realize their common interest in opposing male supremacy.

In 1971, NYFW member Susan Brownmiller held a consciousness-raising "Speak-Out on Rape." Women heard horrifying stories about sexual assault and discovered that rape was far more common than was typically thought. One woman told of missing her bus as she returned from home to Harvard University and accepting a ride with a young man who took her out for coffee and donuts. The young man picked up male friends and then drove the woman to a deserted garage. "They told me I'd better cooperate or I'd be buried there and nobody would ever know," the woman said. "There were three of them and one of me. It was about 1 a.m. and no people were around. I decided to cooperate."

Another woman told of being on a date with a New York University intern that had been arranged by her mother. He asked her if she wanted to see where he lived before they went to dinner and when they got to his room, "he threw me on the bed and raped me, just like that . . . Afterwards, he got up as if nothing had happened," she said. "I thought to myself, I wonder what happens now. I kept thinking about my mother, she'd never believe it. I'll tell you what happened next. We went out to have dinner. We proceeded along with the date as if nothing had happened. I was in such a state of shock I just went along with the rest of the date."

The speakout led to Brownmiller's landmark 1975 study, *Against Our Will: Men, Women and Rape*. The author detailed the brutal history of that crime and its pervasiveness. Brownmiller noted that rape laws evolved primarily as a way for men to protect their female "property" and to ensure the paternity of potential heirs. She described in painful detail how women were blamed for being raped because of how they dressed or if they acted in an allegedly sexually provocative way and documented the lengthy history of rape of children and the elderly.

If they filed charges against their assailants, rape victims routinely suffered humiliation in court as defense attorneys accused such women of being sexually promiscuous and of telling lies about a consensual lover out of spite. In any case, men routinely escaped conviction in rape cases because of the almost impossibly high bar set by the law. New York's rape statute, for instance, required prosecutors to prove that the victim was raped "by force" (thus requiring a victim to physically resist), that "penetration" occurred, and that an additional witness had seen the accused near the location where the rape allegedly occurred.

Brownmiller also provided pioneering research advancing the notion of "marital rape" and "date rape": the idea that violent sexual coercion of a wife by her husband or a girlfriend by a boyfriend is a crime. More controversial was her theory as to the political meaning of rape. In her most contentious passage, she suggests that all men see benefit in rape. "Men's discovery that his genitalia could serve as a weapon to generate fear must rank as one of the most important discoveries of prehistoric time, along with the use of fire and the first crude stone axe," she wrote. "From prehistoric times to the present, I believe, rape has played a critical function. It is nothing more or less than a conscious process of intimidation by which all men keep all women in a state of fear."

THOUGHT QUESTIONS:

1. What did 1970s feminists mean by "consciousness raising"?

2. How did feminist author Susan Brownmiller explain the origins of rape?

3. What obstacles did Brownmiller document that women encountered when they reported rapes?

Roots

Black nationalism transformed depictions of African Americans in movies and television in the 1970s. In 1979, ABC broadcasted the "mini-series" *Roots: The Saga of an American Family*, based on African American author Alex Haley's book of the same name. Haley said the book was based on his research into his family's history, which carried him back to its origins in West Africa. His book sat on top of the national bestseller list for 22 weeks. Like the book, the series told the story of Haley's family, from the capture of an African ancestor named Kunta Kinte as a slave in the 1700s, to the life of "Chicken" George, who lives to see emancipation in the Reconstruction era.

Although the TV networks broadcast several series in the 1970s starring African Americans, comedies such as *Good Times* and *Sanford and Son*, black thinkers said that many of these programs still rested on stereotypes with the characters mostly living in poverty and sometimes committing petty crime. Slavery had been ignored for most of the history of American television. With *Roots*, African Americans dominated a drama and, for the first time, TV audiences were exposed to an extended depiction of slavery that focused on the cruelty of the slave trade, whippings and other sadistic punishments by slave owners, and which portrayed slaves as dignified, brave, and intelligent.

ABC executives worried about the show and its unflinching depiction of white racism, scheduling the program in January when TV audiences were smaller than other parts of the year. As author Dominic Sandbrook pointed out, the mini-series "had almost no sympathetic white characters and depicted a brutal world of rape and racism." TV critics at the time of the broadcast, such as *Time Magazine's* Richard Schickel, in fact did criticize the mini-series for being heavy-handed and featuring no positive white characters. "As always, the native tongue of the persecuted minority is rendered in English as fake-childish poetry," Schickel wrote in an acid-dripping review. "As always, slave-ship captains and plantation owners are shown as psychopathic hypocrites—consulting Scripture in one scene, condoning, even participating in violence and rape in the next."

The broader TV viewing public held a markedly different view. ABC presented *Roots* as what was then called a "mini-series"—a show with a limited number of episodes and a definitive conclusion. The 12-hour series aired over eight consecutive nights and drew an estimated audience of 130 million. Seventy-one percent of all households with a television set watched the final episode on January 30, 1977. The show proved that white Americans would watch entertainment featuring African-American actors and telling black stories. During the week, bars and restaurants closed early, knowing that customers would leave to watch the program. *Roots* earned thirty-seven Emmy nominations and won nine.

The series served as a cathartic moment for a massive black and white audience. "My children and I just sat there crying," recalled an African-American public relations director in Nashville. "We couldn't talk. We just cried."

For many African Americans, *Roots* instilled pride in the strength and endurance of their ancestors and prompted black families to explore their genealogy. African Americans booked tours to Africa in large numbers. Among white viewers, the show provoked an awareness of American injustice and empathy for the African-American freedom struggle. "I never knew such horrible things happened," a high school senior in Missouri said. "I wasn't very proud of my ancestors. Since the movie I have felt sorry for our black population and whenever I see a black person I wonder if any of my ancestors tortured them."

It would be later revealed that Haley plagiarized part of his book and may have fabricated other parts. But for many African Americans, *Roots* became the moment when the black past, in all its pain and heartbreak, would occupy the nation's attention.

THOUGHT QUESTIONS:

1. Why did the ABC television network worry about whether *Roots* would draw ratings?

2. What were some criticisms of the TV series *Roots* when it was originally broadcast?

3. What did the mini-series *Roots* mean to white audiences in 1977?

The People's Temple

In the 1970s, the search for truth and happiness for some Americans turned desperate, leaving them vulnerable to ruthless con artists. Jim Jones, a preacher and faith healer, founded the Peoples Temple Christian Church Full Gospel in Indianapolis in 1956. A crusader against racism who embraced Marxism, Jones launched programs to aid the poor and the hungry. He presided over an integrated congregation that often met hostility from white residents in a city that had been dominated by the Ku Klux Klan in the 1920s.

At Jones' services, church members often helped poor visitors get health care and to access public assistance programs for disabilities and other issues. Appointed to the Indianapolis Human Rights Commission, Jones used his position and the support of local civil rights groups like the NAACP to advance desegregation of the city police department, local businesses and other institutions. Jones received numerous threats as he began adopting Korean, Native American and African-American children.

His outspoken condemnation of racism earned him an ever-larger following in the African-American community. He was a talented entertainer in the pulpit. Jones's inner demons soon overwhelmed his idealism. He staged fake miracle cures to bring in more congregants and to fill church coffers. Dependent on drugs and alcohol, and sexually exploiting members of his church, Jones became obsessed with what he saw as the pending end of the world.

Jones relocated his congregation to Northern California, which he believed would be spared a coming nuclear war. He eventually established a headquarters in San Francisco where his charitable work and anti-racism activism earned him enough credibility that Mayor George Moscone appointed him to lead the city's Housing Authority Commission. Jones cultivated relationships with some of the state's most powerful political figures, with Gov. Jerry Brown and Willie Brown, a member of the California State Assembly and future Assembly Speaker, attending a dinner held in his honor in 1977.

Such fame did nothing to ease Jones' growing paranoia, which was likely intensified by his increasing drug use. Now insisting that the United States government wanted to kill him and destroy the People's Temple, Jones in 1973 rented a remote plot of land surrounded by jungle in Northern Guyana (in South America) for a communal farm that he dubbed "Jonestown."

More than 900 members emigrated there, where they found a life of relentless labor, clearing the jungle, building housing, cultivating crops, and listening to Jones's increasingly doomsday-oriented sermons. The work was hard and carried out in miserably hot weather. Preaching that U.S. government forces would soon come to destroy the Temple, Jones led his followers in suicide drills in which members drank what they were told was Flavor-Aid filled with the poison cyanide.

Reports from relatives of Temple members that their loved ones were being held against their will in South America led the San Francisco-area Congressman Leo Ryan to travel to Jonestown on November 14, 1978. With him were 17 concerned relatives of People's Temple members and an NBC News crew.

After difficult wrangling, the group was allowed to inspect Jonestown on November 17. When Ryan left the next day, 14 Temple defectors joined him. Jones ordered the assassination of Ryan and his group. Temple hit men murdered the Congressmen and four others at a nearby airstrip. Jones's long awaited apocalypse had arrived, and the heavily sweating and stern minister called on members to engage in an act of "revolutionary suicide." Eventually 909 people in Jonestown, including more than 300 children, were found dead. Most drank cups of poisoned Flavor-Aid under the watchful gaze of Jones's private army. Jones shot himself in the head.

THOUGHT QUESTIONS:

1. How did Jim Jones build such a large congregation in Indiana and California from the 1950s to the 1970s?

2. By what means did Jones gain access to powerful political figures during his career?

3. What events led to what Jones called an act of "revolutionary suicide" in northern Guyana?

Spiritual Quests and the "New Narcissism"

Discontent with the establishment form the 1950s to the 1970s extended to religion, as young people broke away from the religions of their parents such as Catholicism, Protestantism and Judaism. They experimented with the wisdom offered by Asian traditions such as Hinduism and Buddhism, as well as so-called "new religions" such as the Church of Scientology founded by one-time science fiction writer L. Ron Hubbard. "A civilization without insanity, without criminals and without war, where the able can prosper and honest beings can have rights, and where man is free to rise to greater heights, are the aims of Scientology," Hubbard once wrote to his followers.

Hubbard served in the United States Navy during World War II and later claimed that he received serious injuries that left him a blinded cripple. Hubbard told his followers that he miraculously healed himself while lying in a military hospital bed, using the methods that later became Church of Scientology practice. Hubbard said he discovered that the mental exercises he used to repair his body could cure depression, alcoholism, and other mental maladies.

He codified these techniques in a 1950 book *Dianetics: The Modern Science of Mental Health*, which charted 28 weeks on the *New York Times* bestseller list. Hubbard said that pain and fear came from what he called the "reactive mind," the location of traumatic memories he labeled "engrams." From the engrams came nightmares, psychosomatic illnesses and all neuroses. Scientology, Hubbard claimed, frees subjects from these maladies, draining the engrams of their negative powers and leaving a person "clear."

Scientologists paid for ever more expensive courses that progressively revealed the cosmic truth as understood by Hubbard, that humans are occupied by the souls of aliens tormented in a disastrous war that unfolded millions of years ago and that these alien presences cause the mental illnesses Scientology claims to cure.

California meanwhile served as the home base for a number of so-called human potential groups like Erhard Sensitivity Training, nickname est. Born Jack Rosenberg, Werner Hans Erhard had already experimented with Scientology and Zen Buddhism and had failed at selling cars and encyclopedias before launching est.

Erhard vaguely claimed to have had some profound spiritual insight while driving on a California freeway. He told prospective students that est would make them "throw away" their belief systems, break down their old personalities and let them recreate a healthier version of themselves.

Students who attended the group training seminars, which cost $250, were given infrequent food, little sleep and few bathroom breaks and were sometimes stuck in a conference room for eight hours with trainers who shouted verbal abuse in order to break down their defense mechanisms. Once beaten down, the students took "responsibility" for their failures and were told they could now achieve virtually anything they wanted as long as they did not defeat themselves. "You are omnipotent," Erhard would tell his devotees. "You are a god in your universe."

In the 1960s and 1970s, transactional analysis, primal scream therapy, Esalen, Rolfing and other psychology therapies, as well as the endless list of bestselling self-help books like *I'm OK, You're OK* and *Looking Out For Number One*, shared what journalist Peter Marin labeled "the new narcissism."

Perhaps Sixties youth grew tired of battling intractable problems like poverty and racism, but these fads all reflected a withdrawal from the wider world and what Marin called "selfishness and moral blindness." Marin described how he heard two speakers at the Esalen Institute claim "the Jews must have wanted to be burned by the Germans." Marin asked the women what they would say to a child trapped in a famine and one said, "What can I do if a child is determined to starve?" If the journalist Tom Wolfe called the 1970s the "me decade," Marin characterized it as an era of "retreat from the worlds of morality and history, an unembarrassed denial of human reciprocity and community."

THOUGHT QUESTION:

1. What characteristics do groups like The Church of Scientology, est, and others that arose in the United States after World War II have in common?

2. From where did the new religions and "human potential" groups gain their inspiration?

3. What criticisms have some scholars of the 1960s and 1970s made of such groups?

Chapter 31

A Period of Transition: The Reagan Revolution, End of the Cold War, and the Gulf War 1980-1992

Documents

A Post-Summit Letter from Ronald Reagan to Mikhail Gorbachev

Since the end of World War II, American presidents starting with Harry Truman had met a dozen times with Soviet leaders to discuss their country's differences. Ronald Reagan held his first meeting with General Secretary Mikhail Gorbachev on November 19, 1985, in Geneva, Switzerland. While the two men began to establish a rapport with each other, mutual mistrust still prevailed. Reagan and his advisers understood the Soviet Union was suffering from severe economic hardships and the continuing military stalemate in Afghanistan, hoping to use these developments to bring the Russians to the negotiating table on a variety of issues. For his part, Gorbachev was under pressure not to concede too much to the U.S. while he sought to further institute reforms at home to prevent the Soviet Union from collapsing. A week after the ice-breaking Geneva Summit ended, Reagan penned this letter to Gorbachev, expressing his desire for further discourse. Four additional summits between the two leaders, including with personal visits to each other's countries as guests of honor, led to tension-reducing agreements on nuclear weapons and cleared the way to six subsequent summits and additional arms agreements between Gorbachev and Reagan's successor, George H.W. Bush, as the Soviet Union was nearing its end.

Dear General Secretary Gorbachev

Now that we are both home and facing the task of leading our countries into a more constructive relationship with each other, I wanted to waste no time in giving you some of my initial thoughts on our meetings. Though I will be sending shortly, in a more formal and official manner, a more detailed commentary on our discussions, there are some things I would like to convey very personally and privately.

First, I want you to know that I found our meetings of great value. We had agreed to speak frankly, and we did. As a result, I came away from the meeting with a better understanding of your attitudes. I hope you also understand mine a little better. Obviously there are many things on which we disagree, and disagree very fundamentally. But if I understand you correctly, you too are determined to take steps to see that our nations manage their relations in a peaceful fashion. If this is the case, then this is one point on which we are in total agreement—and it is after all the most fundamental one of all.

As for our substantive differences, let me offer some thoughts on two of the key ones.

Regarding strategic defense and its relation to the reduction of offensive nuclear weapons, I was struck by your conviction that the American program is somehow designed to secure a strategic advantage—even to permit a first strike capability. I also noted your concern that research and testing in this area could be a cover for developing and placing offensive weapons in space.

As I told you, neither of these concerns is warranted. But I can understand, as you explained so eloquently, that these are matters which cannot be taken on faith. Both of us must cope with what the other side is doing, and judge the implications for the security of his own country. I do not ask you to take my assurances on faith.

However the truth is that the United States has no intention of using its strategic defense program to gain any advantage, and there is no development underway to create space-based offensive weapons. Our goal is to eliminate any possibility of a first strike from either side. This being the case, we should be able to find a way, in practical terms, to relieve the concerns you have expressed....

Regarding another key issue we discussed, that of regional conflicts, I can assure you that the United States does not believe that the Soviet Union is the cause of all the world's ills. We do believe, however, that your country has exploited and worsened local tensions and conflict by militarizing them and, indeed, intervening directly and indirectly in struggles arising out of local causes. While we both will doubtless continue to support our friends, we must find a way to do so without use of armed force. This is the crux of the point I tried to make.

One of the most significant steps in lowering tension in the world—and tension in U.S.-Soviet relations—would be a decision on your part to withdraw your forces from Afghanistan. I gave careful attention to your comments on this issue at Geneva, and am encouraged by your statement that you feel political reconciliation is possible. I want you to know that I am prepared to cooperate in any reasonable way to facilitate such a withdrawal, and that I understand that it must be done in a manner which does not damage Soviet security interests. During our meetings I mentioned one idea which I thought might be helpful and I will welcome any further suggestions you may have.

These are only two of the key issues on our current agenda. I will soon send some thoughts on others. I believe that we should act promptly to build the momentum our meetings initiated.

In Geneva I found our private sessions particularly useful. Both of us have advisors and assistants, but, you know, in the final analysis, the responsibility to preserve peace and increase cooperation is ours. Our people look to us for leadership, and nobody can provide it if we don't. But we won't be very effective leaders unless we can rise above the specific but secondary concerns that preoccupy our respective bureaucracies and give our governments a strong push in the right direction.

So, what I want to say finally is that we should make the most of the time before we meet again to find some specific and significant steps that would give meaning to our commitment to peace and arms reduction. Why not set a goal—privately, just between the two of us—to find a practical way to solve critical issues—the two I have mentioned—by the time we meet in Washington?

Please convey regards from Nancy and me to Mrs. Gorbachev. We genuinely enjoyed meeting you in Geneva and are already looking forward to showing you something of our country next year.

Sincerely yours,
Ronald Reagan

Source: National Archives

THOUGHT QUESTIONS:

1. What were the two differences on issues that Reagan identified as the most pressing concern for the two countries moving forward to improved relations between the United States and the Soviet Union? How did Reagan seek to allay Gorbachev's anxiety about American intentions in these areas?

2. What overall tone did Reagan express in this letter? What are some of the more noteworthy examples that show how he displayed this tone? How did it complement or contradict his often belligerent public rhetoric of the Soviet Union as "the Evil Empire"?

3. While friendship among allied leaders is always important, how necessary do you think it is for leaders of opposing nations to establish rapport and close personal relationships in order to lessen tensions? Is the threat of force and other deterrents the primary way to operate? Is a balance between the two methods preferred? Explain.

"Senator, You're No Jack Kennedy"

Though most remembered for delivering a devastating line during the 1988 vice-presidential debate, Lloyd Bentsen, Jr. enjoyed a long and successful political career representing Texas in Congress before that famous moment on the national stage. After serving as a bomber pilot in Europe during World War II, he returned to his native Rio Grande Valley and was elected to the U.S. House of Representatives in 1948. After serving three terms, he entered the private sector, eventually founding an insurance company and serving on the board of directors of Lockheed Corporation, as well as several oil and gas companies. In the 1970 Democratic Party senatorial primary, Bentsen upset the incumbent, Ralph Yarborough, who led the party's liberal faction in Texas, by lambasting the senator for his votes in favor of the Civil Rights Act of 1964, the Voting Rights Act of 1965, and his opposition to the Vietnam War. Bentsen went on to win the general election against his Republican opponent, future president George H. W. Bush. Over time, Bentsen came to be viewed as an effective centrist Democrat, gaining re-election two more times before the Democratic presidential nominee in 1988, Governor Michael Dukakis of Massachusetts, asked the senator to be his running mate in his race against Bush, the Republican presidential nominee.

Bentsen registered a fine performance in his one and only televised vice-presidential debate on October 5, 1988, when he sparred with Bush's running mate, Dan Quayle, the 41-year-old junior senator from Indiana. Showing fine preparation, Bentsen and his aides had noticed that when Senator Quayle was asked about his youth and relative inexperience at the national level, he frequently cited the fact that President John Kennedy had as much overall national experience as he did when running for president in 1960. If Quayle responded along those lines again during the debate, Bentsen would be ready. When his opponent did indeed fall into his familiar pattern, Bentsen, almost on cue, retorted with a seemingly improvised and heartfelt response: "Senator, I served with Jack Kennedy. I knew Jack Kennedy. Jack Kennedy was a friend of mine. Senator, you're no Jack Kennedy." Bentsen's partisans in the audience roared in approval, and millions watching the event at home realized that it would be one of the unforgettable moments of the 1988 presidential campaign. Though the debate did not affect the ultimate outcome of the race—the Dukakis-Bentsen ticket lost the election overwhelmingly to Bush and Quayle—the exchange (excerpted below) has become a classic in the history of modern American politics. Though disappointed at losing out on the vice presidency, state law allowed him to run concurrently for re-election to his Senate seat, and Bentsen won another term by garnering almost 60 percent of the vote. Texas voters still liked Lloyd Bentsen, and did not care when political pundits pointed out that the senator and John Kennedy were never close friends.

MODERATOR, JUDY WOODRUFF: Brit Hume, a question for Senator Quayle.

HUME: Senator, I want to take you back to the question that I asked you earlier about what would happen if you were to take over in an emergency, and what you would do first and why. You said you would say a prayer, and you said something about a meeting. What would you do next? [Laughter]
QUAYLE: I don't believe that it's proper for me to get into the specifics of a hypothetical situation like that. The situation is that if I was called upon to serve as the president of this country, or the responsibilities of the president of this country, would I be capable and qualified to do that? And I've tried to list the qualifications of twelve years in the United States Congress. I have served in the Congress and served eight years on the Senate Armed Services Committee. I have traveled a number of times—I've been to Geneva many times to meet with our negotiators as we were hammering out the INF Treaty; I've met with the western political leaders—Margaret Thatcher, Chancellor Kohl—I know them, they know me. I know what it takes to lead this country forward. And if that situation arises, yes, I will be prepared, and I will be prepared to lead this country, if that happens. [Applause] . . . .
WOODRUFF: Tom Brokaw, a question for Senator Quayle.
BROKAW: Senator Quayle, I don't mean to beat this drum until it has no more sound in it. But to follow up on Brit Hume's question, when you said that it was a hypothetical

situation, it is, sir, after all, the reason that we're here tonight, because you are running not just for Vice President [Applause]

And if you cite the experience that you had in Congress, surely you must have some plan in mind about what you would do if it fell to you to become President of the United States, as it has to so many Vice Presidents just in the last 25 years or so.

QUAYLE: Let me try to answer the question one more time. I think this is the fourth time that I've had this question.

BROKAW: The third time.

QUAYLE: Three times that I've had this question—and I will try to answer it again for you, as clearly as I can, because the question you are asking is what kind of qualifications does Dan Quayle have to be president, what kind of qualifications do I have and what would I do in this kind of a situation. And what would I do in this situation? I would make sure that the people in the cabinet and the people that are advisors to the president are called in, and I would talk to them, and I will work with them. And I will know them on a firsthand basis, because as vice president I will sit on the National Security Council. And I will know them on a firsthand basis, because I'm going to be coordinating the drug effort. I will know them on a firsthand basis because Vice President George Bush is going to recreate the Space Council, and I will be in charge of that. I will have day-to-day activities with all the people in government. And then, if that unfortunate situation happens—if that situation, which would be very tragic, happens, I will be prepared to carry out the responsibilities of the presidency of the United States of America. And I will be prepared to do that. I will be prepared not only because of my service in the Congress, but because of my ability to communicate and to lead. It is not just age; it's accomplishments, it's experience. I have far more experience than many others that sought the office of vice president of this country. I have as much experience in the Congress as Jack Kennedy did when he sought the presidency. I will be prepared to deal with the people in the Bush administration, if that unfortunate event would ever occur.

WOODRUFF: Senator Bentsen.

BENTSEN: Senator, I served with Jack Kennedy, I knew Jack Kennedy, Jack Kennedy was a friend of mine. Senator, you're no Jack Kennedy. [Prolonged shouts and applause] What has to be done in a situation like that is to call in the—

WOODRUFF: [to the audience] Please, please, once again you are only taking time away from your own candidate.

QUAYLE: That was really uncalled for, Senator. [Shouts and applause]

BENTSEN: You are the one that was making the comparison, Senator—and I'm one who knew him well. And frankly I think you are so far apart in the objectives you choose for your country that I did not think the comparison was well-taken.

WOODRUFF: Tom, a question for Senator Bentsen.

BROKAW: Since you seem to be taking no hostages on the stage, let me ask you a question—[Laughter]—about the American hostages, nine, still in brutal captivity in the Middle East....

Source: Commission on Public Debates

THOUGHT QUESTIONS:

1. How did Senator Quayle's attempt to answer a question about his level of political experience by invoking the name of John Kennedy create an opening for Bentsen to exploit as he did? How well had the senator been doing up to that point?

2. What did you think about the way that the reporters (Hume and Brokaw) addressed the issue of Senator Quayle's experience? Were they fair in trying the clarify matters by following up with additional questions on the issue after not being satisfied with the answers they first received?

3. How important are televised political debates in helping you and people that you know well choose which candidate to support for president or governor? If important, how and why? If not, why not?

Former President Reagan Reveals His Alzheimer's Diagnosis

In August 1994, at the age of 83, Ronald Reagan was diagnosed with Alzheimer's disease, an incurable condition that slowly destroys brain cells, causing dementia and ultimately leading to death. In the later stages of the disease, victims cannot perform basic life functions such as dressing and eating without assistance and most cannot remember who even their closest relatives are let alone memories of their previous life. Over the last ten years of his life, Reagan's mental capacity gradually diminished as memories withered away, and he could no longer distinguish close friends who served under him nor recognize his wife Nancy, who he adored above all others. After Reagan died in 2004 at the age of 93, Nancy Reagan became a public advocate for congressional funding for stem-cell research, believing that it would eventually lead to a cure for Alzheimer's and other diseases.

Though some cited Reagan's occasional forgetfulness in the later years of his presidency as signs that he may have begun suffering the effects of Alzheimer's while still serving as chief executive, there is yet no historical consensus on whether that was actually the case. (His son Ron Reagan believes that he showed early signs of the illness, but the president's doctors at the time disagree.) Three months after his diagnosis, Reagan published the following letter announcing his affliction to the American people, showing courage in the face of adversity as he faced a killer disease that currently impacts over 5 million Americans.

My fellow Americans,

I have recently been told that I am one of the millions of Americans who will be afflicted with Alzheimer's disease.

Upon learning this news, Nancy and I had to decide whether as private citizens we would keep this a private matter or whether we would make this news known in a public way.

In the past, Nancy suffered from breast cancer and I had cancer surgeries. We found through our open disclosures we were able to raise public awareness. We were happy that as a result many more people underwent testing. They were treated in early stages and able to return to normal, healthy lives.

So now we feel it is important to share it with you. In opening our hearts, we hope this might promote greater awareness of this condition. Perhaps it will encourage a clear understanding of the individuals and families who are affected by it.

At the moment, I feel just fine. I intend to live the remainder of the years God gives me on this earth doing the things I have always done. I will continue to share life's journey with my beloved Nancy and my family. I plan to enjoy the great outdoors and stay in touch with my friends and supporters.

Unfortunately, as Alzheimer's disease progresses, the family often bears a heavy burden. I only wish there was some way I could spare Nancy from this painful experience. When the time comes, I am confident that with your help she will face it with faith and courage.

In closing, let me thank you, the American people, for giving me the great honor of allowing me to serve as your president. When the Lord calls me home, whenever that may be, I will leave the greatest love for this country of ours and eternal optimism for its future.

I now begin the journey that will lead me into the sunset of my life. I know that for America there will always be a bright dawn ahead.

Thank you, my friends.

Sincerely,
Ronald Reagan

Source: Ronald Reagan Presidential Library

THOUGHT QUESTIONS:

1. What did Reagan say was a primary motivating factor in coming public with his diagnosis rather than keeping such news private?

2. What themes and overall tones do you think Reagan project as you read this letter?

3. Do you know anyone who suffers, or has suffered, from Alzheimer's disease? If so, what can you say about that person's experience? If not, what do you know about the potential of the illness to affect the victim and their loved ones?

When AIDS Was Funny

During the 1980s, the United States experienced the first mass outbreak of AIDS (Acquired Immune Deficiency Syndrome)--the potentially fatal disease caused by an individual's infection with a specific virus (HIV) that attacks the human immune system. Initially, the condition was viewed by the public solely as a "gay disease" because of its rapid spread in homosexual communities, but as time passed it became evident that anybody having unprotected sex with infected individuals, drug users sharing needles previously used by infected individuals, or those receiving infected blood transfusions were also highly susceptible.

Officials in the Reagan administration adopted a fairly cavalier attitude toward early news reports of a growing epidemic, as evidenced by the replies of White House Press Secretary Larry Speakes to questions posed by conservative political talk-radio host Lester Kinsolving (himself an outspoken opponent of gay rights organizations) during an October 15, 1982 press briefing:

Kinsolving: Larry, does the president have any reaction to the announcement—the Centers for Disease Control in Atlanta, that AIDS is now an epidemic and have over 600 cases?

Speakes: What's AIDS?

Kinsolving: Over a third of them have died. It's known as "gay plague." [laughter] No, it is. I mean it's a pretty serious thing that 1 in every 3 people that get this have died. And I wondered if the president is aware of it?

Speakes: I don't have it. Do you? [laughter]

Kinsolving: No, I don't.

Speakes: You didn't answer my question.

Kinsolving: Well, I just wondered, does the President --

Speakes: How do you know? [laughter]

Kinsolving: In other words, the White House looks on this as a great joke?

Speakes: No, I don't know anything about it, Lester.

Kinsolving: Does the President, does anybody in the White House know about this epidemic, Larry?

Speakes: I don't think so. I don't think there has been any --

Kinsolving: Nobody knows?

Speakes: There has been no personal experience here, Lester.

Kinsolving: No, I mean, I thought you were keeping --

Speakes: I checked thoroughly with Dr. Ruge this morning and he's had no – [Laughter] – no patients suffering from AIDS or whatever it is.

Kinsolving: The President doesn't have gay plague, is that what you're saying or what?

Speakes: No, I didn't say that.

Kinsolving: Didn't say that?

Speakes: I thought I heard you on the State Department over there. Why didn't you stay there? [Laughter]

Kinsolving: Because I love you Larry, that's why. [Laughter]

Speakes: Oh I see. Just don't put it in those terms, Lester. [Laughter]

Kinsolving: Oh, I retract that.

Speakes: I hope so.

THOUGHT QUESTIONS:

1. What was the nature of the attempt at humor expressed by Speakes and Kinsolving toward the outbreak of the AIDS epidemic?

2. What do you think the jocular attitude said about the degree of interest that the Reagan administration had in seeking to combat the growing epidemic? How might the attitude of Reagan's political base toward gay rights and homosexuality in general influence the administration's priorities in this regard?

3. Are there any issues today that you believe are very important but are not being addressed by the current administration because of politics? Are there ways to seek bipartisan compromises on those issues or would it totally depend upon voting in a new administration?

Vignettes

The U.S. Aids Muslim Insurgents in Afghanistan

In late 1979, the Soviet Union sent tens of thousands of troops into Afghanistan, intervening in a civil war for the purposes of supporting a wavering regime on its southern border that had been receiving Russian support but was in danger of falling to rebel forces. Many soon began to see a parallel with the failed effort of the United States to prop up the noncommunist government in South Vietnam, which had also resulted in direct U.S. military intervention. Just as the Soviet Union and China had supported the efforts of the North Vietnamese under Ho Chi Minh to provide aid to Viet Cong guerilla fights in South Vietnam, many in the U.S. government saw an opportunity to turn the tables by supplying arms and other war materiel through the Central Intelligence Agency (CIA) to the Afghan rebels, known as the Mujahideen.

The Carter administration formally protested the Soviet military move before announcing a series of steps designed to force a Russian withdrawal. Economic sanctions and trade embargoes were instituted. The U.S. would also lead a boycott of the 1980 Summer Olympic Games in Moscow (the Soviets responded by boycotting the 1984 Games in Los Angeles). Quietly, Carter arranged for the CIA to start aiding Afghan insurgents, a policy continued vehemently throughout the 1980s by the Reagan administration.

While Afghan government troops and their Soviet allies controlled the major towns and cities, the Mujahideen roamed the countryside in small units undertaking a sustained guerilla insurgency with supplies funneled into the country by the CIA via nearby Pakistan, including assault rifles, land mines, artillery rockets, and anti-aircraft Stinger missiles, which were used to down over 450 Soviet helicopters and jet fighters. In their effort, the Mujahideen were aided by the arrival of thousands of volunteers from various countries in the Middle East willing to take up the cause of driving the non-Muslim Russians from the region. Among those arriving in Afghanistan and eventually receiving military help was Osama bin Laden, who 20 years later became the mastermind of the 9/11 attacks.

For the next ten years, the Mujahideen and their Muslim allies with American help wore down their opponents through sabotage operations, such as downing power lines, bombing radio stations and government buildings, destroying oil pipelines and bridges, and attacking military convoys. The elusive victory and growing discontent at home due to the mounting casualties contributed to the downfall of the Soviet Union. By the time Mikhail Gorbachev ordered the withdrawal of Russian troops in late 1988 and early 1989, the Russians had lost almost 15,000 men and expended the equivalent of billions of U.S. dollars. A shattered country remained, and the civil war continued for three more years until the Mujahideen triumphed in April 1992. Within four years, an Islamic fundamentalist faction, the Taliban, would seize control with the goal of liberating the country from corrupt warlords and instituting a pure Islamic society. They would rule Afghanistan for the next five years, enforcing a harsh adherence to sharia law while harboring Osama bin Laden, granting him sanctuary and allowing him to establish a training base from which to launch terrorist attacks worldwide. Both the Taliban regime and its protection of Bin Laden were ended with the U.S. invasion of Afghanistan in 2001 after the 9/11 attacks.

THOUGHT QUESTIONS:

1. Why did the Soviet Union send troops to Afghanistan? How did the U.S. respond?

2. What types of aid did the CIA provide the insurgents? Who else arrived to right alongside the Mujahideen?

3. In what way can the Soviet moves into Afghanistan be seen as that country's "Vietnam"?

The Once Controversial Vietnam Veterans Memorial

Between 4 and 5 million Americans and foreign tourists visit Vietnam Veterans Memorial in Washington, D.C.'s National Mall every year to see the famous work dedicated to the U.S. military personnel who gave their full measure of devotion to their country during the Vietnam conflict. A somber place, the large black granite wall in the shape of a V rising from recessed earth contains the etched names of every U.S. serviceman and servicewoman who died in the war. Some come to see names of relatives, others to find the names of those they served with, while many others still arrive just to pay their respects.

Though immensely popular today, the monument designed by Yale architecture student Maya Lin was actually quite controversial after it was announced by Congress that a selection committee had chosen Lin's design over 1,441 competing submissions. Critics immediately found fault with the granite's black color, arguing that it emphasized defeat. The lack of ornamentation and grandeur to relay honor and sacrifice was also noted by the design's opponents who preferred a traditional monument ordained with heroic sculptures. Assistant Secretary of Defense James Webb, a Vietnam War veteran and strong supporter of a memorial for veterans of the fight, believed that the design looked like a "mass grave" and recommended at least the use of white walls and the presence of American flags. He refused to support the current design, stating "I never in my wildest dreams imagined such a nihilistic slab of stone." Texas billionaire H. Ross Perot, who helped to fund the design competition, also withdrew his support, claiming that Lin's work only honored "the guys that died."

Intense public pressure eventually forced a compromise. After the memorial was opened to the public in 1982, work was underway to create a bronze sculpture of three servicemen, one white, one Hispanic, and the other black, eventually placed in 1984 a short distance away from the granite wall, facing toward the monument. Nine years later, a Vietnam Women's Memorial was also added, depicting two female nurses heroically caring for a wounded soldier. Unhappy with the inclusion of these celebratory-style works, Lin refused to attend the dedication ceremony for either addition to her memorial.

THOUGHT QUESTIONS:

1. What criticisms did some opponents of the Memorial express about Maya Lin's design? Was Maya Lin correct in objecting to the inclusion of later additions to her Memorial as a compromise? Why or why not?

2. Explain what you believe to be the purpose of commemorative memorials. What types of messages should they portray? Should they be in a set style, or is variation sometimes acceptable?

3. What personal opinions do you have about the design of the Vietnam Veterans Memorial (including the later additions)? Generally favorable or unfavorable? Explain.

A Window to the Universe: The Hubble Space Telescope

Humans have looked at the night sky in wonder for as long as there have been humans. It was not until the 1600s, however, that astronomers and scientists began to develop rudimentary telescopes to give them a better glimpse of the stellar bodies making up the outer universe. Not only did they allow for objects to be seen more clearly, the first telescopes also provided observable evidence to support new theories of the workings of the universe. Galileo, for example, was able to prove Nicholas Copernicus's theory that the Sun was the center of the solar system rather than the Earth.

As telescopes greatly improved over the next four centuries, ever more amazing phenomenon became observable, but one major limitation to professional astronomers remained—distortion created by the Earth's atmosphere. As early as the mid-1940s, Princeton astronomer Lyman Spitzer promoted the benefits of an orbiting space telescope to act as an observatory in space. By the 1960s, the National Academy of Sciences endorsed the idea of incorporating an orbiting telescope into the U.S. space program and Spitzer soon headed a committee in charge of developing specific objectives for such a project.

In 1968, the National Aeronautical and Space Administration (NASA) firmly committed to the deployment of a large space-based reflecting telescope, with a planned start date of 1979. Helping the chances for the project was the need for routine maintenance of the telescope by astronauts, providing steady work for the planned reusable space shuttle program already in development.

After a decade of debate in Congress, funding was finally secured in the late 1970s, with 1983 set as the expected launch date. Delays in construction slowed matters, but in 1983 the decision was made to name the telescope after astronomer Edwin Hubble, who was the first scientist to demonstrate that the universe, in fact, was expanding. By early 1986, signs were finally pointing to a launch later that year, but the entire space shuttle program was placed on an indefinite hold when the *Challenger* exploded soon after take-off from Cape Canaveral, Florida. Four years later, with the resumption of shuttle flights, the shuttle *Discovery* finally deployed the Hubble Space Telescope into its sustained orbit on April 24, 1990.

Soon after pictures from Hubble began to be relayed to NASA, however, a major problem with the telescope's optical system was discovered. Blurred pictures indicated issues caused by a slightly misshapen primary mirror leading to an inability to obtain clearly focused images. While basic observations were still possible, NASA's reputation took a severe hit as most of the ambitious plans for the Hubble were suspended until corrections could be devised. Subsequent investigations revealed that the problem lay with the contractor who constructed the faulty primary mirror. After determining that it would be too expensive and time-consuming to replace the primary mirror in orbit or to bring the entire telescope back for a refitting, the decision was made to have Space Shuttle astronauts install a new secondary mirror calibrated to balance out the error and therefore correct the aberration.

The mission to fix the error took place in 1993 and was successful. Once fully operational, the Hubble Space Telescope has performed beyond the ambitious expectations of its fervent supporters in the astronomical community. The telescope has certainly captured brilliant detailed images of distant objects, such as galaxies, nebulae, and quasars, but it has also helped scientists make observations enabling them to more accurately date the beginning of the universe, as well as change the way that they understand the birth and death of stars and has allowed them to detect the presence of black holes.

Despite the Hubble Telescope's success, its days are numbered. Due to a decaying orbit, the telescope has anywhere from 15 to 25 years of operation remaining. When originally deployed, NASA had planned to eventually retrieve the Hubble via a space shuttle mission and display the telescope in the Smithsonian Institution, but the decision to cancel the shuttle program after the *Columbia* disaster instead led to a later shuttle mission in 2009 designed to modify the telescope to allow it to break apart over the Pacific Ocean once its orbit could not be sustained. Nevertheless, due to Hubble's breakthroughs, the next generation of space telescope is already in the queue. Due to be launched into orbit in October 2018, the James Webb Space Telescope will continue the Hubble's path-breaking exploration of outer space with a more powerful optical system capable of observing some of the most distant objects in the universe beyond the reach of Hubble and the most powerful ground-based telescopes.

THOUGHT QUESTIONS:

1. Describe the purpose of the Hubble Space Telescope and its advantage over ground-based telescopes.

2. What problems were encountered after the Hubble was deployed? How were these problems overcome? What significant discoveries did the Hubble make once fully operational?

3. What are your personal opinions regarding how much the federal government should spend on space exploration? Which projects do you know of that show promise and are worth the expenditures of vast funds and which do you feel are less worthy of public support?

The Impact of the Americans with Disabilities Act

In Hugh Gallagher's illuminating book *FDR's Splendid Deception*, the author detailed the sometimes elaborate staging arrangements that Franklin Roosevelt and his staff would often undertake in order to keep awareness of the president's inability to walk unassisted from the general public. If Roosevelt planned to attend an event where the only way to enter a particular building was through steps, White House personnel frequently arranged for FDR to arrive early after carpenters (working behind draping to conceal their project) had quickly assembled a ramp or other means for the president to gain access without the glaring eye of onlookers.

Over fifty years later, average Americans with physical disabilities that they were not trying to conceal still faced daily challenges trying enter buildings constructed without any consideration for how people in wheelchairs could gain easy entry, let alone move about easily once they got inside. Equal access to public accommodations has become the most recognizable part of the Americans with Disabilities Act (ADA), a landmark piece of federal legislation passed by Congress and signed into law by President George H.W. Bush on July 26, 1990, after overcoming opposition from business groups who complained about the supposedly burdensome cost of retrofitting buildings. The law requires places of accommodation, such as retail stores, hotels, restaurants, doctor's offices, sports stadiums, theaters, and modes of transportation, to abide by standards of reasonable accessibility. This entails altering the structure of an existing building to allow wheelchair access to enter and to navigate, or constructing a new building with these accommodations integrated into the design.

The equal accommodations feature, while the most well known of the law's features, is not the only significant piece of the legislation. The ADA has other important elements, probably none other as important as the provision outlawing employment discrimination. The law states that government entities and businesses with over 15 employees are subject to oversight with respect to hiring and protection from discrimination in their everyday work environment. The ADA helps ensure that employers will not refuse to hire, choose not to promote, or decide to fire Americans with physical and mental challenges simply because they have a documented disability. They also need to be provided with such accommodations as special equipment or scheduling modifications that would allow them to perform their job adequately.

Today, Americans barely give a second thought to ramps providing access to a building or the ubiquitous sight of handicapped parking spots close to a building—a testament to their overall approval by the public. People with disabilities in the workplace have benefited greatly from improved environments and are less likely to lose their jobs. Overall, the provisions of the ADA have produced positive changes in the country, greatly enhancing the ability of people with disabilities to live more independent lives and enabling them to contribute more to American society.

THOUGHT QUESTIONS:

1. How has the ADA improved the ability of Americans with disabilities to obtain access to buildings or ride in various modes of transportation when compared to past decades?

2. How has the ADA improved the ability of disabled American workers to gain and maintain meaningful employment when compared to past decades?

3. Given that the private sector prior to 1990 failed to address the needs of Americans with disabilities, and the fact that many business groups lobbied against passage of the ADA, do you agree with the manner in which the changes were finally implemented via federal legislation? Why or why not?

Chapter 32

America Divided and United, 1993-2008

Documents

Bill Clinton Calls for a "New Covenant"

Bill Clinton accepted the Democratic Party presidential nomination on July 16, 1992 with a speech delivered in New York City's Madison Square Garden. In keeping with his image as a moderate "New Democrat," the nominee used the occasion to lay out his goals for the general election and his presidency were he to be elected. In this excerpt from his address, he stresses the theme of national unity while promoting his middle-road approach to government that he labeled the "New Covenant," whereby a "leaner" but active government would work with citizens who accepted increased personal responsibility for solving personal and societal problems.

. . . Now, I don't have all the answers, but I do know the old ways don't work. Trickle-down economics has sure failed. And big bureaucracies, both private and public, they've failed too.

That's why we need a new approach to government, a government that offers more empowerment and less entitlement. More choices for young people in the schools they attend—in the public schools they attend. And more choices for the elderly and for people with disabilities and the long-term care they receive. A government that is leaner, not meaner; a government that expands opportunity, not bureaucracy; a government that understands that jobs must come from growth in a vibrant and vital system of free enterprise.

I call this approach the New Covenant, a solemn agreement between the people and their government based not simply on what each of us can take but what all of us must give to our Nation.

We offer our people a new choice based on old values. We offer opportunity. We demand responsibility. We will build an American community again. The choice we offer is not conservative or liberal. In many ways, it is not even Republican or Democratic. It is different. It is new. And it will work. It will work because it is rooted in the vision and the values of the American people.

Of all the things that George Bush has ever said that I disagree with, perhaps the thing that bothers me most is how he derides and degrades the American tradition of seeing and seeking a better future. He mocks it as the "vision thing." But just remember what the Scripture says: "Where there is no vision, the people perish."

I hope nobody in this great hall tonight, or in our beloved country has to go through tomorrow without a vision. I hope no one ever tries to raise a child without a vision. I hope nobody ever starts a business or plants a crop in the ground without a vision. For where there is no vision, the people perish.

One of the reasons we have so many children in so much trouble in so many places in this nation is because they have seen so little opportunity, so little responsibility, so little loving, caring community, that they literally cannot imagine the life we are calling them to lead.

And so I say again: Where there is no vision, America will perish. What is the vision of our New Covenant? An America with millions of new jobs and dozens of new industries, moving confidently toward the 21st century.

An America that says to entrepreneurs and businesspeople: We will give you more incentives and more opportunity than ever before to develop the skills of your workers and to create American jobs and American wealth in the new global economy. But you must do your part, you must be responsible. American companies must act like American companies again, exporting products, not jobs. That's what this New Covenant is all about.

An America in which the doors of colleges are thrown open once again to the sons and daughters of stenographers and steelworkers. We will say: Everybody can borrow money to go to college. But you must do your part. You must pay it back, from your paychecks or, better yet, by going back home and serving your communities.

Just think of it. Think of it. Millions of energetic young men and women serving their country by policing the streets or teaching the children or caring for the sick. Or working with the elderly and people with disabilities. Or helping young people to stay off drugs and out of gangs, giving us all a sense of new hope and limitless possibilities. That's what this New Covenant is all about.

An America in which health care is a right, not a privilege, in which we say to all of our people: Your government has the courage finally to take on the health care profiteers and make health care affordable for every family. But you must do your part. Preventive care, prenatal care, childhood immunization—saving lives, saving money, saving families from heartbreak. That's what the New Covenant is all about.

An America in which middle-class incomes, not middle-class taxes, are going up. An America, yes, in which the wealthiest few, those making over $200,000 a year, are asked to pay their fair share. An America in which the rich are not soaked, but the middle class is not drowned, either. Responsibility starts at the top. That's what the New Covenant is all about.

An America where we end welfare as we know it. We will say to those on welfare: You will have, and you deserve, the opportunity, through training and education, through child care and medical coverage, to liberate yourself. But then, when you can, you must work, because welfare should be a second chance, not a way of life. That's what the New Covenant is all about....

But the New Covenant is about more than opportunities and responsibilities for you and your families. It's also about our common community. Tonight every one of you knows deep in your heart that we are too divided. It is time to heal America.

And so we must say to every American: Look beyond the stereotypes that blind us. We need each other—all of us—we need each other. We don't have a person to waste, and yet for too long politicians have told the most of us that are doing all right that what's really wrong with America is the rest of us—them. Them, the minorities. Them, the liberals. Them, the poor. Them, the homeless. Them, the people with disabilities. Them, the gays. We've gotten to where we've nearly them'ed ourselves to death. Them, and them, and them. But this is America. There is no them. There is only us.

One nation, under God, indivisible, with liberty and justice for all. That is our Pledge of Allegiance, and that's what the New Covenant is all about....

Source: CSPAN

THOUGHT QUESTIONS:

1. What examples can you provide that demonstrate Clinton's effort to promote a middle-of-the road approach between liberals and conservatives with his talk of promoting a "New Covenant"?

2. In what ways did Clinton try to promote national unity within this speech excerpt?

3. Explain your overall impressions, both positive and negative, of this excerpt from Clinton's address.

Bill Clinton's 1996 State of the Union Address

On January 23, 1996, President Bill Clinton delivered his State of the Union Address with thoughts of the upcoming congressional elections and his own reelection campaign very much on his mind. In addition to commenting on the past year's accomplishments and his goals for the coming years that he wished Congress to act upon, he also used the occasion to reiterate his "New Democrat" approach of active but limited government. During the course of his speech, he garnered press attention, and the ire of devout liberals, by boldly proclaiming that "the era of big government is over." That memorable phrase, and its context within the speech, are given in the excerpt below.

Thank you very much. Mr. Speaker, Mr. Vice President, Members of the 104th Congress, distinguished guests, my fellow Americans all across our land: Let me begin tonight by saying to our men and women in uniform around the world and especially those helping peace take root in Bosnia and to their families, I thank you. America is very, very proud of you.

My duty tonight is to report on the state of the Union, not the state of our Government but of our American community, and to set forth our responsibilities, in the words of our Founders, to form a more perfect Union.

The state of the Union is strong. Our economy is the healthiest it has been in three decades. We have the lowest combined rates of unemployment and inflation in 27 years. We have completed—created nearly 8 million new jobs, over a million of them in basic industries like construction and automobiles. America is selling more cars than Japan for the first time since the 1970s. And for 3 years in a row, we have had a record number of new businesses started in our country.

Our leadership in the world is also strong, bringing hope for new peace. And perhaps most important, we are gaining ground in restoring our fundamental values. The crime rate, the welfare and food stamp rolls, the poverty rate, and the teen pregnancy rate are all down. And as they go down, prospects for America's future go up.

We live in an age of possibility. A hundred years ago we moved from farm to factory. Now we move to an age of technology, information, and global competition. These changes have opened vast new opportunities for our people, but they have also presented them with stiff challenges. While more Americans are living better, too many of our fellow citizens are working harder just to keep up, and they are rightly concerned about the security of their families.

We must answer here three fundamental questions: First, how do we make the American dream of opportunity for all a reality for all Americans who are willing to work for it?

Second, how do we preserve our old and enduring values as we move into the future? And third, how do we meet these challenges together, as one America?

We know big government does not have all the answers. We know there's not a program for every problem. We know, and we have worked to give the American people a smaller, less bureaucratic government in Washington. And we have to give the American people one that lives within its means. The era of big government is over. But we cannot go back to the time when our citizens were left to fend for themselves.

Instead, we must go forward as one America, one nation working together to meet the challenges we face together. Self-reliance and teamwork are not opposing virtues; we must have both. I believe our new, smaller government must work in an old-fashioned American way, together with all of our citizens through state and local governments, in the workplace, in religious, charitable, and civic associations. Our goal must be to enable all our people to make the most of their own lives, with stronger families, more educational opportunity, economic security, safer streets, a cleaner environment in a safer world. To improve the state of our Union, we must ask more of ourselves, we must expect more of each other, and we must face our challenges together. . . .

I know that this evening I have asked a lot of Congress and even more from America. But I am confident: When Americans work together in their homes, their schools, their churches, their synagogues, their civic groups, their workplace, they can meet any challenge.

I say again, the era of big Government is over. But we can't go back to the era of fending for yourself. We have to go forward to the era of working together as a community, as a team, as one America, with all of us reaching across these lines that divide us—the division, the discrimination, the rancor—we have to reach across it to find common ground. We have got to work together if we want America to work. . . .

Source: William J. Clinton Presidential Library

THOUGHT QUESTIONS:

1. What did Clinton mean when he stated that "the era of big government" had ended?

2. How did Clinton envision that goals would still be achieved if there was a reduced effort on the part of government to try and solve them? In your view, was his vision realistic?

3. Do you agree with Clinton's statement that "the era of big government is over"? Is there support for a federal government role in solving at least some national problems? Support for state and local governments to solve state and local problems? Explain.

Excerpts from President George W. Bush's "Mission Accomplished" Speech aboard the *USS Abraham Lincoln*

*On May 1, 2003, President George W. Bush famously landed (as a passenger) aboard the aircraft carrier **USS Abraham Lincoln** in a Lockheed S-3 Viking aircraft in order to congratulate the ship's crew on their service during the Iraq War and to deliver a national television address. The publicity stunt would garner much criticism over the years, not so much for the overly macho image of Bush confidently strutting on the deck of the ship donning a pilot's flight suit, but for his bold statement at the beginning of his speech that "major combat operations in Iraq have ended" while a banner appeared behind him with the words "Mission Accomplished" emblazoned across the image of an American flag. Though the conventional phase of the war against the Iraqi military ended, the guerilla war that the Bush administration did not anticipate against American occupation forces had already begun. By October 2008, over 98 percent of American casualties sustained since the start of hostilities occurred after Bush's speech. The following excerpt from that speech demonstrates the high hopes that Bush had for American success in the region after the war, his belief that most Iraqis would welcome the arrival of American forces as liberators, and the definite connection that the president made between operations in Iraq and the "war on terror" following the 9-11 attacks that he believed justified the war:*

Admiral Kelly, Captain Card, officers and sailors of the *USS Abraham Lincoln*, my fellow Americans: Major combat operations in Iraq have ended. In the Battle of Iraq, the United States and our allies have prevailed. And now our coalition is engaged in securing and reconstructing that country.

In this battle, we have fought for the cause of liberty, and for the peace of the world. Our nation and our coalition are proud of this accomplishment—yet it is you, the members of the United States military, who achieved it. Your courage—your willingness to face danger for your country and for each other—made this day possible. Because of you, our nation is more secure. Because of you, the tyrant has fallen, and Iraq is free.

Operation Iraqi Freedom was carried out with a combination of precision, and speed, and boldness the enemy did not expect, and the world had not seen before. From distant bases or ships at sea, we sent planes and missiles that could destroy an enemy division, or strike a single bunker. Marines and soldiers charged to Baghdad across 350 miles of hostile ground, in one of the swiftest advances of heavy arms in history. You have shown the world the skill and the might of the American Armed Forces. . . .

In the images of fallen statues, we have witnessed the arrival of a new era. For a hundred years of war, culminating in the nuclear age, military technology was designed and deployed to inflict casualties on an ever-growing scale. In defeating Nazi Germany and imperial Japan, Allied Forces destroyed entire cities, while enemy leaders who started the conflict were safe until the final days. Military power was used to end a regime by breaking a nation. Today, we have the greater power to free a nation by breaking a dangerous and aggressive regime. With new tactics and precision weapons, we can achieve military objectives without directing violence against civilians. No device of man can remove the tragedy from war. Yet it is a great advance when the guilty have far more to fear from war than the innocent.

In the images of celebrating Iraqis, we have also seen the ageless appeal of human freedom. Decades of lies and intimidation could not make the Iraqi people love their oppressors or desire their own enslavement. Men and women in every culture need liberty like they need food, and water, and air. Everywhere that freedom arrives, humanity rejoices. And everywhere that freedom stirs, let tyrants fear.

We have difficult work to do in Iraq. We are bringing order to parts of that country that remain dangerous. We are pursuing and finding leaders of the old regime, who will be held to account for their crimes. We have begun the search for hidden chemical and biological weapons, and already know of hundreds of sites that will be investigated. We are helping to rebuild Iraq, where the dictator built palaces for himself, instead of hospitals and schools. And we will stand with the new leaders of Iraq as they establish a government of, by, and for the Iraqi people. The transition from dictatorship to democracy will take time, but it is worth every effort. Our coalition will stay until our work is done. And then we will leave—and we will leave behind a free Iraq.

The Battle of Iraq is one victory in a war on terror that began on September the 11th, 2001, and still goes on. That terrible morning, 19 evil men—the shock troops of a hateful ideology—gave America and the civilized world a glimpse of their ambitions. They imagined, in the words of one terrorist, that September the 11th would be the "beginning of the end of America." By seeking to turn our cities into killing fields, terrorists and their allies believed that they could destroy this nation's resolve, and force our retreat from the world. They have failed.

In the Battle of Afghanistan, we destroyed the Taliban, many terrorists, and the camps where they trained. We continue to help the Afghan people lay roads, restore hospitals, and educate all of their children. Yet we also have dangerous work to complete. As I speak, a special operations task force, led by the 82nd Airborne, is on the trail of the terrorists, and those who seek to undermine the free government of Afghanistan. America and our coalition will finish what we have begun.

From Pakistan to the Philippines to the Horn of Africa, we are hunting down al-Qaida killers. Nineteen months ago, I pledged that the terrorists would not escape the patient justice of the United States. And as of tonight, nearly one-half of al-Qaida's senior operatives have been captured or killed.

The liberation of Iraq is a crucial advance in the campaign against terror. We have removed an ally of al-Qaida, and cut off a source of terrorist funding. And this much is certain: No terrorist network will gain weapons of mass destruction from the Iraqi regime, because the regime is no more.

In these 19 months that changed the world, our actions have been focused, and deliberate, and proportionate to the offense. We have not forgotten the victims of September the 11th—the last phone calls, the cold murder of children, the searches in the rubble. With those attacks, the terrorists and their supporters declared war on the United States. And war is what they got.

Our war against terror is proceeding according to principles that I have made clear to all: Any person involved in committing or planning terrorist attacks against the American people becomes an enemy of this country, and a target of American justice.

Any person, organization, or government that supports, protects, or harbors terrorists is complicit in the murder of the innocent, and equally guilty of terrorist crimes.

Any outlaw regime that has ties to terrorist groups, and seeks or possesses weapons of mass destruction, is a grave danger to the civilized world, and will be confronted.

And anyone in the world, including the Arab world, who works and sacrifices for freedom has a loyal friend in the United States of America. . . .

Our mission continues. Al-Qaida is wounded, not destroyed. The scattered cells of the terrorist network still operate in many nations, and we know from daily intelligence that they continue to plot against free people. The proliferation of deadly weapons remains a serious danger. The enemies of freedom are not idle, and neither are we. Our government has taken unprecedented measures to defend the homeland—and we will continue to hunt down the enemy before he can strike.

The war on terror is not over, yet it is not endless. We do not know the day of final victory, but we have seen the turning of the tide. No act of the terrorists will change our purpose, or weaken our resolve, or alter their fate. Their cause is lost. Free nations will press on to victory. . . .

Those we lost were last seen on duty. Their final act on this earth was to fight a great evil, and bring liberty to others. All of you—all in this generation of our military—have taken up the highest calling of history. You are defending your country, and protecting the innocent from harm. And wherever you go, you carry a message of hope—a message that is ancient, and ever new. In the words of the prophet Isaiah: "To the captives, 'Come out!' and to those in darkness, 'Be free!'"

Thank you for serving our country and our cause. May God bless you all, and may God continue to bless America.

Source: The White House

THOUGHT QUESTIONS:

1. What images of common Iraqis and their former leader, Saddam Hussein, did President Bush employ in the speech? How did these images color the argument he was trying to make?

2. What claims did Bush make in the speech with regard to the ability of modern technology to limit civilian casualties? Do you agree or disagree with his claims? Why or why not?

3. Most importantly, how did Bush directly link the war effort in Iraq with the 9-11 attacks and the "war on terror"? Cite with multiple examples.

President George W. Bush Discusses the No Child Left Behind Act

Frequently when governors are elected President of the United States, they tout programs created in their states that they wish to extend to the national level. During the Great Depression, Governor Franklin Roosevelt and the New York legislature established a state-level conservation agency for unemployed youths. In 1933, President Roosevelt and the Congress created the Civilian Conservation Corps built upon the much-smaller state-level model from New York. When George W. Bush became president in 2001, he called for education reform at the national level based upon the general concept of teacher and school accountability to improve student educational outcomes that he advocated while serving as Governor of Texas. Congress soon obliged him by passing the No Child Left Behind Act, signed into law in January 2002. The legislation required states to develop assessment markers in basic skills for grades 3-8 in order to continue receiving federal funding. Schools not showing improvement in their assessment scores would trigger initial actions such as requiring tutoring for underperforming students and allowing students to transfer to a better-performing school within the same district. Continued underperformance on assessments could lead to replacement of staff, conversion into a charter school, allowing a private company to administer the school, or permanently closing the school. On January 8, 2009, as Bush was preparing to leave office, he visited the General Philip Kearny School in Philadelphia, Pennsylvania to give his last major policy-related speech—an appeal to Congress to renew the provisions of the law. Excerpts from that speech are given below.

After 13 years of operation, Congress eventually replaced the No Child Left Behind Act, with the Every Student Succeeds Act, signed by President Barack Obama in April 2015. The new law retained annual testing but allowed the states (with U.S. Department of Education approval) more latitude in establishing standards and improvement markers, as well as the consequences for low-performing schools.

THE PRESIDENT: Thank you for the warm welcome. And Laura and I are thrilled to be here at Kearny School. We have come because this is one of the really fine schools in the city of Philadelphia. We bring greetings from the Nation's Capital, but more importantly, we bring appreciation for those who are working so hard to make sure that every child can learn.

You know, seven years ago today, I had the honor of signing a bill that forever changed America's school systems. It was called the No Child Left Behind Act. I firmly believe that thanks to this law, more students are learning, an achievement gap is closing. And on this anniversary, I have come to talk about why we need to keep the law strong. If you find a piece of legislation that is working, it is important to make sure the underpinnings of that law remain strong....

I hope you can tell that education is dear to my heart. I care a lot about whether or not our children can learn to read, write, and add and subtract. When I was a governor of Texas, I didn't like it one bit when I'd go to schools in my state and realize that children were not learning so they could realize their God-given potential. I didn't like it because I knew the future of our society depended upon a good, sound education.

I was sharing this story with people that Laura and I just met with, and at the time I went to a high school in my state, one of our big city high schools. And I said, thanks for teaching—I met this teacher. I think his name is Brown, if I'm not mistaken....Nelson Brown. And he taught geography and history, if I'm not mistaken. I said, "How is it going, Mr. Brown?" He said, "It's going lousy." I said, "Why?" He said, "Because my kids cannot read and they're in high school." You see, the system was just satisfied with just shuffling kids through—if you're 14 you're supposed to be here, if you're 16 you're supposed to be there. Rarely was the question asked: Can you read? Or can you write? Or can you add and can you subtract?

And so we decided to do something about it. We said such a system is unacceptable to the future of our state. And that's the spirit we brought to Washington, D.C. It's unacceptable to our country that vulnerable children slip through the cracks. And by the way, guess who generally those children are? They happen to be inner-city kids, or children whose parents don't speak English as a first language. They're the easiest children to forget about.

We saw a culture of low expectations. You know what happens when you have low expectations? You get lousy results. And when you get lousy results, you have people who say, there's no future for me in this country.

And so we decided to do something about it. We accepted the responsibility of the office to which I had been elected. It starts with this concept: Every child can learn. We believe that it is important to have a high quality education if one is going to succeed in the 21st century. It's no longer acceptable to be cranking people out of the school system and saying, okay, just go—you know, you can make a living just through manual labor alone. That's going to happen for some, but it's not the future of America, if we want to be a competitive nation as we head into the 21st century.

We believe that every child has dignity and worth. But it wasn't just me who believed that. Fortunately, when we got to Washington, a lot of other people believed it -- Democrats and Republicans. I know there's a lot of talk about how Washington is divided, and it has been at times—at times. And it can get awfully ugly in Washington. But, nevertheless, if you look at the history over the past eight years, there have been moments where we have come together. And the No Child Left Behind Act is one such moment....

The philosophy behind the law is pretty straightforward: Local schools remain under local control. In exchange for federal dollars, however, we expect results. We're spending money on schools, and shouldn't we determine whether or not the money we're spending is yielding the results society expects?

So states set standards. One reason this school makes sense is because you have a principal who sets high standards, keeps that bar high. And we hold schools accountable for meeting the standards. There—we set an historic goal, and that is to—every child should learn to read and do math at grade level by 2014.

The key to measuring is to test. And by the way, I've heard every excuse in the book why we should not test—oh, there's too many tests; you teach the test; testing is intrusive; testing is not the role of government. How can you possibly determine whether a child can read at grade level if you don't test? And for those who claim we're teaching the test, uh-uh. We're teaching a child to read so he or she can pass the test.

Testing is important to solve problems. You can't solve them unless you diagnose the problem in the first place. Testing is important to make sure children don't slip too far behind. The facts are, if you get too far behind in reading, for example, it's nearly impossible to catch up. That's why it's important to test early.

Measuring results allows us to focus resources on children who need extra help. And measuring gives parents something to compare other schools with. You oftentimes hear, oh, gosh, I wish parents were more involved. Well, one way to get parental involvement is to post results. Nothing will get a parent's attention more than if he or she sees that the school her child goes to isn't performing as well as the school around the corner.

Measurement is essential to success. When schools fall short of standards year after year, something has to happen. In other words, there has to be a consequence in order for there to be effective reforms. And one such thing that can happen is parents can enroll their children in another school. It's—to me, measurement is the gateway to true reform, and measurement is the best way to ensure parental involvement.

By the way, school choice was only open to rich people up until No Child Left Behind. It's hard for a lot of parents to be able to afford to go to any other kind of school but their neighborhood school. Now, under this system, if your public school is failing, you'll have the option of transferring to another public school or charter school. And it's—I view that as liberation. I view that as empowerment....

There's a new Teacher Incentive Fund in place, as a result of No Child Left Behind reforms, and a city like Philadelphia are rewarding educators for taking jobs in this city's toughest classrooms, and those who are achieving results. In other words, there's an incentive to make sure good teachers get in the classrooms all throughout the city. And by the way, this is happening all across our country.

You know, I mentioned disclosure. More and more districts are producing annual report cards, and that's really important. And I did mention to you what they call supplemental services. Under the No Child Left Behind Act, when you find a disadvantaged child falling behind where he or she should be, there's extra money for tutoring. And across the country there's now about a half a million students benefitting from the tutoring that comes from No Child Left Behind. It makes sense, doesn't it? It says we're going to measure, and if we determine you need extra help, here's some money to help you—so that you don't fall behind, so that you catch up.

The number of charter schools, by the way, has more than doubled over the past seven years. Charter schools provide good outlets. And I met the head of the—president of the Charter School Association here in Philadelphia. He said 10 years ago there were four, and today there are—yes, a lot. (Laughter.) When you get over 60, it's hard to hear. (Laughter.)

The most important result of the No Child Left Behind is this: Fewer students are falling behind; more students are achieving high standards. We have what's called the Nation's Report Card. For those who wonder whether or not we should strengthen No Child Left Behind, I want you to hear this: 4th graders earned the highest reading and math scores in the history of the test. Minority and disadvantaged students made some of the largest gains, with African Americans and Hispanics posting all-time highs in several categories. (Applause.)...

And we've seen the resolve here at Kearny. That's why we're here. Every year—we met a mom, who told us her twins now come to this school. You know, it's interesting what happens when you post scores. Nobody cares more about a child's education, obviously, than the first teacher a child has, which is a parent. And this notion about how parents really don't seem to care—they care, believe me. And when there's transparency in the system it helps them make informed choices. And so the mom was saying her twins come here.

She also said, by the way, they weren't really reading up to snuff initially, and yet they got extra help. And now, guess what. They're reading up to snuff. Kearny School works.

They commute for miles. Some of the families commute for miles because they understand it's a place of excellence. This is a school where a lot of community and faith-based groups come to help. And that is really, really great of you to do that. And by the way, it happens in other schools, too. And if you're interested in how you can serve America, why don't you volunteer in your local school? If you want to be a member of the army of compassion in America, help your schools. Help your schools help each child realize their God-given potential.

I believe that it is going to be important for our citizens to take a hard look at No Child Left Behind, and listen to the facts of No Child Left Behind, and then say with clear voice, for the sake of our children's future, this good law needs to be strengthened and reauthorized by the United States Congress. (Applause.)

There is a growing consensus across the country that now is not the time to water down standards or to roll back accountability. There is a growing consensus that includes leaders of the business communities across America who see an increasingly global economy and, therefore, believe in standards and accountability. There's a growing consensus amongst leaders of civil rights organizations—like La Raza, and the Urban League, and the Education Equality Project. These leaders refuse to accept what I have called the soft bigotry of low expectations. There's a growing consensus -- includes a lot of parents, and superintendents, and mayors, and governors who insist that we put our children first.

And so I've come to herald the success of a good piece of legislation. I have come to talk to our citizens about the results that this reform has yielded. And I call upon those who can determine the fate of No Child Left Behind in the future to stay strong in the face of criticism, to not weaken the law—because in weakening the law, you weaken the chance for a child to succeed in America—but to strengthen the law for the sake of every child.

Thank you for letting us come by for the last policy address that we have been honored to make. God bless you. (Applause.)

Source: www.whitehouse.gov

THOUGHT QUESTIONS:

1. What aspects of No Child Left Behind does Bush cite as the best aspects of the policy?

2. What criticisms of the program did Bush bring up and how did he try to dispense with such opposition?

3. Do you agree or disagree with Bush's emphasis upon standardized testing as the proper means of monitoring student achievement and improvement? What are some positive and negative aspects of reliance on standardized testing in judging overall school performance?

Vignettes

Proposition 187 and the End of Republican Control of California

During the 1990s, growing discontent among many Californians over the migration of large numbers of Mexican immigrants led the state's Republican Party leaders to push for passage of a ballot initiative known as Proposition 187, designed to end access to vital social services such as prenatal and childbirth care, child welfare, public education, and non-emergency health care for undocumented immigrants. The measure, which voters approved in 1994 by a 59-41 percent margin, arose not only from a desire to provide disincentives for illegal aliens to remain in the state, but also from the continuous straining effects of the 1978 property tax revolt in California, which had frozen most property tax rates, costing local government budgets more than $200 billion in sorely needed funds. The passage of Proposition 187 also reflected white Californians' historical tendency toward nativism and racism. Similar to the bigotry toward Asians in the late twentieth and early twenty-first centuries, conservative white Californians were greatly dismayed by the large numbers of Mexican immigrants flooding into their state, believing that they were un-American and an economic drain on the state.

Before the provisions of the law could be carried out, however, the legislation was immediately challenged in court by opponents who argued against its constitutionality. A federal judge issued a permanent injunction against implementation of most provisions until a court decided the matter. Three years later, in November 1997, a federal court determine the law to be unconstitutional on the basis of infringement upon the federal government's sole jurisdiction on matters related to immigration.

While the law was dead, the political ramifications of the deceased statute has continued on in California to the present day. The campaign for Proposition 187 galvanized the state's Hispanic population to organize politically, involving Latinos, especially of the younger generation, in politics like never before. While Governor Pete Wilson, Attorney General Dan Lundgren, and other GOP politicians were able to use their support for the measure to gain reelection in 1994, that year proved to be the high-water mark for Republicans in California. Beginning in 1996, Mexican-American voters began to take out their anger against Republican politicians, resulting not only in the loss of a majority of Latino votes in the state for at least a generation, but also the Republican loss of state government control. Prior to the 1990s, Republicans were a powerful institution in the state government of California, frequently ruling over the state assembly while electing conservative U.S. senators such as Richard Nixon, and governors like Ronald Reagan. Those days, however, were now over as Democrats began to consistently control most state-wide offices and Republicans were relegated to control over a shrinking number of enclaves in the wealthy urban pockets, as well as the less populous rural areas of the state.

THOUGHT QUESTIONS:

1. What political, racial, and economic factors contributed to support for passage of Proposition 187 in California?

2. How did the law, though never implemented, completely change the political landscape in California in subsequent decades?

3. Can you think of a similar issue in today's times that similarly galvanized voters in a way that changed politics, at either the local, state, or national level? What factors came into play to facilitate that mobilization of voters? Will that mobilization have "staying power" or will it eventually fade? Explain.

The Capture of the Unabomber

In 1995, the Federal Bureau of Investigation (FBI) received word from a crazed bomber that he would stop his extended campaign of violence if arrangements were made for a 50-page essay that he wrote entitled "Industrial Society and Its Future" to be published verbatim by a major newspaper or magazine in the United States. FBI Director Louis Freeh and U.S. Attorney General Janet Reno discussed the pros and cons of such a deal before making the decision to allow the "Unabomber Manifesto" to be released in the hope that it would provide clues to a reader on the identity of the killer.

The terrorist had been mailing explosive packages to universities, corporate executives, and business owners since 1978, beginning with a small package mailed to an engineering professor at Northwestern University that injured a campus police officer. The following year, one of his bombs in the cargo hold of an American Airlines flight created immense smoke but failed to fully detonate, likely sparing the aircraft and the lives of its passengers. The FBI then created and led a task force code-named UNABOM (University and Airline Bomber) to bring him to justice. Nevertheless, over the next 17 years, the "Unabomber" remained unidentified and uncaptured as he sent out package bombs in spurts to various individuals and causing a host of injuries—in 1980, to the president of United Airlines (resulting in cuts and burns to the body and face), in 1982 to a UC Berkeley engineering professor (causing severe burns and shrapnel wounds to hands and face), and in 1985 to another professor but opened by a graduate student who lost fingers and partial vision in one eye, just to name a few. In late 1985, the first fatality occurred when a computer store owner in Sacramento, California opened a package mailed to him. In 1994 and 1995, two more deaths attributed to the Unabomber took place as bombs killed a New Jersey advertising executive and a Sacramento timber industry lobbyist. In all, before the publication of his lengthy manuscript, the Unabomber had mailed 16 package bombs resulting in 3 deaths and 23 cases of severe physical injury and psychological trauma.

On September 19, 1995, the *Washington Post* and *New York Times* released the Unabomber's lengthy manifesto, primarily a diatribe against the Industrial Revolution, which he stated denied people their freedom, their community with nature, and made them behave in ways that deviated from the "natural pattern of human behavior." He ended his essay with a call for a revolution against technology. Among the many Americans who bothered to read the Unabomber Manifesto was David Kaczynski, a social worker who fairly quickly recognized the writing style as that of his brother Ted. After discovering copies of some old letters written by Ted to newspapers during the 1970s in which he decried the effects of technology on society and which contained similar phrasing to the manifesto, David alerted the FBI, and Ted Kaczynski was arrested in the secluded Montana cabin that he built himself where he lived without electricity or running water.

While many saw Ted Kaczynski as an evil monster, his decent into violence actually paralleled a slow personal descent into madness. While growing up in suburban Chicago during the 1940s and 1950s, he was found to have an extremely high IQ, excelling in mathematics. Finishing high school by the age of 15, the prodigy had entered Harvard University and graduated by the age of 20. Kaczynski entered the University of Michigan, earning a PhD in Mathematics while publishing scholarly articles before accepting an assistant professorship at the University of California at Berkeley in 1967. At the time, he was the youngest professor ever hired by that institution but was unable to hold his position due to student complaints about his extreme nervousness in front of classes and general anti-social behavior. In 1969, he abruptly resigned and lived with his parents for a while before deciding to move to Montana to build his cabin and live in seclusion. Finding it impossible to live self-sufficiently with nature due to the constant encroachment of land development and industry, Kaczynski mentally snapped and began to plan to fight back through his bombing campaign. In reality, he was unable to see that he had been slowly losing touch with reality, exhibiting signs that many mental health professionals identified in hindsight as classic signs of schizophrenia, including extreme anti-social behavior and recurring delusions.

At his trial, Kaczynski's lawyers planned to argue that he suffered from schizophrenia and therefore could not legally commit a premeditated crime. Kaczynski asked the judge to allow him to represent himself in order to prevent his lawyers from labeling him as mentally ill. The judge would only agree to do so if he submitted to a psychological evaluation. After the court-appointed psychologist diagnosed Kaczynski as a paranoid schizophrenic, the judge denied his petition for self-representation. Prosecutors then offered Kaczynski a plea deal of life in prison without parole, which he reluctantly accepted. His brother David has recently written a book to tell the Unabomber story from his family's perspective in order to clarify much misinformation that has been spread by others without direct knowledge of his brother. As he has stated in interviews promoting the book, "a lot of people have stereotypical notions about mental illness, i.e., that a person is completely disconnected from reality, or that none of Ted's ideas could be valid if he's "crazy." I think it is much more complicated. What I see in his diaries [which he meticulously kept over 40 years] is a person drowning in their pain and loneliness and totally losing perspective on who they are, what the world is and what it means to be human."

THOUGHT QUESTIONS:

1. What bold move by authorities eventually led to the Unabomber's capture? What risks do you think they were possibly taking in resorting to such a desperate effort?

2. How did Ted Kaczynski's social inadequacies and mental illness destroy a promising academic career?

3. How important do you think it is to weigh a defendant's psychological history and current mental health diagnosis in deciding punishment for certain crimes and/or eventual release back into society?

They Called Him "Dr. Death"

During the 1990s, Jack Kevorkian, a medical doctor from Michigan, gained tremendous publicity as he began to help some terminally ill patients end their lives painlessly. His efforts to promote societal acceptance of doctor-assisted suicide sparked intense debate at the time but was hampered by his frequent arrests, multiple lawsuits filed against him, and a generally disapproving media quick to label him as "Dr. Death."

Kevorkian began his medical career quietly, graduating from the University of Michigan Medical School in 1952, eventually working as a pathologist in Pontiac. During the 1980s, he began to speak out and publish his thoughts on euthanasia and began advertising his services locally as a "death counselor." In 1990, Kevorkian assisted his first suicide, helping a 54-year-old woman diagnosed with Alzheimer's disease. Though initially brought up on murder charges, they were eventually dropped as there was no Michigan statute specifically outlawing assisted suicide. The state medical board, however, revoked the doctor's medical license over the incident.

Despite these actions, Kevorkian assisted in over a hundred suicides of terminally ill people over the next eight years, in each instance the patient performed the act which resulted in the death, by pressing a button on devices that he invented which transferred lethal doses of either drugs or carbon monoxide gas into their bodies. Critics pointed out that over half of those who killed themselves with Kevorkian's assistance were not yet in a terminal state, and five patients' autopsies revealed that they had no disease at all, let alone a life-threatening one, suggesting that Kevorkian did not perform an extensive enough medical evaluation including an adequate psychological screening for each patient. In response to criticism, Kevorkian stated "What difference does it make if someone is terminal? We are all terminal." Thus, he believed that a patient did not have to be near death to be assisted in committing suicide, but they should be suffering in a significant way—a view not held by all supporters of decriminalizing assisted suicide.

From 1994 to 1997, Kevorkian was tried for murder four times in Michigan, leading to three acquittals and one hung jury. He was finally convicted in 1999, after he deviated from his traditional practice by personally injecting a lethal drug into a patient (with his consent) who was in the final stages of Lou Gehrig's disease and allowed a videotape of the act to go public. After defending himself in a two-day trial, Kevorkian was found guilty and sentenced to 10-25 years in prison. After eight years in prison, he was paroled for good behavior in June 2007 under the terms that he would no longer assist patients in committing suicide. He kept his promise but lectured frequently on euthanasia issues in a continued effort to change public opinion. After a failed 2008 congressional bid as an independent (receiving only 2.6 percent of the vote), he allowed a movie to be made about his life—You Don't Know Jack—starring Al Pacino in the lead role. His health declined in 2011 as he suffered from recurring kidney problems, and he eventually died from a blood clot in his heart a few days after his 83rd birthday. No artificial attempts were made to keep him alive, and he died without pain.

Though the controversial messenger was gone, Kevorkian's movement continues to this day under new leaders who use less attention-getting means to persuade others that people should have the right to die with dignity on their own terms. Today, while euthanasia (in which a doctor commits the final act) is still illegal in all states, doctor-assisted suicide (whereby the patient willingly performs the deed with the help of medical personnel) is slowly gaining traction, having been made legal in California, Colorado, Oregon, Vermont, and Washington.

THOUGHT QUESTIONS:

1. What did Kevorkian initially do to assist suicide and how did he change his practices, leading to his arrest and conviction for murder?

2. What other movements have had a clear message but were not as successful until they obtained a "better messenger"?

3. How do you personally feel about both doctor-assisted suicide and euthanasia? Under what circumstances, if any, do you think it should be allowed?

Al Gore Becomes an Environmental Rock Star

After failing to win the presidency in 2000, Al Gore had to decide what to do with the rest of his life. After serving as a congressman for eight year, then a U.S. senator for eight years, followed by another eight years as vice president, he knew that he did not want to remain in politics, let alone seek the presidency again. After laying low for a while, he emerged for a few appearances famously sporting a beard for the first time in his public life, symbolically leaving behind his previous self (though he eventually shaved it off).

Gore eventually found his footing as a media executive (founding Current TV, which he later sold for a $70 million profit), a board member for Apple Computer, and an environmental advocate increasingly concerned with climate change. His initial work to directly combat global warming trends had taken place when he served as vice president, pushing for a carbon emission tax to encourage more efficient energy consumption as well as strongly urging the Senate to approve the 1997 Kyoto Protocol—an international agreement that sought to have cooperating nations seek targeted reductions of greenhouse gas emissions into the atmosphere. The Senate, however, passed a resolution expressing disapproval of any agreement that did not specifically require developing countries to make emission reductions, citing undue harm to the U.S. economy. Though the Clinton administration signed the protocol, it was never submitted to the Senate for consideration of ratification.

The work that strongly cemented Gore's connection with the movement to alert the public about the effects of climate change was his involvement with *An Inconvenient Truth*—a 2006 documentary that built upon the information that he had been relaying in lectures across the country. Film producer and environmental activist Laurie David had attended one of Gore's presentations and thought it was the most powerful and clearest explanation of global warming that she had ever heard and immediately sought to work with Gore to produce an expanded movie version of his talk, who eventually agreed to participate.

The main thrust of *An Inconvenient Truth* is Gore's argument, backed by an overwhelming consensus of the scientific community, that despite what critics say, climate change is real, has the potential to cause cataclysmic damage to the environment, and that it is largely man-made. Gore cites a wide variety of collected data, including the documented consistent rise in the concentration of carbon dioxide in the atmosphere since the late 1950s, the proven retreat of glaciers around the world in recent decades, and the destruction of coral reefs due to rising ocean temperatures. The film was a critical and box office success, praised by climate change advocates for its scientific accuracy and educational power. It won the 2006 Academy Award for Best Documentary Feature and has been credited with jump-starting the conversation about climate change, informing the public about core issues and providing information and talking points in lay terms to allow advocates to debate opponents and promote the cause.

The following year, Gore shared the 2007 Nobel Peace Prize with the United Nation's Intergovernmental Panel on Climate Change for their efforts "to build up and disseminate greater knowledge about man-made climate change, and to lay the foundations for the measures that are needed to counteract such change." Gore seemed to have finally found his calling and comfort in life outside of politics, enjoying the positive publicity and the ability to mobilize his newfound celebrity status to his cause. As Davis Guggenheim, the director of *An Inconvenient Truth* observed after the film's release, "Everywhere I go with him, they treat him like a rock star."

THOUGHT QUESTIONS:

1. Describe how Al Gore was able to morph himself from a recently retired politician into a popular environmental activist following his loss in the 2000 presidential election.

2. Do you agree with the current scientific evidence that the planet is currently undergoing impactful climate? Why or why not?

3. To what extent do you believe that human activity is contributing to global warming?

Chapter 33

Barack Obama, Donald Trump, and Contemporary America

Documents

President Obama's Bin Laden Death Announcement

In the late evening on May 2, 2011, President Obama informed a stunned and relieved nation via a televised address that U.S. Navy SEALs had successfully carried out a mission to kill the 9/11 mastermind once his hideout in Pakistan had been discovered and verified. Spontaneous crowds began to appear in Lafayette Square across from the White House, with many jubilant people chanting the ubiquitous rallying cry: "USA! USA!" The fight against the remnants of Al Qaeda would continue, but for one moment, a definite and significant success in the "war on terror" could be acknowledged. Below is the president's announcement in its entirety.

Good evening. Tonight, I can report to the American people and to the world that the United States has conducted an operation that killed Osama bin Laden, the leader of al Qaeda, and a terrorist who's responsible for the murder of thousands of innocent men, women, and children. It was nearly 10 years ago that a bright September day was darkened by the worst attack on the American people in our history. The images of 9/11 are seared into our national memory—hijacked planes cutting through a cloudless September sky; the Twin Towers collapsing to the ground; black smoke billowing up from the Pentagon; the wreckage of Flight 93 in Shanksville, Pennsylvania, where the actions of heroic citizens saved even more heartbreak and destruction.

And yet we know that the worst images are those that were unseen to the world. The empty seat at the dinner table. Children who were forced to grow up without their mother or their father. Parents who would never know the feeling of their child's embrace. Nearly 3,000 citizens taken from us, leaving a gaping hole in our hearts.

On September 11, 2001, in our time of grief, the American people came together. We offered our neighbors a hand, and we offered the wounded our blood. We reaffirmed our ties to each other, and our love of community and country. On that day, no matter where we came from, what God we prayed to, or what race or ethnicity we were, we were united as one American family.

We were also united in our resolve to protect our nation and to bring those who committed this vicious attack to justice. We quickly learned that the 9/11 attacks were carried out by al Qaeda—an organization headed by Osama bin Laden, which had openly declared war on the United States and was committed to killing innocents in our country and around the globe. And so we went to war against al Qaeda to protect our citizens, our friends, and our allies.

Over the last 10 years, thanks to the tireless and heroic work of our military and our counterterrorism professionals, we've made great strides in that effort. We've disrupted terrorist attacks and strengthened our homeland defense. In Afghanistan, we removed the Taliban government, which had given bin Laden and al Qaeda safe haven and support. And around the globe, we worked with our friends and allies to capture or kill scores of al Qaeda terrorists, including several who were a part of the 9/11 plot.

Yet Osama bin Laden avoided capture and escaped across the Afghan border into Pakistan. Meanwhile, al Qaeda continued to operate from along that border and operate through its affiliates across the world.

And so shortly after taking office, I directed Leon Panetta, the director of the CIA, to make the killing or capture of bin Laden the top priority of our war against al Qaeda, even as we continued our broader efforts to disrupt, dismantle, and defeat his network.

Then, last August, after years of painstaking work by our intelligence community, I was briefed on a possible lead to bin Laden. It was far from certain, and it took many months to run this thread to ground. I met repeatedly with my national security team as we developed more information about the possibility that we had located bin Laden hiding within a compound deep inside of Pakistan. And finally, last week, I determined that we had enough intelligence to take action, and authorized an operation to get Osama bin Laden and bring him to justice.

Today, at my direction, the United States launched a targeted operation against that compound in Abbottabad, Pakistan. A small team of Americans carried out the operation with extraordinary courage and capability. No Americans were harmed. They took care to avoid civilian casualties. After a firefight, they killed Osama bin Laden and took custody of his body.

For over two decades, bin Laden has been al Qaeda's leader and symbol, and has continued to plot attacks against our country and our friends and allies. The death of bin Laden marks the most significant achievement to date in our nation's effort to defeat al Qaeda.

Yet his death does not mark the end of our effort. There's no doubt that al Qaeda will continue to pursue attacks against us. We must—and we will—remain vigilant at home and abroad.

As we do, we must also reaffirm that the United States is not—and never will be—at war with Islam. I've made clear, just as President Bush did shortly after 9/11, that our war is not against Islam. Bin Laden was not a Muslim leader; he was a mass murderer of Muslims. Indeed, al Qaeda has slaughtered scores of Muslims in many countries, including our own. So his demise should be welcomed by all who believe in peace and human dignity.

Over the years, I've repeatedly made clear that we would take action within Pakistan if we knew where bin Laden was. That is what we've done. But it's important to note that our counterterrorism cooperation with Pakistan helped lead us to bin Laden and the compound where he was hiding. Indeed, bin Laden had declared war against Pakistan as well, and ordered attacks against the Pakistani people.

Tonight, I called President Zardari, and my team has also spoken with their Pakistani counterparts. They agree that this is a good and historic day for both of our nations. And going forward, it is essential that Pakistan continue to join us in the fight against al Qaeda and its affiliates.

The American people did not choose this fight. It came to our shores, and started with the senseless slaughter of our citizens. After nearly 10 years of service, struggle, and sacrifice, we know well the costs of war. These efforts weigh on me every time I, as Commander-in-Chief, have to sign a letter to a family that has lost a loved one, or look into the eyes of a service member who's been gravely wounded.

So Americans understand the costs of war. Yet as a country, we will never tolerate our security being threatened, nor stand idly by when our people have been killed. We will be relentless in defense of our citizens and our friends and allies. We will be true to the values that make us who we are. And on nights like this one, we can say to those families who have lost loved ones to al Qaeda's terror: Justice has been done.

Tonight, we give thanks to the countless intelligence and counterterrorism professionals who've worked tirelessly to achieve this outcome. The American people do not see their work, nor know their names. But tonight, they feel the satisfaction of their work and the result of their pursuit of justice.

We give thanks for the men who carried out this operation, for they exemplify the professionalism, patriotism, and unparalleled courage of those who serve our country. And they are part of a generation that has borne the heaviest share of the burden since that September day.

Finally, let me say to the families who lost loved ones on 9/11 that we have never forgotten your loss, nor wavered in our commitment to see that we do whatever it takes to prevent another attack on our shores.

And tonight, let us think back to the sense of unity that prevailed on 9/11. I know that it has, at times, frayed. Yet today's achievement is a testament to the greatness of our country and the determination of the American people.

The cause of securing our country is not complete. But tonight, we are once again reminded that America can do whatever we set our mind to. That is the story of our history, whether it's the pursuit of prosperity for our people, or the struggle for equality for all our citizens; our commitment to stand up for our values abroad, and our sacrifices to make the world a safer place.

Let us remember that we can do these things not just because of wealth or power, but because of who we are: one nation, under God, indivisible, with liberty and justice for all.

Thank you. May God bless you. And may God bless the United States of America.

Source: The White House

THOUGHT QUESTIONS:

1. What overall tone did President Obama exude in this announcement? Why did you think he adopted that tone?

2. How did President Obama, while not celebrating Bin Laden's death, make the case that his demise was a good thing for Americans and other citizens of the world?

3. While Bin Laden's death was a significant development, how was it largely a symbolic victory in the ongoing war on terror rather than a definite end to it?

President Obama's Eulogy
for Reverend Clementa Pinckney of the Charleston Nine

On the evening of June 17, 2015, Dylann Roof, a 21-year-old white supremacist wishing to start a race war joined a Bible study group led by the Reverend Clementa Pinckney and attended by a dozen black worshippers at the historic Emanuel African Methodist Episcopal Church in downtown Charleston, South Carolina. After not speaking for 45 minutes, Roof suddenly took out a Glock .45-caliber handgun and proceeded to methodically fire 77 rounds into the members, killing nine of them include Reverend Pinckney. Three other victims survived. The morning after the attack, police arrested Roof in North Carolina. He was later found guilty of federal hate crimes and sentenced to death by a jury.

Roof's hoped-for race war did not come. Photographs posted on social media showing Roof posing with the Confederate flag and other white supremacist emblems enraged many, leading to his heinous act becoming the force that finally convinced the South Carolina assembly to remove the Confederate battle flag—long a source of contention for African Americans in the Palmetto State and around the country—from the State Capitol Grounds.

On June 26, President Obama delivered the eulogy at Clementa Pinckney's funeral, held in the basketball arena of the College of Charleston and televised nationally. The climax of the emotional tribute proved to be his surprise decision, after making a long reflection on the power of grace, to begin leading the audience in the singing of "Amazing Grace." Never before had an American president sung during a speech. Initially advised to reconsider by his advisers and his wife Michelle when he told them beforehand what he was considering, they eventually relented, telling him to follow whatever the spirit moved him at the time to do. The unanticipated act immediately uplifted and energized the crowd and soon came to be seen as one of the indelible moments of Obama's second term. The eulogy, excerpted below, is already viewed as one of the most memorable addresses of his presidency.

Giving all praise and honor to God. (Applause.)

The Bible calls us to hope. To persevere, and have faith in things not seen. "They were still living by faith when they died," Scripture tells us. "They did not receive the things promised; they only saw them and welcomed them from a distance, admitting that they were foreigners and strangers on Earth."

We are here today to remember a man of God who lived by faith. A man who believed in things not seen. A man who believed there were better days ahead, off in the distance. A man of service who persevered, knowing full well he would not receive all those things he was promised, because he believed his efforts would deliver a better life for those who followed.

To Jennifer, his beloved wife; to Eliana and Malana, his beautiful, wonderful daughters; to the Mother Emanuel family and the people of Charleston, the people of South Carolina.

I cannot claim to have the good fortune to know Reverend Pinckney well. But I did have the pleasure of knowing him and meeting him here in South Carolina, back when we were both a little bit younger. (Laughter.) Back when I didn't have visible grey hair. (Laughter.) The first thing I noticed was his graciousness, his smile, his reassuring baritone, his deceptive sense of humor—all qualities that helped him wear so effortlessly a heavy burden of expectation.

Friends of his remarked this week that when Clementa Pinckney entered a room, it was like the future arrived; that even from a young age, folks knew he was special. Anointed. He was the progeny of a long line of the faithful—a family of preachers who spread God's word, a family of protesters who sowed change to expand voting rights and desegregate the South. Clem heard their instruction, and he did not forsake their teaching....

What a good man. Sometimes I think that's the best thing to hope for when you're eulogized—after all the words and recitations and resumes are read, to just say someone was a good man. (Applause.)

You don't have to be of high station to be a good man. Preacher by 13. Pastor by 18. Public servant by 23. What a life Clementa Pinckney lived. What an example he set. What a model for his faith. And then to lose him at 41—slain in his sanctuary with eight wonderful members of his flock, each at different stages in life but bound together by a common commitment to God....

To the families of the fallen, the nation shares in your grief. Our pain cuts that much deeper because it happened in a church. The church is and always has been the center of African-American life—(applause)—a place to call our own in a too often hostile world, a sanctuary from so many hardships....

That's what the black church means. Our beating heart. The place where our dignity as a people is inviolate. When there's no better example of this tradition than Mother Emanuel—(applause)—a church built by blacks seeking liberty, burned to the ground because its founder sought to end slavery, only to rise up again, a Phoenix from these ashes. (Applause.)...

We do not know whether the killer of Reverend Pinckney and eight others knew all of this history. But he surely sensed the meaning of his violent act. It was an act that drew on a long history of bombs and arson and shots fired at churches, not random, but as a means of control, a way to terrorize and oppress. (Applause.) An act that he imagined would incite fear and recrimination; violence and suspicion. An act that he presumed would deepen divisions that trace back to our nation's original sin.

Oh, but God works in mysterious ways. (Applause.) God has different ideas. (Applause.)

He didn't know he was being used by God. (Applause.) Blinded by hatred, the alleged killer could not see the grace surrounding Reverend Pinckney and that Bible study group—the light of love that shone as they opened the church doors and invited a stranger to join in their prayer circle. The alleged killer could have never anticipated the way the families of the fallen would respond when they saw him in court—in the midst of unspeakable grief, with words of forgiveness. He couldn't imagine that. (Applause.)

The alleged killer could not imagine how the city of Charleston, under the good and wise leadership of Mayor Riley—(applause)—how the state of South Carolina, how the United States of America would respond—not merely with revulsion at his evil act, but with big-hearted generosity and, more importantly, with a thoughtful introspection and self-examination that we so rarely see in public life.

Blinded by hatred, he failed to comprehend what Reverend Pinckney so well understood—the power of God's grace. (Applause.)

This whole week, I've been reflecting on this idea of grace. (Applause.) The grace of the families who lost loved ones. The grace that Reverend Pinckney would preach about in his sermons. The grace described in one of my favorite hymnals—the one we all know: Amazing grace, how sweet the sound that saved a wretch like me. (Applause.) I once was lost, but now I'm found; was blind but now I see. (Applause.)

According to the Christian tradition, grace is not earned. Grace is not merited. It's not something we deserve. Rather, grace is the free and benevolent favor of God—(applause)—as manifested in the salvation of sinners and the bestowal of blessings. Grace.

As a nation, out of this terrible tragedy, God has visited grace upon us, for he has allowed us to see where we've been blind. (Applause.) He has given us the chance, where we've been lost, to find our best selves. (Applause.) We may not have earned it, this grace, with our rancor and complacency, and short-sightedness and fear of each other—but we got it all the same. He gave it to us anyway. He's once more given us grace. But it is up to us now to make the most of it, to receive it with gratitude, and to prove ourselves worthy of this gift.

For too long, we were blind to the pain that the Confederate flag stirred in too many of our citizens. (Applause.) It's true, a flag did not cause these murders. But as people from all walks of life, Republicans and Democrats, now acknowledge—including Governor Haley, whose recent eloquence on the subject is worthy of praise—(Applause)—as we all have to acknowledge, the flag has always represented more than just ancestral pride. (Applause.) For many, black and white, that flag was a reminder of systemic oppression and racial subjugation. We see that now.

Removing the flag from this state's capitol would not be an act of political correctness; it would not be an insult to the valor of Confederate soldiers. It would simply be an acknowledgment that the cause for which they fought—the cause of slavery—was wrong—(Applause)—the imposition of Jim Crow after the Civil War, the resistance to civil rights for all people was wrong. (Applause.) It would be one step in an honest accounting of America's history; a modest but meaningful balm for so many unhealed wounds. It would be an expression of the amazing changes that have transformed this state and this country for the better, because of the work of so many people of goodwill, people of all races striving to form a more perfect union. By taking down that flag, we express God's grace.... (Applause.)

That's what I've felt this week—an open heart. That, more than any particular policy or analysis, is what's called upon right now, I think—what a friend of mine, the writer Marilyn Robinson, calls "that reservoir of goodness, beyond, and of another kind, that we are able to do each other in the ordinary cause of things." That reservoir of goodness. If we can find that grace, anything is possible. (Applause.) If we can tap that grace, everything can change. (Applause.)

Amazing grace. Amazing grace.

(Begins to sing)—Amazing grace—(applause)—how sweet the sound, that saved a wretch like me; I once was lost, but now I'm found; was blind but now I see. (Applause.)

Clementa Pinckney found that grace.
Cynthia Hurd found that grace.
Susie Jackson found that grace.
Ethel Lance found that grace.
DePayne Middleton-Doctor found that grace.
Tywanza Sanders found that grace.
Daniel L. Simmons, Sr. found that grace.
Sharonda Coleman-Singleton found that grace.
Myra Thompson found that grace.

Through the example of their lives, they've now passed it on to us. May we find ourselves worthy of that precious and extraordinary gift, as long as our lives endure. May grace now lead them home. May God continue to shed His grace on the United States of America. (Applause.)

Source: The White House

THOUGHT QUESTIONS:

1. What elements did Obama include in the eulogy to present an uplifting tone rather than one dominated by sadness?

2. What major points about God's grace was the president trying to impart to the audience?

3. How did his decision to sing near the end of the eulogy make Obama's address one of his most memorable as president?

Excerpts from President Obama's Farewell Address

After eight years as president, Barack Obama prepared to hand over the reins of executive power to Donald Trump, a completely different type of man with few shared values between them. Knowing that many of his followers were distraught and angry that Trump had won a majority of electoral votes despite losing the popular vote by almost 3 million, Obama characteristically chose to send a hopeful message in his farewell address to the American people in mid-January 2017, noting some of his administration's accomplishments and reminding everyone of goals that were yet unfulfilled. At the same time, Obama used the opportunity, as revealed in the following excerpts, to comment on the extreme partisan rancor in the country at the time and the threat of this intense polarization to the country's democracy.

THE PRESIDENT: In 10 days, the world will witness a hallmark of our democracy.

AUDIENCE: Nooo —

THE PRESIDENT: No, no, no, no, no—the peaceful transfer of power from one freely elected President to the next. (Applause.) I committed to President-elect Trump that my administration would ensure the smoothest possible transition, just as President Bush did for me. (Applause.) Because it's up to all of us to make sure our government can help us meet the many challenges we still face....

We have what we need to do so. We have everything we need to meet those challenges. After all, we remain the wealthiest, most powerful, and most respected nation on Earth. Our youth, our drive, our diversity and openness, our boundless capacity for risk and reinvention means that the future should be ours. But that potential will only be realized if our democracy works. Only if our politics better reflects the decency of our people. (Applause.) Only if all of us, regardless of party affiliation or particular interests, help restore the sense of common purpose that we so badly need right now.

That's what I want to focus on tonight: The state of our democracy. Understand, democracy does not require uniformity. Our founders argued. They quarreled. Eventually they compromised. They expected us to do the same. But they knew that democracy does require a basic sense of solidarity—the idea that for all our outward differences, we're all in this together; that we rise or fall as one. (Applause.)....

To begin with, our democracy won't work without a sense that everyone has economic opportunity. And the good news is that today the economy is growing again. Wages, incomes, home values, and retirement accounts are all rising again. Poverty is falling again. (Applause.) The wealthy are paying a fairer share of taxes even as the stock market shatters records. The unemployment rate is near a 10-year low. The uninsured rate has never, ever been lower. (Applause.) Health care costs are rising at the slowest rate in 50 years. And I've said and I mean it—if anyone can put together a plan that is demonstrably better than the improvements we've made to our health care system and that covers as many people at less cost, I will publicly support it. (Applause.)....

There's a second threat to our democracy—and this one is as old as our nation itself. After my election, there was talk of a post-racial America. And such a vision, however well-intended, was never realistic. Race remains a potent and often divisive force in our society. Now, I've lived long enough to know that race relations are better than they were 10, or 20, or 30 years ago, no matter what some folks say. (Applause.) You can see it not just in statistics, you see it in the attitudes of young Americans across the political spectrum.

But we're not where we need to be. And all of us have more work to do. (Applause.) If every economic issue is framed as a struggle between a hardworking white middle class and an undeserving minority, then workers of all shades are going to be left fighting for scraps while the wealthy withdraw further into their private enclaves. (Applause.) If we're unwilling to invest in the children of immigrants, just because they don't look like us, we will diminish the prospects of our own children—because those brown kids will represent a larger and larger share of America's workforce. (Applause.) And we have shown that our economy doesn't have to be a zero-sum game. Last year, incomes rose for all races, all age groups, for men and for women.

So if we're going to be serious about race going forward, we need to uphold laws against discrimination—in hiring, and in housing, and in education, and in the criminal justice system. (Applause.) That is what our Constitution and our highest ideals require. (Applause.)

But laws alone won't be enough. Hearts must change. It won't change overnight. Social attitudes oftentimes take generations to change. But if our democracy is to work in this increasingly diverse nation, then each one of us need to try to heed the advice of a great character in American fiction—Atticus Finch—(applause)—who said "You never really understand a person until you consider things from his point of view…until you climb into his skin and walk around in it."

For blacks and other minority groups, it means tying our own very real struggles for justice to the challenges that a lot of people in this country face—not only the refugee, or the immigrant, or the rural poor, or the transgender American, but also the middle-aged white guy who, from the outside, may seem like he's got advantages, but has seen his world upended by economic and cultural and technological change. We have to pay attention, and listen. (Applause.)

For white Americans, it means acknowledging that the effects of slavery and Jim Crow didn't suddenly vanish in the '60s—(applause)—that when minority groups voice discontent, they're not just engaging in reverse racism or practicing political correctness. When they wage peaceful protest, they're not demanding special treatment but the equal treatment that our Founders promised. (Applause.)

For native-born Americans, it means reminding ourselves that the stereotypes about immigrants today were said, almost word for word, about the Irish, and Italians, and Poles—who it was said we're going to destroy the fundamental character of America. And as it turned out, America wasn't weakened by the presence of these newcomers; these newcomers embraced this nation's creed, and this nation was strengthened. (Applause.)

So regardless of the station that we occupy, we all have to try harder. We all have to start with the premise that each of our fellow citizens loves this country just as much as we do; that they value hard work and family just like we do; that their children are just as curious and hopeful and worthy of love as our own. (Applause.)

And that's not easy to do. For too many of us, it's become safer to retreat into our own bubbles, whether in our neighborhoods or on college campuses, or places of worship, or especially our social media feeds, surrounded by people who look like us and share the same political outlook and never challenge our assumptions. The rise of naked partisanship, and increasing economic and regional stratification, the splintering of our media into a channel for every taste—all this makes this great sorting seem natural, even inevitable. And increasingly, we become so secure in our bubbles that we start accepting only information, whether it's true or not, that fits our opinions, instead of basing our opinions on the evidence that is out there. (Applause.)

And this trend represents a third threat to our democracy. But politics is a battle of ideas. That's how our democracy was designed. In the course of a healthy debate, we prioritize different goals, and the different means of reaching them. But without some common baseline of facts, without a willingness to admit new information, and concede that your opponent might be making a fair point, and that science and reason matter— (applause)—then we're going to keep talking past each other, and we'll make common ground and compromise impossible. (Applause.)...

Which brings me to my final point: Our democracy is threatened whenever we take it for granted. (Applause.) All of us, regardless of party, should be throwing ourselves into the task of rebuilding our democratic institutions. (Applause.) When voting rates in America are some of the lowest among advanced democracies, we should be making it easier, not harder, to vote. (Applause.) When trust in our institutions is low, we should reduce the corrosive influence of money in our politics, and insist on the principles of transparency and ethics in public service. (Applause.) When Congress is dysfunctional, we should draw our congressional districts to encourage politicians to cater to common sense and not rigid extremes. (Applause.)

But remember, none of this happens on its own. All of this depends on our participation; on each of us accepting the responsibility of citizenship, regardless of which way the pendulum of power happens to be swinging....

In his own farewell address, George Washington wrote that self-government is the underpinning of our safety, prosperity, and liberty, but "from different causes and from different quarters much pains will be taken...to weaken in your minds the conviction of this truth." And so we have to preserve this truth with "jealous anxiety;" that we should reject "the first dawning of every attempt to alienate any portion of our country from the rest or to enfeeble the sacred ties" that make us one. (Applause.)

America, we weaken those ties when we allow our political dialogue to become so corrosive that people of good character aren't even willing to enter into public service; so coarse with rancor that Americans with whom we disagree are seen not just as misguided but as malevolent. We weaken those ties when we define some of us as more American than others; when we write off the whole system as inevitably corrupt, and when we sit back and blame the leaders we elect without examining our own role in electing them. (Applause.)

It falls to each of us to be those anxious, jealous guardians of our democracy; to embrace the joyous task we've been given to continually try to improve this great nation of ours. Because for all our outward differences, we, in fact, all share the same proud title, the most important office in a democracy: Citizen. (Applause.) Citizen.

So, you see, that's what our democracy demands. It needs you. Not just when there's an election, not just when your own narrow interest is at stake, but over the full span of a lifetime. If you're tired of arguing with strangers on the Internet, try talking with one of them in real life. (Applause.) If something needs fixing, then lace up your shoes and do some organizing. (Applause.) If you're disappointed by your elected officials, grab a clipboard, get some signatures, and run for office yourself. (Applause.) Show up. Dive in. Stay at it.

Sometimes you'll win. Sometimes you'll lose. Presuming a reservoir of goodness in other people, that can be a risk, and there will be times when the process will disappoint you. But for those of us fortunate enough to have been a part of this work, and to see it up close, let me tell you, it can energize and inspire. And more often than not, your faith in America—and in Americans—will be confirmed. (Applause.)....

Source: The White House

THOUGHT QUESTIONS:

1. What multiple threats to democracy to President Obama identify in his farewell address? Do you agree with many, all, or none of his points? Why or why not?

2. What developments did the president believe contributed to extreme political polarization in the country? Do you agree or disagree with his analysis? Why or why not?

3. What solutions did Obama offer to help alleviate the deep partisan rancor that existed among many Americans by the end of his presidency? How realistic do you find his suggestions?

President Trump Discusses His Desire for a Border Wall

Donald Trump made his insistence for a border wall with Mexico to supposedly prevent illegal immigration a hallmark of his 2016 presidential campaign. The call appealed to nativist elements in American society looking to blame immigrants for national problems, yet did so in an effective way politically by providing a simplistic but tangible symbol for a complex issue. Trump continued to promote the idea of a border wall throughout his presidency as a means of showing his political base that he had not forgotten their concerns.

An example of Trump's efforts to keep the issue alive occurred on February 11, 2019, as Trump met with border-county sheriffs from Arizona for a discussion of immigration-related issues. Following the meeting, Trump held a photo opportunity in the Diplomatic Reception room of the White House before leaving for a political rally in El Paso, Texas. Excerpts from that event appear below:

THE PRESIDENT: Thank you very much. I'm heading out to El Paso, Texas right now. And we are going to do a job. We're going to continue to do what we're doing. I think we've made a lot of progress.

We've actually started a big, big portion of wall today in a very important location. And it's going to go up pretty quickly over the next nine months. That whole area will be finished. It's fully funded. Construction, which I know a lot about, has begun. And it's a much better wall, much stronger wall, and a much less expensive wall than we've been building. And we're going to have a lot of wall being built in the last — in the next period of time.

I'm with some of the great law enforcement people. A lot of them are friends of mine. I've known them for a long time, and they've been fantastic people. Fantastic men and women. And they know what we're up against. We're up against people who want to allow criminals into our society. Can you explain that one?

You know, most things you understand, but they want to allow criminals into our society. Convicted felons—people of tremendous—like, big problems.

I just got this from Homeland Security. And you look at this — thousands of people. Dangerous drugs: 76,000 people. Then you have traffic offenses. That's not so good, but that's — every crime. Assault: 63,000 people. Larceny: 20,000 people. Fraudulent activities: 12,000 people. Burglaries: 12,000 people. These, again, are just a different crime. Robberies —

These are the people coming into our country that we are holding and we don't want in our country. And the Democrats want them to go into our country, that's why they don't want to give us what we call "the beds." It's much more complicated than beds. But we call them "the beds."

Robberies: 5,991. Sexual Assaults: 6,350. Forgeries: 5,158. Stolen property: 4,462. These are people we're talking about. Kidnapping — these are people that kidnap people. The Democrats want them to come into our society. I don't think so. Anybody here who would like to have a lot of kidnappers left in our society? I don't think — I won't bother waiting for you to raise your hand, right? Kidnappings: 2,085. Homicides — that means murder — murderers: 2,028. I mean, it's incredible. Sexual offenses: 1,739. Just came out two minutes ago. Homeland Security. The Department of Homeland Security. I don't know, maybe we're in a different country than I know of.

And we're going to El Paso. We have a line that is very long already. I mean, you see what's going on. And I understand our competitor has got a line too, but it's a tiny, little line. Of course, they'll make it sound like they had more people than we do. That's not going to happen.

But we're going there for a reason. We're going there to keep our country safe. And we don't want murderers and drug dealers and gang members, MS-13, and some of the worst people in the world coming into our country.

Now, Mexico has had the worst year they've ever had. Almost 40,000 killings in Mexico this year. One of the most unsafe places, unfortunately. We need a wall. And all of the other things are nice to have. But without a wall, it's not going to work. We can have technology, we can have beautiful drones flying all over the place, but it doesn't work without the wall.

Now, we need a wall. We can call it anything. We'll call it barriers. We'll call it whatever they want. But now, it turns out not only don't they want to give us money for the wall, they don't want to give us the space to detain murderers, criminals, drug dealers, human smugglers. How bad is that? Human smuggling. People think of that as an ancient art. There are more human smugglers right now — traffickers, they call them — than at any time in the history of our world, because of the Internet, unfortunately.

So, I'm heading out and we have a tremendous crowd. Like, tremendous. They have 75,000 people signed up. I think the arena holds like 8,000 people, unfortunately. I like the old days when I was allowed to make outdoors speeches. It was a lot easier because you could have very big crowds.

But we have a tremendous crowd. We have screens on the outside of the arena, so we'll have a lot of people coming. And again, if you look at your own newscasts, you'll see people lined up for a long way. A lot of people....

You know, I have to say, before leaving — and again, we're going on the plane. I guess a lot of you are coming on the plane with me to El Paso. ICE [Immigration and Customs Enforcement] is an incredible group of people. They help all of you a lot with some of the most vicious characters you meet anywhere in the world. No matter where you go, you're not going to find worse than the MS-13 gangs and some of these gangs that came over from countries that we don't even know about. And they're very disrespected by the Democrats, and we can't let that happen. They're heroes. And these people will tell you that too. They're heroes. And these people are heroes — and heroines.

But I just want to say that the people working at ICE are brave, tough, strong people that love our country. And they help the sheriffs and they help law enforcement, and they've done an incredible job, and I really appreciate your support. And the Democrats want to cut — you know, think of it: They want to cut ICE. They take out MS-13 and others by the thousands, and they want to cut ICE. So we're not going to let that happen. Thank you all very much. I appreciate it. (Applause.)

Source: www.whitehouse.gov

THOUGHT QUESTIONS:

1. What approaches did Trump tend to use in an effort to mobilize support for his border wall? An appeal to reason? An appeal to fear? Explain with examples.

2. How does Trump characterize those opposed to his immigration policies?

3. What do you believe should be done, if anything, about the nation's immigration issues? Explain.

Vignettes

President Obama's "Beer Summit"

The mainstream public has become more aware of the issue of racial profiling, the assumption that a person looks suspicious based on some distinguishing characteristic (usually race) has long been a complain within the African-American community, as black citizens innocent of any wrongdoing have frequently been stopped by police and accused of a crime or nefarious activity without any overt action justifying the suspicion. In July 2009, an overt case of racial profiling occurring early in Barack Obama's tenure made national headlines, leading the nation's first African-American president to seek to diffuse the situation and calm racial tensions in a unique way.

The case garnered national attention because it involved Henry Louis Gates—a renowned 58-year-old African-American scholar at Harvard University—who was not happy that he was arrested after trying to enter his own home in Cambridge, Massachusetts. Returning from a trip to China where he researched the family background of the cellist Yo-Yo Ma for a PBS series, Gates found that his front door was jammed. As he and his driver sought to force it open, they caught the attention of a nearby resident who did not recognize his own neighbor and called the police, suspecting a burglary was taking place even though it was the middle of the day.

When Sgt. James Crowley arrived, he met the woman who had called the police, and she stated the men were inside the house. When the officer entered, he confronted Gates and told him why he was there, asking for some identification. Gates got upset and exploded that he was being asked for an ID in his own living room, shouting "This is what happens to black men in America!" He then telephoned the Cambridge Police Department, demanding to speak with the chief about "a racist officer." When Crowley asked Gates to speak further outside, Gates continued his tirade while other officers and some citizens on the street looked on. After a couple of warnings, Crowley handcuffed Gates and arrested the professor for disorderly conduct, sending him to the local jail where he was held for a few hours then released.

The resulting furor generated much publicity, because of Gates's celebrity status, the perceived racial profiling by the neighbor, and the officer's seemingly quick decision to arrest Gates who was understandably upset. African American civil rights groups denounced the arrest, as did Deval Patrick, Massachusetts's first black governor. President Barack Obama even entered the fray when asked about the incident at a press conference, responding with his belief that Officer Crowley had "acted stupidly." After law enforcement organizations protested the president's words, Obama stated that he regretted his comments and expressed his hope that the whole affair would provide a "teachable moment" for everyone in the country. In that vein, he formally invited Professor Gates and

Sergeant Crowley to the White House for an outdoor beer along with casual conversation in an effort to move beyond the incident.

With this meeting in the White House Garden, quickly labeled the "Beer Summit" by the press, Obama characteristically wished to send a message about cooler heads prevailing in times of discord, especially regarding racial matters. Through calm dialogue and mutual understanding, the two sides could move forward and put the incident behind them. Though Officer Crowley nor Professor Gates offered any apologies for their actions, the visuals from the photo op inherently relayed the feel of the president as a fatherly figure trying to get each side to at least feel that they were both wrong and could have handled the situation better—the cop was just doing his job but probably overreacted to Gates's outbursts; but also, that Gates should have remained calm despite his legitimate frustrations as an African American who was genuinely peeved at the continued way in which he and others of his race are treated differently than white Americans when placed in similar circumstances.

THOUGHT QUESTIONS:

1. Do you feel that Professor Gates's arrest was justified? Do you believe that the situation would have been different had Professor Gates not been an African American? Why or why not?

2. What are your feelings about President Obama's attempt to diffuse the situation by calling for a "beer summit"?

3. Are you aware of any other instances of profiling (racial or otherwise) of individuals who become suspected of taking part in some nefarious activity simply because of the way that they look? What are some ways in which such profiling can be minimized?

The Controversial "Sequel" to Harper Lee's *To Kill a Mockingbird*

Harper Lee's *To Kill a Mockingbird* has stood the test of time as a classic of American literature. The novel, set in 1930s Alabama, centers on the trial of an African American man named Tom Robinson who is falsely accused of raping a young white woman. Robinson is passionately defended by a local white attorney, Atticus Finch, who seeks to convince the jury to look beyond their prejudices and free Robinson. Finch's courtroom soliloquies echoed the feelings of civil rights advocates at the time that the Pulitzer Prize-winning book was written (1960) and its message would resonate further with the American public when it was turned into an immensely popular Hollywood film in 1962 starring Gregory Peck as Atticus.

The story behind the novel is more interesting and convoluted than simply a case of Harper Lee, a white Alabama woman, writing *To Kill a Mockingbird* to shed light on the injustices inherent in racial prejudice. We now know that *Mockingbird* was actually a much-revised draft of a previous story written by Lee—*Go Set a Watchman*—that her publisher had first passed on. (The publisher saw promise in the material and worked with Lee to revise the author's original story by having the 1930s trial, referenced only in flashback scenes from the perspective of Scout Finch, Atticus's young daughter, become the main focus.) In the original story, Scout Finch, who is now an adult woman, returns home to her Alabama town and has to deal with her father who has turned into a classic bigot. No longer the idealistic attorney of Scout's youth who did his best to defend a black man from injustice, the Atticus Finch of *Go Set a Watchman* is a disillusioned older man who rails against those wishing to upend traditional society by ending segregation.

Many would have never known about this future Atticus Finch had Harper Lee's publisher, HarperCollins, not decided to publish *Watchman* after becoming aware of the existence of the original manuscript among the author's private papers. Though the publisher originally tried to push *Watchman* as a sequel to *Mockingbird*, Lee released a statement through her lawyer stating that she was informed of the original manuscript's existence and that she agreed to have it published as its own novel. Some disagreed with the notion that the 87-year-old Lee gave her willing consent to publish the book. Citing her refusal to publish any novel after *Mockingbird*, they repeated a rumor that her lawyer simply waited until the recent death of Lee's protective sister, who had previously handled all her legal and business affairs, to make the push to release *Watchman*. Accusations of elderly abuse began to fly as critics denounced the release of what they believed would be a lesser literary work that would tarnish the lasting power of *Mockingbird*. An investigation was carried out by Alabama state social services authorities. They determined that Lee was in failing health but still legally competent to make decisions. *Go Set a Watchman* was published by HarperCollins in July 2015. Lee died eight months later.

Regardless of the controversy surrounding Harper Lee's true intent regarding the publication of the original story, *Go Set a Watchman* has the power, if seen as *To Kill a Mockingbird*'s sequel, to demonstrate the power of racism despite the positive changes resulting from the civil rights movement. Even if the structure of society does not revert back to older times, intense prejudice can indeed linger. As times change, people's attitudes may also change, but not always in a more progressive direction. Rather than detracting from *To Kill a Mockingbird*, the existence of *Go Set a Watchman* has added a fascinating dimension to the story that will be studied in literary classes for decades to come.

THOUGHT QUESTIONS:

1. Why do you think *To Kill a Mockingbird* (both the book and the film) was so popular when it was released in the early 1960s and continues to resonate with readers and audiences today?

2. How was the basic story of *Go Set a Watchman* changed into *To Kill a Mockingbird*? Explain the main differences in the depiction of Atticus Finch.

3. Regardless of Harper Lee's intentions, do you agree with the decision to publish *Go Set a Watchman* as a separate novel? Does it make you view *To Kill a Mockingbird* in a different way? If so, how? If not, why not?

The Growing Public Awareness of CTE

During the early decades of the twenty-first century, an increased understanding of chronic traumatic encephalopathy (CTE)—a progressive degenerative disease of the brain caused by repeated blows to the head—made many begin to more seriously consider athlete safety in high contact sports, such as boxing, hockey, wrestling, and rugby, but especially football. The heightened awareness came from a series of notable cases of athletes and former athletes exhibiting bizarre behavior and/or diminished mental capacity before their deaths that became connected to CTE by neurologists.

The death of former All-Pro center Mike Webster of the four-time Super Bowl champion Pittsburgh Steelers in 2002 began to shed light on CTE for the general public. Retired in 1990 after a 17-year professional career, Webster's post-playing days were increasingly characterized by memory loss, depression, dementia, and bizarre personal behavior ranging from his preference to sleep in trucks or at train stations to tasering himself and huffing ammonia to maintain consciousness. After he died in 2002 from a heart attack at the age of 50, Dr. Bennet Omalu, a Nigerian neuropathologist who knew very little about American football, was assigned to perform Webster's autopsy and was astounded by his findings. The brain samples, in his opinion, should not have matched a 50-year-old man. Dr. Omalu found large accumulations of tau protein in the former player's brain, caused by repeated concussions from extended years of playing football, which would explain Webster's mood swings and other examples of abnormal behavior. (An excess of tau proteins block blood vessels and hamper the ability of nutrients and other essentials to effectively travel through nerve cells in the brain, eventually killing them.)

After Omalu published the results of his report, his conclusions were attacked by the National Football League (NFL) whose medical officials initially attempted to discredit his findings. In 2006, Omalu published an article based on his study of the brain of Terry Long, a former Pittsburgh Steelers guard who suffered from depression and committed suicide at the age of 45. Omalu found reported tau protein concentrations at levels that one would expect in a 90-year-old man with advanced Alzheimer's disease. After studying the brains of several other deceased former players, he formally presented his findings to the NFL, whose officials continued to dispute the doctor, primarily out of legal concerns and fears of reduced enthusiasm for the sport until 2009.

The suicides of high-profile former players Andre Waters, Dave Duerson, and Hall-of-Fame linebacker Junior Seau whose families requested studies of the players' brains, which were found in each case to show extreme CTE, focused more public attention on the condition. Currently, there have been 87 confirmed cases of former NFL players whose deaths have been attributed to the effects of CTE, as a result of multiple concussions playing football. In addition to the 2013 release of "League of Denial," a widely watched PBS Frontline investigation of Omalu's struggle for CTE recognition, the doctor's efforts received further public exposure when he wrote the book *Concussion*, which was turned into a major Hollywood movie of the same name starring Will Smith

The NFL has responded in multiple ways to compensate former players, protect current players, and maintain the immense popularity of their sport. Players are now bound to follow a "concussion protocol" in which they are immediately taken out of games if they display any signs of a concussion and are not allowed to practice or play in subsequent weeks until any lingering symptoms dissipate. The league also settled a class-action lawsuit with 20,000 former players who accused the NFL of covering up knowledge of the link between football-related concussions and CTE by agreeing to set up a fund that could reach up to $1 billion over 65 years to pay medical costs and other benefits to the players who suffered repeated concussions while playing.

THOUGHT QUESTIONS:

1. Describe some of the ways that CTE negatively impacted the lives of former football players, leading to suspicions that they were feeling the long-term effects of playing their sport.

2. Describe Dr. Omalu's contributions to public understanding of the positive link between repeated concussions and the heightened risk of acquiring CTE.

3. Do you think that growing awareness of CTE may harm the popularity of football in America, not just professionally but at the youth and collegiate level as well? Why or why not?

The Deep Water Horizon Explosion and the Gulf Oil Spill

Scientific advances during the early twenty-first century have contributed greatly to revolutionary changes in countless sectors of the economy. The oil industry has been no different as technological developments have led to the enhanced ability to extract petroleum from locations in the earth previously not available. The beginning of hydraulic fracturing (fracking) within shale has released sizeable oil deposits via forced pressure of water and chemicals, though with the downside of contamination of nearby ground water, the creation of moderate-sized earthquakes, and unknown long-term environmental effects.

Another new development has been the extraction of oil from deep water locations further out in the offshore continental shelf, though not without risk. The dangers involved in such operations became evident for all to see when the Deepwater Horizon drilling rig located 40 miles off the coast of Louisiana exploded on the night of April 30, 2010, killing ten crew members whose bodies were never found. Seventeen were injured and evacuated along with 94 other workers before the platform sunk. At the time, the

Horizon was drilling and exploratory well for British Petroleum (BP) in 5,000 feet of water approximately 18,000 feet below sea level.

On top of the tragic circumstances due to the loss of life, the explosion set off the worst environmental disaster in American history as petroleum began to gush out of the well on the ocean floor. For three months, the oil continued to flow. Though BP originally stated that they estimated the flow rate as no more than 5,000 barrels per day, scientists brought in to study the spill concluded that the most accurate estimate was over 60,000 barrels per day, for a total of over 4 million barrels before a proper means was developed to shut the flow from the well by pumping mud then cement into the well head.

The disaster delivered a mighty cost to the economy of the Gulf Coast region, paralyzing recreational fishing along the coast and tourism along beach communities from southern Mississippi to western Florida. The unprecedented oil spill also destroyed a tremendous amount of wildlife in the Gulf of Mexico, killing huge numbers of fish, turtles, and marine fowl in the ocean along with shellfish, crabs, even insects along coastal waterways and marshes.

Investigations looking into the cause of the explosion began even before the spilling ended. For its part, BP blamed Transocean, the company which owned and operated the Deepwater Horizon on behalf of BP, claiming its employees avoided warning signs of the buildup of flammable gases. Transocean responded by accusing BP of having a fatally flawed well design.

Ultimately, a U.S. District Judge ruled in September 2014 that BP was guilty of gross negligence and willful misconduct under the Clean Water Act while Transocean was also negligent. He apportioned two-thirds of the blame for the spill to BP and almost a third to Transocean, with fines to be based on the degree of negligence of the parties multiplied by the total estimated number of barrels of oil spilled (4.2 million) because under the Clean Water Act fines are often based on a cost per barrel basis. BP planned to appeal the court's decision but announced in July 2015 that they had reached an $18.7 billion settlement with the U.S., and the states of Alabama, Florida, Louisiana, Mississippi and Texas. In addition to bearing the financial burden of the cleanup effort, the spill to date had cost BP almost $55 billion.

THOUGHT QUESTIONS:

1. What new developments have occurred to enable the extraction of petroleum from previously inaccessible locations and what risks are involved with them?

2. What was the human and environmental cost of the Deepwater Horizon explosion?

3. Explain your feelings with regard to the issue of exploring new ways of extracting fossil fuels versus focusing more attention on researching the development of renewable energy sources.